Luigi L. Pasinetti, who is professor of economics at Università Cattolica, Milan, is well known to economists for his contributions to the theories of capital, economic growth, and income distribution. He has been a Research Fellow at Nuffield College, Oxford, a Fellow of King's College, Cambridge, and a Lecturer and a Reader in Economics at the University of Cambridge. He has been Wesley Clair Mitchell Visiting Professor of Economics at Columbia University on two occasions. He is the author of *Growth and Income Distribution: Essays in Economic Theory*.

Lectures on the Theory of Production

Columbia Studies in Economics 9

By the same author

Growth and Income Distribution: Essays in Economic Theory

LECTURES ON THE THEORY OF PRODUCTION

Luigi L. Pasinetti

COLUMBIA UNIVERSITY PRESS
New York 1977

Luigi L. Pasinetti is Professor of Economics at the
Università Cattolica, Milan, Italy.

Library of Congress Cataloging in Publication Data

Pasinetti, Luigi L
  Lectures on the theory of production.

  (Columbia studies in economics, 9)
  Translation of Lezioni di teoria della produzione.
  Includes index.
  1. Production (Economic theory)   I. Title.
II. Series.
HB241.P3713 1977   338'.001   77–1541
ISBN 0-231-04100-4

First published as *Lezioni di teoria della produzione* by
Società editrice il Mulino, Bologna, 1975.
English translation published in 1977 in Great Britain by
The Macmillan Press, Ltd., and in the United States of
America by Columbia University Press.
Printed in Great Britain.

Preface

THE theory of production was at the very foundations of Classical economic theory but was later pushed into a secondary and subordinate position by the development of the marginal theories of consumers' behavior and of exchange in competitive markets. It has, however, emerged once more as a focal point in some of the most exciting recent contributions to economic theory.

Renewed theoretical interest in the problems of production began as a consequence of the practical applications of linear programming techniques during the war. Unfortunately, linear programming was all too quickly constrained within the limits of traditional marginal analysis and lost its driving force. But the appearance in 1960 of a small book by Piero Sraffa, *Production of Commodities by means of Commodities*, has given new momentum to the economic analysis of the process of production and has put it into a new light: not only as a continuation of the earlier works of the Classical economists, but also as a critique of the prevalent positions of marginal economic theory. This approach has been developing ever since; and the present work is meant to be a contribution to presenting such an approach at the level of a graduate course.

The content of this book comes from notes for lectures delivered over a period of many years at the Catholic University of Milan, Italy, and at the University of Cambridge, England. It was mainly as a result of the requirements, and insistence, of the Italian students that I was, at various stages, induced to put the lecture notes into writing. Earlier versions of parts of these lectures have thus circulated in Italian universities since 1956. The printed version appeared in 1975 (*Lezioni di Teoria della Produzione*, Soc. Ed. il Mulino, Bologna, 1975).

These *Lectures* are limited in two respects. First, they are confined to the treatment of industries with a single product. The more complex problems concerning joint production and production with fixed capital are not discussed. If this version proves useful, I may feel encouraged to go into such fields as well. But, for the time being, the analysis of single-product industries is, I think, quite sufficient to evince the basic features of the type of production theory that is emerging. Secondly, the introduction to dynamic models sketched in the final chapter concerns economic systems with proportional expansion due to population growth only and no technical change. Here the shortcomings are not, alas, my fault (elsewhere I have actually tried to make a contribution to this subject). They are due to the present state of economic theory, which is still very unsatisfactory as far as technical change is concerned.

In the exposition I have made extensive use of matrix algebra, which has recently become an increasingly familiar analytical tool of economic analysis. Nevertheless, for the benefit of readers who may not be acquainted with it, I have added a Mathematical Appendix which presents all the notions of matrix algebra used in the text. In this way the book is rendered both self-contained and accessible to readers whose initial mathematical knowledge does not go beyond that of usual elementary algebra.

In the preparation of the manuscript from the lecture notes I have benefited from the critical comments, encouragement, and help of many friends and students. I am particularly grateful to Salvatore Baldone, Mario Faliva, Alberto Quadrio-Curzio, Luigi Filippini, and Paolo Varri, who provided constructive criticism and generous help, though on different subjects and at different times. I also received helpful comments from Pier Carlo Nicola, Terenzio Cozzi, and Alessandro Roncaglia.

For this English version I am most grateful to Ian Steedman, of the University of Manchester, who kindly provided me with a first draft of an English translation of the whole Italian text and also made numerous comments and suggestions. Without his help this English edition would perhaps never have appeared. Since I have revised and modified that first draft extensively, I must take full responsibility for the present text. I have not always adhered to the Italian version. At some points, excisions have become necessary; at others, substantial additions have been made, as for Sections 10.2 and 10.3 of Chapter V, Section 10 of the Appendix to Chapter V, Sections 6.1, 6.2, and 6.3 of Chapter VI, the entire Appendix to Chapter VI, and Sections 2.10, 3.4, and 3.5 of Chapter VII – all of which appear here for the first time.

Most of the revision work was carried out in the autumn of 1975 during my stay as Wesley Clair Mitchell Research Professor at the Economics Department of Columbia University, New York. I should like to express my appreciation for all the facilities and opportunities I enjoyed there.

Cambridge, England   L.L.P.
July 1976

Contents

CHAPTER ONE

A Brief Historical Excursus

1 Introduction

1.1. *Production as a characteristic of human societies.* One of the most outstanding characteristics of human societies is, without doubt, that they *produce* the goods and services which they need. This phenomenon was less conspicuous in primitive societies. Early man lived on what was immediately offered to him by nature; by hunting, fishing, gathering berries and wild fruit. In the course of progress, however, man has learned to transform what he finds in his surroundings, to use and control those processes of nature which are useful to him, and to eliminate or tame those which are harmful. The history of mankind is also the history of the continual improvement of the process of production of goods and services, of the increasing emancipation of man from the caprice and whims of nature, of his persistent effort at making the goods and services which he consumes and the very environment in which he lives.

This evolution in the process of production has taken place continuously, but it has also undergone qualitative leaps and remarkable discontinuities. In particular, the Agricultural Revolution, about 8000 B.C., which led to the cultivation of land and the domestication of animals (i.e., to the production of the means of subsistence), was the first major step toward the independence of human societies from the variability and consequent unreliability of the natural surroundings. A second remarkable, qualitative leap occurred much more recently with the Industrial Revolution of the 18th century, which led to the production of the very environment (the factory) in which the process of production was going to take place.

It is of course the Industrial Revolution which is particularly important for our purposes. The economists of the day saw the rapid and enormous increase in productive capacity which it brought as an increase in the wealth of nations. The phenomenon was, however, far more complex and deep-rooted. The very concept of wealth had itself evolved because of the evolution in the process of production.

1.2. *Two notions of "wealth."* The concept of "wealth" appears, at first sight, to be perfectly clear and familiar. It is traditionally defined as "the abundance of goods and services at the disposal of an individual or of a community." But closer consideration immediately reveals sources of ambiguity in this as in other definitions.

The principal distinction to be made is that "abundance of goods" might mean an endowment, or fund, of existing goods, i.e., wealth as a stock of commodities or claims, or it might mean a sizable periodic flow of goods and services, i.e., wealth as a flow of commodities or income. These two meanings are often confused, even today. Yet they embody very different concepts. Although the two kinds of wealth are not, of course, unconnected, the relation between the two is not at all simple or clear; nor is it unchanging with the evolution of the economic systems themselves.

The fact is that, when speaking of the wealth of single individuals, one usually finds it most convenient to refer to the concept of wealth as a stock (to the size of their total ownership). But, when speaking of rich and poor countries, one usually refers to the average income per head of their inhabitants, i.e., to their average annual ability to produce goods and services. Thus the concept of wealth as a flow seems to become increasingly relevant in thinking of the wealth of nations.

1.3. *Natural resources and produced wealth.* For centuries the wealth of a nation was identified with the wealth of its king. It is not surprising, therefore, that the concept of wealth as a stock, to which one usually refers in relation to single individuals, was extended to nations and to the whole world. This is particularly evident in the work of economists who wrote before the Industrial Revolution. For the Mercantilists in the 15th, 16th, and 17th centuries wealth meant the endowment of available economic resources with particular reference to the precious metals. The dominant idea was that the total stock of wealth is given for the world as a whole and that the wealth of one country can therefore increase only at the expense of some other country.[1] (Hence the close connection between Mercantilism and the aggressive policies of the national states.)

The considerable merit of having broken with this tradition goes to the French Physiocratic school, toward the middle of the 18th century. It was at that time that Quesnay drew a *Tableau Economique*, in which

---

[1] Consider, for example, statements like the following, reported by Heckscher [5, vol. II, p. 26]: "It is said that no one ever loses without another gaining. This is true and is borne out in the realm of commerce more than anywhere else" (Montchrétien). "It is likewise to be remembered that...an increase in any Estate must be upon the Foreigner, for whatsoever is somewhere gotten is somewhere lost" (Francis Bacon).

he focused attention precisely on the net annual product of a nation. In the various analyses of the *Tableau*, the *production et distribution des richesses* are continually referred to. And the synthesis of Physiocratic thought which Turgot wrote toward the end of the 18th century was, indeed, entitled: *Réflexions sur la formation et la distribution des richesses*. The terms *production* and *distribution* clearly refer to the concept of wealth as a flow. Yet the implications had already reached much further. When the "stock" consists of produced goods, it is itself continually consumed and replaced by the very process of production; it is no longer something given but something which is itself produced, renewed, and enlarged.

The English Classical economists fully accepted this approach and developed it further. Adam Smith singled out the productivity of labor as the cause of the wealth of nations, seeing in labor productivity the principal source of every increase in the productive capacity of an economic system. Torrens entitled his work *An essay on the production of wealth*; and Ricardo centred his analysis on the distribution of the national product among rents, profits, and wages. Jean-Baptiste Say himself divided his *Traité d'économie politique* into three books: (i) *De la production des richesses*; (ii) *De la distribution des richesses*; (iii) *De la consommation des richesses*.

A radical change of view had gradually asserted itself. It was no longer, or not so much, the distinction between wealth as a stock and wealth as a flow that was seen as important, but rather the contrast between *produced* wealth (whether as an annual flow or as an accumulation of means of production) and exogenously given natural resources. And the Classical economists were in no doubt over this matter: Whatever the endowments of natural resources and the climatic characteristics of a country might be, it was in their conviction produced wealth (as a flow and as a stock), which was going to increasingly characterize and condition the emerging industrial societies.[2]

1.4. *Beyond economic analysis.* Karl Marx went further. The process of production of material goods seemed so important to him that he thought it possible to base an entire conception of history and of social relations on that very process (hence the emergence of historical materialism). In brief, according to this conception of history,

> "Men . . . begin to distinguish themselves from animals as soon as they begin to *produce* their means of subsistence, a step which is conditioned by their physical organisation. By producing their means of subsistence men are indirectly producing their actual material life.

[2] See the very first pages of Adam Smith [16].

"The way in which men produce their means of subsistence depends first of all on the actual means of subsistence they find in existence and have to reproduce. This mode of production must not be considered simply as being the production of the physical existence of the individuals. Rather it is a definite form of activity of these individuals, a definite form of expressing their life, a definite *mode of life* on their part. As individuals express their life, so they are. What they are, therefore, coincides with their production, both with *what* they produce and with *how* they produce. The nature of individuals thus depends on the material conditions determining their production." (Marx-Engels [11, p. 42]. Italics in original.)

Marx had clearly gone beyond economic analysis, to enter territory fraught with philosophico-sociological controversy. There was bound to be a reaction, and the repercussions thereof could not but affect the foundations of economic analysis itself.

1.5. *Interindustry analysis*. Toward the end of the 19th century the Marginalist school returned to the pre-Classical tradition and revived the attempt to build theoretical economic models on the concept of wealth as an endowment of given resources. Marginal theory had a remarkable initial success, due principally to the associated introduction of mathematics into economic analysis. But its many shortcomings for the purpose of interpreting the typical problems of industrial societies have by now laid it open to a whole barrage of criticism. The controversies on these matters belong to contemporary economic literature.

The fact remains that, over the past 40 years, the theories of production developed by the Classical economists have been taken up again.

The most remarkable contributions in this connection have come from what has been called interindustry analysis, which has direct links with the Physiocratic *Tableau Economique* and with the theoretical concerns of the Classical economists. Interindustry analysis has proved to be a fruitful field of enquiry in which economic theory, analytico-mathematical tools, and direct empirical applications have been very successfully combined. But precisely because these new formulations have again taken up, although with new analytical tools, concepts developed some two centuries ago, it seems necessary to start by considering them, if only briefly, within their historical background. This is done in the following pages with specific reference to the theories of some of the most representative economists. These sketches, however, are confined to those ideas which are important in their own right for present-day analysis, without any intention or claim to provide a survey of the theories of the authors mentioned.

2 François Quesnay[3]

2.1. *The Tableau Economique*. François Quesnay has become famous as the author of a *Tableau Economique*[4] which represents the circulation of commodities in an economic system and can be considered the first input-output schema ever to have been formulated.

Two ideas in Quesnay's *Tableau* reappear continually in subsequent writings: (a) the idea of a "surplus" or "net product" (*produit net*), i.e., of a physical excess of goods produced over the goods which have to go back to the production process; (b) the idea of economic activity as a circular process which, in addition to producing a surplus, reproduces all the material goods consumed, so that the production process itself may continue in the following period.

Quesnay's schema is very simple. It contains first of all an identification of social classes with specific roles in economic activity (an identification which was to be taken up and developed by the Classical economists and by Marx). The members of society are grouped into three classes: the landlord class, the "productive" class, and the so-called "sterile" class. Each class has particular rights and carries out particular duties. The "productive" class consists of those employed in agriculture and mining. This class is termed "productive" because the physical quantity of goods it obtains by working on the land can directly be seen to be greater than the physical quantity of the same goods which had to be used up. The land thus comes to be thought of as the only factor capable of producing a "net product." The "sterile" class consists of the artisans and those engaged in manufacturing. This class is called "sterile" because, in Quesnay's view, it adds nothing to the net product; it merely transforms what has been produced by the productive class. Finally, the landlord class consists of the king and of the noble and ecclesiastical aristocracy. This class does not work, owns the land, and receives the rents from its property.

Given this social structure, it is clear that exchanges must occur, i.e., flows of commodities from one class to another must take place at the

---

[3] François Quesnay (1694–1774), the son of a countryman, was by no means a professional economist. His main occupation was that of surgeon-physician. He became Secretary General of the French Academy of Surgery, and first physician to the king. Economics was for him a secondary occupation; yet his economics writings have made him famous. He became the leader of a school of economic thought which, because of its insistence on the idea of a *natural order* in society, was called the "Physiocratic school."

[4] The *Tableau* was first published in Versailles in 1758 and was immediately acclaimed as one of the greatest discoveries of all times. (Louis XV himself is said to have been concerned with the correction of the proofs.) Abridged versions were elaborated by Quesnay himself and by Mirábeau. It has since been reproduced many times. For some of the most recent reproductions, comments, and interpretations see [6], [8] and [12].

end of each production period in order that the wealth produced may be distributed among the various members of society, and in order that the production process may continue in the following period. The purpose of the *Tableau Economique* is to represent all these flows.

2.2. *A graphical representation.* The *Tableau Economique* has been presented in various forms. The form originally used by Quesnay (known as the "zigzag," because of the crossed, slanting lines joining the various figures) is rather cumbersome and is now only of historical interest. Here we shall use two alternative devices—a graphical representation and a double-entry table.

Suppose that the production process takes place within a finite period of time (which we may call a "year") and that the exchanges take place at the end of such period. Quesnay's *Tableau* could be represented as shown in Fig. I.1.[5] Each rectangle represents a physical quantity of commodities having a value, say, of 1 million *livres*. Total gross production is therefore worth 5 million *livres*. F denotes production of foodstuffs; *RM*, production of raw materials; and *M*, production of manufactured goods. The two finer and dashed rectangles

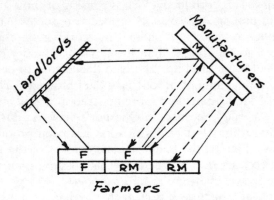

FIG. I.1. Graphical representation of the "Tableau Economique" (before exchange)

represent 2 million *livres* in money (i.e., means of payment, introduced here merely for accounting purposes). Finally, the broken arrows show the monetary flows, and the solid arrows show the real flows (opposite to but symmetrical with the monetary flows).

When the process of exchange is completed, the situation is as shown in Fig. I.2. The 2 million *livres* in money which are shown in the possession of the farmers will, at the begining of the following period, return to the landlords as rents for the use of the land. The initial

---

[5] This graphical representation follows the one given by Shigeto Tsuru [19].

situation will thus be reestablished, the production process will go on, and at the end of that period the same circular flows of commodities will take place all over again.

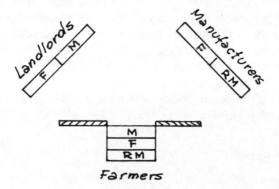

FIG. I.2. Graphical representation of the "Tableau Economique" (after exchange)

At the end of every period the landlord class is thus able to obtain goods to the value of 2 million *livres*. These 2 million *livres* worth of goods, which constitute the physical excess emerging over and above what is needed to maintain the production process, represent for Quesnay the "net product" of society.

As will be seen, Quesnay's schema is very simple and may appear rather primitive to us. Yet, in order to find any markedly superior schema of interindustry relationships, we had to wait until the contemporary economic literature, and more precisely until Leontief's input-output analysis, which is considered in following chapters.

2.3. *A double-entry table.* It is not difficult to express Quesnay's *Tableau Economique* in the more modern form of a double-entry

TABLE I.1

The "Tableau Economique" as an input-output table (the figures are in million livres)

		Outputs			
Inputs		Farmers	Manufacturers	Landlords	Totals
Farmers {	foodstuffs	1	1	1 }	5
	raw materials	1	1	— }	
Manufacturers		1	—	1	2
Landlords		2	—	—	(2)
Totals		5	2	(2)	7

table, as used by Leontief.[6] The flows of material goods considered by Quesnay may be rewritten as in Table I.1.

This table, as will appear more clearly below, is a genuine input-output table. The farmers and the manufacturers (first two rows and columns) represent what is today called the interindustry part of the table, while the landlord class (third row and third column) represents the "final sector." The surplus, or net product, of the system – all of which, according to Quesnay, goes to the landlords – is shown in both the third column and the third row. It appears in the third column as the bundle of material goods available to the final sector; and it appears in the third row as the "value-added" to the means of production.

3 David Ricardo[7]

3.1. *A one-sector model.* It is worthwhile to consider at somewhat greater length the economic theories of at least one of the Classical economists who, of the two Quesnaysian ideas mentioned above – that of a surplus and that of production as a circular process – developed principally the former, in a theoretical rather than in a purely descriptive direction. For this purpose, I have chosen to consider David Ricardo, whose theories are undoubtedly the most logically consistent among those of the Classical economists.

Like Quesnay, Ricardo postulates a strict identification of social classes with specific roles in economic activity. The three social classes which Ricardo considers are: the landlords who rent out land; the workers who provide labor services in return for a certain wage; and the capitalists who provide capital, with which they hire labor, and organize the process of production.

The simplest way to grasp the principal ideas of Ricardo is to consider a highly simplified economic system in which only one commodity – corn – is produced (a one-sector model). It will be assumed that the production process takes exactly one year and that the only kind of capital required is the fund needed for the advancing of wages to the workers (until the end of the year, when the availability of the gross product will make it possible to renew such fund).

---

[6] The first to notice this seems to have been Phillip [14].

[7] A few biographical notes: David Ricardo (1772–1823) was born in England of a Jewish family of continental origin. He entered a business career very early in his life. He was, in succession, a broker, a jobber, and a stock-exchange dealer. At 42, after accumulating a considerable amount of personal wealth, he retired and devoted himself to economic theory and policy. His major contributions are the *Essay on the Influence of a Low Price of Corn on the Profits of Stocks* (1815) and the *Principles of Political Economy and Taxation* (1817). The most accurate edition of his works is the one edited by Piero Sraffa, in 11 volumes [18].

In such a simplified economic system, the Ricardian theory can be represented by the following set of equations:

$$X = f(N) \qquad\qquad (\text{I.3.1})$$

with the properties

$$f(0) \geq 0 \qquad\qquad (\text{a})$$
$$f'(1) > \bar{x} \qquad\qquad (\text{b})$$
$$f''(N) < 0 \qquad\qquad (\text{c})$$
$$R = f(N) - Nf'(N) \qquad\qquad (\text{I.3.2})$$
$$W = Nx \qquad\qquad (\text{I.3.3})$$
$$K = W \qquad\qquad (\text{I.3.4})$$
$$P = X - R - W \qquad\qquad (\text{I.3.5})$$

where X denotes the quantity of corn produced in a year, N the number of workers employed, R total rents, W total wages, K the circulating capital, P profits, and x the wage rate.

Equation (I.3.1) represents what may be called, in a certain sense, the production function. This function has the three properties shown as (a), (b), and (c). The meaning of (a) is that, if no workers are employed, then the output obtained will be either zero or positive. (This rules out the possibility of negative output, which would have no economic meaning.) The meaning of (b) is that, if just one worker is employed, the resulting output of corn must exceed, or at the very least be equal to, a certain quantity $\bar{x}$, which represents what may, for the sake of brevity, be called the "subsistence wage." If this condition were not satisfied, the production process would not be maintained over time (the economic system would not be *viable*). Finally, the meaning of (c) is that production is subject to decreasing returns to scale. The reason for this is that capitalists behave rationally, under the pressure of competition. If there are various plots of land and each of them is of a different fertility, the capitalists will begin by cultivating the more fertile plots. Then, as population increases, they will go on to cultivate ever less fertile plots. From this property of $f(N)$, it follows immediately that the owners of the more fertile plots of land will be able to reap a "net gain" or *rent* (a differential rent) with respect to the owners of the last plot of land brought under cultivation. The sum of all these "net gains" makes up the total rent in the economic system which is shown by (I.3.2).[8] The remaining equations are self-explanatory.

It will be noted that the equation system (I.3.1)–(I.3.5) is not yet complete. It contains five equations in seven unknowns. In order to close it, we could add the two equations

$$N = \bar{N} \tag{I.3.6}$$

$$K = \bar{K} \tag{I.3.7}$$

where $\bar{N}$ and $\bar{K}$ denote the existing number of workers and the existing quantity of capital. Ricardo maintains, however, that the system (I.3.1)–(I.3.7) is unstable unless the wage rate is equal to what has been called the "subsistence" wage, i.e., unless $x = \bar{x}$.

Ricardo is convinced (on Malthusian grounds) that the population will increase (if $x > \bar{x}$) or decrease (if $x < \bar{x}$) until the equality $x = \bar{x}$ is reestablished.

Taking this demographic mechanism into account, it is better to close the system (I.3.1)–(I.3.5), not with equations (I.3.6)–(I.3.7), but rather with the alternative pair of equations

$$x = \bar{x} \tag{I.3.6a}$$

$$K = \bar{K} \tag{I.3.7a}$$

The system (I.3.1)–(I.3.5), (I.3.6a), (I.3.7a) now represents a Ricardian system in what might be called a situation of "natural" equilibrium. It should be noted that in this "natural" equilibrium the number of workers (and thus, in effect, population) is a variable determined by the economic system itself. Since all the variables are expressed in physical terms, it may be helpful to consider the graphs of the functions $f(N)$ and $f'(N)$ in Fig. I.3 and I.4, respectively. The second of these graphs, in Fig. I.4, shows the derivative of the graph in Fig. I.3 and thus represents the physical product of the last worker employed.

The graphs in the two figures have, of course, been drawn to different scales. Total output X is shown by $f(N)$ in the first graph and by the area beneath the function $f'(N)$ in the second graph. Similarly, the distribution of total output among rents, wages, and profits is shown by the segments of a line in Fig. I.3 and by areas in Fig. I.4.

---

[8] This is the so-called "extensive" rent. But Ricardo also considers the "intensive" rent, emerging from the applications of ever greater quantities of labor *cum* capital to the same plot of land. In our analysis, $f'(N)$ may be regarded as the joint marginal product of labor *cum* capital with reference to both types of rent.

The situation explicitly represented in Figs. I.3 and I.4 is one of "natural" equilibrium in which the number of workers employed is $\bar{N}$.[9]

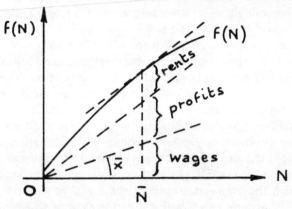

FIG. I.3. Distribution of income in the Ricardian system (in terms of total product)

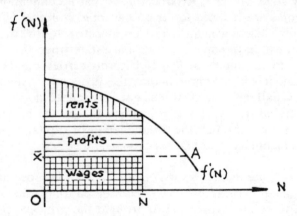

FIG. I.4. Distribution of income in the Ricardian system (in terms of marginal product)

It should be added that wages, being at the subsistence level, constitute a fund which is essential to the process of production. Ricardo therefore thinks of them as being a necessary part of the "means of production." In other words, for Ricardo only rents and profits enter the net product, or surplus of the economic system.

Now, if the surplus – rents plus profits – is consumed (by the landlords and the capitalists), the production process and all economic activity will be repeated in the following period, in exactly the same

[9] The one-sector Ricardian model presented here corresponds to the one used by Kaldor [7].

way as in the current period. But Ricardo also considers the case in which part of the surplus – or, more precisely, part of profits – is accumulated, i.e., added to the circulating capital. In this case a complex dynamic process is set into motion: the dynamics of accumulation. If capital increases, the wage fund and hence the wage rate will increase. But, if the wage rate increases, the number of workers will increase (via the above-mentioned demographic mechanism). New, less fertile, land will have to be brought under cultivation. The production activity will thus be expanded. This process can continue as long as accumulation is possible, i.e., as long as there are profits to be accumulated. But, if the subsistence wage rate is fixed and the expansion of the production process involves the cultivation of ever less fertile land, total profits will eventually begin to fall (as can be seen immediately from Fig. I.4). Indeed, a point will come (point *A* in Fig. I.4) at which the area representing profits will be reduced to zero. At this point all accumulation will cease; the system will have reached a stationary state. (In fact, Ricardo thinks that accumulation will cease before profits are reduced to zero. One could conceive of a minimum rate of profit below which there is no incentive to invest. In this case the system will have entered a stationary state when the rate of profit has fallen to its minimum level.) Ricardo carries out nearly all his analysis under the assumption that the economic system is moving toward the stationary state but has not yet reached it.

It will be clear that this is a genuine theory of the growth of an economic system through the accumulation of capital, albeit a rather simple, rudimentary, and highly pessimistic theory.

3.2. *A two-sector model.* No problem of valuation arose in the model just examined because we have considered only one commodity. However, if we also wish to bring to light the principal properties of the Ricardian theory of value, we must go further and examine a more complex Ricardian system. We begin with a two-sector model.

Ricardo divides produced commodities into two broad categories: *necessities* (or wage goods) and *luxuries* (or luxury goods). Hence the simplest two-sector Ricardian model one can build is one in which a single necessity, which we shall call corn, and a single luxury, which we shall call gold, are produced. It will be assumed that the production of the former is subject to decreasing returns to scale, as in the previous section, while the production of the latter takes place at constant returns to scale. Thus only the corn-producing sector will give rise to rents. We shall assume furthermore that, in both sectors, capital simply consists of the wages, which are advanced at the beginning of the production period or "year"; and that this production period is the same for both sectors. We shall use the same symbols as in the preceding section, subscript 1 being added for the corn-producing sector and subscript 2 for the gold-producing sector.

We can at once write down the seven equations referring to the production of corn:

$$X_1 = f(N_1) \tag{I.3.8}$$

$$f(0) \geq 0 \tag{a}$$

$$f'(1) > \bar{x} \tag{b}$$

$$f''(N_1) < 0 \tag{c}$$

$$R = f(N_1) - N_1 f'(N_1) \tag{I.3.9}$$

$$W = Nx \tag{I.3.10}$$

$$K = W \tag{I.3.11}$$

$$P_1 = X_1 - R - N_1 x \tag{I.3.12}$$

$$x = \bar{x} \tag{I.3.13}$$

$$K = \bar{K} \tag{I.3.14}$$

We must now add the equations referring to the production of gold. We have, first,

$$X_2 = \alpha N_2 \tag{I.3.15}$$

$$N = N_1 + N_2 \tag{I.3.16}$$

where α denotes the quantity of gold produced in one year by one worker, X_2 the total quantity of gold produced in a year, N the total number of workers, and N_1 and N_2 denote the number of workers employed in the corn-producing sector and the gold-producing sector, respectively. Assuming that free competition makes the wage rate and the rate of profit uniform in the two sectors, let w denote the money wage rate (in both sectors), π the rate of profit (in both sectors), p_1 the price of corn, and p_2 the price of gold. Then, in general,

$$w = x p_1 \tag{I.3.17}$$

$$\pi = \frac{P_1 p_1 + P_2 p_2}{K p_1} \tag{I.3.18}$$

where P_1 denotes total profits in the corn sector, in terms of corn, and P_2 denotes total profits in the gold sector, in terms of gold. We can also add

$$P_2 p_2 = X_2 p_2 - N_2 w \tag{I.3.19}$$

We thus arrive at the crux of the Ricardian argument. Disregarding the temporary oscillations of market prices, Ricardo argues that what fundamentally determines the "value" or "natural price" of produced commodities is their cost of production. Thus, in equilibrium, the price p_2 must cover the cost of production of gold (wages plus profits at the ruling rate of profit); and the price p_1 must cover the cost of production of the corn produced on the last plot of land brought under cultivation, or "marginal" land (for this land would otherwise not be cultivated). Since the wage rate and the rate of profit are both uniform in the two sectors as a result of free competition, and since the capital per worker is also uniform, by assumption,[10] it follows that

$$\frac{p_2 X_2}{N_2} = \frac{p_1(X_1 - R)}{N_1} \tag{I.3.20}$$

that is, in equilibrium the cost of production, or value, of the output of gold per worker[11] must be equal to the cost of production, or value, of the output of corn per worker, exclusive of rent.

The convention to follow in measuring prices must be chosen. In the present context it is convenient to adopt as *numéraire*, or basis for the price system, the quantity α of gold, which is equivalent to setting its value equal to unity, i.e.,

$$\alpha p_2 = 1 \tag{I.3.21}$$

The equations of our system now contain a theory of value and a theory of income distribution but do not yet contain a theory of demand. Ricardian theory is, however, rather primitive in this respect. It can be expressed as follows: The workers spend all their wages on the purchase of necessities (corn); the capitalists spend all their profits (apart from a supposedly negligible portion) also on the purchase of corn, but in order to add most of it to capital for the following period; finally, the landlords, whom Ricardo sees as spendthrifts (by contrast with the capitalists who are very thrifty), spend all their rents, apart from a supposedly negligible portion, in purchasing luxuries. This can all be expressed by the single equation

$$p_2 X_2 = p_1 R \tag{I.3.22}$$

No further equation is needed. The determination of the demand for one of the two commodities (gold in our example) also determines, implicitly, the demand for the other commodity (corn), since total output is already functionally determined.

---

[10] Remember that we have supposed capital to consist of the wage fund only.

[11] That is, wages per worker plus profits per worker.

As the reader may see, we have obtained a system of 15 equations – (I.3.8)–(I.3.22) – in 15 unknowns: X_1, X_2, N, N_1, N_2, R, W, K, P_1, P_2, x, w, π, p_1, p_2. The system is thus determinate. The solution of (I.3.8)–(I.3.22) represents what may be called the "natural" equilibrium of a two-sector Ricardian system.

3.3. *The essential features of the Ricardian system.* This two-sector model, while still a simplification, already displays nearly all the essential features of the Ricardian theory.

We can find in it, first of all, a theory of income distribution which is independent of the theory of value. The national product continues to be distributed among rents, wages, and profits, via the process already described in Section 3.1. At the same time the "natural prices" or values of the produced commodities are, from (I.3.20) and (I.3.21),

$$p_1 = \frac{1}{f'(N_1)} \tag{I.3.20a}$$

$$p_2 = \frac{1}{\alpha} \tag{I.3.21a}$$

It will be noted that $1/f'(N_1)$ is simply the quantity of labor required to produce one physical unit of corn on the marginal land; and that $1/\alpha$ is merely the quantity of labor required to produce one physical unit of gold. The value of each commodity is thus proportional (and in our example, owing to the special choice of *numéraire*, is actually exactly equal) to the quantity of labor "embodied" in it, whatever the rate of profit may be. The system (I.3.8)–(I.3.22) thus contains a pure labor theory of value.

It follows from (I.3.8)–(I.3.22), furthermore, that wage goods and luxury goods do not play symmetrical roles in the system. After some obvious substitutions, (I.3.17) and (I.3.18) may be written as

$$w = \frac{\bar{x}}{f'(N_1)} \tag{I.3.17a}$$

$$\pi = \frac{f'(N_1)}{\bar{x}} - 1 \tag{I.3.18a}$$

from which it is immediately apparent that the two distributive variables, the wage rate and the rate of profit, depend on the technical conditions of production of the wage good but are completely independent of the technical conditions of production of the luxury good.

Indeed, the technical function for the production of luxury goods, (I.3.15), has very limited effects on the system as a whole, because it contributes to the determination of only two variables, X_2 and p_2. By contrast, the technical function for the production of corn, (I.3.8), plays a fundamental role by contributing to the determination of every variable except p_2. It follows, for example, that a change in technique or the imposition of a tax, when either takes place in the luxury goods sector, has effects which are confined to the purchasers of the luxury good; whereas, when either takes place in the wage good sector, it has effects that are felt (via the change in the wage rate and the rate of profit) by all people participating in the process of production and distribution.

Finally, from the system of equations (I.3.8)–(I.3.22) it is not difficult to deduce the type of dynamics that the economic system will follow, as it moves from one period to the next, provided that one maintains the assumption that the capitalists save most of their profits and add them to the capital stock. In analytical terms, one can study this problem by finding the derivative of each variable with respect to K. It can then be verified that, until the stationary state is reached, all the macro-economic variables of the system, apart from total profits, will follow a monotonically rising trend. One can show, furthermore, that: (a) if the price of gold remains constant, the price of corn will follow a rising trend, as can be inferred from (I.3.20a); (b) the money wage will rise through time, while the rate of profit will fall [see (I.3.17a) and (I.3.18a)]; (c) the economic system will continue to grow until the rate of profit is reduced to a level so low as to deprive capitalists of any incentive to carry out further saving and hence investment. At this point the dynamics of accumulation will come to a standstill and the economic system will settle into the cheerless tranquility of the Ricardian stationary state.

3.4. *Extension to many sectors.* We could easily expand this two-sector Ricardian model into a more complete multisector model with many wage goods and many luxury goods. The conclusions of the previous section would, however, remain substantially unchanged, provided that one maintains the assumption, crucial to the whole of the Ricardian argument, that capital per worker employed is the same in every sector of production.[12]

---

[12] Any reader interested in this extension of the Ricardian system may see Pasinetti [13], where he or she can find the details of the dynamic analysis that leads to the conclusions stated at the end of Section 3.3.

3.5. *Unresolved problems.* At the beginning of the 19th century the Ricardian theory set out above was a remarkable step forward in the evolution of economic thought. When reconsidered more than a century and a half later, it obviously reveals many shortcomings and deficiencies.

Many of Ricardo's pessimistic conclusions have not been borne out by the economic history of the industrial countries. It has been found, for example, that the relation between the growth of income and the growth of population is far more complex than Ricardo, under strong Malthusian influence, would have thought. In general, economists now no longer think of population as a variable to be explained in economic terms; they prefer to accept it as exogenously given. Ricardian pessimism concerning the ultimate effects of economic growth has also shown itself to be largely unjustified. In the countries which have achieved industrialization, technical progress has not merely offset but has actually outweighed the effects of the much-feared "law of decreasing returns to scale." Increasing (not decreasing!) returns to scale by now prevail in many fields of production and have also cast doubt on the Ricardian belief in the tendency to a falling rate of profit.

But the shortcoming within the Ricardian theory which is of greater interest to us here concerns the theory of value. It was seen above that the Ricardian model contains a pure labor theory of value, but it was also noted that the latter depends crucially on the assumption that capital per worker (i.e., in modern terms, the capital intensity) is exactly the same in all sectors of production. Immediately one abandons this assumption, which is certainly very unrealistic, the elegant Ricardian proportionality between value and quantity of labor vanishes. Worse still, once this assumption is dropped, the interdependence between values and income distribution, which Ricardo had carefully set aside, at once reappears. Suppose that, starting from a particular distribution of income between wages and profits, a change in that distribution occurs. Obviously the profit component in any price will vary in one direction, while the wage component will vary in the opposite direction. These two variations will offset one another in part, but in a way which differs from price to price because of the differing capital intensities of the respective production processes. As a result the whole structure of prices will have been changed, even though no change has taken place in the relative quantities of labor. This contradicts, in general, the pure labor theory of value.

Ricardo was, of course, aware of this weakness in his theory of value, but he persisted in rejecting all the criticisms which were directed at it. He thought that the abandonment of the equal-capital-intensity assumption would have led only to unimportant modifications in his conclusions and that the pure labor theory of value, although not perfectly valid, ought therefore to be retained as "the nearest approximation to truth."[13] Ricardo realized, nevertheless, that he would not have made his conviction acceptable until he had suggested a standard of comparison by which the degree of approximation could be assessed. This undertaking was rendered difficult precisely by the interdependence between values and income distribution. The difficulty here is that it is not enough to record the variations of prices of the various commodities in terms of *any* arbitrary commodity chosen as *numéraire*. If the distribution of income changes, the wage component and the profit component of that *numéraire* will themselves change. It therefore proves to be impossible to say what part of a given change in a price is to be attributed to the commodity whose price it is and what part of it is to be attributed to the variation of the wage and profit components of the *numéraire*-commodity itself.

In order to remove this uncertainty, one would have to find a *numéraire*-commodity with the very special property of representing, in a certain sense, an average of all commodities, i.e., having a wage component and a profit component whose variations always exactly counterbalance, and thus eliminate each other in the face of any variations in income distribution. Ricardo thought that, if such a commodity could be found, it would constitute an "invariable standard of value." For, by using it as the *numéraire*-commodity, one would be sure that each variation in any price, following a change in the distribution of income, could confidently be attributed to the commodity whose price it is (and not to any variation in the unit of measurement).[14] Furthermore the use of such a commodity as the *numéraire* would justify treating the problem of income distribution in the manner adopted by Ricardo, i.e., independently of prices.

The problem of the search for an "invariable standard of value" was never solved by Ricardo. It may be of interest to add, however, that one of the most rigorous theoretical schemata of production, to be discussed below – that of Piero Sraffa – has recently sprung from precisely the attempt to solve this Ricardian problem.

[13] Letter to Malthus, October 9, 1920; see [18, vol. VIII, pp. 279–280].

[14] "If, then, I may suppose myself to be possessed of a standard so nearly approaching to an invariable one, the advantage is, that I shall be enabled to speak of the variations of other things, without embarrassing myself on every occasion with the consideration of the possible alteration in the value of the medium in which price and value are estimated." (Ricardo, *Principles*, in Sraffa [18, vol. I, p. 46].)

4 Karl Marx[15]

4.1. *Simple reproduction*. Marx's writings contain a production schema which displays many of the characteristics of Quesnay's *Tableau Economique*. They also contain, though in a different form, the same difficulties faced by Ricardo in the formulation of a pure labor theory of value.

For Marx the "value" of a commodity is, by definition, the quantity of labor "socially necessary" for its production. Human labor has the characteristic of being able to produce more commodities than are strictly necessary for mere survival, and this would be a source of joy and happiness if the capitalist society in which we live were not to cause certain lamentable distortions. Starting from the Classical belief that free market competition reduces the prices of commodities to their cost of production, Marx argues that capitalist society has the peculiarity of reducing human labor itself to a commodity like any other. Thus the ruthless logic of market competition also reduces the price of labor to its cost of production, i.e., to that subsistence wage which is strictly necessary for the maintenance of the worker and his family. The excess of what a worker produces over what is strictly necessary for this maintenance, called "surplus value" by Marx, is appropriated in full by those in the privileged position of owning the means of production – the capitalists. The "surplus value" thus becomes a tangible measure of exploitation.

The "value" of any commodity is represented by Marx as the sum of three components:

$$c + v + s$$

where c denotes the quantity of labor needed to replace the "constant capital," defined as all the commodities and machines consumed in the production process; v denotes the quantity of labor needed to replace the "variable capital," defined as the stock of wage goods advanced for the maintenance of the workers; and s denotes the "surplus value," or the quantity of labor in excess of replacement needs, which ends up into the commodities appropriated by the capitalists.

Consider a simple economic system in which there are three sectors, producing means of production, wage goods, and luxury goods, the

[15] Karl Marx (1818–1883) was born at Triers to a Jewish family of the higher Prussian bourgeoisie; he died in London after a life entirely devoted to the cause of the working class. He occupies an entirely special place in the history of economic thought, in sharp opposition to all "schools" of economists. His principal work, *Das Kapital*, in 3 volumes, was published in 1867 (1st volume) and posthumously in 1885 (2nd volume) and 1894 (3rd volume). Our remarks on Marx's work will be limited to his theory of value.

corresponding variables being denoted by the subscripts 1, 2, 3, respectively. If the system is to be capable of reproducing itself from year to year, the following equations will have to hold:

$$\left.\begin{aligned}
c_1 + v_1 + s_1 &= c_1 + c_2 + c_3 \\
c_2 + v_2 + s_2 &= v_1 + v_2 + v_3 \\
c_3 + v_3 + s_3 &= s_1 + s_2 + s_3
\end{aligned}\right\} \tag{I.4.1}$$

The value of the commodities produced in sector 1 must be equal to the value of the means of production required by all three sectors. The value of the commodities produced in sector 2 must be equal to the value of the wage goods needed by the workers in all three sectors. Finally, the value of the commodities produced in sector 3 will make up the value of the luxury goods purchased by the capitalists, or the surplus value of the economic system as a whole.

This is, in brief, the Marxian schema of simple reproduction. As will be seen, it reveals a close kinship with Quesnay's *Tableau*. Social classes are here completely identified with specific economic roles. As with Quesnay, production is represented as a circular process which reproduces, from year to year, all the means of production used up in the production process and yields, in addition, a surplus of goods, here called the "surplus value," which is appropriated by the owners of the means of production.

4.2. *Marx's own solution of the "transformation problem."* The ratio between surplus value and variable capital, which will be denoted by σ, is called the "rate of surplus value" by Marx:

$$\sigma = \frac{s}{v} \tag{I.4.2}$$

If the subsistence wage is the same in all sectors (as a result of competition) and if the value of each commodity is (by Marx's definition) equal to the quantity of labor socially necessary for its production, then it follows that the rate of surplus value must be the same in all sectors, so that in our example

$$\sigma = \frac{s_1}{v_1} = \frac{s_2}{v_2} = \frac{s_3}{v_3} \tag{I.4.3}$$

In a capitalist system, however, this equality of the rates of surplus value will never be realized because market competition will drive capital into the various sectors in such a way as to tend to equalize, not the rates of surplus value, but rather the rates of profit, which we shall denote by π_i, and which Marx represents by

$$\pi_i = \frac{s_i}{c_i + v_i} \qquad i = 1, 2, 3 \qquad (I.4.4)$$

i.e., as the ratio of surplus value to total capital (constant capital plus variable capital) in each sector.

We can now denote by γ what Marx calls the "organic composition of capital" and define it by the ratio

$$\gamma_i = \frac{c_i}{v_i} \qquad i = 1, 2, 3 \qquad (I.4.5)$$

which obviously is an index of capital intensity in the various sectors. Substituting (I.4.3) and (I.4.5) into (I.4.4), one obtains

$$\pi_i = \frac{\sigma}{1 + \gamma_i} \qquad i = 1, 2, 3 \qquad (I.4.6)$$

from which the following propositions can be deduced immediately:

(a) the rate of profit is positive if, and only if, the rate of surplus value is positive;

(b) the rate of profit is always less than the rate of surplus value, except in the extreme case in which there is no constant capital (in which case $\gamma_i = 0$ and hence $\pi_i = \sigma$);

(c) the rate of profit is a monotonically increasing function of the rate of surplus value.

It can also be seen immediately from (I.4.6) that equality of the rates of profit in the various sectors and equality of the rates of surplus value in the same sectors can hold simultaneously only in the very special case in which the "organic composition of capital" is exactly the same in all sectors.

In the general case, in which the "organic composition of capital" differs from one process of production to another, it will be the equality of the rates of profit which is realized in any capitalist system and not the equality of the rates of surplus value. The result is that prices will come to diverge from quantities of embodied labor (i.e., from what Marx calls "values," by definition). This once again contradicts, in a framework different from Ricardo's, the pure labor theory of value.

But Marx, like Ricardo, did not give up in the face of these difficulties. On the contrary, and by contrast with Ricardo, Marx went on to counterattack. After carrying out the whole of his analysis in Volumes I and II of *Capital* by adhering to the rule of proportionality between values and quantities of embodied labor, in Volume III, Chapter IX (see Marx [10]), he turned to "prices of production" and developed an argument which can, in essence, be expressed as follows.

In a capitalist system, "prices of production" certainly diverge from quantities of embodied labor, or "values." Such a divergence is, nevertheless, nothing more than merely one of the distortions of capitalist economies. The primary magnitudes, Marx argues, are the "values," and thus all the fundamental relationships must be expressed in terms of "values." Prices are *derived* magnitudes. They are derived from the "values" and simply effect a redistribution of surplus value according to the logic of a capitalist system, which needs to place capital at the heart of the production process. What happens in a capitalist system is that the market acts as a kind of pool which receives surplus value and redistributes it in the form of profit. It is as if, ideally, the capitalists would pay surplus value into a common fund and would then redistribute it, through the price system, no longer in proportion to wages (i.e., in the way in which it was created), but rather in proportion to total capital. In the system (I.4.1) above, the common fund would consist of $(s_1 + s_2 + s_3)$ and the average rate of profit would be

$$\frac{s_1 + s_2 + s_3}{c_1 + c_2 + c_3 + v_1 + v_2 + v_3} = \pi \tag{I.4.7}$$

The market would force the prices of the outputs of the three sectors so as to become

$$c_1 + v_1 + \pi(c_1 + v_1)$$

$$c_2 + v_2 + \pi(c_2 + v_2) \tag{I.4.8}$$

$$c_3 + v_3 + \pi(c_3 + v_3)$$

The prices of commodities produced by processes with an above-average capital intensity will prove to be higher than the quantities of embodied labor, while the prices of commodities produced by processes with a below-average capital intensity will prove to be lower than the quantities of embodied labor. Appearances would thus become more complicated, but the substance would nevertheless remain unchanged. Finally, on the basis of two further assertions: i.e., (i) total profits are equal to total surplus value; and (ii) "the sum of the prices of production of the commodities produced is equal to the sum of their values," Marx concludes that the "transformation of values into prices of production" effected by the market serves merely to create the mystification that capital is "productive" and that profit is its reward, while in reality the former is embodied labor and the latter is disguised surplus value.

4.3. *Bortkiewicz' solution.* The ingenuity of these arguments can hardly be disputed. What had been an insurmountable analytical difficulty for Ricardo was turned by Marx into a further indictment of the capitalist system.

However, critics of Marx soon pointed out a logical inconsistency in the Marxian argument. If the conditions of simple reproduction are to be satisfied, the totals of the three rows in (I.4.8) must be equal to the totals of the three corresponding columns, as in (I.4.1). If this were not so, the system would not be able to reproduce itself from year to year. Now it is not difficult to show that, when this condition of logical consistency is met by (I.4.1), it cannot be satisfied by (I.4.8), unless the three sectors all have the same organic composition of capital, in which case the very problem of transformation would simply not arise. The drastic conclusion was therefore drawn that Marx's whole argument was mistaken.

But the whole problem of the "transformation of values into prices of production" was given new life by Ladislaus von Bortkiewicz, a Russian economist of Polish descent, in an article published in 1907 [1]. Bortkiewicz pointed out that, while Marx had certainly fallen into a mistake, this was due not to the intrinsic difficulty of the problem but rather to his inability to formulate the system of equations correctly. In the case of the schema (I.4.1), the appropriate system of equations is not that adopted by Marx, i.e., (I.4.8), but rather

$$
\left.
\begin{aligned}
(c_1 p_1 + v_1 p_2)(1 + \pi) &= (c_1 + c_2 + c_3)p_1 \\
(c_2 p_1 + v_2 p_2)(1 + \pi) &= (v_1 + v_2 + v_3)p_2 \\
(c_3 p_1 + v_3 p_2)(1 + \pi) &= (s_1 + s_2 + s_3)p_3
\end{aligned}
\right\}
\qquad (I.4.9)
$$

where p_1, p_2, p_3 are the prices of the means of production, the wage good, and the luxury good, respectively. This is a system of three equations in four unknowns: π, p_1, p_2, p_3. If one of the three prices is set equal to unity, the corresponding commodity thus being adopted as the *numéraire*, the unknowns reduce to three and it can be shown that the system is determinate.[16]

---

[16] The algebraic solution of system (I.4.9), as it was presented by Bortkiewicz [1, p. 202–203], is:

$$
\pi = \frac{f_2 g_1 + g_2 - \sqrt{(f_2 g_1 - g_2)^2 + 4 f_1 g_1 g_2}}{2(f_2 - f_1)} - 1
\qquad \text{where}
$$

$$
p_3 = 1
$$

$$
f_1 = \frac{v_1}{c_1} \qquad g_1 = \frac{v_1 + c_1 + s_1}{c_1}
$$

$$
p_2 = \frac{g_3}{g_2 + (f_3 - f_2)(1 + \pi)}
$$

$$
f_2 = \frac{v_2}{c_2} \qquad g_2 = \frac{v_2 + c_2 + s_2}{c_2}
$$

$$
p_1 = \frac{f_1 p_2 (1 + \pi)}{g_1 - (1 + \pi)}
$$

$$
f_3 = \frac{v_3}{c_3} \qquad g_3 = \frac{v_3 + c_3 + s_3}{c_3}
$$

It may be interesting to note that the solution for the rate of profit (π) preserves the property, already mentioned with reference to the Ricardian system, of being entirely independent of the condition of production of the luxury goods.

The logical inconsistency between Volumes I, II and Volume III of *Capital* is thus removed. It follows, however, from Bortkiewicz own formulation, that the equality of total surplus value and total profit and the equality of total "values" and total prices cannot be satisfied simultaneously. Moreover, the expression (I.4.7), by which Marx represents the average rate of profit, is not correct, because profit must be expressed in terms of the price system and not in terms of the "value" system. Finally, even the *directions* of the divergences of prices from "values" cannot be predicted with absolute certainty on the basis of the "organic composition of capital" alone, as will clearly appear later.

To conclude, Marx was somewhat over confident and over hasty in thinking that he had solved the problem of the relation between prices and quantities of labor. His two assertions, (i) and (ii), mentioned at the end of the previous section, are incorrect; furthermore, the expressions which he suggested for the rate of profit, (I.4.4) and (I.4.7), are also incorrect. At the same time, however, the accusation made by his critics that there is an inherent logical inconsistency in the problem of the "transformation of values into prices" has been shown to be without foundation. A relation between quantities of labour and prices does exist, even if it is very complex, and not so easy to interpret. In the economic literature on Marx, these problems have thus given rise to a long series of debates which, even today, show no sign of coming to an end. We shall return to these problems in the *Appendix to Chapter V*.

5   The Marginalists

5.1. *The "pure exchange model" and the optimum allocation of resources.* Marginal economic analysis, which has dominated formal economic thinking since 1870, marked a radical change of interests with respect to Classical economics. For reasons not yet adequately clarified by historians of economic thought, the Marginalists left aside the phenomenon of production and began to study the rational behavior of the single consumer. Indeed, it is quite unnecessary to consider any process of production in order to grasp the essential features of marginal economic analysis.

The fundamental construction is a "model of pure exchange," which can be briefly summarized as follows. Consider a single individual who has a given endowment of "resources" and certain preferences, to be represented by a utility function. If the individual is assumed to maximize his utility, subject to the constraint of the "resources" which he possesses, and if the utility function has certain properties (which can be expressed with a certain formal elegance), it can be shown that the individual, for whom prices are given by the market, will go on purchasing physical quantities of each commodity up to the point at which its marginal utility becomes proportional to its price (equilibrium of the consumer). If one then turns to consider the set of all consumers who exchange their goods on the market, one can show that their atomistic, competitive behavior leads to the determination of such a set of market prices that, at these prices, no consumer can be made better off without making some other consumer worse off (a Pareto-optimal, general, economic equilibrium).

This model clearly has nothing whatsoever to do with the phenomenon of production. The problem it deals with is the optimal allocation, through exchange, of a certain initial endowment and distribution of resources. From one point of view it represents a return to the idea of a fixed endowment of resources (i.e., to the concept of wealth as a stock), which had characterized pre-Classical economic thinking.[17] From another point of view, it also represents an attempt to build economic analysis on those foundations. Indeed, to the unacceptable conclusion of the Mercantilists (i.e., securing the greatest possible share of the given resources through an aggressive national policy), the Marginalists counterposed a completely different attitude. They accepted the distribution of the initial resources as given and then concentrated all their analytical efforts on the search for their optimal "allocation" through free exchange. The essential analytical elements that may be said to have emerged from this new model are: (i) the notion of "marginal utility," which presupposes continuous and differentiable utility functions; (ii) the notion of "substitution" among the various goods consumed as prices vary, which presupposes convex utility functions; (iii) an explanation of prices as "scarcity indexes" and hence as "optimal allocators" of the existing resources.

This model of pure exchange was, of course, subsequently modified and extended so as to include also the process of production.[18] To do this, however, it was necessary to adapt the phenomenon of production to the requirements of a preconceived model developed with reference to the concept of wealth as a stock. It was necessary to invent concepts exactly parallel to those of the consumption schema: the concept of "marginal productivity"; the concept of "substitution" among the various factors of production; the treatment of the wage rate and the rate of profit as prices, just like any other price, and hence their interpretation as scarcity indexes and "optimal allocators" of the resources "labor" and "capital." In other words, it became necessary

---

[17] See pp. 2-3 above.

[18] The marginal productivity theory was developed in the 1890s.

to shape a theory of production (which by its very nature is concerned with *flows*) in such a way as to meet the requirements of a preexisting theory concerning the optimal "allocation" of certain *stocks* of resources. This feature of marginal theory has proved itself to be of crucial importance for subsequent theoretical developments, because it has inevitably contributed to keeping the phenomenon of production in a secondary and subordinate position.[19]

The Marginalist theory of production has been given various versions. For our purposes it is of interest briefly to consider two of them associated with the names of Walras and Wicksell, respectively.[20]

5.2. *Léon Walras*.[21] The Walrasian theory is of interest in the context of the present study because, in its original formulation, it introduced the use of production coefficients. This use of production coefficients has resulted in the Walrasian system's often being counted as one of the precursors of Leontief's input-output analysis. Yet, for Walras, as for all the Marginalists, the two basic poles around which the whole analysis gravitates are the utility functions of consumers on the one hand, and the exogenously given quantities of resources on the other. Production is inserted in between as a purely intermediate, and eventually insignificant, process of transformation, which complicates the original theoretical schema without affecting its foundations.

It is in fact here that the typical limitations of Walras' model can be seen most clearly. Walras is obliged to apply his theory, originally developed for the optimal allocation of a given *stock* of resources, to a flow. What he does is to consider the flow of a certain period of time as if it were a stock *within that period of time* taken in isolation from all other periods of time. But in this way he is never able to relate one period of time to another in a satisfactory manner; he is never able to develop a satisfactory theory of capital accumulation.

[19] In dealing with production, whenever anything came to light that was not quite consistent with the model of pure exchange, the typical reaction has been to modify the production side of the picture, i.e., to introduce into the theory of production all the assumptions that are necessary to restore its consistency with the preconceived model of pure exchange.

[20] Marginal theory was developed almost simultaneously by various authors in various countries. Besides Walras and Wicksell, one may recall: C. Menger (1840–1921) and E. Böhm-Bawerk (1851–1914) in Austria; W. S. Jevons (1835–1882), F. Edgeworth (1845–1926), and A. Marshall (1842–1924) in England; M. Pantaleoni (1857–1924), V. Pareto (1848–1923), and E. Barone (1859–1924) in Italy; J. B. Clark (1847–1938) and Irving Fisher (1867–1947) in the U.S.A.; G. Cassel (1866–1945) in Sweden.

[21] Léon Walras (1834–1910) was first a mining engineer, then a journalist, and finally a professor of economics at Lausanne. His principal work, *Elements d'économie politique pure*, was first published in 1874–1877.

Recent extensions of the Walrasian schema have accentuated these features of it. The model of pure exchange has become ever more dominant as the basic frame of reference. The phenomenon of production, if and when it is included, adds nothing essential. Indeed, in the attempt to overcome the difficulties of linking up the various periods of time, the theoretical schema for the "allocation" of a given stock of resources has recently been extended to cover *all* time periods, considered together, from the present to the end of time, as if economic decisions did not have to be taken continually, period by period, but today, once for all time. There is no justification for such an exercise in economic fiction, except that the Walrasian model cannot be developed in any other way. In reality, time is a succession of periods *in each of which* decisions are taken. But the inability of the Walrasian theoretical framework to deal with a succession of decisions has left the theorists with no option but that of singling out one period of time and privileging it to such an extent as to suppose that all economic decisions are to be taken in that period for all time. In this way one may well arrive at models that are extremely elegant from a formal or mathematical point of view. It becomes difficult, however, to resist the persistent trend toward making the process of production increasingly more abstract, insignificant, and irrelevant.

5.3. *Knut Wicksell.*[22] The version of the marginal theory of production which is associated with the name of Wicksell shows features which appear at once of greater relevance. One can, if one wishes, trace this version back to Classical economics by relating it to the analysis of rent given within the Ricardian theory. Ricardo had distinguished between two kinds of rent: extensive rent (which results from the process of bringing less and less fertile plots of land under cultivation), and *intensive* rent (which results from the application of increasing quantities of capital and labor to the same land). The first kind of rent is not congenial to marginal analysis (and has usually been ignored), but the second kind, "intensive rent," lends itself rather well to such analysis. If we assume, to start with, that production is by means of land and labor alone (no capital being required), we may suppose there to be many different *proportions* in which labor and land can be "combined" (many methods of production) and we can therefore write

$$Y = \varphi(L, T) \tag{I.5.1}$$

---

[22] Knut Wicksell (1851–1926) was an economist with considerable mathematical training. He obtained the chair of Economics (at Lund, Sweden) rather late in his life, probably because of the numerous enemies he made by being outspoken on birth control, a subject which fascinated him.

That is, net output (Y) is a function of the physical quantities of labor (L) and land (T).

It is to be noted that, if w denotes the wage rate and r the rent per unit of land, then it necessarily follows (as an accounting relation) that

$$Y = wL + rT \tag{I.5.2}$$

Suppose now that the production function φ is continuous and differentiable, with first partial derivatives which are positive but decreasing (so as to make the function itself convex, just like a utility function) and call $\partial Y/\partial L$ the "marginal product of labor" and $\partial Y/\partial T$ the "marginal product of land." Under conditions of free competition, it can be asserted that, owing to the convexity of the production function, the wage rate w will tend to equality with the marginal product of labor, so that $w = \partial Y/\partial L$. It does not follow, however, that the rent per unit of land, r, should also tend to equality with the marginal product of land (granted that it is the landowners that hire labor and organize the process of production). One can make a further assertion, i.e., that $r = \partial Y/\partial T$, and hence, by substitution into (I.5.2), that

$$Y = \frac{\partial Y}{\partial L}L + \frac{\partial Y}{\partial T}T \tag{I.5.3}$$

only if the function φ is of a particular kind. More precisely, we know, from a mathematical theorem due to Euler, that the relation (I.5.3) holds *only* if the function is homogeneous of the first degree. Thus the Marginalists were obliged to assume that the production function (I.5.1) is homogeneous of the first degree. Only in this way were they enabled to say that, under perfectly competitive conditions, w and r tend to the corresponding marginal products, while Euler's relation (I.5.3) ensures that the net output Y is entirely distributed between workers and landowners in proportion to the marginal products of labor and land respectively, without any residual being left over.

This has become the basic model for the marginal theory of production and the marginal theory of income distribution.[23] It will be noted how perfectly it mirrors the features of the Marginalist theory of consumer behavior, which is sketched out in Section 5.1 above.

One can also see that no difficulties arise in extending the same theoretical schema to a greater number of factors (for example, to different types of labor and to different qualities of land), provided that these factors are all like labor and land, in the sense that they can be

---

[23] The model is common to a whole group of Marginalist economists, from Wicksteed [25] onward.

expressed in physical terms. Difficulties do arise,[24] however, as soon as one attempts to introduce the factor "capital."[25] For, whereas the wage rate and the rent per unit of land refer to *physical units* of labor and land respectively, the rate of profit is a percentage rate referred to the *value* of capital goods. And the value of total capital is a magnitude the determination of which requires a prior knowledge of the rate of profit, which is precisely a variable that one seeks to determine.[26] In other words, the rate of profit is defined with respect to the *value* of capital goods, while the production function is a technical relation which can only include physical quantities. This has given rise to a long series of attempts to overcome the difficulty.

Böhm-Bawerk sought to identify capital with time and to reduce every type of capital good to an "average period of production." This he succeeded in doing for the special case of a simple rate of interest but not for the general case of a compound rate of interest. Wicksell explicitly took up Böhm-Bawerk's work at this point. In his first important theoretical work [22], Wicksell follows Böhm-Bawerk and uses the "average period of production." Subsequently, in his *Lectures* [23], he constructs a more complex theoretical system in which the production functions are conceived in terms of capital goods measured in physical terms, but the total quantity of capital is assumed to be given in terms of value. This system leads him to admit the existence of a divergence between the marginal productivity of capital (obtained as a derivative of the production function) and the rate of profit (which is, by definition, related to the value of the capital goods). Finally, in a work written toward the end of his life, Wicksell [24] sets out a model of production in which, in order to avoid various objections, he has to introduce numerous simplifications. It is in this work that he uses the special production function

$$Y = c L^{1-\alpha} K^\alpha \tag{I.5.4}$$

(where Y denotes net output, L labor, K capital, and c and α are constants). It later became known as the Cobb–Douglas production function, after the names of two American economists who took it up.

---

[24] A detailed analysis of these difficulties may be found in Garegnani [4].

[25] On the wave of initial enthusiasm, many Marginalists did not even perceive these difficulties. John Bates Clark [2] is a typical example. As early as the 1890s he proposed the use of a global quantity, called "capital," along the same lines as those for "land" and "labor."

[26] On the circularity of the arguments into which one falls in this way, see Wicksell [23, pp. 149].

Such a function can, of course, be written more generally as

$$Y = f(L, K) \tag{I.5.5}$$

provided that f is assumed to be a homogeneous function of the first degree, and that one adds all the assumptions which are logically necessary if one is to include a factor "capital," K, such that its partial derivative may be identified with the "rate of profit." Wicksell himself had many doubts and hestitations on this point, and ended up by leaving the whole discussion in a rather inconclusive state.[27] But this has not been the attitude of most of the other Marginalist writers, who have set aside all doubts and hesitations.[28]

---

[27] See the very last pages of Wicksell [24, pp. 297–299].

[28] The production function (I.5.5) has been used both with reference to an economic system as a whole and with reference to a single firm. (See, for example, Schneider [15].) In graphical terms it has been represented by a diagram of isocurves, or isoquants (see Fig. I.5) or by a curve expressing the relation between the capital/labor ratio (k) and the net product/labor ratio (y). (See Fig. I.6.)

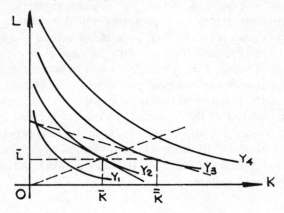

FIG. I.5. Isoquants of a production function

In Fig. I.5 each of the isoquants $Y_1, Y_2, Y_3, \ldots$ represents the infinite number of possible proportions between capital and labor to obtain the same level of net output. Each isoquant is the radial projection of every other isoquant, as the function is homogeneous of the 1st degree. Given the endowments of factors $\bar{K}$ and $\bar{L}$, the optimum equilibrium position is indicated by the point at which the given "endowments" $\bar{K}$ and $\bar{L}$ are fully employed. At this point the slope of the line tangent to the isoquant represents the optimum ratio between the "factor prices," i.e. between the wage rate and the rate of profit. For, the isoquant to which the line is tangent is the highest among all the isoquants touched by the line itself.

Alternatively, in Fig. I.6, given a capital/labor ratio $\bar{k}$, the rate of profit can be read off as the slope of the tangent at the correspondent point $\bar{y}$ of the curve y (AB/wB in Fig. I.6), and the wage rate may be read off as the intercept of such tangent on the ordinate ($0w$ in the same figure).

Thus, after all the attempts in various directions, it has not proved possible to do anything other than return to the Marginal theory of production and distribution based on the factors labor and land and, notwithstanding all the difficulties, simply extend it, just as it is, to the factor "capital," accepting all the additional assumptions which are necessary if the analysis is to remain logically consistent.

Unfortunately, these additional assumptions have turned out to be far more restrictive than the Marginalist writers suspected. In practice, the only case for which it has proved possible to construct a marginal theory of production and income distribution along the lines set out above, without encountering logical difficulties, is the (purely hypothetical and imaginary) case of an economic system producing only one

From simple inspection of the two figures one can see immediately that, if one fixes the quantity of one factor, for example $\bar{L}$, and increases the quantity of the other, K in our case, one obtains a "movement along the production function," with which are associated certain well-defined relations; namely (see, in the two figures, the changes from $\bar{K}$ to $\bar{\bar{K}}$ and from $\bar{k}$ to $\bar{\bar{k}}$, respectively): an increase in the output/labor ratio, an increase in the capital/output ratio, an increase in the wage rate, and a decrease in the rate of profit. More particularly, one can see immediately that the relation between the rate of profit and the capital/output ratio is necessarily inverse and monotonic.

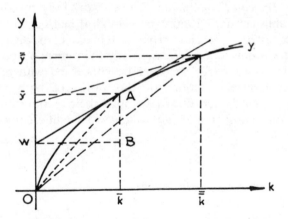

FIG. I.6. Relation between output/labor ratio and capital/labor ratio
in the marginal theory

It is worth noting that the notions of production as a circular process and of net output intended as a surplus (with respect to what it is necessary to produce in order to replace the means of production) have disappeared from this model. The final net product is put directly into relation with the "factors of production," while all the complex intermediate interindustry process has been eliminated completely. Conversely, the theory has accentuated to the utmost the notions of *change in the proportions* and of *substitution* among the factors of production, as a necessary consequence of the variation in the opposite direction of the ratio of their "factor prices" (rate of profit and wage rate).

commodity, which serves both as a consumption good and as a capital good. In this case the difficulties of extending the marginal analysis to capital theory do not arise simply because the same magnitude, K, can express at one and the same time both the physical quantity of the capital good and its value. With respect to the general case, Marginalist writers have only been able to stick to the hope (or, as one writer put it, the "act of faith"[29]) that the relations derived from a one-commodity model also hold good for the general case. We shall return to this question in Chapter VI.

6   Wassily Leontief and Piero Sraffa

As hinted earlier, recent reformulations of the theory of production have derived from a return to interindustry analysis. This has happened mainly on the initiative of two economists of our time: Wassily Leontief and Piero Sraffa. Leontief, of Russian origin, has been a professor at Harvard University, Sraffa, an Italian, has been at the University of Cambridge (in England), since 1926. Leontief's work [9], first published in 1941 and in a second edition in 1951, is inspired by essentially empirical concerns and represents a direct descendant of Quesnay's *Tableau Economique*. Sraffa's work [17], by contrast, which was not published until 1960 even though it had begun to take shape in the late 1920s, descends from a schema of a clearly Ricardian origin and was developed for essentially theoretical purposes.

In the following pages we shall be concerned with matters which form a common foundation for the works of both of these two economists, even though they developed their theories quite independently of one another and with such widely different concerns and intentions.[30]

---

[29] This expression has been used by Ferguson [3, p. xvii].

[30] In the last chapter of the book, which is devoted to dynamic models, we also consider a theoretical model [20], proposed by the Hungarian-born mathematician, John von Neumann (1903–1957). This model was first published in German in 1937, and thus before the works of Leontief and Sraffa. However, it became known only after its English translation (1945), and has since become a constant reference in most theoretical works on dynamic economic theory.

References*

[1] Bortkiewicz, Ladislaus von, "On the Correction of Marx's Fundamental Theoretical Construction in the Third Volume of Capital," in Paul M. Sweezy, ed., *Karl Marx and the Close of his System* by E. von Böhm-Bawerk, and *Böhm-Bawerk's Criticism of Marx* by R. Hilferding, New York: August M. Kelley, 1969, pp. 199–221.

[2] Clark, John Bates, *Theory of Distribution of Wealth*, New York: Macmillan, 1899.

[3] Ferguson, Charles, *The Neoclassical Theory of Production and Distribution*, Cambridge: Cambridge University Press, 1969.

[4] Garegnani, Pierangelo, *Il capitale nelle teorie della distribuzione*, Milano: Giuffrè, 1960.

[5] Heckscher, Eli F., *Mercantilism*, 2 vols., London: George Allen and Unwin, 1955 (first published in Swedish in 1931).

[6] I.N.E.D., "François Quesnay et la Physiocratie," 2 vols., Paris: Institut National d'Etudes Démographiques, 1958.

[7] Kaldor, Nicholas, "Alternative Theories of Distribution," *Review of Economic Studies*, 1955–56, pp. 83–100, reprinted in *Essays on Value and Distribution*, London: G. Duckworth, 1960.

[8] Kuczynski, Marguerite, and Meek, Ronald, *Quesnay's Tableau Economique*, London: Macmillan, 1972.

[9] Leontief, Wassily W., *The Structure of American Economy 1919–1929*, 1st ed., Cambridge, Mass.: Harvard University Press, 1941; *The Structure of American Economy 1919–1939*, 2nd ed., New York: Oxford University Press, 1951.

[10] Marx, Karl, *Capital*, Vol. III, London: Lawrence and Wishart, 1959 (first published in German in 1894).

[11] Marx, Karl, and Engels, Friedrich, *The German Ideology*, ed. by C. J. Arthur, London: Lawrence and Wishart, 1965 (originally written in 1845–1846).

[12] Meek, Ronald, "The Interpretation of the 'Tableau Economique'," *Economica*, 1960, pp. 322–347.

[13] Pasinetti, Luigi L., "A Mathematical Formulation of the Ricardian System," *Review of Economic Studies* 1959–60, pp. 78–98; reprinted in *Growth and Income Distribution – Essays in Economic Theory*, Cambridge: Cambridge University Press, 1974.

[14] Phillip, Almarin, "The 'Tableau Economique' as a Simple Leontief Model," *Quarterly Journal of Economics*, 1955, pp. 137–144.

---

* The references at the end of each chapter are simply a list of the works referred to in the chapter itself. They are not meant to be a complete bibliography.

[15] Schneider, Erich, *Theorie der Produktion*, Vienna: Julius Springer, 1934.

[16] Smith, Adam, *An Enquiry into the Nature and Causes of the Wealth of Nations*, ed. by E. Cannan, London: Methuen & Co., 1904. (First edition: 1776).

[17] Sraffa, Piero, *Production of Commodities by means of Commodities*, Cambridge: Cambridge University Press, 1960.

[18] ———, ed., *Works and Correspondence of David Ricardo*, 11 vols., Cambridge: Cambridge University Press, 1951–1973.

[19] Tsuru, Shigeto, "On Reproduction Schemes," in Paul M. Sweezy, *The Theory of Capitalist Development*, New York: Oxford University Press, 1942, pp. 365–374.

[20] Von Neumann, John, "Über ein ökonomisches Gleichungssystem und eine Verallgemeinerung des Brouwerschen Fixpunktsatzes," in *Ergebnisse eines Matematischen Kolloquiums*, Vienna, 1937, vol. VIII, pp. 73–83, translated as "A Model of General Equilibrium," *The Review of Economic Studies*, 1945, pp. 1–9.

[21] Walras, Léon, *Elements of Pure Economics*, ed. by W. Jaffé, London: George Allen and Unwin, 1954 (first published in French in 1874–1877).

[22] Wicksell, Knut, *Value, Capital and Rent*, London: George Allen and Unwin, 1954 (first published in German in 1893).

[23] ———, *Lectures on Political Economy*, 2 vols., ed. by Lionel Robbins, London: George Routledge and Sons, 1934 (first published in Swedish in 1901).

[24] ———, "A Mathematical Analysis of Dr. Åkerman's Problem," in [23, pp. 274–299] (first published in Swedish in 1923).

[25] Wicksteed, Philip H., *An Essay on the Co-ordination of the Laws of Distribution*, London: Macmillan, 1894.

CHAPTER TWO

The Transactions, or
Input-output, Table

1 A Simple Economic System and its Transactions Table

1.1. *Remarks on method.* The theories of modern economists are sharply distinguished from those of their predecessors by a quite general feature. As may be seen from the discussion in Chapter I, the economists of earlier centuries set themselves the rather ambitious task of studying economic reality in all its complexity, using, however, somewhat crude methods of analysis.

Today economists are more conscious of the complexity of real economic relationships and adopt the procedure of initially assuming a simplified economic system. This simplified economic system is, however, studied in a rigorous way, with analytical methods which, in principle at least, should leave no room for any ambiguity. It is only after having studied a simplified economic system that the attempt is then made to introduce, one at a time, more complex hypotheses. This procedure is of course followed in the present analysis.

1.2. *The commodity flows.* We begin with a numerical example used by Sraffa in Chapter I of his already mentioned book.

Consider an economic system so simple as to consist of only three production processes (or industries), each quite distinct from the others, producing wheat (w), iron (i), and turkeys (t), respectively. Suppose now that we have observed such an economic system over a certain finite period of time (call it a "year") and that we have observed, in that period, the physical flows of commodities shown in Table II.1. The first column lists the physical quantities of wheat (240 tons), iron (12 tons) and turkeys (18 gross)[1] which are observed as entering the wheat industry and, below the arrow, the physical quantity of wheat (450 tons) which are observed as being produced. The second and third columns are to be interpreted similarly. One can thus interpret each column as the set of inputs of the various commodities into each production process.

---

[1] A gross is equal to 12 dozen.

TABLE II.1
Flows of commodities in physical terms

	w		i		t		
w	240	+	90	+	120	=	450
i	12	+	6	+	3	=	21
t	18	+	12	+	30	=	60
	↓		↓		↓		
	450(w)		21(i)		60(t)		

The various commodities are expressed in different units of measurement: the wheat in tons, the iron also in tons, the turkeys in gross; thus the numbers appearing in any column cannot be added. The situation is different with respect to the rows, in each of which there appear physically homogeneous quantities. The latter can be added, as indeed they have been in Table II.1. Each row may thus be interpreted as the set of deliveries of the corresponding commodity to the various industries.

1.3. *A distinction between technical requirements and consumption requirements.* Table II.1 shows the circulation (or set of flows) of commodities that may be observed in the economic system considered during the period of time in question. It does not, however, show how they are used. Clearly the quantities of commodities shown will serve in part as means of production and in part as consumption goods for those working in each industry. Thus Table II.1 must be analyzed in greater depth if one wishes to distinguish the technical relations between the different industries from the relations between these industries and the final demands (consumption and investment).

In order to make this distinction we must carry our analysis a step further. Suppose that the economic system under consideration is found to be in a completely stationary state. The labor force, technical knowledge, and consumption decisions are all constant through time, and the economic system neither expands nor contracts. Exactly the same physical flows of goods and services are reproduced year after year without any change. More specifically, suppose that empirical investigation shows that in the economic system as a whole 60 workers are employed, with 18, 12, and 30 of them, respectively, being allocated to each of the three industries. We assume that, on average, each worker consumes 3 tons of wheat and half a gross of turkeys every year. In this case Table II.1 can be replaced by another table in which a distinction is made between an economic activity of production and an economic activity of consumption (see Table II.2).

TABLE II.2
Flows of commodities and labor services

	w	i	t	Final sector		
w	186	54	30	180	=	450
i	12	6	3	—	=	21
t	9	6	15	30	=	60
Final sector	18	12	30	—	=	60
	↓	↓	↓			
	450	21	60			

There has thus been added a final row which shows the annual flow of labor services to each industry (expressed in man-years) and a final column which shows, in the present example, the total consumption of each commodity expressed in physical terms. The row and the column in question may be referred to as the *final sector*.

The quantities which appear in the last column (180 tons of wheat and 30 gross of turkeys) can all be devoted to consumption, given that, in the present example, the system is in a stationary state. They represent the net product of the economic system or the *net national income*. They thus include both what Quesnay, Ricardo, and Marx thought of as the surplus of the economic system and what they thought of as the means of subsistence (i.e., what is necessary for the mere maintenance of the workers employed in production).

In modern economic theories this Classical distinction between means of subsistence and the surplus is no longer made because of the arbitrariness therein, which results from the fact that the distinction itself ought to vary from place to place and from time to time. It is nevertheless worth remembering that in certain countries, for example in underdeveloped countries and in centrally planned economies, where it is important to know what share of the net national income can be used for purposes other than consumption (notably for investment), the distinction is still made in practice. In the interest of simplicity we shall not make use of the distinction in the following pages, but we shall never preclude the possibilities of introducing it whenever it seems useful to do so.

1.4. *The input-output table.* Table II.2 displays the interdependence of the various industries and, moreover, the interdependence between the industries and the final sector of the simplified economic system considered. Each commodity is produced in the corresponding industry and is then delivered by that industry to all the industries (including itself) according to their production requirements. The output in excess of these industrial requirements is delivered to the final sector for consumption. From the final sector, in turn, labor services flow to the various industries for their production needs.

Given our assumption that the system is completely stationary, this whole network of flows of goods and services is repeated year after year with exactly the same magnitudes and properties.

The reader will perhaps already have realized that, if these flows of goods and services are to be repeated year after year with precisely the same properties, then the various commodities must be exchanged with one another according to certain exchange ratios or "prices." We shall see below how these prices may be "calculated." For the moment, suppose it to be observed that in our system 10 tons of wheat exchange with: 1 ton of iron; 2 gross of turkeys; 1.81818 man-years of labor. Then, if we adopt a physical unit of one of the three commodities, for example a ton of iron, as *numéraire*, we obtain the following prices: the price of one ton of iron is 1, by definition; the price of one ton of wheat is 0.1; the price of a gross of turkeys is 0.5; and the annual wage per worker is 0.555.

We may now rewrite Table II.2 in current value terms after having multiplied each physical quantity by the corresponding price. We obtain Table II.3. As may be seen, the columns are now also summed

TABLE II.3

Flows of commodities and services in terms of iron, used as
numéraire

	w	i	t	Final sector (consumption)	Total
w	18.6	5.4	3	18	45
i	12	6	3	—	21
t	4.5	3	7.5	15	30
Total (partial)	35.1	14.4	13.5	—	
Final sector (value added)	9.9	6.6	16.5	—	(33)
Total	45	21	30	(33)	96

since, by contrast with Tables II.1 and II.2, the commodities and even the labor services are expressed in homogeneous (current value) units, i.e., in terms of the *numéraire* or unit of account adopted (a ton of iron). The sum of each row thus comes, for accounting reasons, to equal the corresponding column sum.

This table represents what has been called *the transactions matrix*, or simply *the transactions table*, or *the input-output table*.

1.5. *Notions of national accounting*. The numerical example considered above, though very simple, brings to light certain important national accounting concepts which it will be appropriate to emphasize. Table II.3 comprises an "interindustry" part, consisting of the first three rows and columns, and a part relating to the "final sector," consisting of the final column and the final row. The interindustry part, which expresses the technical relations between the various industries, absorbs 63 units of account (out of the 96 units which make up the total gross product), those 63 units being needed for the replacement of the means of production used up in the productive process. The final sector can therefore absorb the remaining 33 units, which represent the "fruit" of the productive activity, i.e., the net product of the system or the *net national income*. Since, by hypothesis, our system is in a stationary state, the entire net national income can be devoted to consumption. Table II.3 thus shows at a glance how the net national income can be considered from two distinct points of view: from the standpoint of the composition of final use (the "final sector" column) and from the standpoint of what has been called the *value added* in an economic system (the "final sector" row).

As is well known, value added in an economic system is the sum total of the payments made to the various members of the community. It was so called by reference to what happens in each industry, where the value of the output is identically equal to the sum: (i) of the value of the commodities used up in that industry (raw materials and manufactures, i.e., intermediate commodities); and (ii) of the value of the remuneration to those who have taken part in the productive process in that industry. It is therefore said that the value of this remuneration *is added* to the value of the purchased commodities; hence it has been called *value added*. The sum of the values added in all industries is obviously equal to total net income, i.e., to the value of the physical goods and services which make up the net national product.

Thus the final sector column and row in Table II.3 provide two different ways of considering the net national income, which is set out in the column with respect to its physical composition and in the row with respect to the industry in which it originated. The two totals coincide, although for any single industry the value added will, in general, differ from the value of the commodities which that industry delivers to the final sector. The former (value added) depends fundamentally on the state of technology, while the latter (the value of the commodities delivered to the final sector) depends on decisions concerning consumption (and concerning investment, in the case of a nonstationary system). Thus, in our example, the value added in the wheat industry (9.9 units of account) differs from the value of the quantity of wheat which is included in the net national product (18 units of account). Similarly, the values added in the iron and turkey industries (6.6 and 16.5 units of account respectively) differ from the values of the quantities of iron and turkeys which are included in the net national product (zero and 15 units of account respectively). Nevertheless, the two totals (9.9 + 6.6 + 16.5 = 33; and 18 + 0 + 15 = 33) necessarily coincide.

2　Practical devices and procedures

2.1. *Adjusting the theoretical scheme to meet empirical reality.* The schema considered above, even though it referred to an economic system so simple as to consist of only three industries in a completely stationary state, has sufficed to illustrate, at least in principle, the essential features of a transactions table. Not surprisingly, however, the moment one considers constructing a transactions table for a modern economic system, there immediately arises a whole series of problems of adjusting the theoretical scheme to match empirical reality. We shall briefly consider a few such problems.

2.2. *Problems of aggregation and disaggregation.* In the first place, in a modern economic system, one is confronted by thousands of products and by an extremely complex network of interrelationships.

In principle, one could list all these products one by one (as was done for wheat, iron, and turkeys in our example) and represent all the interrelationships in the way that we have seen above. In practice, this would involve the construction of tables so large as to be quite unmanageable, besides involving a formidable task of data collection and classification, at least in the present state of industrial censuses. It has therefore been normal to work at a certain level of "aggregation" of the productive processes, representing with a single row and corresponding column the whole steel industry, for example, with another row and corresponding column the whole of the chemical industry, and so on.[2]

The transactions tables which have been constructed and published for various countries in fact differ widely from one another principally

---

[2] The aggregation of single-firm data into data for an "industry" and/or of single-industry data into data for a larger "industry" gives rise to a series of complications. The opposite problem may also arise, namely, the problem of firms that produce commodities classified into different "industries," or of firms in which the same production process yields many *joint* products. For all these problems various statistical and accounting procedures have been suggested. See Stone [10] and U.N.O. [12].

with respect to the varying degrees of aggregation or dissaggregation that have been adopted, and their dimensions vary from a minimum of about 10 rows and columns (tables of dimension 10 × 10) to a maximum of about 450 rows and columns (tables of dimension 450 × 450).

2.3. *The calendar year as the time unit.* It will be evident, furthermore, that an actual economic system is hardly ever in a stationary state. The interindustry relations can vary from one year to another for various reasons, the improvement in technical knowledge being an especially important one. These changes normally have a cumulative effect which can, after a few years, lead to significant differences in the interindustry relations. Hence, in every country, every transactions table that has been constructed has been compiled with reference to a specific calendar year.

2.4. *Peculiar "industries."* In compiling transactions tables one is faced, furthermore, with certain rows and columns which refer to very special "industries," for which the inputs and outputs do not reflect flows of a strictly technical nature. The rows and columns in question are those referring to commercial services (wholesale and retail trade), transport, public adminstration, and importing and exporting. The following remarks on the treatment of such "industries" may prove helpful.

The commercial sector actually receives almost the whole output of all industries and then delivers it to the final sector or to other industries. To only a minor extent, however, do these transactions correspond to technical relations. It is therefore normally preferred not to trace the actual commodity flows in the table but rather to make the various products flow, from their respective industries, directly to the final demand sector (or to the other industries that require them), at a price including the payment for the commercial service. Then, in the row for the commercial sector, a payment is recorded, from each industry to the commercial sector, for the commercial services rendered to that industry. When this procedure is followed, the column for the commercial sector includes only the materials actually needed by that sector (which correspond to genuine technical relations), while the corresponding row represents the commercial services rendered in the handling of the products of the various industries.

The transport sector exhibits features similar to those of the commercial sector and has usually been treated analogously.

The public administration sector is also a very special one, although in a different way. In its column are shown the commodities needed in the provision of certain services, public consumption, and public investment. In the corresponding row there ought to appear, in theory, the services rendered, by public administration, to each industry; in fact, there appear the taxes and duties collected, the amount thereof being conventionally assumed to equal the value of the services rendered by public administration to each industry. It will be clear that these relationships are to only a minimal degree of a technical nature. It has therefore often been preferred to subdivide the row and column referring to public administration into several parts, some – or occasionally even all of them – being placed right outside the interindustry part of the table.

Finally, exports and imports constitute a column and a row, respectively, relating to international trade. In theory, imports ought to be divided into two parts: complementary imports (to be kept within the interindustry part of the table, because they relate to commodities which cannot be produced in the country in question, the demand for which is therefore governed by technical relations); and competitive imports (to be placed, by contrast, outside the interindustry part of the table, because they relate commodities which can be produced in that country). In practice such a distinction is not always made; it is sometimes preferred to place all imports outside the interindustry part of the table.[3] A more simple rule is followed for exports – they are always set completely outside the interindustry part of the transactions table.

The common aim of all these particular devices is that of maintaining, as far as possible, the technical nature of the interindustry relations which are represented.[4]

2.5. *The final sector.* The row and column representing the final sector must also be completed, with respect to the features of our simple example, as soon as one wishes to proceed to a concrete application. As has already been noted, an actual economic system is hardly ever in a stationary state. This implies that only part of the net national income can be devoted to consumption. Another part (which in modern economic systems may vary from about 10% to about 20%) has to be devoted to new investment for the expansion of productive capacity. The final sector column is therefore usually divided into two parts, relating to the goods and services devoted to consumption and those devoted to new investment.

[3] An interesting accounting procedure which has been adopted (especially in countries where imports are a high proportion of total transactions) consists in classifying imports both by industry of origin and by industry of destination. In practice this amounts to compiling two different input-output tables: one for the domestic flows and another for the flows coming from abroad.

[4] For all these special "industries" too, see Stone [10] and U.N.O. [12].

In its turn the final sector row is also usually divided into two parts, referring to the different kinds of income which make up value added: incomes from labor (wages and salaries), and nonlabor incomes (profits and rents).[5]

2.6. *The intermediate stages in the formation of prices.* In a transactions table in which the final sector is subdivided into consumption and investment, and in which the corresponding row is subdivided into wages and salaries, profits and rents, the two standpoints from which the net national product can be viewed, that of its physical composition and that of the distribution of value added, stand out more clearly.

It may be useful to emphasize that the equality between the row and column totals for the final sector does not merely represent an accounting identity, but represents a result of a real significance. The value of each commodity entering the final sector column is of course equal to the total costs of its production in the industry from which it comes; that is to say, it is equal to the cost of the (intermediate) commodities which were used up in that industry, plus the value added (i.e., wages, salaries, profits and rents) in that industry. But those intermediate commodities, in turn, were produced in a preceding stage of production. Thus their value will again be the sum of the cost of the (intermediate) commodities which were needed for their production, plus the value added in that stage of production; and so on, further and further back in the chain. Thus, as one traces the productive process backwards through time, all the intermediate commodities come to be "eliminated" from the calculation. And the value of each commodity eventually turns out to be nothing but the sum of all the values added (wages, salaries, profits, and rents) which have been distributed in all the stages of production necessary to obtain it as a final good.

2.7. *Replacement of the means of production.* As has been said above, Table II.3 shows the flows of goods and services among the various industries and between those industries and the final sector, which are observed in a well-defined period of time (usually a calendar year). In the interindustry part of the table these flows of goods and services represent the replacement of those means of production that have been used up in the process of production. But the means of production are of two kinds: those constituting the so-called "circulating capital," which are completely used up in the production process

---

[5] It goes without saying that the row (or rows) and column (or columns) of the final sector may also include such items as public administration and international trade, when these items are placed outside the interindustry table, according to the criteria discussed above.

within the year and must therefore be replaced in full, and those constituting the so-called "fixed capital," which are used up only partially during the year, and for which only the used-up part need be replaced. The flows of goods and services which appear in the transactions table thus represent the complete replacement of circulating capital and the replacement of that portion of the fixed capital which is made good during the year in question.

2.8. *A practical procedure concerning net and gross investment.* It follows from the last two sections that, with respect to investment goods, a transactions table ought to show all replacements (of circulating capital and of fixed capital) in the interindustry part and all new investments in the final sector column. Here, again, however, another procedure is usually adopted for practical reasons. As is well known, while it is relatively easy for statisticians to record gross investment in fixed capital, the attempt to distinguish between new investment and depreciation is far more difficult (and, in practice, arbitrary to a large extent). In order not to introduce arbitrary elements into the transactions table, it is therefore preferred to move all fixed capital replacements from the interindustry part of the table to the final sector column, showing there not just new investment but gross investment in fixed capital (including, that is, both new investments and replacements). Correspondingly, in the final sector row, the depreciation figure for each industry is shown alongside the value added.

2.9. *An interindustry table for the stocks of capital goods.* There is another implication to be drawn from the discussion above. When there are fixed capital goods in an economic system, a transactions table that shows the flows of commodities in the system can no longer be considered to be a complete representation of the whole economic system. For, "behind" all the flows of goods and services that take place during the year considered, there is also a set of stocks, consisting of the fixed capital goods (to which could be added all the natural resources).

Alongside the *table of flows*, one could therefore also construct a *table of stocks*, drawn up similarly to the flow table, thus containing for each single industry all the existing fixed capital stocks, listed according to their industry of origin, and finally all the existing natural resources. Although a table of stocks involves no more conceptual difficulties than does a table of flows, it has very rarely been constructed in practice,[6] not least because of the many statistical difficulties (and the

---

[6] From among the few attempts at constructing a table of stocks, it may be worth mentioning those made in the U.S.A., in Japan, and in India. In the U.S.A. the leading role has been taken by Professor Leontief's "Harvard Economic Research Project." See Leontief [8] and Carter [2].

costs) of obtaining the data. Furthermore, for planning purposes, it is the table of flows that has been found to be far more important.

3 Actual Applications

3.1. *The main input-output tables compiled so far*. Transactions tables have been constructed in many countries,[7] principally as useful adjuncts to, and checks on, national accounting. As is well known, the national accounts relate to value added and to final demand, while transactions tables record, in addition, all the interindustry flows.

The first transactions tables ever constructed for the U.S.A. are due to Leontief. They are of size 41 × 41 and relate to the years 1919 and 1929, respectively. In 1951 the *Bureau of Labor Statistics*, in collaboration with Leontief's research group, prepared a 96 × 96 table for 1939 and two others of the same size for 1919 and 1929. Then, in 1951, the *Bureau of Labor Statistics*, in collaboration with many other government agencies, and Harvard University, with financial assistance from the American government, completed the construction of a table with 450 rows and columns. This table relates to the year 1947. There are also two simplified versions of it, with dimensions 50 × 50 and 200 × 200, respectively. Other tables, of various dimensions, have been constructed more recently for the United States for the years 1958, 1963, 1967 and 1972.[8]

Various transactions tables were constructed in Great Britain too: the first, for 1935 and with 34 industries, was prepared by Tibor Barna in 1952. Tables of small and medium dimensions have been prepared by the *Central Statistical Office* for various years from 1948 onward.[9] A table with 400 industries was constructed at the University of Cambridge (Department of Applied Economics) for 1948 and then brought up to date for various subsequent years.

In Italy the first transactions table (of size 25 × 25) was constructed in 1950 on the initiative of the *U.S. Mutual Security Agency*.[10] It was later updated to 1953 and published in [9]. Subsequently, the Italian Central Statistical Institute (ISTAT), in collaboration with the Statistical Institute of the European Economic Community (ISCE), prepared transactions tables for 1959 and 1965. These tables are of size 77 × 77, but simplified versions have also been produced of sizes 33 × 33 and 16 × 16.

---

[7] A good survey, up to the end of the 1950s, is contained in Chenery and Clark [3].

[8] The transactions tables for the U.S.A. are normally published in the *Survey of Current Business*.

[9] For details, see Berman [1].

[10] See di Fenizio [4].

In fact, a joint project has been undertaken by the Central Statistical Institutes of all the countries belonging to the European Economic Community, whereby with a common plan and hence uniform principles, transactions tables have been constructed for Italy, France, West Germany, Holland, and Belgium, all with reference to the same years, 1959 and 1965.[11] Since the adoption in 1970 of the European system of integrated economic accounts, it has been expected that transactions tables will soon be published annually for all the E.E.C. countries.

The construction of input-output tables is by now widely practiced throughout the world, and there are very few countries for which one or more transactions tables have not been compiled.

An interesting question is the extent to which transactions tables have been constructed and used in the socialist countries. Certainly, from the beginning of Soviet planning in the 1920s, rudimentary systems of interindustry accounting were widely used. These systems were then gradually improved, particularly in the direction of greater disaggregation with respect to single industries and the various regions. Genuine transactions tables, of far greater dimensions than those constructed in the West, are said to have been prepared more recently (in the Soviet Union, they seem to have reached a size of 1500 × 1500). Precise information concerning such tables is not publicly available, however, owing to the secrecy which, particularly in the Soviet Union, surrounds this kind of work.[12]

3.2. *Planning aims and theoretical aims.* The transactions table, as presented above, appears as a tool of a purely descriptive nature. Even in these terms, it certainly represents an extremely useful source of information besides being a device for checking the results of national accounting.

Given that the methods for the compilation of transactions tables have been widely tested, the possibility of actually constructing them simply depends, nowadays, on the level of organization of the various government statistical agencies for processing the necessary data. In other words, what could only be a dream for Quesnay (the possibility of actually constructing a table representing the commodity flows taking place in an economy) has now become a reality.

It will be clear, however, that the scholars who have concerned themselves with the analysis of interindustry relations have had interests and aims reaching far beyond those of mere description. It is with these further interests and aims (mainly relating to planning and economic theory) that we shall be concerned in the following pages.

[11] See ISCE [6] and [7].
[12] See the references given by Ellman [5] and Treml [11].

References

[1] Berman, L., "Development in Input-Output Statistics," *Statistical News*, No. 3, November 1968 (HMSO, London).

[2] Carter, Anne P., *Structural Change in the American Economy*, Cambridge, Mass.: Harvard University Press, 1970.

[3] Chenery, Hollis B., and Clark, Paul G., *Interindustry Economics*, New York: John Wiley and Sons, 1959.

[4] Di Fenizio, Ferdinando, (ed.), special issue of *l'industria*, No. 4, 1952.

[5] Ellman, Michael, *Planning Problems in the U.S.S.R.*, Cambridge: Cambridge University Press, 1973.

[6] ISCE, *Tableaux Entrées-Sorties pour les pays de la Communauté Economique Européenne* (2nd version), Brussels, December 1965.

[7] ISCE, *Tableaux Entrées-Sorties pour les pays de la Communauté Economique Européene* (serie speciale), Brussels, 1970.

[8] Leontief, Wassily W., et al., *Studies in the Structure of the American Economy*, New York: Oxford University Press, 1953.

[9] Ministero del Bilancio e Tesoro, *Relazione generale sulla situazione economica del paese* (1954), Rome: Istituto Poligrafico dello Stato, 1955.

[10] Stone, Richard, *Input-Output and National Accounts*, Paris: OECE 1961.

[11] Treml, Vladimir, "Input-Output Analysis and Soviet Planning," in J. P. Hardt et al. (eds.), *Mathematics and Computers in Soviet Economic Planning*, New Haven: Yale University Press, 1967.

[12] U.N.O., *Input-Output Tables and Analysis* (*Studies in Methods, Series F*), No. 14, New York, 1973.

Other sources of bibliographical references are: (a) the periodical bibliographies published by the U.N.O.; (b) the *Proceedings* of the conferences on input-output, which have been held since 1950, roughly every three years, in various places.

CHAPTER THREE

A Linear Model of Production

1 The Transactions Table in Algebraic Terms

1.1. *Back to a simplified economic system.* In order to develop our analysis beyond the purely descriptive stage of the input-output table, we now return to a simplified economic system. Once again we adopt the simplifying assumptions of the numerical example of the previous chapter, namely, the assumptions that the economic system is in a perfectly stationary state with respect to the labor force, technical knowledge, and consumption decisions. We shall assume that exactly the same physical flows of goods and services are taking place year after year.

1.2. *The transactions table.* A representation in numerical terms becomes too restrictive for analytical purposes. But a more general treatment can be carried out in algebraic terms.

Suppose, quite generally, that the input-output table contains n rows and n columns, representing the outputs and the inputs, respectively, of n industries (where the term "industry" is broadly interpreted). Denote by: $q_{i1}, q_{i2}, \ldots, q_{ij}, \ldots, q_{in}$, the physical quantities of the ith commodity which are delivered to industries $1, 2, \ldots, j, \ldots, n$; and by p_i the price of the ith commodity. Since $i, j = 1, 2, \ldots, j, \ldots n$, (i.e., there are n rows and n columns), the transactions table will appear as in Table III.1.

As will be seen, in this table there appear n prices p_i, $i = 1, 2, \ldots, n$, and n^2 physical quantities q_{ij}; $i, j = 1, 2, \ldots, n$. These physical quantities are classified both by the kind of commodity (classification by the rows) and by the type of industry (classification by the columns). The symbol q_{ij} thus denotes the physical quantity of the ith commodity which is used in the jth industry. In other words, the two subscripts indicate the position of the corresponding physical quantity in the table – the first shows the number of the row and the second shows the number of the column.

The physical quantities which appear in the same row are clearly homogeneous (the first row might refer to the commodity wheat, for example), while the physical quantities which appear in any column are

TABLE III.1
Transactions table

Inputs	Outputs			
	Industry 1	Industry 2	Industry j	Final sector (column n)
Commodity 1	$q_{11}p_1$	$q_{12}p_1$ $\cdots$	$q_{1j}p_1$ $\cdots$	$q_{1n}p_1$
Commodity 2	$q_{21}p_2$	$q_{22}p_2$ $\cdots$	$q_{2j}p_2$ $\cdots$	$q_{2n}p_2$
	$\vdots$	$\vdots$	$\vdots$	$\vdots$
Commodity i	$q_{i1}p_i$	$q_{i2}p_i$ $\cdots$	$q_{ij}p_i$ $\cdots$	$q_{in}p_i$
	$\vdots$	$\vdots$	$\vdots$	$\vdots$
Final sector (row n)	$q_{n1}p_n$	$q_{n2}p_n$ $\cdots$	$q_{nj}p_n$ $\cdots$	$q_{nn}p_n$

heterogeneous (for example: wheat, coal, iron, etc., used in the wheat producing industry). Nevertheless, since every physical quantity has been multiplied by the corresponding price, the magnitude appearing in every cell is expressed in current values. It is thus possible to carry out the sums both across the rows and down the columns. From the purely accounting nature of the table it follows that the sum of each row will be identically equal to the sum of the corresponding column. Thus, if we denote by $Q_1, Q_2, \ldots, Q_n$ the total quantities of the commodities $1, 2, \ldots, n$ we have:

$$\sum_{j=1}^{n} q_{ij} = Q_i, \qquad\qquad i = 1, 2, \ldots, n$$

Table III.1 can also be expressed by two systems of accounting identities corresponding to the row sums and the column sums, respectively. We obtain

$$\left.\begin{array}{l} q_{11}p_1 + q_{12}p_1 + \quad\cdots\quad q_{1n}p_1 \equiv Q_1p_1 \\ q_{21}p_2 + q_{22}p_2 + \quad\cdots\quad q_{2n}p_2 \equiv Q_2p_2 \\ \vdots \qquad\quad \vdots \qquad\qquad \vdots \qquad \vdots \\ q_{n1}p_n + q_{n2}p_n + \quad\cdots\quad q_{nn}p_n \equiv Q_np_n \end{array}\right\} \qquad \text{(III.1.1)}$$

$$\left.\begin{array}{l} q_{11}p_1 + q_{21}p_2 + \quad\cdots\quad q_{n1}p_n \equiv Q_1p_1 \\ q_{12}p_1 + q_{22}p_2 + \quad\cdots\quad q_{n2}p_n \equiv Q_2p_2 \\ \vdots \qquad\quad \vdots \qquad\qquad \vdots \qquad \vdots \\ q_{1n}p_1 + q_{2n}p_2 + \quad\cdots\quad q_{nn}p_n \equiv Q_np_n \end{array}\right\} \qquad \text{(III.1.2)}$$

2 An Algebraic Reformulation

The two systems of accounting identities (III.1.1) and (III.1.2), as set out above, are somewhat unmanageable for mathematical purposes because they present a marked asymmetry. Each equality in (III.1.1), for example, can be immediately simplified by dividing through by the price (which is the same for each term). This cannot be done in (III.1.2). Yet it is possible to introduce some definitions which, by rendering the algebraic formulation symmetrical, make it analytically more interesting. Let

$$\frac{q_{ij}}{Q_j} = a_{ij}$$

and hence

$$q_{ij} = a_{ij}Q_j, \qquad\qquad i, j = 1, 2, \ldots, n$$

Using these definitions to eliminate the q_{ij} from (III.1.1) and (III.1.2) and then simplifying, we obtain

$$\left.\begin{aligned}
a_{11}Q_1 + a_{12}Q_2 + &\cdots + a_{1n}Q_n \equiv Q_1 \\
a_{21}Q_1 + a_{22}Q_2 + &\cdots + a_{2n}Q_n \equiv Q_2 \\
\vdots \qquad \vdots \qquad\quad &\qquad \vdots \qquad \vdots \\
a_{n1}Q_1 + a_{n2}Q_2 + &\cdots + a_{nn}Q_n \equiv Q_n
\end{aligned}\right\} \qquad \text{(III.2.1)}$$

$$\left.\begin{aligned}
a_{11}p_1 + a_{21}p_2 + &\cdots + a_{n1}p_n \equiv p_1 \\
a_{12}p_1 + a_{22}p_2 + &\cdots + a_{n2}p_n \equiv p_2 \\
\vdots \qquad \vdots \qquad\quad &\qquad \vdots \qquad \vdots \\
a_{1n}p_1 + a_{2n}p_2 + &\cdots + a_{nn}p_n \equiv p_n
\end{aligned}\right\} \qquad \text{(III.2.2)}$$

It will be seen that the two systems (III.2.1) and (III.2.2) are now perfectly symmetrical. The first sets out relationships between the physical quantities $Q_1, Q_2, \ldots, Q_n$, and the second, relationships between the prices, $p_1, p_2, \ldots, p_n$. Both contain the same magnitudes a_{ij} $(i, j = 1, 2, \ldots, n)$, but the rows and columns are interchanged – the same a_{ij}, which in (III.2.1) appear on the rows, in (III.2.2) appear on the columns, and *vice versa*.

3 The Accounting Nature of the Formulation Used So Far

One must not be misled by the definitions used above. Nothing has been added to, or subtracted from, the transactions table by our having represented it in terms of systems of equalities. In particular, (III.2.1) and (III.2.2), as set out above, are no more than accounting identities, being merely another way of writing the transactions Table III.1.

For example, if we wished to write down the table for the numerical example of Chapter II, using the definitions of the last section, we would obtain for the row equalities the expressions

$$\left.\begin{array}{l}
\dfrac{186}{450}450 + \dfrac{54}{21}21 + \dfrac{30}{60}60 + \dfrac{180}{60}60 \equiv 450 \\[2ex]
\dfrac{12}{450}450 + \dfrac{6}{21}21 + \dfrac{3}{60}60 \qquad\qquad \equiv 21 \\[2ex]
\dfrac{9}{450}450 + \dfrac{6}{21}21 + \dfrac{15}{60}60 + \dfrac{30}{60}60 \equiv 60 \\[2ex]
\dfrac{18}{450}450 + \dfrac{12}{21}21 + \dfrac{30}{60}60 \qquad\qquad \equiv 60
\end{array}\right\} \qquad \text{(III.3.1)}$$

The sums across the rows are now written in a way which is apparently more complicated but is, as will be seen shortly, analytically more interesting.

4   An Interpretation of the a_{ij}'s as Coefficients of Production

The significance of (III.2.1) and (III.2.2), as compared to (III.1.1) and (III.1.2), lies in the fact that they contain a whole new set of magnitudes – the ratios a_{ij}, $i, j = 1, 2, \ldots, n$ – which have an important economic meaning. If, in our numerical example, we consider more closely the ratios which appear in the first column of (III.3.1):

$$\frac{186}{450} \qquad \frac{12}{450} \qquad \frac{9}{450} \qquad \frac{18}{450}$$

(or, more generally, $a_{11}, a_{21}, a_{31}, \ldots, a_{n1}$), it will be noted that they represent the physical quantities of wheat, iron, turkey, and labor, respectively (or, more generally, of the commodities, broadly interpreted, $1, 2, 3, \ldots, n$) that were necessary on average, in the observed economy, for the production of 1 physical unit of wheat. They are merely the so-called *coefficients of production* for the wheat industry (i.e., for industry 1). The ratios appearing in the other columns are to be interpreted similarly. These average production coefficients a_{ij} are magnitudes which contrast sharply with the Q_i and p_j, $i, j = 1, 2, \ldots, n$. The former belong to the world of techniques of production, while the latter belong to the world of economic decisions. The separation of these two kinds of magnitudes, which appear mixed together in the transactions table, is indeed the most interesting feature of (III.2.1) and (III.2.2), since there is a whole series of problems for which this distinction becomes important.

The case in which the production coefficients would remain constant in the face of variations in the physical quantities produced would clearly correspond to the case in which the technical processes of production yield neither increasing nor decreasing returns to scale (constant returns to scale). When this is so, it becomes legitimate to interpret (III.2.1) and (III.2.2) as systems of linear equations with coefficients $a_{11}, a_{12}, \ldots, a_{1n}, a_{21}, a_{22}, \ldots, a_{nn}$, in the unknowns $Q_1, Q_2, \ldots, Q_n$ and $p_1, p_2, \ldots, p_n$, respectively. The same procedure could be justified when the returns to scale, while not exactly constant, depart from constancy only slightly.

5 Two Systems of Equations

At the end of Section 4 we referred to systems of equations, and no longer to systems of identities as before, since reference was being made to a specific hypothesis: that of constant returns to scale.

Indeed, as soon as one introduces a hypothesis concerning the a_{ij} coefficients into (III.2.1) and (III.2.2) – as in the present case in which reference was made to the hypothesis of constant returns to scale – the equalities cease to be identically true. They remain true only if the hypothesis holds. They thus become equations, expressing a "theory," which could, for example, be rejected after empirical tests.

One could, of course, adopt assumptions other than that of constant returns to scale. It will therefore be necessary, henceforth, to specify with care the assumptions made concerning the technical coefficients a_{ij}. In some cases it may also be important to specify the hypotheses which it is *not* necessary to make. (We shall consider a remarkable example of this in Section 12 of Chapter V.) These statements should not be taken to mean, however, that the production coefficients must necessarily remain constant and that the physical quantities and the prices must necessarily vary. (In practice it might very well be that the technical coefficients change, while the outputs remain constant. Or it might be of interest to analyze problems which do not necessarily involve changes in the Q_i or in the p_j.) Our contrasting of the ratios a_{ij} to the quantities Q_i and prices p_j ($i, j = 1, 2, \ldots, n$) is therefore based not on a distinction between *constants* and *variables* but rather on a distinction between magnitudes considered as *given* and magnitudes considered as *unknown*. The technical coefficients are magnitudes which, for economists, are *given* by the technique of production, while the Q_i and p_j are magnitudes which are the subject of economic analysis. More generally, we shall think of (III.2.1) and (III.2.2) as two systems of equations which allow us to analyze the properties of the solutions for the Q_i and p_j, in relation to certain hypotheses concerning the technical coefficients a_{ij}, $i, j = 1, 2, \ldots, n$.

6   On the Use of Matrix Algebra

At this point it becomes important to investigate the mathematical properties of (III.2.1) and (III.2.2) considered as two systems of linear equations.

The solutions and the properties of systems of two or three linear equations are well known from elementary algebra. In the present context, however, the number of equations could become very large indeed. To facilitate and speed up our analysis, an extensive use will be made of matrix algebra.

For the reader's convenience, the basic concepts of matrix algebra used in the following pages are reviewed in a *Mathematical Appendix* at the end of the book. The reader who is not familiar with matrix algebra is thus advised to turn to the *Mathematical Appendix* before proceeding.

CHAPTER FOUR

The Leontief System

1 Two Systems of Linear Equations

CONSIDER once again the two systems of equations (III.2.1) and (III.2.2) which, in matrix notation, may be written out in full as

$$
\begin{bmatrix}
(a_{11} - 1) & a_{12} & a_{13} & \cdots & a_{1n} \\
a_{21} & (a_{22} - 1) & a_{23} & \cdots & a_{2n} \\
\vdots & \vdots & \vdots & \vdots & \vdots \\
a_{n1} & a_{n2} & & \cdots & (a_{nn} - 1)
\end{bmatrix}
\begin{bmatrix}
Q_1 \\
Q_2 \\
\vdots \\
Q_n
\end{bmatrix}
=
\begin{bmatrix}
0 \\
0 \\
\vdots \\
0
\end{bmatrix}
\qquad \text{(IV.1.1)}
$$

$$
\begin{bmatrix}
(a_{11} - 1) & a_{21} & a_{31} & \cdots & a_{n1} \\
a_{12} & (a_{22} - 1) & a_{32} & \cdots & a_{n2} \\
\vdots & \vdots & \vdots & \vdots & \vdots \\
a_{1n} & a_{2n} & & \cdots & (a_{nn} - 1)
\end{bmatrix}
\begin{bmatrix}
p_1 \\
p_2 \\
\vdots \\
p_n
\end{bmatrix}
=
\begin{bmatrix}
0 \\
0 \\
\vdots \\
0
\end{bmatrix}
\qquad \text{(IV.1.2)}
$$

where the a_{ij} denote the coefficients of production (broadly interpreted), the Q_i denote the physical quantities, and the p_j denote the prices $(i, j = 1, 2, \ldots, n)$.

From the economic meaning of the coefficients, it follows of course that

$$a_{ij} \geq 0, \qquad\qquad i, j = 1, 2, \ldots, n \qquad\qquad \text{(IV.1.3)}$$

That is, the coefficients of production and of consumption are all positive or, at the very least, equal to zero. Negative coefficients would have no economic meaning.

As will be seen, the matrices of coefficients for these two systems of equations contain exactly the same elements, but each matrix is the transpose of the other.

If the assumption of constant returns to scale is now added, i.e., the assumption that all the technical coefficients a_{ij} remain constant when the Q_i and the p_j vary $(i, j = 1, 2, \ldots, n)$, the two systems of equations, (IV.1.1) and (IV.1.2), come to represent what has been called the Leontief system (or schema or model), closed with respect to final demand, or more simply the *closed Leontief system.*[1]

2   The Closed Leontief System

2.1. *The term "closed" explained.* The reason for calling (IV.1.1) and (IV.1.2) a *closed* system is that the final sector is treated there as if it were an ordinary industry. The nth column, which contains final demand, is treated, in the same way as every other column, as showing the *inputs* required by the industry to which it refers. And the nth row, which contains the value added in the various industries, is treated, in the same way as every other row, as representing the outputs distributed to the various industries.

This interpretation acquires an immediate meaning in the context of a stationary system in which the labor is constant from year to year and new investment is zero (since only that investment needed to replace the used-up means of production is carried out). This is, in effect, the case to which Leontief referred the theoretical formulations of his closed model. The nth column and the nth row appear as an industry that requires a set of consumptions as inputs and produces a set of services as outputs. These services are composite services – of labor and productive resources – which are, however, simply paid an all inclusive income – value added – comprising wages, salaries, profits, and rents. In other words, at this stage of his analysis, Leontief preferred in fact not to distinguish between the various kinds of income and to accept value added as an entity in itself, irrespective of its composition.

2.2. *A necessary condition for economically meaningful solutions.* Consider now the formal aspects of our two systems of equations. These equation systems are linear and homogeneous. From the *Mathematical Appendix* we know that systems of this kind always have at least one solution, namely,

$$Q_i = 0, \qquad\qquad i = 1, 2, \ldots, n \qquad\qquad\qquad \text{(IV.2.1)}$$

$$p_j = 0, \qquad\qquad j = 1, 2, \ldots, n \qquad\qquad\qquad \text{(IV.2.2)}$$

These, however, are the so-called "trivial" solutions. When all outputs and all prices are equal to zero, the economic system does not exist. This is, indeed, a solution to our systems of equations but it is a solution completely devoid of any economic interest. We are obviously

---

[1] This system was presented by Leontief in the first edition of his work [1].

interested in situations in which there are other solutions, namely, solutions with economic meaning – positive solutions.

Now, if linear and homogeneous systems are to have solutions other than zero, the determinant of the matrix of coefficients must be equal to zero. Since, in our economic example, the matrix of coefficients is the same for both systems, although transposed, this condition is the same for both systems:

$$
\begin{vmatrix}
(a_{11} - 1) & a_{12} & \cdots & a_{1n} \\
a_{21} & (a_{22} - 1) & \cdots & a_{2n} \\
\vdots & \vdots & & \vdots \\
a_{n1} & a_{n2} & \cdots & (a_{nn} - 1)
\end{vmatrix} = 0
\qquad\text{(IV.2.3)}
$$

In other words, a necessary condition for the existence of nonzero solutions is that at least one column of the coefficient matrix is linearly dependent on the others.

We must therefore reconsider the economic meaning of the various columns to see whether they permit the satisfaction of (IV.2.3). Now we know that the first $(n - 1)$ columns represent the technical coefficients of the production processes. These coefficients are *given* by technology. In general, then, we cannot expect to find among the first $(n - 1)$ columns one that just happens to be linearly dependent on the others (i.e., that is a linear combination of the others). If that were to occur, it would be a truly exceptional coincidence indeed. And even then that coincidence could be observed only at a precise moment in time. The very smallest change, in even only one coefficient among the production processes concerned, would suffice to destroy that coincidence. For all practical purposes, therefore, one must exclude the possibility that the first $(n - 1)$ columns are linearly dependent.

Only the nth column remains to be considered. This column clearly *can* be linearly dependent on the others, since it contains a set of magnitudes concerning consumption which are not technically given and which can be adjusted. Condition (IV.2.3) therefore simply amounts to stating that this column *must* be linearly dependent on the others for the two systems of equations to have nonzero solutions. And that is fairly obvious. There can be no economic system in which per capita consumption levels are independent of the matrix of technical coefficients. In common sense terms the consumption possibilities (represented here by the nth column) are limited by the technical production possibilities (represented by the other $n - 1$ columns). Or, alternatively, we may say that in a stationary system it is physically impossible to devote to consumption more than can physically be produced.

Yet the above does not exhaust the full meaning of condition (IV.2.3). This condition does not merely say that the determinant in question cannot be greater than zero, it says also that the determinant must be *equal* to zero. This implies that final demand not only cannot exceed the technical production possibilities (which would be physically impossible) but must not fall short of them either. Actually, a final demand smaller than the technical production possibilities is quite possible, physically at least. It is just this eventuality which is ruled out by (IV.2.3), which implies that, if final demand were less than the technical production possibilities, at least one of the equations would not be satisfied. More precisely, the sum of the outputs of each industry would be less than the sum of the inputs to that industry (accumulation of stocks, i.e., underutilized productive capacity) and/or the sum of the labor requirements would be less than the total supply of labor power (unemployment).

Condition (IV.2.3) can thus also be interpreted in economic terms as expressing the well-known Keynes condition[2] that the total volume of final demand must be equal to the productive capacity of the system, if full employment is to be ensured.

3   The Solutions of the Closed System

3.1. *Relative prices and relative quantities.* Suppose, then, that the condition (IV.2.3) is satisfied so that, in economic terms, final demand is such as to require full employment of the existing productive capacity and labor force. In this case there are also nonzero solutions, i.e., economically meaningful solutions.

From the arguments of the previous section (leading to the conclusion that for all practical purposes the matrix of the two systems contains $(n - 1)$ linearly independent columns), it follows that the matrix itself is of rank $(n - 1)$. This implies that each of the two systems (IV.1.1) and (IV.1.2) contains $(n - 1)$ independent equations. Since there are n unknowns, any one of them may be fixed arbitrarily. Then the solutions for the other $(n - 1)$ unknowns will be uniquely determined.

For the price system (IV.1.2) the meaning of these conclusions is immediately apparent. The system determines only *relative prices* and not the absolute level of prices. The price of any commodity can thus

---

[2] See, on this point, my own *Growth and Income Distribution*, Cambridge: Cambridge University Press, 1974, pp. 41–42.

be fixed arbitrarily; the system will then determine all the other prices relative to the arbitrarily chosen price. In other words, any commodity can be adopted as the *numéraire* (which is equivalent to setting its price equal to unity) and all the other prices can then be expressed in terms of that *numéraire*-commodity. As is well-known, for centuries the commodity adopted as *numéraire* was gold. In modern economic systems the determination of the price level has become more complex. However, without going into questions of a monetary nature, it will suffice to point out that the real system offers the possibility of a choice here. As is apparent from the set of relations considered, each price only expresses a ratio – the exchange ratio between physical units of two goods. The absolute level is open to choice.

The interpretation of these same formal conclusions is rather less obvious with respect to the system of physical quantities (IV.1.1). Here, too, one could say that the system of equations determines the relative quantities or the proportions in which the various commodities are produced, but not the absolute levels of the outputs; that is, it determines the *structure* of the economic system but not the *scale* of operation (provided, of course, that the assumption of constant returns to scale holds good). However, the concept of a relative quantity is not so intuitively evident as that of a relative price. There is, moreover, a more compelling question, resulting from the fact that in practice not all of the Q_i, $i = 1, 2, \ldots, n$, are open to being determined within the economic system. One of these quantities – Q_n in our formulation, the available labor force – is, as it is normally put, an *exogenous* quantity; in the sense that, for the purposes of economic argument, it is generally taken as given. In other words, while $Q_1, Q_2, \ldots, Q_{n-1}$ – the physical quantities of commodities to be produced – are subject to economic decisions, the total labor supply is not. Therefore, in system (IV.1.1), if Q_n is thought of as an exogenous quantity, the unknowns are reduced to $(n - 1)$ and they will all be determined by the $(n - 1)$ independent equations of the system.

3.2. *A sufficient condition to ensure non-negative solutions.* The reader will perhaps have noticed that condition (IV.2.3), when it is satisfied, ensures that there are nonzero solutions but does not necessarily ensure that they are positive. Since negative solutions for $Q_1, Q_2, \ldots, Q_n, p_1, p_2, \ldots, p_n$, would have no economic meaning, some further condition in addition to (IV.2.3) must be satisfied to ensure that the two systems of equations (IV.1.1) and (IV.1.2) have positive solutions.

This condition can be stated quite simply by taking advantage of the fact that the coefficients matrix of the two systems (IV.1.1) and (IV.1.2) is, from (IV.1.3), a non-negative matrix. It may be noted, in fact, that the coefficients matrix of the two systems (IV.1.1) and (IV.1.2) is the special case of the matrix $(\lambda \mathbf{I} - \mathbf{A})$ in which $\lambda = 1$. Thus, when condition (IV.2.3) is satisfied (i.e., when the determinant of the coefficients matrix is zero), unity is an eigenvalue of the coefficients matrix of the two systems. It is easy to show that this eigenvalue is also the maximum eigenvalue.[3] Then the Perron-Frobenius theorems[4] guarantee immediately that the solutions of the two systems (IV.1.1) and (IV.1.2), i.e., the components of the two eigenvectors associated with the maximum eigenvalue, are all non-negative.

To conclude, given the way in which the coefficients have been obtained, condition (IV.1.3) suffices, in conjunction with condition (IV.2.3), to ensure that the solutions are not only nonzero but are actually non-negative, i.e., economically meaningful.

4 The Open Leontief System

4.1. *Asymmetry between interindustry relations and the final sector.* The schema considered thus far in this chapter, the closed Leontief system, has interested scholars principally on account of its formal mathematical properties and of the theoretical interpretation of the various input-output relationships which it permits. It has been somewhat neglected, however, for practical purposes, for reasons which are not difficult to grasp.

The last column of the coefficients matrix considered thus far is, in fact, of a quite different character from the other $(n - 1)$ columns. Admittedly, it has been treated just like any other column but only on the grounds of mathematical symmetry and formal elegance. The fact remains that it contains consumption coefficients which are open to economic decisions, whereas the other $(n - 1)$ columns contain coefficients which are *given* by technology.

[3] Call $\mathbf{Z}$ the matrix of the quantities q_{ij} of the previous chapter $(i, j = 1, 2, \ldots, n)$. In order to go from the q_{ij} to the a_{ij} $(i, j = 1, 2, \ldots, n)$, we divided each column of matrix $\mathbf{Z}$ by the corresponding total quantity Q_j $(j = 1, 2, \ldots, n)$, i.e., we performed the operation $\mathbf{Z}\hat{\mathbf{Q}}^{-1}$, where $\hat{\mathbf{Q}}$ is a diagonal matrix with the $Q_1, Q_2, \ldots, Q_n$ on its main diagonal. If, instead of performing the operation $\mathbf{Z}\hat{\mathbf{Q}}^{-1}$, we had performed the operation $\hat{\mathbf{Q}}^{-1}\mathbf{Z}$ (which means dividing the rows of $\mathbf{Z}$, instead of its columns by the corresponding quantities $Q_1, Q_2, \ldots, Q_n$), we would have obtained a matrix in which, by construction, the sum of each row is equal to unity. Such a matrix, i.e., $\hat{\mathbf{Q}}^{-1}\mathbf{Z}$, has a maximum eigenvalue equal to unity (owing to Perron-Frobenius Theorem 6; see *Mathematical Appendix*, p. 274). But matrices $\hat{\mathbf{Q}}^{-1}\mathbf{Z}$ and $\mathbf{Z}\hat{\mathbf{Q}}^{-1}$ are similar, and this implies that they have the same eigenvalues (see *Mathematical Appendix*, p. 261). It therefore follows that (all q_{ij}'s and Q_j's being non-negative) matrix $\mathbf{Z}\hat{\mathbf{Q}}^{-1}$, i.e., the coefficients matrix $[a_{ij}]$, has a maximum eigenvalue equal to unity.

[4] See *Mathematical Appendix*, Theorems 1 and 1b, p. 269 and 275.

It is thus easy to understand why the closed Leontief system cannot give reliable results for practical purposes (notably for forecasting or programming purposes). Its coefficients matrix contains two parts – that relating to technology and that relating to final consumption – which are not of the same nature and therefore involve different principles and necessitate the use of different methods. And, since the final column is, after all, open to direct investigation, attention has been concentrated on the other $(n - 1)$ columns, which represent the technical input-output relationships of the economic system.

4.2. *The open system.* We know, from the arguments above, that the technique of the economic system is represented by the square matrix of coefficients relating to the inputs and outputs of *commodities* (we shall call it the matrix of *interindustry coefficients*):

$$
\begin{bmatrix}
a_{11} & a_{12} & \cdots & a_{1,n-1} \\
a_{21} & a_{22} & \cdots & a_{2,n-1} \\
\vdots & \vdots & \cdots & \vdots \\
a_{n-1,1} & a_{n-1,2} & \cdots & a_{n-1,n-1}
\end{bmatrix}
\tag{IV.4.1}
$$

and by the vector of labor coefficients:

$$
\begin{bmatrix} a_{n1} & a_{n2} & \cdots & a_{n,n-1} \end{bmatrix}
\tag{IV.4.2}
$$

which we shall call the vector of *direct labor coefficients.*

Hence, if we now think of the final demand column as containing terms which are known (or at least predetermined on the basis of a separate investigation), which we shall call $\bar{Y}_1, \bar{Y}_2, \ldots, \bar{Y}_{n-1}$, we can write the system of equations

$$
\begin{bmatrix}
(1 - a_{11}) & -a_{12} & \cdots & -a_{1,n-1} \\
-a_{21} & (1 - a_{22}) & \cdots & -a_{2,n-1} \\
\vdots & \vdots & \cdots & \vdots \\
-a_{n-1,1} & -a_{n-1,2} & \cdots & (1 - a_{n-1,n-1})
\end{bmatrix}
\begin{bmatrix}
Q_1 \\
Q_2 \\
\vdots \\
Q_{n-1}
\end{bmatrix}
=
\begin{bmatrix}
\bar{Y}_1 \\
\bar{Y}_2 \\
\vdots \\
\bar{Y}_{n-1}
\end{bmatrix}
\tag{IV.4.3}
$$

and the equation

$$
a_{n1}Q_1 + a_{n2}Q_2 + \cdots a_{n,n-1}Q_{n-1} = L
\tag{IV.4.4}
$$

where L is the number of workers employed per year.

This procedure has the further advantage that it does not necessarily confine our analysis to a stationary system (in which new investment is zero), as was the case with the closed Leontief system. Final demand might very well consist of both consumption and new investment, provided that it is thought of as given in total.

The system of equations (IV.4.3) can also be written in a more compact form:

$$(\mathbf{I} - \mathbf{A})\mathbf{Q} = \bar{\mathbf{Y}} \tag{IV.4.5}$$

where: $\mathbf{I}$ is the identity matrix of order $(n - 1)$, $\mathbf{A}$ is the non-negative square matrix of interindustry coefficients, of order $(n - 1)$, $\mathbf{Q}$ is the column vector of the $(n - 1)$ physical quantities of commodities to be produced, and $\bar{\mathbf{Y}}$ is the column vector of the $(n - 1)$ physical quantities making up the final demand (consumption plus investment), which is assumed to be given. This system of equations represents what has been called the Leontief system (or schema or model) *open* with respect to final demand, or more simply the *open Leontief system*.

It is to be noted that in this system of equations the matrix of technical coefficients, $\mathbf{A}$, is of order $(n - 1)$, by contrast with the nth order matrix of the closed system, because it excludes the last column (the consumption coefficients) and the last row (the labor coefficients) of the latter matrix.

4.3. *A "dual" price system.* By analogy with the procedure adopted above for the physical quantities, one could write a system of equations, "dual" to the system (IV.4.5), with $(n - 1)$ prices as unknowns and $(n - 1)$ values added: $\bar{V}_1, \bar{V}_2, \ldots, \bar{V}_{n-1}$, as the known terms, namely,

$$\mathbf{p}(\mathbf{I} - \mathbf{A}) = \bar{\mathbf{V}} \tag{IV.4.6}$$

where $\mathbf{p}$ is the row vector of $(n - 1)$ prices and $\bar{\mathbf{V}}$ is the row vector of the $(n - 1)$ magnitudes, taken as known, representing the values added in the $(n - 1)$ industries.

However, this system of equations, at least in the form (IV.4.6), has not found any important practical applications. "Open Leontief system" is generally taken to mean the system of physical quantities (IV.4.5).[5]

5 The Solution of the Open System

5.1. *A unique solution.* Consider then the system of $(n - 1)$ linear equations, in $(n - 1)$ unknowns, (IV.4.5). It will be seen immediately that the square matrix of order $(n - 1)$, $(\mathbf{I} - \mathbf{A})$, has as its columns the $(n - 1)$ production processes, which are given by the technique. From the argument of Section 3 the matrix $(\mathbf{I} - \mathbf{A})$ can, for all practical

---

[5] The *open* system was proposed by Leontief in the second edition of his work [1].

purposes, be assumed to contain $(n - 1)$ linearly independent vectors and thus to be a matrix of rank $(n - 1)$. It follows that the augmented matrix of the system, $[(\mathbf{I} - \mathbf{A}), \bar{\mathbf{Y}}]$, obtained by adjoining the vector $\bar{\mathbf{Y}}$ to the matrix $(\mathbf{I} - \mathbf{A})$, will be a rectangular $(n - 1) \times n$ matrix. A matrix of this type cannot be of rank greater than $(n - 1)$; and since $r(\mathbf{I} - \mathbf{A}) = (n - 1)$, it follows that $r[(\mathbf{I} - \mathbf{A}), \bar{\mathbf{Y}}] = (n - 1)$, or

$$r[(\mathbf{I} - \mathbf{A}), \bar{\mathbf{Y}}] = r(\mathbf{I} - \mathbf{A}) = n - 1 \qquad \text{(IV.5.1)}$$

This implies that the system (IV.4.5) has one, and only one, solution (i.e., it is a determinate system).

We may also state that, since $r(\mathbf{I} - \mathbf{A}) = (n - 1)$, then $(\mathbf{I} - \mathbf{A})$ is a nonsingular matrix, that is, a matrix which has an inverse. Multiplying both sides of (IV.4.5) by this inverse matrix yields

$$\mathbf{Q} = (\mathbf{I} - \mathbf{A})^{-1}\bar{\mathbf{Y}} \qquad \text{(IV.5.2)}$$

This is the solution of the open Leontief system.

5.2. *Solution with economic meaning.* The result expressed by (IV.5.2) is still too general. For our purposes only those solutions for $\mathbf{Q}$ which are non-negative make economic sense. We know that both the vector $\bar{\mathbf{Y}}$ and the matrix $\mathbf{A}$ are necessarily non-negative. (Negative commodity components of the net product or negative production coefficients would have no economic meaning.) And moreover we know that the solution (IV.5.2) depends both on $\bar{\mathbf{Y}}$ and on $\mathbf{A}$. Now, if *all* the elements of $(\mathbf{I} - \mathbf{A})^{-1}$ were non-negative, then the non-negativity of $\mathbf{Q}$ would be ensured for all possible non-negative vectors $\bar{\mathbf{Y}}$. We only have therefore to reexpress this condition in terms of restrictions on the matrix $\mathbf{A}$. This can be done immediately by noting that matrix $(\mathbf{I} - \mathbf{A})^{-1}$ is the special case of the matrix $(\mu\mathbf{I} - \mathbf{A})^{-1}$ in which $\mu = 1$. Applying the Perron-Frobenius theorems,[6] we can infer that the necessary and sufficient condition for the non-negativity of all the elements of the matrix $(\mathbf{I} - \mathbf{A})^{-1}$, and hence of all the components of $\mathbf{Q}$, is that the maximum eigenvalue of $\mathbf{A}$, λ_m, should be less than unity,[7] or $1 = \mu > \lambda_m$.

Although this mathematical formulation seems somewhat abstruse at first sight, its economic meaning is extremely simple. It implies, as will

---

[6] See *Mathematical Appendix*, Theorems 5 and 5a, pp. 273 and 276.

[7] Compare this condition with the one considered for a *closed* system in Section 3.2, where the maximum eigenvalue is required to be exactly equal to unity.

become clear in Chapter V, Section 9.2, and Chapter VII, Section 3.3, that the technical properties of the economic system must bé such as to permit the production of *at least* some commodity in addition to those needed for the replacement of the means of production used up in the production process. If an economic system were technically so backward that it was not even capable of reproducing the inputs which it had used up, then it could not survive (i.e., it would not be *viable*). It is true that, even in such cases, the equations representing the system could have mathematical solutions, but these solutions, which would include some negative elements, would have no economic meaning.

We exclude the economically meaningless cases from our analysis. In other words, we confine the whole of our analysis to cases in which the economic system is viable; more precisely, to the cases in which $\lambda_m < 1$.

6 The Labor Requirements

The reader will have noticed that, in the open Leontief system, our having taken the final demand column as given has obliged us to disregard the nth row of the transactions table even though it contains elements of a technical nature – the labor coefficients. It has obliged us, in other words, to consider only the equation system (IV.4.3) and to disregard (IV.4.4). This implies that, if we wanted to add (IV.4.4), it would be necessary, in order not to render the system overdetermined, to add also another unknown, which in the present context could only be the variable L, i.e., the number of man-years required.

Hence, in the open Leontief system, the quantity L, being an unknown, must be interpreted as expressing the labor requirements of the system (and not, as before, the exogenously given number of man-years available, which was denoted by Q_n). It follows, of course, that we have the further constraint

$$L \leq \bar{Q}_n \tag{IV.6.1}$$

That is, the labor requirements of the economic system cannot exceed the available labor force.

7 An Economic Interpretation of the Inverse Matrix

7.1. *The direct and indirect requirements.* The expression (IV.5.2), which represents in matrix notation the solution of the system (IV.4.5), deserves further investigation.

Denoting by α_{ij} $(i, j = 1, 2, \ldots, n)$ the elements of the inverse matrix, we can write the solution (IV.5.2) out in full:

$$
\begin{bmatrix} Q_1 \\ Q_2 \\ \vdots \\ Q_i \\ \vdots \\ Q_{n-1} \end{bmatrix} = \begin{bmatrix} \alpha_{11} & \alpha_{12} & \cdots & \alpha_{1j} & \cdots & \alpha_{1,n-1} \\ \alpha_{21} & \alpha_{22} & \cdots & \alpha_{2j} & \cdots & \alpha_{2,n-1} \\ \vdots & \vdots & \cdots & \vdots & \cdots & \vdots \\ \alpha_{i1} & \alpha_{i2} & \cdots & \alpha_{ij} & \cdots & \alpha_{i,n-1} \\ \vdots & \vdots & \cdots & \vdots & \cdots & \vdots \\ \alpha_{n-1,1} & \alpha_{n-1,2} & \cdots & \alpha_{n-1,j} & \cdots & \alpha_{n-1,n-1} \end{bmatrix} \begin{bmatrix} \bar{Y}_1 \\ \bar{Y}_2 \\ \vdots \\ \bar{Y}_i \\ \vdots \\ \bar{Y}_{n-1} \end{bmatrix} \qquad \text{(IV.7.1)}
$$

This expression shows the physical quantities $Q_1, Q_2, \ldots, Q_{n-1}$, of the commodities $1, 2, \ldots, n - 1$, which must be produced in total for these commodities to be available in the quantities $\bar{Y}_1, \bar{Y}_2, \ldots, \bar{Y}_{n-1}$ for final demand (i.e., for consumption and new investment). Thus, for every possible set of final uses chosen at will, with the aid of the inverse matrix we can compute directly the total quantities of all commodities which have to be produced. All these quantities $Q_1, Q_2, \ldots, Q_{n-1}$ will clearly be greater than, or at least equal to, the quantities $\bar{Y}_1, \bar{Y}_2, \ldots, \bar{Y}_{n-1}$, since they must provide for the quantities $\bar{Y}_1, \bar{Y}_2, \ldots, \bar{Y}_{n-1}$, which are required for consumption and new investment purposes, and the quantities $(Q_1 - \bar{Y}_1), (Q_2 - \bar{Y}_2), \ldots, (Q_{n-1} - \bar{Y}_{n-1})$, needed for intermediate use (i.e., as replacements for the means of production used up in the production process).

From this we can infer the economic meaning of each element α_{ij} $(i, j = 1, 2, \ldots, n - 1)$ of the inverse matrix $(\mathbf{I} - \mathbf{A})^{-1}$, by contrast with the economic meaning of each element a_{ij} $(i, j = 1, 2, \ldots, n - 1)$ of the original matrix $\mathbf{A}$. We know, of course, that each element a_{ij} of $\mathbf{A}$ represents the physical quantity of the ith commodity needed *in the jth industry* for the production of 1 physical unit of the jth commodity. Thus the a_{ij} $(i, j = 1, 2, \ldots, n - 1)$ may be said to represent the *direct requirements* of commodities for the production of commodities. In $(\mathbf{I} - \mathbf{A})^{-1}$, by contrast, each element α_{ij} represents the physical quantity of the ith commodity needed *in the economic system as a whole* in order to obtain eventually the availability of 1 physical unit of the jth commodity as a final good. The α_{ij} $(i, j = 1, 2, \ldots, n - 1)$ thus represent the *total* requirements (or the *direct and indirect requirements*) of commodities for the production of final commodities (i.e., of consumption and new investment goods).

We can also consider the individual rows or columns of $(\mathbf{I} - \mathbf{A})^{-1}$, one at a time. The jth column of $(\mathbf{I} - \mathbf{A})^{-1}$ clearly represents the

heterogeneous set of commodities $1, 2, \ldots, n - 1$, which it is necessary to produce, in total, in order to make 1 physical unit of the jth
commodity available for final use. By contrast, the ith row of $(\mathbf{I} - \mathbf{A})^{-1}$
represents the quantities of the ith commodity which have to be
produced in order to make 1 physical unit of each of the commodities
$1, 2, \ldots, n - 1$ available for final use.

7.2. *Numerical example.* To clarify these concepts it may be helpful to
consider a numerical example. It will suffice to examine the very simple
two-equation system used in Section 8.1 of the *Mathematical Appendix*
to illustrate the economic meaning of the inverse matrix, namely,

$$\begin{bmatrix} 1 & -0.6 \\ -0.3 & 1 \end{bmatrix}\begin{bmatrix} Q_1 \\ Q_2 \end{bmatrix} = \begin{bmatrix} \bar{Y}_1 \\ \bar{Y}_2 \end{bmatrix} \qquad \text{(IV.7.2)}$$

with solution

$$\begin{bmatrix} Q_1 \\ Q_2 \end{bmatrix} = \begin{bmatrix} 1.2195 & 0.7317 \\ 0.3658 & 1.2195 \end{bmatrix}\begin{bmatrix} \bar{Y}_1 \\ \bar{Y}_2 \end{bmatrix} \qquad \text{(IV.7.3)}$$

As the reader will realize, (IV.7.2) and (IV.7.3) represent a minia-
ture open Leontief system in which

$$\mathbf{A} = \begin{bmatrix} 0 & 0.6 \\ 0.3 & 0 \end{bmatrix} \qquad \text{(IV.7.4)}$$

and

$$(\mathbf{I} - \mathbf{A})^{-1} = \begin{bmatrix} 1.2195 & 0.7317 \\ 0.3658 & 1.2195 \end{bmatrix} \qquad \text{(IV.7.5)}$$

Assuming that industry 1 produces wheat and industry 2 produces
iron, and that both wheat and iron are measured in tons, the matrix
(IV.7.4) shows that to produce 1 ton of wheat the wheat industry (first
column) needs 0 tons of wheat and 0.3 tons of iron. (These are the
direct requirements for the production of wheat.) The corresponding
first column of the matrix (IV.7.5) shows that to produce 1 ton of
wheat for final use the economic system as a whole must produce
1.2195 tons of wheat (of which 1 ton is for use as a final commodity
and 0.2195 ton must go back to the production process), and 0.3658
ton of iron (all to go back to the production process). In the same way
the second column of (IV.7.4) shows that the direct requirements for
the production of 1 ton of iron are 0.6 ton of wheat and 0 tons of iron.
And the corresponding second column of (IV.7.5) shows that the total

(direct and indirect) requirements for the production of 1 ton of iron for final use are 0.7317 ton of wheat (all to go back to the production process) and 1.2195 tons of iron (of which 1 ton is for use as a final commodity and 0.2195 ton must go back to the production process). Thus, in order to have both 1 ton of wheat and 1 ton of iron available as final commodities, it is necessary to produce, in total, 1.2195 + 0.7317 = 1.9512 tons of wheat and 0.3658 + 1.2195 = 1.5853 tons of iron. The total requirements of wheat and iron for the production of any final quantity of wheat and iron can be found by multiplying the requirements per unit by the corresponding physical quantities.

Knowledge of the inverse matrix $(\mathbf{I} - \mathbf{A})^{-1}$ thus makes possible the direct calculation of the total outputs necessary for all possible patterns of final use (consumption plus new investment) that one may wish to consider. It should be quite clear how very important such an analytical tool may become for programming purposes.

8   An Iterative Method of Computing the Leontief Inverse Matrix

8.1. *Expansion as power series.* In order to use the Leontief model for programming purposes it is, of course, necessary to compute the numerical values of all the elements of the inverse matrix $(\mathbf{I} - \mathbf{A})^{-1}$. This involves laborious calculations for which, in practice, a computer is almost always essential as soon as the matrix $\mathbf{A}$ has more than a dozen rows and columns.

The most general method for the calculation of an inverse matrix is the method of determinants.[8] The Leontief inverse, however, has special properties which permit the use of an iterative method of computation which is usually much faster. We know that the special square matrix $\mu^{-1}(\mu\mathbf{I} - \mathbf{A})^{-1}$ can be expanded as a convergent power series:

$$\mathbf{I} + \frac{1}{\mu}\mathbf{A} + \left(\frac{1}{\mu}\mathbf{A}\right)^2 + \left(\frac{1}{\mu}\mathbf{A}\right)^3 + \cdots$$

provided that $\mu > |\lambda_M|$, where λ_M is the eigenvalue of $\mathbf{A}$ of greatest modulus.[9] Now the Leontief inverse $(\mathbf{I} - \mathbf{A})^{-1}$ is the special case of the matrix $\mu^{-1}(\mu\mathbf{I} - \mathbf{A})^{-1}$ in which $\mu = 1$. Thus we can always write the power series expansion:

$$(\mathbf{I} - \mathbf{A})^{-1} = \mathbf{I} + \mathbf{A} + \mathbf{A}^2 + \mathbf{A}^3 + \cdots \tag{IV.8.1}$$

[8] See *Mathematical Appendix*, pp. 248–249.
[9] See *Mathematical Appendix*, pp. 265–266.

provided that the eigenvalue of **A** with greatest modulus is in modulus less than unity.[10]

In our case, since **A** is a non-negative matrix, its largest eigenvalue will necessarily be its eigenvalue of greatest modulus. And, as has already been seen in Section 5.2, the greatest eigenvalue of **A** *must* be less than unity if **A** is to have an economic meaning. The **A** matrix in the Leontief system is therefore always convergent and the expression (IV.8.1) can always be used.

The interest of (IV.8.1) lies of course in the fact that it provides a simple iterative method for computing the Leontief inverse matrix $(\mathbf{I} - \mathbf{A})^{-1}$. The solution thus obtained is obviously approximate, but any desired degree of approximation can be achieved by an appropriate choice of the number of iterations; the speed of the calculation will depend on the degree of convergence of the matrix involved. Sometimes quite a few iterations (i.e., the sum of quite a few terms in the series) might be needed to obtain an acceptable degree of approximation. In other cases (of rapid convergence) one can get very close to the "exact" solution after only a few iterations. In any event this iterative method is nearly always the quickest method for computing the Leontief inverse.

8.2. *Economic meaning of the power series expansion.* It is of interest to note that the power series expansion of the matrix $(\mathbf{I} - \mathbf{A})^{-1}$ has a quite precise economic meaning. Conceptually, one can interpret the terms of the power series as successive (conceptual) *rounds* of production required for obtaining the final net product.

All this may be illustrated with the aid of the numerical example used in Section 7.2. Consider the system of two equations (IV.7.2) and set $\bar{Y}_1 = 1$ and $\bar{Y}_2 = 1$. Then, by using the iterative method, the

---

[10] It may be of interest to note the analogy with the algebra of numbers. If x is a real number such that $|x| < 1$, we can always write the power series expansion:

$$(1 - x)^{-1} = 1 + x + x^2 + x^3 + \dots \qquad (\text{IV.8.2})$$

As

$$\sum_{i=0}^{N} x^i = 1 + x + x^2 + x^3 + \dots + x^N$$

$$(1 - x) \sum_{i=0}^{N} x^i = 1 - x^{N+1}$$

$$\sum_{i=0}^{N} x^i = \frac{1 - x^{N+1}}{1 - x}$$

from which, if $|x| < 1$, one obtains (IV.8.2) as $N \to \infty$.

solution can be written

$$
\begin{bmatrix} Q_1 \\ Q_2 \end{bmatrix} = \begin{bmatrix} 1+0 \\ 0+1 \end{bmatrix} + \begin{bmatrix} 0 & +0.6 \\ 0.3+0 \end{bmatrix} + \begin{bmatrix} 0.18+0 \\ 0 & +0.18 \end{bmatrix} + \begin{bmatrix} 0 & +0.108 \\ 0.054+0 \end{bmatrix}
$$

$$
+ \begin{bmatrix} 0.0324+0 \\ 0 & +0.0324 \end{bmatrix} + \begin{bmatrix} 0 & +0.01944 \\ 0.00972+0 \end{bmatrix}
$$

$$
+ \begin{bmatrix} 0.005832+0 \\ 0 & +0.005832 \end{bmatrix} + \cdots \tag{IV.8.3}
$$

Now it can be seen that the first term on the right-hand side

$$
\begin{bmatrix} 1+0 \\ 0+1 \end{bmatrix} \tag{IV.8.4}
$$

shows the final quantities of the two goods required. (To produce 1 unit of wheat and 1 unit of iron as final commodities, one must obviously produce, first of all, 1 unit of wheat and 1 unit of iron). Then the second term on the right of (IV.8.3)

$$
\begin{bmatrix} 0 & +0.6 \\ 0.3+0 \end{bmatrix} \tag{IV.8.5}
$$

shows the quantities of the two goods that are directly required for the production of the quantities (IV.8.4). The third term on the right of (IV.8.3)

$$
\begin{bmatrix} 0.18+0 \\ 0 & +0.18 \end{bmatrix}
$$

shows the quantities of the two goods that are directly required for the production of the quantities (IV.8.5), and thus indirectly required for the production of the quantities (IV.8.4); and so on. All the terms coming after the term (IV.8.5), taken together, therefore show the sum of the indirect requirements. Obviously, the more remote the stage of production, the smaller are the residual requirements that remain to be added.

The exact solution, which we obtained above

$$
\begin{aligned}
Q_1 &= 1.9512 \quad \text{(i.e., } 1.2195 + 0.7317) \\
Q_2 &= 1.5853 \quad \text{(i.e., } 0.3658 + 1.2195)
\end{aligned} \tag{IV.8.6}
$$

is, of course, given by the complete sum of the infinite series of ever-decreasing requirements. Nevertheless, as may be seen from

(IV.8.3), the summing up of merely the first seven terms yields the quantities

$$Q_1 = 1.9457$$

$$Q_2 = 1.5819$$

which are already very close to the exact solution (IV.8.6).

This exact solution therefore represents, in a consolidated manner, the overall result of aggregating the infinite number of rounds of production, which in the power series expansion appear as individually specified one by one.

9 The Limitations of the Leontief System

After having brought out the significance of the Leontief model, particularly for programming purposes, it is appropriate also to mention its limitations. These limitations may all be traced back to the basic assumption which was adopted in its construction, namely, the assumption that the technical coefficients are constant.

In practice, changes in the technical coefficients can arise from two quite distinct sources. The first one is that the returns to scale may be increasing or decreasing. When this is the case, the technical coefficients are no longer independent of the scale of production. The extent to which the Leontief system might nevertheless be useful, at least as an approximation, will of course depend on the degree of nonlinearity of the production processes. A linear relation is, after all, a good approximation to any function, provided that the variations around the point under consideration are small (this is a remarkable and well-known analytical result deriving from the Taylor series expansion). When changes are large, though, the nonlinearity of the production relations could lead to deceptive conclusions. Yet it must be said that this fact, by itself, ought not to present an insuperable difficulty, since in cases of marked nonlinearity one could always try other functions (of higher degree).

But there is a second source of variations of the technical coefficients: technical progress. And this is much more awkward to deal with. Technical progress acts upon the various coefficients quite autonomously, sometimes independently of the scale of production, and sometimes in conjunction with it. The important factor therefore, in this respect, is *time*. For short periods of time, changes in technical knowledge can normally be neglected, but when periods of some years are considered (especially in markedly dynamic economic systems), technical changes can become highly relevant, and it would be unreasonable to rely on conclusions based on a model in which it is assumed that the coefficients matrix remains constant.

Reference

[1] Leontief, Wassily W., *The Structure of American Economy* 1919–1929, 1st ed., Cambridge Mass.: Harvard University Press, 1941; *The Structure of American Economy* 1919–1939, 2nd ed., New York: Oxford University Press, 1951.

CHAPTER FIVE

The Sraffa System

1 Production of Commodities by Means of Commodities

THE relationships considered in Chapter IV can be reformulated in terms of a theoretical schema, recently presented by Piero Sraffa [1] for preeminently theoretical purposes. It has been called one of *production of commodities by means of commodities.*

The version presented in this chapter is the less complex one – that concerning single product industries. Unlike Sraffa, whose analysis is in terms of elementary algebra, we shall be able to make extensive use of the notions of matrix algebra, which are reviewed in the *Mathematical Appendix.*

2 The Assumptions

The assumptions underlying the analysis of this chapter can be briefly stated as follows:

(i) We assume that we are observing a certain economic system which is in a perfectly stationary state. Each "year" the system produces exactly the same physical quantities of commodities.

(ii) The methods of production are such that each industry produces a single commodity by using a certain physical quantity of labor and certain physical quantities of commodities. These commodities (required as means of production) are completely used up in each period, so that they have to be replaced entirely.[1] At the end of each "year" the total output of the system must therefore be divided into two parts: one part must be devoted to the replacement of those commodities which have been used up in the production process; the remainder represents the final net output, or net national income, or

---

[1] This is the assumption of "single-product industries." Sraffa also carries out his analysis with reference to the more general case of "joint production," which he uses for his treatment of fixed capital and land. The principal theoretical results thereby obtained do not, however, basically differ from those obtained for the case of single product industries.

net product, and can be devoted to consumption (the system being in a stationary state).

The technical methods of production will be represented by a matrix of interindustry coefficients, denoted by $\mathbf{A}$, and by a row vector of direct labor coefficients, denoted by $\mathbf{a}_n$:

$$
\mathbf{A} = \begin{bmatrix}
a_{11} & a_{12} & \cdots & a_{1,n-1} \\
a_{21} & a_{22} & \cdots & a_{2,n-1} \\
\vdots & \vdots & \cdots & \vdots \\
a_{n-1,1} & a_{n-1,2} & \cdots & a_{n-1,n-1}
\end{bmatrix}
\tag{V.2.1}
$$

$$
\mathbf{a}_n = \begin{bmatrix} a_{n1} & a_{n2} & \cdots & a_{n,n-1} \end{bmatrix}
\tag{V.2.2}
$$

where

$$
a_{ij} \geq 0, \qquad j = 1, 2, \ldots, n-1; i = 1, 2, \ldots, n
$$

We shall call $[\mathbf{A}, \mathbf{a}_n]'$ the *technique* of the system. It is important to add that, unlike Leontief, Sraffa does *not* introduce the assumption of constant returns to scale, although he warns that "If such a supposition is found helpful, there is no harm in the reader's adopting it as a temporary working hypothesis. In fact, however, no such assumption is made".[2]

(iii) The value added in the economic system, which is equal to the value of the commodities which make up its net national income (or net product), is distributed to the members of the community at the end of each "year" in two forms: *wages* and *profits*. Wages are distributed in proportion to the physical quantity of labor which has been contributed; profits are distributed in proportion to the value of the means of production. It is assumed that labor is of a uniform quality and that both the wage rate and the rate of profit are uniform all over the economic system.

3   The Price System

We begin by considering the system of prices. What has been said above immediately allows us to pursue a more detailed analysis of that system than the one provided by Leontief. The value added in the economic system is here divided into two categories: wages and profits. Let us denote the wage rate by w (a scalar) and the rate of profit by π (also a scalar).

---

[2] Sraffa [1, p. v]. The reason why Sraffa's analysis is kept free from any assumption on returns to scale is that he is interested in investigating an economic system in which nothing changes except the distribution of income between wages and profits.

Given the technique $[\mathbf{A}, \mathbf{a}_n]'$ and assumption (iii) concerning the distribution of value added, the prices will be defined by the system of equations

$$
\left.
\begin{aligned}
&(a_{11}p_1 + a_{21}p_2 + \quad\cdots\quad + a_{n-1,1}p_{n-1})(1 + \pi) \\
&\quad + a_{n1}w = p_1, \\
&(a_{12}p_1 + a_{22}p_2 + \quad\cdots\quad + a_{n-1,2}p_{n-1})(1 + \pi) \\
&\quad + a_{n2}w = p_2 \\
&\;\vdots \\
&(a_{1,n-1}p_1 + a_{2,n-1}p_2 + \quad\cdots\quad + a_{n-1,n-1}p_{n-1})(1 + \pi) \\
&\quad + a_{n,n-1}w = p_{n-1}
\end{aligned}
\right\}
\qquad \text{(V.3.1)}
$$

where, as in earlier chapters, $p_1, p_2, \ldots, p_{n-1}$ are the prices of the commodities $1, 2, \ldots, n - 1$. In a more compact notation, system (V.3.1) can be rewritten

$$
\mathbf{p}\mathbf{A}(1 + \pi) + \mathbf{a}_n w = \mathbf{p}
\qquad \text{(V.3.1a)}
$$

where $\mathbf{p}$ denotes the (row) vector of prices.

As may be easily verified, this sytem contains $(n - 1)$ equations in $(n + 1)$ unknowns, namely w, π, and the $(n - 1)$ prices $p_1, p_2, \ldots, p_{n-1}$. We therefore have two more unknowns than we have equations; this means that two of the unknowns can be fixed exogenously.

Following the procedure adopted above, we may begin by setting the price of any arbitrarily chosen commodity equal to unity. The number of prices (which thereby become relative prices) is reduced to $(n - 2)$, and the total number of unknowns is reduced to n. We still have one degree of freedom. To render the system determinate we have to fix another unknown. And, since it would have no economic meaning to fix arbitrarily a relative price, we are left with a choice between the wage rate and the rate of profit. Within the context of (V.3.1) we can therefore fix arbitrarily either the wage rate or the rate of profit.

It must not, of course, be inferred from this conclusion that in a real economic system the wage rate or the rate of profit can be fixed at will. Our conclusion simply means that the system of equations (V.3.1) is not sufficient to determine all the unknowns. The determinants of one of these unknowns will have to be sought outside the equations (V.3.1).

4 Search for a Relation that may Render the Price System Determinate

The problem just referred to has behind it a long history in the evolution of economic thought. The Classical economists were aware of the indeterminateness of the system of prices (V.3.1) and solved the problem by taking the wage rate as determined by a relation outside the economic system. They thought of the biological needs of subsistence, appropriately assessed with reference to social conditions. Specific examples of this approach were encountered in the brief discussion of the theories of Ricardo and Marx in Chapter I. And, if we accept this approach (by setting $w = \bar{w}_{subsistence}$), the system of equations (V.3.1) does indeed become determinate.

It need hardly be added that this approach is not normally followed today. At most one might think of the wage rate as consisting of two parts: a part which is necessary for subsistence and which is comparable to the commodities constituting the means of production (its composition being rigidly determined by biological necessity), and a part which represents a "surplus" relative to subsistence requirements. But, if this distinction is accepted, the subsistence part of the wage rate takes up a character which is similar to that of the technical data and could therefore be thought of as being already included in the matrix of technical coefficients. We would then have to reinterpret our system, taking w to mean the surplus wage. Thus the problem of the division of the total surplus between π and w would remain unchanged.

The inclination of most modern economists with reference to system (V.3.1) is to reverse the Classical approach and seek a relation from outside the system (V.3.1) which may determine the rate of profit. Sraffa himself gives a clear indication that he thinks in these terms, although he does not explicitly state which relation might determine the rate of profit. Rather he confines himself to considering the alternative solutions to system (V.3.1) for all possible given values of the rate of profit. In this chapter, we shall follow Sraffa's approach. (But we shall come back to the problem of the determination of the rate of profit in Chapter VII).

5 Relative Prices Corresponding to Various Levels of the Rate of Profit

5.1. *Extreme cases and intermediate cases.* To examine the properties of the possible solutions of the system of equations (V.3.1), corresponding to various assumptions about the level of the rate of profit, it is instructive to consider the two extreme cases in which the rate of profit is at its minimum level and at its maximum level, respectively, separately from the general case in which the rate of profit is fixed at any intermediate level in between the two extremes.

5.2. *A pure labor theory of value.* We may begin by considering the extreme case in which $\pi = 0$. In this case, profits being zero, the entire net product, or surplus of the economic system, goes to wages. Equations (V.3.1) become a system of $(n - 1)$ linear equations in n unknowns: the wage rate and the $(n - 1)$ prices. There is only one degree of freedom. If any one of the commodities is chosen as the *numéraire*, its price being set equal to unity, the equation system determines uniquely the wage rate and the other $(n - 2)$ prices in terms of the chosen commodity. Alternatively, if we take the wage rate as the *numéraire* (by setting $w = 1$), the system determines uniquely the $(n - 1)$ prices in terms of the wage rate.

Whichever convention is adopted, when $\pi = 0$, the system (V.3.1a) becomes

$$\mathbf{p}(\mathbf{I} - \mathbf{A}) = \mathbf{a}_n w \tag{V.5.1}$$

Since the matrix $(\mathbf{I} - \mathbf{A})$ is nonsingular, we can multiply both sides of (V.5.1) by $(\mathbf{I} - \mathbf{A})^{-1}$ to obtain

$$\mathbf{p} = \mathbf{a}_n(\mathbf{I} - \mathbf{A})^{-1} w \tag{V.5.2}$$

which, for the special case $w = 1$, becomes

$$\mathbf{p} = \mathbf{a}_n(\mathbf{I} - \mathbf{A})^{-1} \tag{V.5.3}$$

Since $\mathbf{a}_n$ is a non-negative vector (see Section 2) and $(\mathbf{I} - \mathbf{A})^{-1}$ is a non-negative matrix (see Section 5.2 of Chapter IV), it follows that the prices $\mathbf{p}$ are all non-negative in both systems (V.5.2) and (V.5.3).

These expressions have an economic meaning which deserves to be emphasized. Each component of the vector $\mathbf{a}_n(\mathbf{I} - \mathbf{A})^{-1}$ is the scalar product of $\mathbf{a}_n$ (the vector of direct labor coefficients) and the corresponding column of the inverse matrix $(\mathbf{I} - \mathbf{A})^{-1}$. But from the discussion in Section 7.1 of Chapter IV, we know that the ith column of $(\mathbf{I} - \mathbf{A})^{-1}$ represents the physical quantities of commodities which have been used, directly and indirectly in the economic system as a whole, to obtain one physical unit of the ith commodity as a final commodity. Multiplying each of these physical quantities by the corresponding labor coefficient and summing the products thus obtained, we clearly obtain the quantity of labor used, directly and indirectly in the economic system as a whole, to obtain one physical unit of the ith commodity as a final commodity, $i = 1, 2, \ldots, n - 1$. Therefore the vector **v** defined as

$$\mathbf{v} = \mathbf{a}_n (\mathbf{I} - \mathbf{A})^{-1} \tag{V.5.4}$$

contains what may be called the *vertically integrated labor coefficients*. In Classical terminology, we can also say that **v** represents the quantities of labor directly and indirectly "embodied" in each physical unit of the commodities which make up the net product of the economic system (what Marx called "values," by definition).[3]

Thus equations (V.5.2) state that, when $\pi = 0$, prices are proportional to the physical quantities of "embodied labor". Indeed, in the particular case $w = 1$ prices are precisely equal to these physical quantities of labor. This conclusion should cause no surprise. Profits being equal to zero and the entire net product being absorbed by wages, prices cannot but be proportional to quantities of labor. We have thus arrived at a rigorous definition of the case for which the pure Classical labor theory of value holds.

5.3. *The maximum rate of profit.* We now turn to the other extreme case: that in which the rate of profit is at a level so high as to render the wage rate equal to zero. Profits are so high as to absorb the whole net product.[4] In this case the rate of profit is at its maximum possible level, which we may denote by Π, defined as

$$\Pi = \pi_{(w=0)} \tag{V.5.5}$$

i.e., as the rate of profit corresponding to a zero wage rate.

We can find the system of prices for this case by setting $w = 0$ in equation system (V.3.1a), which thus becomes

$$\mathbf{p}\mathbf{A}(1 + \Pi) = \mathbf{p} \tag{V.5.6}$$

or

$$\mathbf{p}[\mathbf{I} - (1 + \Pi)\mathbf{A}] = \mathbf{0} \tag{V.5.7}$$

Further, writing for convenience,

$$\frac{1}{1 + \Pi} = \lambda \tag{V.5.8}$$

---

[3] See p. 123.

[4] The reader may find it hard to imagine a hypothetical economic system in which wages are reduced to zero. But one may use the device of interpreting w as the "surplus" wage rate, in the sense suggested in Section 4 above. In other words, that part of the wage rate which represents subsistence (duly specified in physical terms) may be considered as already included in the technical interindustry coefficients. With this reinterpretation of matrix **A** the whole analysis of the present section remains formally unchanged.

we obtain

$$\mathbf{p}(\lambda \mathbf{I} - \mathbf{A}) = \mathbf{0} \qquad\qquad (V.5.9)$$

This is a homogeneous system. A necessary condition for its having solutions other than zero is that the determinant of the matrix of coefficients, i.e., $\det(\lambda \mathbf{I} - \mathbf{A})$, be zero. We can find the values of λ which satisfy this condition by solving the characteristic equation

$$\det(\lambda \mathbf{I} - \mathbf{A}) = 0 \qquad\qquad (V.5.10)$$

As the reader will note, the roots of equation (V.5.10) are the eigenvalues of matrix $\mathbf{A}$. As we know from the *Mathematical Appendix*, there are $(n - 1)$ such eigenvalues (although some of them might be repeated). There are therefore $(n - 1)$ values of λ that satisfy the system of equations (V.5.9). These eigenvalues might not have an economic meaning, however. Indeed, since $\mathbf{A}$ is a non-negative matrix, we can say immediately that only one of the $(n - 1)$ eigenvalues, i.e., the maximum eigenvalue, λ_m, is certainly such as to yield an eigenvector with no negative components.[5] Since in the present context the components of such an eigenvector are prices (and negative prices would have no economic meaning), it follows that only the solutions corresponding to the maximum eigenvalue will certainly have an economic meaning. Thus, even though from a mathematical point of view there are $(n - 1)$ values of λ satisfying (V.5.10), only one of them, the maximum eigenvalue λ_m, is certainly such as to have an economic meaning. Hence we shall always take Π to be the rate of profit which is associated with λ_m.[6]

If we substitute this rate of profit Π into (V.5.7) and λ_m into (V.5.9), we obtain a linear and homogeneous system of equations with a zero determinant.

By arguments similar to those carried out in Section 5.1 of Chapter IV it can be shown that the $(n - 1) \times (n - 1)$ matrix $[\mathbf{I} - (1 + \Pi)\mathbf{A}]$ will, in general, be of rank $(n - 2)$, i.e., the system (V.5.7) will contain $(n - 2)$ independent equations. This ensures the existence of determinate solutions for the prices, which we shall call $\mathbf{p}^*$, if any one of them is fixed arbitrarily. To conclude, substituting the rate of profit Π into (V.5.7) and λ_m into (V.5.9), we are enabled to obtain determinate, non-negative solutions for all the $(n - 2)$ relative prices.

[5] See *Mathematical Appendix* pp. 269, 275, Theorems 1 and 1a (of Perron-Frobenius).

[6] Actually the non-negative solution for relative prices, which is associated with the maximum eigenvalue λ_m, is also a unique solution. The only proviso needed is a condition to be discussed later (Section 10.7).

5.4. *The viability condition.* There is a further condition which must be satisfied in the case $w = 0$. The unique rate of profit

$$\Pi = \frac{1}{\lambda_m} - 1 \qquad\qquad (V.5.11)$$

to which there certainly correspond non-negative prices (i.e., prices with an economic meaning) must itself be economically meaningful. It must not be negative or

$$\Pi \geq 0 \qquad\qquad (V.5.12)$$

which implies, from (V.5.11),

$$\lambda_m \leq 1 \qquad\qquad (V.5.13)$$

If (V.5.13) were not satisfied, we should be dealing with an economic system so technically backward that it could not generate a profit even with a zero wage rate. Such an economic system could clearly not survive; it would not be *viable*.

It will be noted that (V.5.13) is precisely the condition for the viability of an economic system discussed in Section 5.2 of Chapter IV. Thus relation (V.5.11) between Π and λ_m provides a new interpretation of the economic meaning of that condition.

5.5. *A pure capital theory of value.* It might be asked what kind of theory of value is implicit in the prices $\mathbf{p}^*$, corresponding to a zero wage rate. To give an answer to this question, it is useful to adopt the device suggested in Section 4 of supposing that the goods constituting the subsistence wage are already included in the matrix of technical coefficients; so that $w = 0$ may be taken to mean a zero *surplus* wage.

In such a system the quantities of labor required in the process of production come to be treated in the same way as any commodity. "Men are like horses," so to speak. The inputs to the production process, including the workers, are all represented by commodities evaluated at their mere cost of reproduction. This is obviously a slave economy. Prices become proportional to the cost of the means of production, i.e., to the cost of the capital goods. The prices $\mathbf{p}^*$ – the solution to (V.5.6) – thus express a theory of value which, bearing in mind the proportionality to the cost of the capital goods, we could call a "pure capital theory of value."[7]

It is interesting to note that the theories of both Ricardo and Marx can be interpreted as referring to such an economic system.[8] We can

[7] Torrens [7, pp. 25, ff] and, later, the Russian economist Dmitriev [5, pp. 50–80] both came very close to this conclusion.

[8] See Chapter I.

now better understand the nature of their theoretical difficulties. They both thought, intuitively, in terms of a pure labor theory of value, i.e., of exchange ratios such as those given by (V.5.2). But they found themselves grappling with an analytical scheme the logic of which led them to the opposite extreme, i.e., to prices such as those given by (V.5.6), which imply a pure capital theory of value. Ricardo responded by building his theories largely on the special case in which the ratio of capital to labor is the same in every sector, i.e., as we may now realize, precisely on the special case in which the prices (V.5.2) come to coincide with the prices (V.5.6).[9] (He then thought of the more general case as giving rise to only insignificant deviations from this case). For his part, Marx faced the difficulty by resorting to the analytically equivalent device of assuming the "organic composition of capital" to

---

[9] In an economic system in which the proportions of capital to labor are the same in all production processes, prices proportional to capital are clearly also proportional to labor. The conditions under which this happens are, however, very restrictive indeed. In analytical terms it must be possible to substitute prices (V.5.3) for prices (V.5.7), which we have called $\mathbf{p}^*$, so that

$$\mathbf{a}_n(\mathbf{I} - \mathbf{A})^{-1}[\mathbf{I} - (1 + \Pi)\mathbf{A}] = \mathbf{0}$$

or rather, owing to definition (V.5.4),

$$\mathbf{v}[\mathbf{I} - (1 + \Pi)\mathbf{A}] = \mathbf{0} \qquad (V.5.14)$$

It should be clear that these expressions hold only for very particular vectors $\mathbf{a}_n$ and $\mathbf{v}$. More precisely, we can see immediately that (V.5.14) holds if, and only if, $\mathbf{v}$ is a left-hand eigenvector of matrix $\mathbf{A}$ (corresponding to its maximum eigenvalue λ_m, since $\mathbf{v} \geq \mathbf{0}$). Now call $\mathbf{v}^*$ that particular vector of vertically integrated labor coefficients which is an eigenvector of $\mathbf{A}$, and $\mathbf{a}_n^*$ the vector of direct labor coefficients from which it derives. Since by definition

$$\mathbf{v}^* = \mathbf{a}_n^*(\mathbf{I} - \mathbf{A})^{-1}$$

we have

$$\mathbf{a}_n^* = \mathbf{v}^*(\mathbf{I} - \mathbf{A}) = \mathbf{v}^* - \mathbf{v}^*\mathbf{A}$$

or

$$\mathbf{a}_n^* = \mathbf{v}^* - \lambda_m\mathbf{v}^* = (1 - \lambda_m)\mathbf{v}^* = \frac{\Pi}{1 + \Pi}\mathbf{v}^* \qquad (V.5.15)$$

That is, $\mathbf{a}_n^*$ too, by being proportional to $\mathbf{v}^*$, is an eigenvector of $\mathbf{A}$. We may conclude that the necessary and sufficient condition for prices such as those given by (V.5.2) to coincide with prices such as those given by (V.5.6) – in other words, for a pure labor theory of value to coincide with a pure capital theory of value – is that the vector of vertically integrated labor coefficients (which also implies the vector of direct labor coefficients) be a left-hand eigenvector of the matrix $\mathbf{A}$.

be the same in all industries,[10] and then, for the general case, by resorting to the problem of the "transformation of values into prices of production."[11]

5.6. *The general case.* We can at last turn to the more general case in which the rate of profit lies between the two extremes. Setting $\pi = \bar{\pi}$, such that $0 < \bar{\pi} < \Pi$, we can write (V.3.1a), after a few obvious algebraic manipulations, as

$$\mathbf{p} = \frac{1}{1 + \bar{\pi}} \, \mathbf{a}_n \left[\frac{1}{1 + \bar{\pi}} \mathbf{I} - \mathbf{A} \right]^{-1} w \tag{V.5.17}$$

or

$$\mathbf{p} = \mathbf{a}_n [\mathbf{I} - (1 + \bar{\pi})\mathbf{A}]^{-1} w \tag{V.5.18}$$

[10] In analytical terms this assumption also may be expressed by saying that the vector of direct labor coefficients must be a left-hand eigenvector of matrix $\mathbf{A}$, i.e., must be a particular eigenvector $\mathbf{a}_n^*$ such that

$$\mathbf{a}_n^*(\lambda_m \mathbf{I} - \mathbf{A}) = \mathbf{0}$$

For, if this expression holds, then

$$\mathbf{v}^* = \mathbf{a}_n^*(\mathbf{I} - \mathbf{A})^{-1} = \mathbf{a}_n^*(\mathbf{I} + \mathbf{A} + \mathbf{A}^2 + \mathbf{A}^3 + \cdots)$$

$$\mathbf{v}^* = \mathbf{a}_n^* + \lambda_m \mathbf{a}_n^* + \lambda_m^2 \mathbf{a}_n^* + \lambda_m^3 \mathbf{a}_n^* + \cdots$$

$$\mathbf{v}^* = \mathbf{a}_n^* \left[1 + \frac{1}{1 + \Pi} + \frac{1}{(1 + \Pi)^2} + \frac{1}{(1 + \Pi)^3} + \cdots \right] \tag{V.5.16}$$

And since

$$\lambda_m \equiv \frac{1}{1 + \Pi} < 1$$

by applying the formula of footnote 10 on p. 67,

$$\mathbf{v}^* = \mathbf{a}_n^* \frac{1}{1 - \lambda_m} = \mathbf{a}_n^* \frac{1 + \Pi}{\Pi} \tag{V.5.15a}$$

which is the same expression as obtained in footnote 9. Thus if $\mathbf{a}_n^*$ is an eigenvector of $\mathbf{A}$, then $\mathbf{v}^*$ is also an eigenvector of $\mathbf{A}$ (while it was found in footnote 9 that, if $\mathbf{v}^*$ is an eigenvector of $\mathbf{A}$, then $\mathbf{a}_n^*$ is also an eigenvector of $\mathbf{A}$).

It is now easy to grasp the economic meaning of (V.5.15a). The proportion between each component of vector $\mathbf{v}^*$ and the corresponding component of vector $\mathbf{a}_n^*$ is exactly the same for all components. This means that the quantity of direct plus indirect labor required by each commodity (in Marxian terminology, the quantity of labor embodied in constant plus variable capital) is *for all commodities* the same proportion of the corresponding quantity of direct labor. This is precisely the meaning of a uniform "organic composition of capital." (Cf. Chapter I, pp. 21–22, and the Appendix to this chapter, pp. 137–139).

[11] The Appendix to this chapter is specifically devoted to this problem.

Here, again, any one price can be set equal to unity, so that a determinate system will be obtained for the other $(n - 2)$ prices and for the wage rate w. Or we can adopt the wage rate as the *numéraire*, setting $w = 1$, so that (V.5.17) and (V.5.18) become, respectively,

$$\mathbf{p} = \frac{1}{1 + \bar{\pi}} \mathbf{a}_n \left[\frac{1}{1 + \bar{\pi}} \mathbf{I} - \mathbf{A} \right]^{-1} \qquad \text{(V.5.19)}$$

and

$$\mathbf{p} = \mathbf{a}_n [\mathbf{I} - (1 + \bar{\pi}) \mathbf{A}]^{-1} \qquad \text{(V.5.20)}$$

Expression (V.5.19), or (V.5.20), is a determinate system of equations in the $(n - 1)$ prices, expressed in terms of the wage rate.

Since $\bar{\pi} > 0$, $\mathbf{a}_n \geq 0$, and, moreover, $[1/(1 + \bar{\pi})] > \lambda_m$ (which implies that

$$\left[\frac{1}{1 + \bar{\pi}} \mathbf{I} - \mathbf{A} \right]^{-1} \geq \mathbf{O}),^{12}$$

it follows that all the prices (V.5.19), and thus all the prices (V.5.17), are non-negative.[13]

It can now be verified that, when $\bar{\pi} = 0$, (V.5.17) and (V.5.19), or (V.5.18) and (V.5.20), reduce to (V.5.2) and (V.5.3), respectively, and prices become proportional to the quantities of embodied labor. But, as soon as $\bar{\pi} > 0$, this is no longer so. The quantities of indirect labor come to acquire a greater "weight" relative to the quantities of direct labor because of the profit which has to be reckoned on them. In general, therefore, the proportionality between prices and quantities of embodied labor (i.e., the pure labor theory of value), which was so dear to the Classical economists, breaks down. As is clear from (V.5.17), the structure of prices depends, in general, on both the technical coefficients (i.e., on the quantities of embodied labor) and the particular level of the rate of profit.[14] Given the technique of the economic system, a particular structure of prices, corresponding to each level of the rate of profit, will obtain.

It is to this general case that most of the following analysis will be referred. Note that, in this general case, the rate of profit is taken as exogenously given and the *numéraire* is chosen arbitrarily. Of course,

[12] See *Mathematical Appendix* pp. 273, 276, Theorems 5 and 5a (of Perron-Frobenius).

[13] In the system of equations (V.3.1) the prices are therefore non-negative at each of the two extreme levels $\pi = 0$ and $\pi = \Pi$, as well as at all intermediate levels $0 < \pi < \Pi$.

[14] These assertions will be further illustrated in Section 7.2 below.

any time that the choice of the *numéraire* does make a difference to our arguments, the *numéraire* itself will be explicitly specified. But in most cases our arguments will be such as to hold whichever *numéraire* is chosen. We shall, however, make a point of always specifying the *numéraire* explicitly whenever the wage rate is set equal to unity. In other cases this will be unnecessary. Therefore, whenever in the following pages we refer to vector **p** without any specification, we shall mean a vector of $n - 1$ prices in which it does not matter which one of them (or which linear combination of them) is set equal to unity.

5.7. *Price changes as an effect of changes in the rate of profit.* A question that may be asked at this point is how prices change, relative to one another, as a consequence of changes in the rate of profit. Unfortunately, this is not a question to which any simple answer can be given.

One can infer from (V.5.20), in which $w = 1$, that, as π increases, *all* prices in terms of the wage rate will increase or, in extreme cases, remain constant[15] (the extreme cases in question being those of commodities, if there are any, which require for their production only direct labor unassisted by any intermediate commodity).

However, although all prices in terms of the wage rate increase (or do not decrease) as π increases, some of them will increase faster than others, so that, relative to any given *numéraire*-commodity, some prices will increase and others will decrease.

Returning to equation system (V.3.1) and setting $w = 1$, we can consider the ratio

$$\frac{p_j}{p_1} = \frac{a_{nj} + (1 + \pi) \sum_{i=1}^{n-1} a_{ij}p_i}{a_{n1} + (1 + \pi) \sum_{i=1}^{n-1} a_{i1}p_i}, \qquad j = 2, 3, \ldots, n - 1$$

which is equivalent to changing the *numéraire* or, more precisely, to expressing the price of the jth commodity, $j = 2, \ldots, n - 1$, in terms of commodity 1. By finding the derivative of this ratio with respect to π, one can verify immediately that, at least in the neighborhood of π,

$$\frac{d}{d\pi} \left(\frac{p_j}{p_1} \right) \gtrless 0$$

[15] This follows from Theorems 5 and 5a (of Perron-Frobenius, see the *Mathematical Appendix* pp. 273, 276). According to these theorems each single element of matrix $[\mathbf{I} - (1 + \pi)\mathbf{A}]^{-1}$ is an increasing (or at least a nondecreasing) function of π.

according as

$$\left[p_1 \sum_{i=1}^{n-1} a_{ij}p_i - p_j \sum_{i=1}^{n-1} a_{i1}p_i \right]$$

$$+ (1 + \pi)\left[p_1 \sum_{i=1}^{n-1} a_{ij}\frac{dp_i}{d\pi} - p_j \sum_{i=1}^{n-1} a_{i1}\frac{dp_i}{d\pi} \right] \gtreqless 0 \tag{V.5.21}$$

$$j = 2, \ldots, n - 1.$$

In other words the price of the jth commodity in terms of commodity 1 will increase or decrease (as π increases) according as the expression (V.5.21) is positive or negative.

Expression (V.5.21) is rather complex. However, it has been possible to split it up into two parts which have been enclosed in square brackets. The first square bracket expresses a comparison between the proportion of the price of the jth commodity ($j = 2, 3, \ldots, n - 1$), which is due to the cost of its means of production, and the proportion of the price of commodity 1, which is due to the cost of its means of production. The effect exerted on (V.5.21) by the expression in this bracket can therefore be called the *capital intensity effect*. This effect will always be positive for all commodities produced by technical processes having a capital intensity greater than that of commodity 1 (used as the standard of comparison or *numéraire*); and it will always be negative for all commodities produced by technical processes having a capital intensity lower than that of commodity 1. By contrast, the expression in the second square bracket cannot be related to any property which may be defined in a simple manner. It depends on how *all* the prices change in the whole system. Its effect on (V.5.21) can thus be called the *price effect*. This effect could be either positive or negative, depending on the entire network of interindustry relationships. Thus, whereas the capital intensity effect always acts on each single price in a well-defined direction (which can be determined unambiguously at the level of the corresponding production process by a simple comparison with the production process of the *numéraire*-commodity), the price effect depends on the entire economic system and is therefore not predictable at the level of any single industry. In some cases it will strengthen the first effect (when it works in the same direction) and in other cases weaken it, when it works in the opposite direction, or indeed even reverse it, when it is particularly strong.

To conclude, in predicting price changes in the neighborhood of any particular rate of profit,[16] a probable, but not absolutely certain,

---

[16] This qualification is necessary. The degree of capital intensity (defined as the ratio of the means-of-production component to the wage component in each price) is a notion which is itself dependent on the rate of profit. Some production processes might turn out to be more capital intensive at some rates of profit, and less capital intensive at other rates of profit, than the production process of the *numéraire*-commodity.

indicator is provided by the degree of capital intensity of the various processes of production. Thus we can say that an increase in the rate of profit will be associated in most cases with an increase in the prices of commodities which for their production require a ratio of means of production to direct labor which is greater than that required by the *numéraire*-commodity (processes with high capital intensity). And, at the same time, that it will be associated in most cases with a decrease in the prices of commodities which require a ratio of means of production to direct labor which is lower than that required by the *numéraire*-commodity (productive processes with low capital intensity). However, as has already been said, these propositions hold *in most but not all cases*. There might always be commodities for which the price effect is not only in the direction opposite to the capital intensity effect but also is so strong as to more than offset it and cause a reversal of the overall effect.

This would seem to be about all that can be said concerning the changes of the prices (V.5.17) corresponding to changes in the rate of profit. The relationships are highly complex precisely because the structure of prices depends both on the technical coefficients and on the particular level of the rate of profit.

6   The Relationship Between the Wage Rate and the Rate of Profit

6.1. *Income distribution and changes in relative prices.* There is an important relation, that between the wage rate and the rate of profit, which is influenced in a very complicated way by the unpredictable behavior of prices, examined above. When the structure of prices changes as the rate of profit varies, the relation between the wage rate and the rate of profit is influenced by two different phenomena: the change in the distribution of income between wages and profits and the variation of the structure of prices as this distribution changes.

The role played by the distribution of income stands out clearly if we start with a particular net product in physical terms, $(\mathbf{I} - \mathbf{A})\bar{\mathbf{Q}}$, and then consider the distribution of shares of this net product (in physical terms) to wages and to profits. If we denote by ω the proportion or share of $(\mathbf{I} - \mathbf{A})\bar{\mathbf{Q}}$ distributed to wages and by $(1 - \omega)$ the share distributed to profits, all the possible distributions of income are obviously represented by a straight line with a slope of 45° (see Fig. V.1).

However, as soon as we consider not just the *shares* of the net product which go to wages and to profits (which can be thought of in physical terms) but rather the wage rate and the rate of profit, the introduction of the price vector **p** becomes unavoidable, and the relation immediately becomes more complicated.

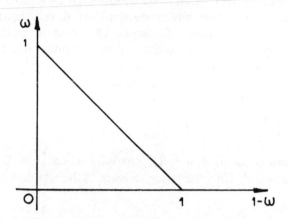

FIG. V.1. Distribution of net income by shares to wages and profits

It is still always possible to preserve the equality of the wage rate and the share of the net product which goes to wages (i.e., of ω and w) by adopting the convention of setting the net product per worker of the system equal to unity, i.e., of setting $\mathbf{p}(\mathbf{I} - \mathbf{A})\mathbf{Q} = Q_n$. But, with respect to profits, the transition to considering their *rate* rather than their share involves the introduction of the total value of capital. Indeed, the rate of profit is precisely a ratio between the value of that part of the net product which goes to profits and the value of total capital. In general, it can be represented here as

$$\pi = (1 - \omega)\frac{\mathbf{p}(\mathbf{I} - \mathbf{A})\bar{\mathbf{Q}}}{\mathbf{p}\mathbf{A}\bar{\mathbf{Q}}} \qquad (V.6.1)$$

Now, when $\omega = 0$ and the prices become those given by the solution of (V.5.6), i.e., $\mathbf{p}^*$, we have

$$\frac{\mathbf{p}^*(\mathbf{I} - \mathbf{A})\bar{\mathbf{Q}}}{\mathbf{p}^*\mathbf{A}\bar{\mathbf{Q}}} = \Pi \qquad (V.6.2)$$

But, as soon as $\omega > 0$, we have $\mathbf{p} \neq \mathbf{p}^*$. And, since the composition of capital, $\mathbf{A}\bar{\mathbf{Q}}$, differs in general from the composition of the net product, $(\mathbf{I} - \mathbf{A})\bar{\mathbf{Q}}$, the ratio $\mathbf{p}(\mathbf{I} - \mathbf{A})\bar{\mathbf{Q}}/\mathbf{p}\mathbf{A}\bar{\mathbf{Q}}$ will vary continually, as the distribution of income changes, because of variations in **p**. This means that (V.6.1) will be influenced both by the variation of ω and by the variation of **p**.

6.2. *The special case of uniform capital intensity*. It may be of interest to note that there is a special case in which these complications disappear. It is the very special case (considered by Ricardo and Marx) in which the price vector, which we shall call $\bar{\mathbf{p}}$, remains invariant to changes in the distribution of income (the case of uniform capital intensity or uniform "organic composition of capital" in all sectors). In this case, since $\mathbf{p} = \bar{\mathbf{p}}$, we have

$$\frac{\bar{\mathbf{p}}(\mathbf{I} - \mathbf{A})\bar{\mathbf{Q}}}{\bar{\mathbf{p}}\mathbf{A}\bar{\mathbf{Q}}} = \Pi \tag{V.6.3}$$

for all values of ω ($0 \le \omega \le 1$), not only when $\omega = 0$, so that, by substituting into (V.6.1), the latter reduces to the simple linear relation

$$\pi = \Pi(1 - \omega) \tag{V.6.4}$$

If we then adopt the convention of taking the net product per worker of the system as the *numéraire*, i.e., of setting $\mathbf{p}(\mathbf{I} - \mathbf{A})\mathbf{Q} = Q_n$, ω coincides with w and the relation even becomes

$$\pi = \Pi(1 - w) \tag{V.6.5}$$

a linear relation between the rate of profit and the wage rate (see Fig. V.2). This relation reflects the income distribution phenomenon alone,

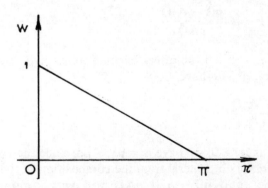

FIG. V.2. Relation between the wage rate and the rate of profit in the special case of uniform capital intensity

simply because the price structure remains invariant to changes in the distribution of income.[17]

6.3 *The general case.* In the general case the relation between the rate of profit and the wage rate is very complicated. For the purpose of analyzing its properties it is helpful to return to our earlier convention of expressing prices in terms of an arbitrary commodity, chosen as *numéraire*. We might start by choosing, for example, commodity 1, i.e.,

---

[17] The same linear relation may be obtained (but in a more laborious way) from the expressions of footnote 10 on p. 80. It was proved there that, if the vector of direct labor coefficients is the particular vector $\mathbf{a}_n^*$, defined as the eigenvector of $\mathbf{A}$ corresponding to λ_m, then relative prices turn out to be the same at the two extreme points $\pi = 0$ and $\pi = \Pi$. It is not difficult to prove now that relative prices remain the same also at *all* intermediate levels of the rate of profit $0 < \pi < \Pi$. If we put $\mathbf{a}_n = \mathbf{a}_n^*$ in (V.3.1), i.e., if we consider the special case

$$\mathbf{p}\mathbf{A}(1 + \pi) + \mathbf{a}_n^* w = \mathbf{p} \qquad (V.6.6)$$

it is sufficient for us to verify that (V.6.6) holds if we substitute in it the price vector $\mathbf{p}^*$ (which is by definition an eigenvector of $\mathbf{A}$). Since $\mathbf{p}^*\mathbf{A} = \lambda_m \mathbf{p}^*$, by substitution we obtain

$$\mathbf{p}^* = \mathbf{a}_n^* \frac{w}{1 - (1 + \pi)\lambda_m} \qquad (V.6.7)$$

We may therefore say that this expression holds if $\mathbf{p}^*$ and $\mathbf{a}_n^*$ are proportional to each other. But $\mathbf{p}^*$ is an eigenvector of $\mathbf{A}$ by definition, and $\mathbf{a}_n^*$ is an eigenvector of $\mathbf{A}$ by hypothesis (i.e., the two are indeed proportional to each other). Therefore, whatever the scalar

$$\frac{w}{1 - (1 + \pi)\lambda_m}$$

may be, i.e., whatever the rate of profit, π, and the wage rate, w, may be, expression (V.6.7) does indeed hold. (Note that for no other $\mathbf{a}_n$, which is not an eigenvector of $\mathbf{A}$, does (V.6.7) hold.)

We know also from footnote 10 on p. 80 that $\mathbf{v}^*$ is proportional to $\mathbf{a}_n^*$. And, since the price vector contains one degree of freedom (i.e., prices are determined up to an arbitrary constant), we may well set $\mathbf{p}^* = \mathbf{v}^*$, which is equivalent to choosing the unit of embodied labor as the *numéraire* of the price system (and therefore to fixing at $0 \le w \le 1$ the range of variation of the wage rate). In this case the coefficient of proportionality between $\mathbf{p}^*$ and $\mathbf{a}_n^*$, from (V.6.7), must coincide with the coefficient of proportionality between $\mathbf{v}^*$ and $\mathbf{a}_n^*$ from (V.5.15a), i.e.,

$$\frac{w}{1 - (1 + \pi)\lambda_m} = \frac{1}{1 - \lambda_m}$$

from which we obtain

$$\pi = \Pi(1 - w)$$

which is precisely the linear relation obtained in the text.

by setting $p_1 = 1$. By post-multiplying expression (V.5.18) by the first unit (column) vector $\mathbf{e}_1$, we obtain

$$1 = \mathbf{a}_n[\mathbf{I} - (1 + \pi)\mathbf{A}]^{-1}\mathbf{e}_1 w^{(1)} \tag{V.6.8}$$

where $w^{(1)}$ denotes the wage rate expressed in terms of commodity 1.

It will now be noted that (V.6.8) is an implicit function, of polynomial form, relating π and $w^{(1)}$. More specifically, (V.6.8) is in general an $(n-1)$th degree polynomial in π (where $n-1$ is the order of the matrix $\mathbf{A}$, which we shall here assume, for simplicity, to be irreducible). If the graph of this polynomial is drawn, using the usual Cartesian axes, its shape will therefore be far more complex than that of a straight line. One could, for example, obtain a curve such as that shown in Fig. V.3.

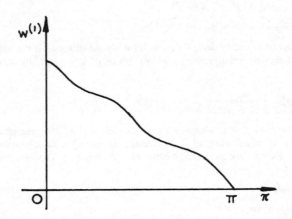

FIG. V.3. The wage rate – rate of profit relationship in the general case

Unfortunately, one can really say very little about the shape of this curve. One can only state that: (i) its intercept on the horizontal axis is necessarily Π (by definition); and (ii) the curve itself is everywhere strictly decreasing throughout the positive quadrant. Actually, every element of the matrix $[\mathbf{I} - (1 + \pi)\mathbf{A}]^{-1}$ is a strictly increasing function of π.[18] And this necessarily implies that each of π and $w^{(1)}$ is a monotonically decreasing function of the other.

One could, of course, repeat this argument with respect no longer to commodity 1 but to commodity j, j being any one of the other

[18] See Theorem 5 (of Perron-Frobenius), *Mathematical Appendix*, p. 273.

commodities $2, \ldots, n - 1$. In general, for each commodity j, $j = 1, 2, \ldots, n - 1$, one obtains a particular relation of the type (V.6.8) and a particular curve of the type shown in Fig. V.3. Each of these relations (and each corresponding curve) is different from each of the others, being dependent on the particular production conditions for the commodity in question. These relations are all polynomial functions of degree $(n - 1)$, they all intersect the π axis at Π, and they are all strictly decreasing in the positive quadrant. However, nothing whatever can be said in general about their shape.

We may now conclude. In an economic system with single product industries, the wage rate, expressed in terms of any commodity, is a monotonically decreasing function of the rate of profit.[19] However, this function is expressed by a complicated polynomial curve which assumes a specific shape for each particular commodity chosen as *numéraire*. This prevents a clear perception of the phenomenon of the distribution of income between wages and profits, since this phenomenon becomes intertwined with the other complex phenomenon of the variation of the entire structure of prices.

At first sight this conclusion might appear to destroy not only the Classical pure labor theory of value, but also the Ricardian attempt to separate the problem of income distribution from the problem of value. But we shall return to this question in Section 12 below.

7 Reduction of Prices to "Dated" Quantities of Labor

7.1. *A convergent series of quantities of labor.* Despite the difficulties met thus far, which might seem to stand in the way of any attempt to consider the system of prices in terms of quantities of labor, equation (V.5.20) lends itself to an interesting analysis which actually places the quantities of embodied labor at the center of the stage once again. The matrix $[\mathbf{I} - (1 + \pi)\mathbf{A}]^{-1}$ can be expanded as a power series in $\mathbf{A}$ provided only [20] that $(1 + \pi) < 1/|\lambda_M|$, where λ_M is the eigenvalue of $\mathbf{A}$ with the greatest modulus. In the present context the eigenvalue of greatest modulus coincides with the maximum eigenvalue, and this condition is therefore satisfied for every

$$\pi < \Pi \equiv \frac{1}{\lambda_m} - 1$$

---

[19] Not even this proposition holds when there is joint production.

[20] See *Mathematical Appendix*, p. 265.

Equation (V.5.20) can therefore be written as

$$\mathbf{p} = \mathbf{a}_n[\mathbf{I} + (1 + \pi)\mathbf{A} + (1 + \pi)^2\mathbf{A}^2 + (1 + \pi)^3\mathbf{A}^3 + \cdots]$$

$$(V.7.1)$$

or

$$\mathbf{p} = \mathbf{a}_n + (1 + \pi)\mathbf{a}_n\mathbf{A} + (1 + \pi)^2\mathbf{a}_n\mathbf{A}^2 + (1 + \pi)^3\mathbf{a}_n\mathbf{A}^3 + \cdots$$

$$(V.7.2)$$

Consider first the special case in which $\pi = 0$. Since $w = 1$, $\mathbf{p} = \mathbf{v}$ from (V.5.4); and (V.7.2) reduces to

$$\mathbf{p} = \mathbf{v} = \mathbf{a}_n + \mathbf{a}_n\mathbf{A} + \mathbf{a}_n\mathbf{A}^2 + \mathbf{a}_n\mathbf{A}^3 + \cdots \qquad (V.7.3)$$

It is not difficult to realize that this sequence of powers of $\mathbf{A}$, pre-multiplied by $\mathbf{a}_n$, has a precise economic meaning. It has already been seen[21] in fact that in the series of powers $\mathbf{I}, \mathbf{A}, \mathbf{A}^2, \mathbf{A}^3, \ldots$ the columns of each matrix represent the quantities of commodities which are (conceptually) required in each "round" of production in order to obtain each unit of the corresponding commodities as final commodities. The pre-multiplication of these matrices by the vector of direct labor coefficients therefore yields an infinite series of vectors which represent the quantities of labor required in the various successive rounds of production. Since the elements of the matrix $\mathbf{A}^s$, $s = 1, 2, 3, \ldots$, become ever smaller as s increases, these labor requirements become ever smaller as one moves backwards in time through the various rounds. They actually tend to zero as s tends to infinity. Thus the first term on the right side of (V.7.3) is the vector of direct labor requirements, while the sum of all the following terms is the vector of indirect labor requirements. The total sum thus represents the vector of the total (direct and indirect) labor requirements, i.e., the vector of the vertically integrated labor coefficients or quantities of embodied labor, which was obtained earlier in a compact, timeless way from (V.5.4).

But each of these quantities of labor also appears in (V.7.2). The latter expression, indeed, contains exactly the same quantities of labor as (V.7.3), with the difference that they are multiplied by the factor $(1 + \pi)^s$, where s is the round of production in which the quantity of labor is required. Thus the same quantities of labor, which in (V.7.3)

---

[21] See pp. 67–69.

are summed as they stand, in (V.7.2) are *dated*; a different weight is attributed to each quantity of labor according to the particular date, in time, at which it is required. It is to be noted that each term in the series, and thus also the sum of them, is an increasing function of π. Hence all the prices increase as the rate of profit increases. In the limit, (V.7.2) ceases to be convergent and the prices, in terms of the wage rate, tend to infinity. This occurs, however, only at the extreme limiting point at which the rate of profit reaches its maximum level, Π. For all rates of profit in the interval $0 \leq \pi < \Pi$, the series (V.7.2) is convergent and effects the reduction of all the prices to quantities of labor of different "dates," appropriately weighted by the corresponding compound interest factor $(1 + \pi)^s$.

7.2. *A series of "layers" of wages and profits.* We can now make use of the series (V.7.2) to illustrate the assertion made at the end of Section 5.6 that each price depends on both the quantity of labor directly and indirectly embodied in the respective commodity and the particular level of the rate of profit. Writing (V.7.2) in terms of an arbitrary *numéraire* as

$$\mathbf{p} = \mathbf{a}_n w + (1 + \pi)\mathbf{a}_n \mathbf{A} w + (1 + \pi)^2 \mathbf{a}_n \mathbf{A}^2 w + \cdots \qquad (V.7.4)$$

it can be seen at once that, with each variation in the distribution of income, each term in the series is pulled in opposite directions by the variations in the wage rate and the rate of profit.

The net result of these opposing pulls will, however, differ from term to term and from commodity to commodity, being dependent on the particular characteristics of the various powers of the matrix $\mathbf{A}$. As w and π vary in opposite directions, some terms will increase while others will decrease,[22] and each price will increase or decrease in accordance with the net effect of the sum of all these complicated variations.

Expression (V.7.4) can also be thought of as representing the superposing, backwards through time, of the infinitely many "layers" of profits and wages of which the price of each commodity consists. For each commodity each "layer" of wages and profits depends on the particular proportions of labor to means of production required, at the corresponding "date," by the technical characteristics of the production methods for that commodity. The reason for the variations in prices as the distribution of income between profits and wages varies

---

[22] A detailed analysis (with numerical example and graphical illustration) of the variations of all these addenda as an effect of changes in the rate of profit can be found in Sraffa [1, pp. 35–38].

can thus be traced back to the particular proportions of labor to means of production required by each commodity in each of the infinitely many "layers" of wages and profits which make up its price.[23]

8   The System of Physical Quantities

We turn now to the system of equations relating to the physical quantities to be produced, and we begin by formulating this system as "dual" to the price system. Leaving aside the last row of the transactions table, just as in (V.3.1) we left aside the last column, we can write

$$\left.\begin{aligned}
a_{11}Q_1 + a_{12}Q_2 + \quad \cdots \quad + a_{1,n-1}Q_{n-1} + Y_1 &= Q_1 \\
a_{21}Q_1 + a_{22}Q_2 + \quad \cdots \quad + a_{2,n-1}Q_{n-1} + Y_2 &= Q_2 \\
\vdots \qquad\qquad\qquad\qquad\qquad\qquad & \\
a_{n-1,1}Q_1 + a_{n-1,2}Q_2 + \quad \cdots + a_{n-1,n-1}Q_{n-1} + Y_{n-1} &= Q_{n-1}
\end{aligned}\right\} \quad \text{(V.8.1)}$$

If we were now to make explicitly the assumption of constant returns to scale, this system of equations would appear to be nothing but the "open" Leontief system, the quantities $Y_1, Y_2, \ldots, Y_{n-1}$ being displayed on the left-hand sides in order to draw attention to these

---

[23] Consider, by contrast, the very special case in which the proportions between labor and means of production are the same everywhere in the economic system (uniform capital intensity). In this case, a_n^* is an eigenvector of $\mathbf{A}$ (see footnotes 9 and 10 above). Therefore

$$a_n^* \mathbf{A} = a_n^* \lambda = a_n^* \frac{1}{1 + \Pi}$$

so that (V.7.4) becomes

$$\begin{aligned}
\mathbf{p} &= a_n^* w + \frac{1+\pi}{1+\Pi} a_n^* w + \left(\frac{1+\pi}{1+\Pi}\right)^2 a_n^* w + \left(\frac{1+\pi}{1+\Pi}\right)^3 a_n^* w + \cdots \\
&= a_n^* w \left[1 + \frac{1+\pi}{1+\Pi} + \left(\frac{1+\pi}{1+\Pi}\right)^2 + \left(\frac{1+\pi}{1+\Pi}\right)^3 + \cdots \right]
\end{aligned} \qquad \text{(V.7.5)}$$

The succession is perfectly regular. As may be seen, there appears within square brackets a geometric progression which is exactly the same for all prices. Therefore, whatever variations may take place in w and π, these variations affect each price by exactly the same multiplicative factor, thereby leaving their ratios (relative prices) unchanged.

It also follows from (V.7.5) that for all commodities the proportions of labor to means of production are exactly the same *at each single* conceptual stage of the production process, and not only at the vertically integrated stage. (As we saw, $\mathbf{v}^*$ is proportional to a_n^*). The remarkable consequence is that it makes no difference whether one talks of uniform capital intensity at the level of the single industries, at the level of the vertically integrated sectors, or at any one of the intermediate stages. Uniformity at one level necessarily entails uniformity at *all* levels.

quantities as constituting those portions of the total physical quantities which are in surplus relative to those portions which must go back into the production process.[24] To emphasize this point further it will be useful to express the various quantities of commodities which are devoted to final use in relative terms, i.e., in terms of physical rates of surplus, which we shall call R_i, $i = 1, 2, \ldots, n - 1$, and which we define as

$$R_1 = \frac{Y_1}{Q_1 - Y_1}, \qquad R_2 = \frac{Y_2}{Q_2 - Y_2}, \qquad \ldots, \qquad R_{n-1} = \frac{Y_{n-1}}{Q_{n-1} - Y_{n-1}}$$

$$(V.8.2)$$

The system of physical quantities may now be written in the alternative form

$$\left. \begin{aligned} (a_{11}Q_1 + a_{12}Q_2 + \ \cdots \ + a_{1,n-1}Q_{n-1})(1 + R_1) &= Q_1 \\ (a_{21}Q_1 + a_{22}Q_2 + \ \cdots \ + a_{2,n-1}Q_{n-1})(1 + R_2) &= Q_2 \\ \vdots \\ (a_{n-1,1}Q_1 + a_{n-1,2}Q_2 + \ \cdots \ + a_{n-1,n-1}Q_{n-1})(1 + R_{n-1}) &= Q_{n-1} \end{aligned} \right\}$$

$$(V.8.3)$$

Just as the quantities $Y_1, Y_2, \ldots, Y_{n-1}$ in (V.8.1) have been considered as given from outside, so in the alternative version (V.8.3) the $R_1, R_2, \ldots, R_{n-1}$ can now be considered as given from outside. In version (V.8.1) the problem is to find the total quantities $Q_1, Q_2, \ldots, Q_{n-1}$ which must be produced in order to obtain the given set of final commodities $Y_1, Y_2, \ldots, Y_{n-1}$. In version (V.8.3) the corresponding problem is that of finding the total quantities $Q_1, Q_2, \ldots, Q_{n-1}$, which must be produced in order to obtain a given set of physical rates of surplus $R_1, R_2, \ldots, R_{n-1}$. These physical rates of surplus will, of course, normally differ from one commodity to another (just as the proportions among the quantities $Y_1, Y_2, \ldots, Y_{n-1}$ are usually different from one another in (V.8.1)). Moreover, they must be

---

[24] It may also be pointed out that in this chapter we are considering a stationary system, so that all physical quantities $Y_1, Y_2, \ldots, Y_{n-1}$, making up the net product, are entirely devoted to consumption.

non-negative, i.e.,

$$R_i \geq 0, \qquad\qquad i = 1, 2, \ldots, n - 1 \qquad (V.8.4)$$

(just as $Y_i \geq 0$, $i = 1, 2, \ldots, n - 1$).[25]

The two formulations carry different implications, however. This becomes apparent as soon as one considers the solution of (V.8.3), which can be written

$$
\begin{bmatrix}
\left(a_{11} - \dfrac{1}{1 + R_1}\right) & a_{12} & \cdots & a_{1,n-1} \\[2mm]
a_{21} & \left(a_{22} - \dfrac{1}{1 + R_2}\right) & \cdots & a_{2,n-1} \\[2mm]
\vdots & \vdots & \ddots & \vdots \\[2mm]
a_{n-1,1} & & \cdots & \left(a_{n-1,n-1} - \dfrac{1}{1 + R_{n-1}}\right)
\end{bmatrix}
\begin{bmatrix}
Q_1 \\[2mm] Q_2 \\[2mm] \vdots \\[2mm] Q_{n-1}
\end{bmatrix}
=
\begin{bmatrix}
0 \\[2mm] 0 \\[2mm] \vdots \\[2mm] 0
\end{bmatrix}
$$

$$(V.8.5)$$

It will be noted that this system, by contrast with (V.8.1), is homogeneous. A necessary condition for the existence of nonzero solutions is therefore that the determinant of the coefficient matrix be zero, i.e.,

$$
\begin{vmatrix}
\left(a_{11} - \dfrac{1}{1 + R_1}\right) & a_{12} & \cdots & a_{1,n-1} \\[2mm]
a_{21} & \left(a_{22} - \dfrac{1}{1 + R_2}\right) & \cdots & a_{2,n-1} \\[2mm]
\vdots & & \ddots & \vdots \\[2mm]
a_{n-1,1} & & \cdots & \left(a_{n-1,n-1} - \dfrac{1}{1 + R_{n-1}}\right)
\end{vmatrix}
= 0
$$

$$(V.8.6)$$

If this equation is to be satisfied, it is necessarily implied that the physical rates of surplus $R_1, R_2, \ldots, R_{n-1}$ cannot all be taken as given. At most $(n - 2)$ of them can be taken as given; the remaining one must be such as to satisfy the algebraic equation (V.8.6).

[25] To get an idea of the meaning of these physical rates of surplus, it may be useful to refer them to the numerical example of Chapter II, Section 1.3, where the physical

Let us assume therefore that at least one of the R_i, $i = 1, 2, \ldots, n - 1$, is determined so as to satisfy (V.8.6). Then (V.8.5) becomes a linear and homogeneous system of equations with a zero determinant. Such a system will yield solutions for the physical quantities $Q_1, Q_2, \ldots, Q_{n-1}$, which are determined only up to a scalar multiple, i.e., it will determine the *structure* of production in the economic system, leaving the scale of operation indeterminate.

The contrast between this formulation and Leontief's now becomes clear. In system (V.8.1) all the Y_i, $i = 1, 2, \ldots, n - 1$, can be taken to be exogenously given; in system (V.8.3) at least one of the R_i, $i = 1, 2, \ldots, n - 1$, since it has to satisfy equation (V.8.6.), cannot be taken as given but itself becomes an unknown. On the other hand, the solutions to (V.8.1) refer to a well-defined scale of production, while the solutions to (V.8.3) relate to "relative quantities" and thus are independent of the scale of operation.

Version (V.8.3) has the advantage of retaining a degree of freedom, which might be used, for example, to take account of the last row of the transactions table, which could not be considered in version (V.8.1). In other words, we could now add equation (IV.4.4) to system (V.8.3), after having replaced the unknown quantity L (the requirements of labor) by the exogenous quantity $\bar{Q}_n$ (the total available labor). By means of this equation the size of the available labor force would determine the scale of operation of the economic system under consideration.[26]

9   The "Standard System"

9.1. *A logical exercise.* We now set ourselves a particular problem which we shall, for the moment, face as a purely logico-mathematical

quantities corresponding to the above notation are those given in Table V.1.

TABLE V.1

	Q_i	$Q_i - Y_i$	Y_i	$R_i = \dfrac{Y_i}{Q_i - Y_i}$
Tons of wheat (1)	450	270	180	66.66%
Tons of iron (2)	21	21	0	0%
Gross of turkeys (3)	60	30	30	100%

[26] The elaborations of this section have been presented in such a way as to make them directly comparable with those of the Leontief system. It may therefore be easier for the reader to consider them under the assumption of constant returns to scale. It must be specified, however, that Sraffa himself always keeps his analysis free from such an assumption. His arguments on the proportions among various industries are carried out on a purely hypothetical basis, as a preparation for the construction of the standard commodity, which we consider in following sections.

exercise. Since all but one of the R_i, $i = 1, 2, \ldots, n - 1$, can be taken to be determined from outside the system of equations (V.8.5), we may set all the R_i equal to one another, i.e.,

$$R_1 = R_2 = R_3 = \cdots = R_{n-1} = R \qquad \text{(V.9.1)}$$

where R denotes a uniform rate of surplus throughout the economic system.

Substituting a single R for the various R_i in system (V.8.5), $i = 1, 2, \ldots, n - 1$, and defining, for convenience,

$$\frac{1}{1 + R} = \eta \qquad \text{(V.9.2)}$$

we obtain a system of equations which can be written in compact form as

$$\mathbf{A}\mathbf{Q} = \eta\mathbf{Q} \qquad \text{(V.9.3)}$$

or

$$(\eta\mathbf{I} - \mathbf{A})\mathbf{Q} = \mathbf{0} \qquad \text{(V.9.3a)}$$

This system of equations is formally the same as system (V.5.9), although here the (column) vector $\mathbf{Q}$ multiplies the rows of $\mathbf{A}$, while in (V.5.9) the (row) vector $\mathbf{p}$ multiplies the columns of $\mathbf{A}$. Here too a necessary condition for the existence of nonzero solutions is that the determinant $|\eta\mathbf{I} - \mathbf{A}|$ be zero. Thus we can obtain the solution (or solutions) for η from the characteristic equation

$$\det (\eta\mathbf{I} - \mathbf{A}) = 0 \qquad \text{(V.9.4)}$$

which has, in general, $(n - 1)$ roots, although some of them could be repeated roots. These roots are simply the eigenvalues of the matrix $\mathbf{A}$, while $\mathbf{Q}$ is a right-hand eigenvector of $\mathbf{A}$. But $\mathbf{A}$ is non-negative and is the same matrix as appears in system (V.5.9), where $\mathbf{p}$ is its left-hand eigenvector. It follows that the values of η satisfying (V.9.4) coincide with the values of λ satisfying (V.5.10), so that

$$\eta_i = \lambda_i, \qquad\qquad i = 1, 2, \ldots, n - 1$$

As before, however, not all of these eigenvalues have an economic meaning. In fact, only one of them, the maximum eigenvalue η_m, is certainly associated with a strictly non-negative eigenvector,[27] the elements of which represent physical quantities in the present context. It is therefore to this eigenvalue that there corresponds, via (V.9.2), the unique R having an economic meaning, i.e., the unique R which,

---

[27] The result of Theorems 1 and 1a (of Perron-Frobenius). See *Mathematical Appendix*, pp. 269, 275.

on being substituted into (V.9.3), always yields non-negative solutions. Moreover, since $\eta_m \equiv \lambda_m$, it also follows that

$$R \equiv \frac{1}{\eta_m} - 1 \equiv \frac{1}{\lambda_m} - 1 \equiv \Pi \qquad\qquad (V.9.5)$$

i.e., the uniform rate of surplus of the system is identically equal to the maximum rate of profit. This is a remarkable result, deriving from the mathematical properties of the equations which represent a production system.

Thus R and Π provide two different economic interpretations of the maximum eigenvalue of $\mathbf{A}$, the matrix of the interindustry technical coefficients. Every $\mathbf{A}$ matrix is characterized by a particular maximum eigenvalue, which is related, by the same relation (V.9.5), both to the uniform rate of surplus and to the maximum rate of profit, which consequently coincide.

9.2. *The viability condition once again.* A further condition must, of course, be satisfied by system (V.9.3):

$$R \geq 0$$

which implies that

$$\eta_m \leq 1$$

But, since $\eta_m \equiv \lambda_m$, this is nothing other than condition (V.5.13), which we have already discussed. Thus the identity $\eta_m \equiv \lambda_m$ now provides an alternative interpretation of that condition. If the condition were not satisfied, it would mean that the economic system considered is so technically backward as to yield a negative rate of surplus, i.e., to use as means of production greater quantities of commodities than it would then be able to produce. Such an economic system could obviously not survive; it would not be viable. This is in effect the interpretation of the viability condition for the system which was anticipated in Chapter IV (Section 5.2).

9.3. *"Standard commodity" and "standard net product."* Once the uniform rate of surplus, R, has been found, it can be substituted into system (V.9.3), thus enabling us to obtain the solutions for the Q_i, $i = 1, 2, \ldots, n - 1$, which satisfy the problem which we posed at the outset. Since the system (V.9.3) becomes linear and homogeneous with a zero determinant, it yields solutions for the physical quantities Q_i, $i = 1, 2, \ldots, n - 1$, which are determined up to a scalar multiple. It thus determines the structure of the production system but not its scale of operation. To determine the latter a further relation is required.

We may now suppose such a relation to be introduced by adding, for example, equation (IV.4.4), with L replaced by the available labor force $\bar{Q}_n$, assumed to be exogenously given. We may thus write

$$(1 + R)\mathbf{AQ} = \mathbf{Q} \tag{V.9.6}$$

$$\mathbf{a}_n \mathbf{Q} = \bar{Q}_n \tag{V.9.7}$$

Equations (V.9.6) and (V.9.7) now form a system of n equations in n unknowns: R and the $(n - 1)$ physical quantities Q_i, $i = 1, 2, \ldots, n - 1$. We shall denote the solutions for the Q_i by $Q_1^*, Q_2^*, \ldots, Q_{n-1}^*$.

An interesting problem now arises. If the $\mathbf{A}$ matrix is an irreducible matrix, the Perron-Frobenius theorems[28] guarantee that the solutions are all strictly positive. If, on the other hand, the $\mathbf{A}$ matrix is reducible, the same Perron-Frobenius theorems (in their weak form) guarantee only that the solutions are non-negative. This means that some of them will be positive while others might be zero. The positive solutions clearly satisfy the equalities (V.9.1). For the zero solutions, by contrast, a physical rate of surplus cannot be defined. However, precisely because these solutions are zero, we may remove the corresponding rows and columns from the coefficient matrix. This means that we can eliminate the corresponding industries and commodities from the system of equations.

Let the number of positive solutions be k ($k = n - 1$ if the matrix $\mathbf{A}$ is irreducible, and $k < n - 1$ if the matrix $\mathbf{A}$ is reducible). It may now be noted that these solutions possess a very interesting property concerning their proportions. If we denote by $Y_1^*, Y_2^*, \ldots, Y_k^*$ the quantities for final use corresponding to the solutions $Q_1^*, Q_2^*, \ldots, Q_k^*$, we shall have by definition

$$R = \frac{Y_1^*}{Q_1^* - Y_1^*} = \frac{Y_2^*}{Q_2^* - Y_2^*} = \cdots = \frac{Y_k^*}{Q_k^* - Y_k^*}$$

from which it follows that

$$[Y_1^*, Y_2^*, \ldots, Y_k^*]' = R[(Q_1^* - Y_1^*), (Q_2^* - Y_2^*), \ldots, (Q_k^* - Y_k^*)]'$$

$$= \frac{R}{1 + R}[Q_1^*, Q_2^*, \ldots, Q_k^*]' \tag{V.9.8}$$

[28] See the *Mathematical Appendix*, Theorems 1 and 1a (of Perron-Frobenius), pp. 269, 275.

Thus the positive physical quantities which represent the solution of system (V.9.3) are such that the *proportions* in which the various commodities are produced are equal to the proportions in which the same commodities are used as means of production in the economic system as a whole, and are also equal to the proportions in which the same commodities are devoted to final uses (in the present context, consumption).

Sraffa has called an economic system which exhibits these proportionality relations a "standard system." And he has called the net product of that particular standard system in which the scale of operation is such as to require a quantity of labor equal to that employed in the actual economic system, as in (V.9.6). (V.9.7), the "standard net product." It will be noted that vector $[Y_1^*, Y_2^*, \ldots, Y_k^*]'$ represents a particular composite commodity into which the various commodities enter in precisely determined proportions. Sraffa has called this composite commodity, or any multiple or fraction thereof, the "standard commodity." And he has called the ratio R, expressing the uniform rate of surplus, the "standard ratio."

The standard system, as derived above, is, of course, simply a logical construction. For any given economic system, characterized by a particular coefficient matrix $\mathbf{A}$, there logically exists a corresponding standard system in which each commodity from the actual system is either produced in the standard proportions or is not produced at all.

9.4. *Labor embodied in the standard net product.* By calling $\mathbf{Q}^*$ the vector solution to (V.9.6), we have

$$\mathbf{AQ}^* = \frac{1}{1 + R}\mathbf{Q}^* \tag{V.9.9}$$

and thus, in general,

$$\mathbf{A}^s\mathbf{Q}^* = (1 + R)^{-s}\mathbf{Q}^* \tag{V.9.10}$$

It follows that

$$\mathbf{Y}^* = (\mathbf{I} - \mathbf{A})\mathbf{Q}^* = R\mathbf{AQ}^* = \frac{R}{1 + R}\mathbf{Q}^* \tag{V.9.11}$$

and hence, after substitution into (V.9.9), that

$$\mathbf{AY}^* = \frac{1}{1 + R}\mathbf{Y}^* \qquad \mathbf{A}^s\mathbf{Y}^* = (1 + R)^{-s}\mathbf{Y}^* \tag{V.9.12}$$

Thus $\mathbf{Y}^*$ is also found to be an eigenvector of $\mathbf{A}$. ($\mathbf{Q}^*$ and $\mathbf{Y}^*$ are indeed proportional to one another, as they contain the same commodities in exactly the same proportions).

Let us now consider the problem of finding the quantity of direct and indirect labor which is required for the production of the standard commodity, i.e., the total quantity of labor "embodied" in it. By making use of (V.7.3) and post-multiplying by Y^*, we obtain vY^*, the labor embodied in the standard net product expressed as the sum of the (infinite) series:

$$vY^* = a_n Y^* + a_n AY^* + a_n A^2 Y^* + a_n A^3 Y^* + \ldots \qquad (V.9.13)$$

where the first term on the right-hand side is the quantity of direct labor and the sum of the remaining terms is the total quantity of indirect labor, the latter being divided up according to the dates at which the various quantities of indirect labor were required. On substituting from (V.9.12), we obtain

$$vY^* = a_n Y^* \left[1 + \frac{1}{1 + R} + \frac{1}{(1 + R)^2} + \frac{1}{(1 + R)^3} + \ldots \right]$$

$$(V.9.14)$$

and thus[29]

$$vY^* = a_n Y^* \frac{1 + R}{R} \qquad (V.9.15)$$

This is a remarkable expression. The total quantity of labor embodied in the standard net product, vY^*, is obtained by simple multiplication of the quantity of direct labor, $a_n Y^*$ by the scalar $(1 + R)/R$. As is shown by (V.9.11), $(1 + R)/R$ is the ratio between the total quantities of the standard system and the corresponding quantities of the standard net product.[30] The remarkable conclusion obtained is thus that for the standard commodity the quantity of direct labor bears the same ratio to the quantity of embodied labor (direct labor plus indirect labor) as the standard net product Y^* bears to the total outputs Q^*. And, as a consequence, the quantity of direct labor

[29] See the formula in footnote 10, p. 67.

[30] It should be noted that the standard commodity has the remarkable property of reproducing precisely that proportion between direct labor and total embodied labor which characterizes each commodity in the hypothetical case of uniform capital intensity (or uniform "organic composition of capital"). Moreover, it reproduces precisely the same temporal succession of labor requirements. Compare expressions (V.5.15a) and (V.5.16) in footnote 10, p. 80.

From a purely formal point of view this result should not be surprising. There is a clear phenomenon of formal duality. The standard system has been constructed in such a way as to make vector Q^* (and by implication vector Y^*) a right-hand eigenvector of matrix A. And we saw in footnote 10 above (p. 80) that, in the special case of uniform capital intensity, vector a_n^* (and by implication vector v^*) must be a left-hand eigenvector of the same matrix A.

$\mathbf{a}_n \mathbf{Y}^*$ bears the same ratio to the quantity of indirect labor (the latter being $R^{-1}\mathbf{a}_n \mathbf{Y}^*$) as the standard net product $\mathbf{Y}^*$ bears to its means of production $\mathbf{AQ}^*$. Hence the standard ratio R also expresses the proportion between the quantity of labor embodied in the standard net product and the quantity of labor embodied in its means of production.

9.5. *Numerical example.* It may prove helpful to illustrate the algebraic operation of finding the standard system by making use of our numerical example from Chapter II. The matrix of interindustry coefficients for that example can be derived from (III.3.1); it is

$$
\mathbf{A} = \begin{bmatrix} \dfrac{186}{450} & \dfrac{54}{21} & \dfrac{30}{60} \\[2mm] \dfrac{12}{450} & \dfrac{6}{21} & \dfrac{3}{60} \\[2mm] \dfrac{9}{450} & \dfrac{6}{21} & \dfrac{15}{60} \end{bmatrix} \approx \begin{bmatrix} 0.4133 & 2.5714 & 0.5 \\[2mm] 0.0266 & 0.2857 & 0.05 \\[2mm] 0.02 & 0.2857 & 0.25 \end{bmatrix} \qquad \text{(V.9.16)}
$$

This is an irreducible matrix. We can infer immediately that all three commodities will enter the standard net product. The maximum eigenvalue is[31]

$$ \lambda_m \simeq 0.674 \qquad \text{(V.9.17)} $$

from which the maximum rate of profit and the uniform rate of surplus can be derived as

$$ \Pi \equiv R \equiv \frac{1}{\lambda_m} - 1 \simeq 48\% \qquad \text{(V.9.18)} $$

(The sign $\simeq$ is used because some decimal places have been rounded off.) On substituting the matrix (V.9.16) and the corresponding maximum eigenvalue (V.9.17) into (V.9.3), we can now compute the *relative quantities* for the standard system corresponding to the economic system considered in our numerical example.

Furthermore, if we add equation (V.9.7), after having substituted therein the total quantity of labor in the system, which is $\bar{Q}_n = 60$, and the vector of direct labor coefficients, which is

$$ \mathbf{a}_n = \begin{bmatrix} \dfrac{18}{450} & \dfrac{12}{21} & \dfrac{30}{60} \end{bmatrix} \simeq [0.04 \quad 0.5714 \quad 0.5] \qquad \text{(V.9.19)} $$

---

[31] As may easily be verified, the other eigenvalues are 0.2 and 0.074, both positive but smaller than $\lambda_m = 0.674$.

we can compute the absolute quantities of the standard net product. These quantities are

$$Y_1^* \simeq 141.77 \quad Y_2^* \simeq 11.58 \quad Y_3^* \simeq 14.47 \qquad \text{(V.9.20)}$$

The same results may be obtained by an alternative method which proceeds directly from the transactions table (given, for our example, in Chapter II, Section 1.3). We shall consider this alternative procedure since it is the method employed by Sraffa. The procedure consists in finding appropriate multipliers which, when applied to the corresponding industries in the original system, effect an expansion (if greater than 1) or a contraction (if less than 1) of each industry so as to make the total quantities produced stand in the same proportion to the total quantity of the corresponding commodity used as means of production. In our example, with three industries, the respective multipliers being denoted by q_1, q_2, and q_3, the problem becomes that of solving a system of three equations:

$$\left.\begin{aligned}
(186q_1 + 54q_2 + 30q_3)(1 + R) &= 450q_1 \\
(\ 12q_1 + \ 6q_2 + \ 3q_3)(1 + R) &= \ 21q_2 \\
(\ \ 9q_1 + \ 6q_2 + 15q_3)(1 + R) &= \ 60q_3
\end{aligned}\right\} \qquad \text{(V.9.21)}$$

in which there are four unknowns: q_1, q_2, q_3, R. We must therefore add another, normalizing equation which, from (V.9.7), is

$$18q_1 + 12q_2 + 30q_3 = 60 \qquad \text{(V.9.22)}$$

As may readily be checked, the unique positive solution (i.e., economically meaningful solution) of system (V.9.21), (V.9.22), is

$$\begin{aligned}
q_1^* &\simeq 0.968 \\
q_2^* &\simeq 1.695 \\
q_3^* &\simeq 0.741 \\
R &\simeq 0.48
\end{aligned} \qquad \text{(V.9.23)}$$

The meaning of these results will be clear enough. Industry 2 (producing iron) will have to be expanded by a factor of 1.695, while industries 1 and 3 (producing wheat and turkeys, respectively) will have to be contracted, by being multiplied by the factors 0.968 and 0.741, respectively. In this way the sizes of the industries will all be such as to yield a physical rate of surplus of 48% for each of the commodities, while requiring neither more nor less labor than is employed in the actual system.

Using either the solution (V.9.18), (V.9.20), or the solution (V.9.23), we can now construct the hypothetical standard system with a standard net product – which we may call the "normalized standard system" – corresponding to the original economic system considered in Chapters II and III. The results are brought together in Tables V.2 and V.3.

TABLE V.2
Actual economic system

	Industries						
Commodities	(1)	(2)	(3)	$Q_i - Y_i$	Y_i	Q_i	R_i
(1) Wheat (tons)	186	54	30	270	180	450	66.66%
(2) Iron (tons)	12	6	3	21	—	21	0
(3) Turkeys (gross)	9	6	15	30	30	60	100%
Man/years	18	12	30			60	

TABLE V.3
Normalized standard system

	Industries						
Commodities	(1)	(2)	(3)	$Q_i^* - Y_i^*$	Y_i^*	Q_i^*	R
(1) Wheat (tons)	180.04	91.52	22.24	293.80	141.77	435.57	48%
(2) Iron (tons)	11.62	10.17	2.22	24.01	11.58	35.59	48%
(3) Turkeys (gross)	8.72	10.17	11.12	30.01	14.47	44.48	48%
Man/years	17.42	20.34	22.24			60	

It will be seen that both the original economic system and the normalized standard system employ 60 workers. In the former, the workers produce a net product consisting of 180 tons of wheat, 0 tons of iron, and 30 gross of turkeys, with corresponding rates of surplus of 66.6%, 0%, and 100%, respectively. In the normalized standard system the same number of workers produce a standard net product consisting of 141.77 tons of wheat, 11.58 tons of iron, and 14.5 gross of turkeys, with a physical rate of surplus of 48% for each commodity. It will be observed that the proportions between the quantities of wheat, iron, and turkeys are always the same, whether one considers the means of production, the net product, or the total outputs. It is also to be noted that the uniform rate of surplus (48%) lies between the lowest (0%) and the highest (100%) of the rates of surplus in the original system.

10   Basic Commodities and Non-basic Commodities

10.1. *Definitions.* It was pointed out above that, in going from the actual economic system to the corresponding standard system, the latter may prove to contain fewer commodities (and industries) than the former. In such a case there are commodities (and industries) in the actual system which do not appear in the standard system (or, if one prefers, which appear with zero quantities). The methods of production of these commodities, which do not appear in the standard system, therefore play no role whatever in the determination of the prices of those commodities which do enter the standard system and moreover play no role whatever in the determination of the maximum rate of profit and uniform rate of surplus for the economic system as a whole.

These commodities, which do not appear in the standard system and therefore have a limited role to play, are called *non-basic commodities*. By contrast, the other commodities, those which do appear in the standard system, and which therefore contribute to the determination of all prices and of Π and R, are called *basic commodities*.

10.2. *A definition in terms of reducible and irreducible matrices.* The distinction between basic and non-basic commodities clearly derives from certain properties of the technical processes of production. In the case considered in this chapter this distinction can be characterized very precisely in simple mathematical terms. If the matrix of technical interindustry coefficients is an irreducible matrix, then all the commodities in the economic system are basic commodities; on the other hand, if the matrix is reducible, some of the commodities are basic commodities, while others are non-basic commodities.

More precisely, suppose that the interindustry coefficient matrix so far considered, $\mathbf{A}$, is reducible by appropriate interchanges of rows and corresponding columns to the block-triangular form (see *Mathematical Appendix*, p. 267):

$$\mathbf{A} = \begin{bmatrix} \mathbf{A}_{11} & \mathbf{A}_{12} \\ \mathbf{0} & \mathbf{A}_{22} \end{bmatrix} \qquad (V.10.1)$$

where $\mathbf{A}_{11}$ is an irreducible square submatrix of the kth order ($k \le n - 1$), and $\mathbf{A}_{22}$ is a square submatrix of the $(n - 1 - k)$th order (reducible or irreducible). Then the first k commodities on the rows of $\mathbf{A}$ are basic commodities and the remaining $(n - 1 - k)$ are non-basic commodities.

If $\mathbf{A}_{22}$ is an irreducible submatrix, we assume that at least one element of $\mathbf{A}_{12}$ is strictly positive. If $\mathbf{A}_{22}$ is a reducible submatrix, then

(V.10.1) may be reduced further to the general form

$$
\mathbf{A} = \begin{bmatrix} \mathbf{A}_{11} & \mathbf{A}_{12} & \cdots & \mathbf{A}_{1s} \\ \mathbf{O} & \mathbf{A}_{22} & \cdots & \mathbf{A}_{2s} \\ & & \cdot & \\ & & \cdot & \\ & & \cdot & \\ \mathbf{O} & \mathbf{O} & & \mathbf{A}_{ss} \end{bmatrix} \tag{V.10.2}
$$

where all submatrices $\mathbf{A}_{11}, \mathbf{A}_{22}, \ldots, \mathbf{A}_{ss}$ on the principal diagonal are irreducible.

In this case we assume that each of the submatrices $\mathbf{A}_{12}, \ldots, \mathbf{A}_{1s}$ on the first row contains at least one strictly positive element. The reason for this assumption is that we want to consider a single economic system. If the submatrices to the right of $\mathbf{A}_{11}$, on the first row of (V.10.2) or of (V.10.1) were zero matrices, then matrix (V.10.1), or matrix (V.10.2), would not refer to a single economic system, but to a multiplicity of quite separate economic systems, disjoint from, and simply put side by side with one another. (See also Section 10.7.)

By simple inspection of matrix (V.10.1) or matrix (V.10.2) we can now see clearly the economic meaning of the distinction between basic and non-basic commodities. Since the columns of the interindustry coefficient matrix represent production processes, the basic commodities are revealed to be commodities that are required (directly or indirectly) for the production of all commodities (basic and non-basic). By contrast, the non-basic commodities are commodities that are not required for the production of the basic commodities (though they may be required for their own production).

10.3. *A reformulation.* We may partition the vectors $\mathbf{Q}$, $\mathbf{p}$, and $\mathbf{a}_n$, of the previous sections as follows:

$$
\mathbf{Q} = \begin{bmatrix} \mathbf{Q}_1 \\ \mathbf{Q}_2 \end{bmatrix} \tag{V.10.3}
$$

$$
\mathbf{p} = [\mathbf{p}_1, \mathbf{p}_2] \tag{V.10.4}
$$

$$
\mathbf{a}_n = [\mathbf{a}_{n1}, \mathbf{a}_{n2}] \tag{V.10.5}
$$

where subscript 1 refers to the first k components (i.e., to the basic commodities) and subscript 2 refers to the remaining $(n - 1 - k)$ components (i.e., to the non-basic commodities).

It may be noted immediately that, when the matrix $\mathbf{A}$ is of the form (V.10.1), a vector $\mathbf{Q}$ of the form

$$
\mathbf{Q} = \begin{bmatrix} \mathbf{Q}_1 \\ \mathbf{O} \end{bmatrix} \tag{V.10.6}
$$

i.e., a vector $\mathbf{Q}$ in which $\mathbf{Q}_2 = \mathbf{0}$ is a solution of equation system (V.9.6). It follows that the standard system will simply be defined by the solution of the system of equations

$$[\mathbf{I} - (1 + R)\mathbf{A}_{11}]\mathbf{Q}_1 = \mathbf{0} \tag{V.10.7}$$

The non-basic commodities are thus eliminated completely. Vector $\mathbf{Q}_1^*$, the solution of (V.10.7), defines the standard commodity. Hence both $\mathbf{Q}_1^*$, the standard commodity, and R, the standard ratio, depend exclusively on $\mathbf{A}_{11}$, the production processes of the basic commodities, while being entirely independent of $[\mathbf{A}_{12}, \mathbf{A}_{22}]'$, the production processes of the non-basic commodities.

It may be noted, moreover, that, when the matrix $\mathbf{A}$ is of the form (V.10.1), the inverse matrix $[\mathbf{I} - (1 + \pi)\mathbf{A}]^{-1}$ may be obtained by parts (see procedure in *Mathematical Appendix*, pp. 242–243), so that

$$[\mathbf{I} - (1 + \pi)\mathbf{A}]^{-1}$$

$$= \begin{bmatrix} [\mathbf{I} - (1 + \pi)\mathbf{A}_{11}]^{-1} & [\mathbf{I} - (1 + \pi)\mathbf{A}_{11}]^{-1}\mathbf{A}_{12}[\mathbf{I} - (1 + \pi)\mathbf{A}_{22}]^{-1} \\ \mathbf{O} & [\mathbf{I} - (1 + \pi)\mathbf{A}_{22}]^{-1} \end{bmatrix}$$

$$\tag{V.10.8}$$

This means that the general solution for the price system (V.5.18) takes the form

$$\mathbf{p}_1 = \mathbf{a}_{n1}[\mathbf{I} - (1 + \pi)\mathbf{A}_{11}]^{-1}w \tag{V.10.9}$$

$$\mathbf{p}_2 = \mathbf{a}_{n1}[\mathbf{I} - (1 + \pi)\mathbf{A}_{11}]^{-1}\mathbf{A}_{12}[\mathbf{I} - (1 + \pi)\mathbf{A}_{22}]^{-1}w$$

$$+ \mathbf{a}_{n2}[\mathbf{I} - (1 + \pi)\mathbf{A}_{22}]^{-1}w \tag{V.10.10}$$

As may now be seen explicitly, vector $\mathbf{p}_1$ (the prices of basic commodities) depends exclusively on the submatrix $\mathbf{A}_{11}$, i.e., on the production processes of the basic commodities, while being entirely independent of the submatrix $[\mathbf{A}_{12}, \mathbf{A}_{22}]'$, i.e., the production processes of the non-basic commodities. By contrast, vector $\mathbf{p}_2$ (the prices of the non-basic commodities) depends both on $\mathbf{A}_{11}$ and on $[\mathbf{A}_{12}, \mathbf{A}_{22}]'$, i.e., both on the production processes of the basic commodities and on the production processes of the non-basic commodities.

Finally, expression (V.6.8), which gives the relation between π and $w^{(1)}$ (the rate of profit and the wage rate expressed in terms of commodity 1) takes the form

$$1 = \mathbf{a}_{n1}[\mathbf{I} - (1 + \pi)\mathbf{A}_{11}]^{-1}\mathbf{e}_1 w^{(1)} \tag{V.10.11}$$

This means (provided only that the wage rate is expressed in terms of a basic commodity) that the w-π relation depends exclusively on the production processes of the basic commodities and is entirely independent of the production processes of the non-basic commodities.

10.4. *Numerical example.* In order to appreciate the economic meaning of the preceding presentation, it will be helpful to consider again the numerical example of Section 9.5. Let us suppose an economic system which, in addition to producing wheat, iron, and turkeys as previously assumed, also produces a fourth commodity, which we shall call ostriches. And suppose that the production of one unit of this commodity requires, on average, 0.2 ostrich, 0.005 ton of wheat, and 0.005 ton of iron. The matrix of technical coefficients for this new economic system (containing four industries and four commodities) will thus be

$$\begin{bmatrix} 0.4133 & 2.5714 & 0.50 & 0.005 \\ 0.0266 & 0.2857 & 0.05 & 0.005 \\ 0.02 & 0.2857 & 0.25 & 0 \\ 0 & 0 & 0 & 0.200 \end{bmatrix} \qquad (\text{V}.10.12)$$

As can be seen immediately, this is a reducible matrix. One can easily verify that, on moving from the system described by this matrix to the corresponding standard system, the fourth commodity disappears (i.e., the corresponding solution turns out to be zero) and the standard system comes to be characterized simply by the submatrix

$$\begin{bmatrix} 0.4133 & 2.5714 & 0.50 \\ 0.0266 & 0.2857 & 0.05 \\ 0.02 & 0.2857 & 0.25 \end{bmatrix} \qquad (\text{V}.10.13)$$

which is the same matrix (V.9.16) as for our earlier example. Commodities 1, 2, 3, (wheat, iron, turkeys) are thus basic commodities, while the fourth commodity (ostriches) is a non-basic commodity. It is also easy to see that the maximum eigenvalues of (V.10.12) and (V.10.13) are the same, namely 0.674, corresponding to a maximum rate of profit of 48%. (The eigenvalue, which in (V.10.12) is added to the three previous eigenvalues is 0.2, as can be seen by inspection, and is thus smaller than 0.674.)

If the matrix (V.10.12) is now examined more closely, it will be seen that it is the three zeros appearing in the last row which render it reducible. These zeros have a precise economic meaning; they imply that commodity 4 is *not* used in the production of the other three commodities, while these other commodities are required for its production (wheat and iron directly, and turkeys indirectly—through the production of wheat and iron). It follows that a zero output of commodity 4 is compatible with the production of positive quantities of commodities 1, 2, 3. By contrast, it would not be possible to produce a positive quantity of commodity 4 without also producing positive quantities of commodities 1, 2, 3. There is thus a sense in which we can say that the basic commodities are "more necessary" to the system than are the non-basic commodities. This is the reason why the standard system, which represents the system's essential nucleus, so to speak, necessarily includes the basic commodities but excludes the non-basic commodities.

10.5. *The economic meaning of the distinction between basic and non-basic commodities.* The findings above make it necessary for us to emphasize further the economic significance of the contrast between basic and non-basic commodities. We have seen that a basic commodity is a commodity which is technically necessary for the production of all the other commodities. It follows that a zero production of even just one basic commodity necessarily implies zero production of all commodities (basic and non-basic). It also follows that, when any one of the production coefficients for a basic commodity changes, this causes the prices of all commodities (basic and non-basic) to change. It also causes a change of the maximum rate of profit and uniform rate of surplus for the whole system, and a change of the whole w-π relation.

A non-basic commodity, by contrast, is not technically necessary for the production of basic commodities, whereas the latter are required for its production. Even if all the coefficients of the production process for a non-basic commodity changed, while the price of that commodity and of those non-basic commodities which use it as a means of production would certainly change, the prices of all basic commodities in terms of any basic commodity would remain unchanged. The maximum rate of profit and the uniform rate of surplus of the system and the whole relation (V.6.8) between w and π would also remain unchanged.

10.6. *Relations with the distinction between necessary and luxury goods.* It may be of interest to point out that the distinction between basic and non-basic commodities corresponds to the distinction which the Classical economists made between "necessary" or "subsistence" commodities and "luxury" goods. In the theories of the Classical economists, subsistence commodities are always needed in the production of all commodities. By contrast, luxury commodities require subsistence commodities for their production but are not used in the production of the latter.

Yet the Classical economists thought of this distinction as being based on the *use* to which the two categories of commodities were devoted. The novel feature of Sraffa's analysis is that the distinction is shown to arise from the technical properties of the production processes.

10.7. *An assumption on the physical own-rates of reproduction of the basic and non-basic commodities.* The preceding discussion enables us to consider two assumptions which it has not been possible to discuss explicitly until now, even though they have been present throughout the analysis.

The first assumption is that there always exists at least one basic commodity[32] and that it requires labor for its production. This assumption implies that all commodities require, directly or indirectly, both commodities and labor for their production.

The second (rather more complex) assumption concerns the maximum eigenvalue of the matrix of technical coefficients. We know that the eigenvalues of a reducible matrix (when it is reduced to a block-triangular form) coincide with the eigenvalues of the square sub-matrices which lie on its principal diagonal.[33] The assumption which is now to be made explicit is that the maximum eigenvalue of the matrix **A** is the maximum eigenvalue of the submatrix on the principal diagonal which refers to the basic commodities. (This assumption is obviously satisfied in our earlier numerical example, where the maximum eigenvalue of the matrix (V.10.12) is $\lambda_m = 0.674$ and coincides with the maximum eigenvalue of its submatrix (V.10.13), which refers to the basic commodities.)

From a purely mathematical point of view this assumption might seem somewhat arbitrary. It is less so, however, if we consider its economic meaning. To assume that the maximum eigenvalue is that of the submatrix relating to the basic commodities is to assume that the physical own-rate of reproduction of the basic commodities is smaller than the physical own-rate of reproduction of the non-basic com-modities.[34] Given the economic meaning of basic and non-basic com-modities, discussed in Section 10.5 above, this seems to be a rather

---

[32] If this were not so, we should not be considering an economic "system," but a multiplicity of different systems, set alongside each other.

[33] See *Mathematical Appendix*, p. 258.

[34] In our previous numerical example, the physical own-rate of reproduction of basic commodities is 48% (uniform rate of surplus). This means that basic commodities cannot be reproduced at a rate larger than 48%. The non-basic commodity, by contrast, has a physical own-rate of reproduction of

$$\frac{1}{0.2} - 1 = 400\%$$

plausible assumption.[35] This is a case in which our knowledge of the economic system permits us to accept certain assumptions in preference to others, even when they might appear, from a formal point of view, to be symmetrical to one another.

In any case the effect of this assumption is that, at the analytical level, it enables us to make some further important assertions. First of all, if the maximum eigenvalue of the (irreducible) submatrix referring to basic commodities is larger than the maximum eigenvalues of all the other submatrices on the principal diagonal, we know that the maximum eigenvalue of the corresponding characteristic equation is a simple root.[36] This implies that the standard ratio R (a real number) is associated with a vector Q^* which not only has all non-negative components (as was said in Section 9.1) but is also *unique*. Similarly, we can say (in addition to what was said in Section 5.3) that the system of prices, p^*, associated with the same real number $\Pi \equiv R$, is *unique*. Indeed, with respect to the latter vector, we can even assert that its elements are all strictly positive. (In other words, prices are always positive, both for basic commodities and for non-basic commodities.[37])

10.8. *An unusual case.* It is nevertheless natural to ask what would happen in the case (which Sraffa considers a "freak case") of a non-basic commodity whose physical own-rate of reproduction were so unusually low as to be lower than that of the basic commodities; for example, the case in which, in the particular economic system considered in Section 10.4, the own-coefficient of reproduction of ostriches were, say, 0.8 (rather than 0.2), corresponding to an own-rate of reproduction of 25% (rather than 400%).

The answer is that in such a case the non-basic commodity could not be produced at a rate of profit greater than 25%. The basic commodities, by contrast, could perfectly well continue to be produced at rates of profit greater than 25%. In other words, the maximum rate of profit for the economic system would continue to be determined by the maximum eigenvalue of the submatrix which relates to basic products (i.e., in our example it would continue to be 48%); and the whole of our earlier analysis would continue to hold with respect to the basic commodities. However, the price of the non-basic commodity would now behave in a rather peculiar way. The formal solution for the system of prices shows that in this case the price of the non-basic

---

[35] An interesting discussion of this problem has taken place between Piero Sraffa and Peter Newman [2], following Newman [6].

[36] Theorem 1 (of Perron-Frobenius). See *Mathematical Appendix*, p. 269.

[37] This follows from the theorem stated in footnote 9, p. 275, of *Mathematical Appendix*.

commodity (in terms of a basic commodity) is positive for rates of profit less than 25%, but becomes infinite at the singular point $\pi = 25\%$, and becomes negative for rates of profit greater than 25%. In practice, since infinite or negative prices have no meaning, this simply means that, for rates of profit equal to, or greater than, 25%, it would not be possible to maintain the assumptions of a uniform rate of profit in all sectors and of a uniform price for all units of the same commodity.[38]

11   Autonomy of the Two Systems Considered (the Price System and the Physical Quantity System)

Considering the preceding analysis as a whole, it must now be emphasized that, all the similarities and formal analogies notwithstanding, the system of prices and the system of physical quantities are two separate systems, neither of which carries any implications for the other. The standard system, for example, is a logical construction which relates to physical quantities and which implies nothing about the price system. Although, from a formal point of view, the particular system of prices in which $w = 0$ appears as "dual" to the standard system, the former in no way implies the latter and, similarly, the latter in no way implies the former. If, for example, a certain economic system were actually to be in the standard proportions, that would not imply that the system of prices would necessarily have to be that for which $w = 0$. Any other system of prices would be perfectly possible. Similarly, if the (surplus) wage were actually zero in an economic system, that would in no way imply that the proportions of the physical system would necessarily have to be those of the standard system. Any other set of proportions would be possible.

In practice, of course, the ruling price system is usually a system with a rate of profit lying somewhere between the two extremes, while the system of physical quantities actually being observed will usually be a system in which the proportions are not those of the standard system. Thus actual economic systems are usually highly complex and, from a formal point of view, distinctly inelegant. It is precisely this complexity which justifies the analysis of the corresponding (hypothetical) extreme price systems and of the corresponding (hypothetical) standard systems, which, in addition to being formally more elegant, are conceptually easier to grasp. These hypothetical systems possess the important property of having the same coefficients matrix as the actual system. It follows that all those properties *of the actual system* which depend on

[38] A special appendix is devoted to this case in Sraffa [1, pp. 90–91].

the structure of the coefficients matrix can be better analyzed, studied, and understood by considering the standard system and the extreme cases of the price system. The significance of these remarks should already be clear from the preceding analysis; however, a further important illustration is given in the following section.

12   Price System and Income Distribution

12.1. *The standard net product as the numéraire of the price system.* We are now going to consider one of the most interesting applications of the notion of a standard system (and of a standard net product and of a standard commodity). This is an application which has been carried out by Sraffa in order to solve a theoretical problem that had remained unsolved since Ricardo.

Suppose we are observing a certain economic system and suppose that the corresponding physical quantities and prices are represented by the two systems of equations which were obtained earlier, namely,

$$\mathbf{AQ} + \hat{\mathbf{R}}\mathbf{AQ} = \mathbf{Q} \tag{V.12.1}$$

$$\mathbf{pA}(1 + \pi) + \mathbf{a}_n w = \mathbf{p} \tag{V.12.2}$$

where $\hat{\mathbf{R}}$ is a diagonal matrix with $R_1, R_2, \ldots, R_{n-1}$ on the principal diagonal.

We have seen that, although the rate of profit is taken as exogenously fixed, a normalization problem arises with reference both to (V.12.1) and to (V.12.2). For the former determines only relative quantities and the latter only relative prices. In each case there is room for a further equation.

For the quantity system it will prove convenient to add the equation

$$\mathbf{a}_n \mathbf{Q} = 1 \tag{V.12.3}$$

which sets the total quantity of labor equal to unity. This means, in comparison with our previous convention under which the labor coefficients were expressed in terms of workers/year, that here those coefficients have been divided by Q_n and are thus now expressed in terms of the total quantity of labor.

For the price system we know that any commodity, or any linear combination of commodities, can be chosen at will as the *numéraire* by setting its price equal to unity. Now we consider the choice of a very particular *numéraire*, namely, the standard commodity. More specifically, we choose as *numéraire*-commodity that particular bundle of commodities, a composite commodity, which forms the standard net product.

To effect this normalization we must first find the standard system corresponding to the actual system (V.12.1). By using the normalization which also yields the standard net product, we obtain

$$[\mathbf{I} - (1 + R)\mathbf{A}]\mathbf{Q}^* = \mathbf{0} \qquad\qquad (V.12.4)$$

$$\mathbf{a}_n \mathbf{Q}^* = 1 \qquad\qquad (V.12.5)$$

where, of course,

$$\det[\mathbf{I} - (1 + R)\mathbf{A}] = 0$$

The standard net product is represented by the column vector $\mathbf{Y}^* = (\mathbf{I} - \mathbf{A})\mathbf{Q}^*$ and the convention adopted here is thus to set equal to unity the value of the composite commodity represented by this vector, i.e.,

$$\mathbf{p}(\mathbf{I} - \mathbf{A})\mathbf{Q}^* = 1 \qquad\qquad (V.12.6)$$

This is the extra equation we need. By adding it to (V.12.2), the system of prices is closed (for any given rate of profit) and the $(n - 1)$ prices and the wage rate all come to be expressed in terms of the particular composite commodity $\mathbf{Y}^*$, the standard net product.

The value of the standard net product having been set equal to unity it should be noted that the value of the actual net product will, in general, differ from unity so that, in general: $\mathbf{p}(\mathbf{I} - \mathbf{A})\mathbf{Q} \neq \mathbf{p}(\mathbf{I} - \mathbf{A})\mathbf{Q}^* = 1$, except in the special case in which $\pi = 0$. In this case, prices are given by $\mathbf{p} = \mathbf{v}w$, i.e., they are proportional to the quantities of embodied labor; and the value of the net national income, whatever its physical composition, will simply be equal to the total quantity of labor multiplied by the wage rate. In the present case, thanks to normalizations (V.12.3) and (V.12.6), it even follows that, for the special case $\pi = 0$,[39]

$$\mathbf{v}(\mathbf{I} - \mathbf{A})\mathbf{Q} = \mathbf{v}(\mathbf{I} - \mathbf{A})\mathbf{Q}^* = 1 = w$$

In other words, the normalizations adopted here fix the two extreme limits (between which the wage rate can vary) at zero and unity respectively. (As one can easily see, $w = 0$ for $\pi = \Pi$ and $w = 1$ for

---

[39] From (V.12.3) and (V.5.4) we have

$$\mathbf{a}_n(\mathbf{I} - \mathbf{A})^{-1}(\mathbf{I} - \mathbf{A})\mathbf{Q} = 1$$

$$\mathbf{v}(\mathbf{I} - \mathbf{A})\mathbf{Q} = 1$$

and similarly, from (V.12.5),

$$\mathbf{a}_n(\mathbf{I} - \mathbf{A})^{-1}(\mathbf{I} - \mathbf{A})\mathbf{Q}^* = 1$$

$$\mathbf{v}(\mathbf{I} - \mathbf{A})\mathbf{Q}^* = 1$$

$\pi = 0$.) Hence the wage rate w now also expresses the proportion, or relative share, of the standard net product which can be purchased by total wages.

12.2. *The π-w relation in the standard system.* Before going on, a brief digression will prove useful. If the very special case of an actual economic system being exactly in the standard proportions were to occur, and if the net product or net income of that system were to be distributed between profits and wages in such a way that both profits and wages consisted of standard commodity, then the rate of profit could be seen in physical terms, i.e., it would be independent of prices. Indeed, with total profits and means of production consisting of the same commodities, in the same proportions, the ratio between the physical quantity of any commodity in total profits and the physical quantity of the same commodity in the means of production would express the rate of profit as a physical ratio. Even if all the physical quantities were multiplied by their prices, any given price, by appearing both in the numerator and in the denominator, would cancel out, leaving the ratio unchanged.

It follows that the standard system (in which $\mathbf{Q} = \mathbf{Q}^*$) is another special case in which the ratio $\mathbf{p(I - A)Q/pAQ}$, which we met in (V.6.1), remains the same at all levels of the rate of profit. (It will be remembered that the other special case in which this occurs is that in which the prices remain the same at all levels of the rate of profit, i.e., the case of uniform capital intensity in all sectors.) In the standard system therefore (as in the case of uniform capital intensity in all sectors) we always have $[\mathbf{p(I - A)Q^*/pAQ^*}] = \Pi$, for all levels of π within the interval $0 \leq \pi \leq \Pi$.

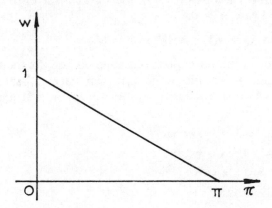

FIG. V.4. Relation between w and π in the standard system

In the present context, since $\omega = w$, owing to (V.12.5) and (V.12.6), the relation (V.6.1) between w and π becomes

$$\pi = \Pi(1 - w) \tag{V.12.7}$$

i.e., it becomes a linear relation between π and w. (See Fig. V.4). The simplicity of the linear relation contrasts sharply with the complexity of the polynomial relation between w and π in the general case discussed in Section 6.3. It is clear, however, that so simple a relation, derived for a special case, will be of interest to us only if it is in some way relevant to the general case.

12.3 *The same linear relation valid for the actual system, with the one proviso that w be expressed in terms of the standard commodity.* Let us return to the actual economic system for which the prices have been expressed in terms of the standard commodity (in the particular size of the standard net product):

$$\mathbf{pA} + \mathbf{pA}\pi + \mathbf{a}_n w = \mathbf{p} \tag{V.12.2}$$

$$\mathbf{p(I - A)Q^*} = 1 \tag{V.12.6}$$

Post-multiplying both sides of (V.12.2) by the column vector $\mathbf{Q^*}$ and rearranging, we obtain

$$\mathbf{pAQ^*}\pi = \mathbf{pQ^*} - \mathbf{pAQ^*} - \mathbf{a}_n \mathbf{Q^*}w$$

$$\mathbf{pAQ^*}\pi = \mathbf{p(I - A)Q^*} - \mathbf{a}_n \mathbf{Q}w$$

But $\mathbf{p(I - A)Q^*} = 1$, from (V.12.6), and $\mathbf{a}_n \mathbf{Q^*} = 1$, from (V.12.5). Hence

$$\mathbf{pAQ^*}\pi = 1 - w$$

or

$$\mathbf{pAQ^*}\pi R = R(1 - w) \tag{V.12.8}$$

Consider now the term $(\mathbf{pAQ^*}R)$. Returning to (V.12.4), pre-multiplying by the row vector of prices $\mathbf{p}$ and rearranging, we obtain

$$\mathbf{pAQ^*}R = \mathbf{pQ^*} - \mathbf{pAQ^*}$$

$$\mathbf{pAQ^*}R = \mathbf{p(I - A)Q^*}$$

But $\mathbf{p(I - A)Q^*} = 1$ from (V.12.6). Thus $\mathbf{pAQ^*}R = 1$; so that, by substituting into (V.12.8),

$$\pi = R(1 - w) \tag{V.12.9}$$

Since $R = \Pi$, this is precisely the same linear relation obtained in the previous section. But here it has been obtained for the actual system (V.12.2), (V.12.6)!

This is a truly remarkable result. The relation (V.12.9) between the wage rate and the rate of profit is found to be valid in general, and not only for the standard system, provided only that the wage rate is expressed in terms of the standard commodity.[40] In the actual system, of course, the rate of profit will no longer appear as a ratio between physical quantities, but as a ratio between values. Nevertheless (the price system being independent of the system of physical quantities), the relation between w and π will always be the same, both for the standard system and for the actual system. To put it the other way round, we can say that, although the w-π relation is the same for both systems, the particular proportions of the standard system have the property of "rendering visible," in terms of ratios between physical quantities, that which in the actual system can only be seen in terms of ratios between values.

Returning to our numerical example, if, in the actual system, we distribute to wages a sum that can purchase $\frac{3}{4}$ of the standard net product, the remaining part of the actual net product, which goes to profits, will be such that, at the corresponding prices, its ratio to the means of production will yield (just as in the corresponding standard system) a rate of profit equal to $\frac{1}{4}$ of 48%, or 12%.[41]

12.4. *No assumptions on returns to scale.* It is important that explicit emphasis be given to the absence of any assumption concerning returns to scale in the preceding sections. The two systems (V.12.1) and (V.12.2) represent observed quantities. Thus no change in those quantities has been considered. For its part, the logical construction (V.12.4), (V.12.5) is an imaginary system, the sole purpose of which is

---

[40] The fact that the wage rate is expressed in terms of the standard commodity does not mean that it will necessarily be spent on buying standard commodities (in the same way as, in our previous cases, the fact that the wage rate is expressed in terms of any commodity, for instance gold, does not mean that it is necessarily spent on buying gold). What it means is that the physical goods which the workers can buy (whatever their physical composition) have a value, at current prices, which is equal to the value of that quantity of standard commodity which makes up the wage rate.

[41] It should be noted that, the actual net product being different from the standard net product, that part of the actual net product which is left over for profits (after deducting $\frac{3}{4}$ of the standard net product for wages) will be equal neither to $\frac{1}{4}$ of the actual net product (since the already deducted $\frac{3}{4}$ refers to the standard net product) nor to $\frac{1}{4}$ of the standard net product, since the already deducted $\frac{3}{4}$ of the standard net product has been deducted from the actual net product. Yet its ratio to the means of production will be exactly 12%.

to define those proportions between the basic commodities which constitute the standard commodity, to be used as *numéraire*. Thus no assumption about returns to scale is needed to obtain the linear relation (V.12.9) between the rate of profit and the wage rate.

Strictly speaking, it is not even necessary to adopt any explicit convention concerning the measurement of prices, since no price appears explicitly. It was shown above that the *numéraire*-commodity (V.12.6) implies the linear relation (V.12.9) between the wage rate and the rate of profit. But the converse is equally true: (V.12.9) implies (V.12.6), since no other *numéraire* would satisfy such a linearity condition. Hence, if we impose the requirement that the system of prices be such as to produce the linear relation (V.12.9) between w and π, then the wage rate and prices will *ipso facto* be expressed in terms of the standard net product. The system of prices (V.12.2), (V.12.6) can therefore also be written more simply as

$$\mathbf{p} = \mathbf{p}\mathbf{A}(1 + \pi) + \mathbf{a}_n w \qquad (\text{V.12.2})$$

$$\pi = R(1 - w) \qquad (\text{V.12.9})$$

where, without explicit reference to any construction, the very simple relation (V.12.9) has replaced (V.12.6). In this way, wages and prices come to be expressed in terms of the standard net product, without it even being necessary to compute the standard system, i.e., without it even being necessary to know what the standard commodity consists of. The only quantity which needs to be calculated is the standard ratio R, i.e., through relation (V.9.5), the maximum eigenvalue of the matrix $\mathbf{A}$.

12.5. *"Labor commanded" and the standard net product*. We may note that, from (V.12.9), it immediately follows that

$$\frac{1}{w} = \frac{\Pi}{\Pi - \pi} \qquad (\text{V.12.10})$$

The total quantity of labor and the value of the standard net product being equal to unity by definition, and the wage being expressed in terms of the standard net product, the ratio $1/w$ clearly represents "the quantity of labor that can be purchased by the standard net product," i.e., Adam Smith's notion of "labor commanded." This quantity of labor varies from 1 to ∞, as π varies from 0 to Π, according to the simple relation (V.12.10). We thus obtain the remarkable result that the quantity of labor which can be purchased by the standard net product, while being a function of (i.e., while varying with) the rate of profit, is entirely *independent of prices*. This means that expressing the prices in terms of standard net product is equivalent to expressing them in terms of that quantity of labor which, at the given rate of profit, can be purchased by the standard net product.[42]

12.6. *Perfect regularity of the "layers" of wages and profit in the standard net product.* It was seen in Section 9.4 that "the quantity of labor embodied in the standard net product" can be obtained by multiplying the corresponding quantity of direct labor by the ratio $(1 + R)/R$. We can now draw attention to a more deeply rooted property. If we reduce the standard net product to quantities of "dated" labor by using the expression (V.7.4) we obtain

$$\mathbf{pY^*} = w\mathbf{a}_n[\mathbf{I} + (1 + \pi)\mathbf{A} + (1 + \pi)^2\mathbf{A}^2 + (1 + \pi)^3\mathbf{A}^3 + \cdots]\mathbf{Y^*}$$

$$(\text{V.12.11})$$

and since

$$\mathbf{AY^*} = \frac{1}{1 + R}\mathbf{Y^*}$$

we have

$$\mathbf{pY^*} = w\mathbf{a}_n\mathbf{Y^*}\left[1 + \frac{1 + \pi}{1 + R} + \left(\frac{1 + \pi}{1 + R}\right)^2 + \left(\frac{1 + \pi}{1 + R}\right)^3 + \cdots\right]$$

$$(\text{V.12.12})$$

As already noted at the end of Section 7.2, this series can be thought of as the sequence, backwards through time, of the "layers" of wages and profits of which the standard net product $\mathbf{Y^*}$, at prices $\mathbf{p}$, consists. But (V.12.12) exhibits another remarkable property. The quantities of labor which follow one another in the various "layers," namely, $\mathbf{a}_n\mathbf{Y^*}$, $\mathbf{a}_n\mathbf{Y^*}(1 + R)^{-1}$, $\mathbf{a}_n\mathbf{Y^*}(1 + R)^{-2}, \ldots$, form a perfectly regular geometric series. The quantity of labor (and hence the wage bill) needed in any "layer" is always equal to $1/(1 + R)$ times the quantity of labor (and the wage bill) which is needed in the "layer" immediately following in time. Consequently, the reckoning of a rate of profit on this regular sequence of wage bills generates a geometric progression of profits which is also perfectly regular through time. It follows that the sum of profits and wages in any "layer" is always equal to $(1 + \pi)/(1 + R)$ times the sum of profits and wages in the "layer" immediately following in time. Thus each "layer" is structurally the same as every other "layer": it differs from the other "layers" only by

---

[42] Sraffa points out that "... it is surprising that the standard commodity which has been evolved ... here should be found to be equivalent to something very close to the standard suggested by Adam Smith, namely 'labor commanded,' to which Ricardo himself was so decidedly opposed." (Sraffa [1, p. 94].)

a scale factor, while having the same proportions. In other words, the proportions between labor and the means of production are always the same, in all the infinitely many "layers" backwards through time.[43]

This is, in fact, the essential property of the standard commodity: that of reproducing exactly the same proportions between labor and the means of production in each of the infinitely many layers backwards through time of which it consists.

12.7. *The standard commodity and the theory of income distribution.* We may now draw some conclusions concerning the theoretical significance of the linear relation (V.12.9), associated with the use of the standard commodity as *numéraire* for the price system.

It was seen above (Section 6.3) that, in general, the relation between w and π is highly complex. This results from the fact that one can never exclude all the prices from that relation; at least one price, that of the commodity in terms of which the wage rate is measured, is always implicitly present. It is precisely the peculiarities of the methods of production of the commodity used as *numéraire* which cause a whole series of complications. We have seen the source of these complications in Section 7.2 above. The peculiarities of the methods of production of any commodity translate themselves into the different proportions between labor and means of production in each of the infinitely many "layers" of wages and profits of which the commodity consists. As wages and profits vary, they give rise to irregular movements in each of these "layers" and, *a fortiori*, in their sum. Thus, in expression (V.6.8) and in the corresponding Fig. V.3, changes in the distribution of income between profits and wages cannot be seen clearly because they are, so to speak, "disturbed" by the many complex effects of the variations in the components of the price of the *numéraire*-commodity. And since these effects or "disturbances" differ from one commodity to another, the relation between w and π will differ, even within the same economic system, according to which particular commodity is used as the unit of measurement for wages.

However, a very special commodity, the standard commodity, has now been discovered, which enables us to formulate the distribution relations independently of prices. A commodity has been found which

---

[43] Compare expression (V.12.12) with expression (V.7.5) in footnote 23 on p. 92. It will be seen that the succession through time is identical. The standard commodity therefore reproduces, *ex constructo*, in all its infinite number of "layers," that constancy of proportions between capital and labor which, in the very special case of uniform capital intensity, is assumed *ex hypothesi*. (The nature of this contrast seems to have escaped many of Sraffa's critics. For example, cf. Burmeister [4]).

has a price whose infinitely many "layers" of wages and profits (which for an arbitrary commodity are superimposed in the most disparate way, depending on the technical characteristics of its methods of production) here always follow one another in a perfectly regular way, at any level of the rate of profit, according to a geometrical progression which always reproduces, to infinity, the same proportions between labor and means of production. The use of such a commodity as the unit of measurement for prices thus has the remarkable analytical property of eliminating any "disturbance" due to the peculiarities of the methods of production of the *numéraire*-commodity from the relation between the wage rate and the rate of profit. With the linear relation (V.12.9) we are at last able "to see," as it were, the alternative possible distributions of the net national income between wages and profits in ideal conditions, free from any interference due to price changes specific to the commodity used as the unit of measurement.

After a century and a half, Sraffa's standard commodity has thus fulfilled Ricardo's dream of an "invariable measure" of value.[44] It would, of course, be merely fanciful to think that such a commodity might be found in the real world (and it is scarcely surprising that Ricardo never found it); yet it can always be constructed from the commodities actually produced, by taking them in the proportions defined by the standard system.

The most remarkable theoretical implication of this construction is to be found in the demonstration that it is possible to treat the distribution of income independently of prices and in the demonstration, moreover, that this possibility is not tied to the pure labor theory of value.[45] It is at last possible to state rigorously that the shortcomings and inadequacies of the Classical pure labor theory of value or, indeed, even the abandonment of such a theory, leave quite unscathed the possibility of treating the distribution of income independently of prices.

---

[44] This, at least, with reference to the property of being "invariable" with respect to changes in income distribution.

[45] Ricardo's insistence on an "approximate" validity of the pure labor theory of value had ended up by hampering awareness of this result. In the economic literature the rejection of Ricardo's pure labor theory of value has generally been associated also with the rejection of his (quite legitimate) claim that his theory of income distribution is independent of his theory of value.

References

[1] Sraffa, Piero, *Production of Commodities by means of Commodities – Prelude to a Critique of Economic Theory*, Cambridge: Cambridge University Press, 1960.

[2] Sraffa, Piero, and Newman, Peter, exchange of letters, published as an appendix to [3].

[3] Bharadwaj, Krishna, "On the Maximum Number of Switches between Two Production Systems," *Schweizerische Zeitschrift für Volkswirtschaft und Statistik*, 1970, pp. 425–429.

[4] Burmeister, Edwin, "On a Theorem of Sraffa," *Economica*, 1968, pp. 83–87.

[5] Dmitriev, V. K., *Economic Essays on Value Competition and Utility*, ed. by D. M. Nuti, Cambridge: Cambridge University Press, 1974 (originally published in Russian in 1904).

[6] Newman, Peter, "Production of Commodities by Means of Commodities," *Schweizerische Zeitschrift für Volkswirtschaft und Statistik*, 1962, pp. 58–75.

[7] Torrens, Robert, *An Essay on the Production of Wealth*, with an introductory essay by Joseph Dorfman, New York: A. M. Kelly, 1965 (originally published in 1821).

APPENDIX TO CHAPTER FIVE

Marx's Problem of the "Transformation of Values into Prices of Production"

1. *Introductory remark.* The type of analysis carried out thus far also allows us to present a general version of the much discussed problem of the "transformation of values into prices of production," which Marx sets out in Volume III of *Das Kapital.*[1]

2. *An "ideal" price system.* Imagine an economic system of the kind considered in Chapter V with single-product industries. The technique of the system is represented by a matrix of interindustry coefficients $\mathbf{A}$, assumed to be viable (i.e., to have a maximum eigenvalue $\lambda_m < 1$), and by a row vector of (direct) labor coefficients $\mathbf{a}_n$.

An "ideal" system of prices, as understood, for example, by the "Ricardian socialists"[2] (who had claimed at the beginning of the 19th century that the whole net product of an economic system ought to go to the workers), might be

$$\mathbf{p}\mathbf{A} + w\mathbf{a}_n = \mathbf{p} \qquad (V.A.1)$$

This is a linear system of $(n - 1)$ equations. It determines $(n - 2)$ relative prices and a wage rate which absorbs the entire net product per worker of the economic system. This was regarded as the "maximum" wage rate in Chapter V, since it corresponds to a profit rate of zero. We may call it the "ideal" wage rate here, or, from a different point of view, the "complete" wage rate and denote it by w^*.

As we know, the system of prices (V.A.1) can be expressed in absolute, rather than in relative, terms by adding an equation defining the *numéraire.* To this end we may adopt our usual procedure of setting the price of an arbitrary commodity, for example the ith commodity, equal to unity, or of setting the wage rate equal to unity.

---

[1] Marx [1, chapter IX]; see pp. 20–22 above. Mathematical formulations of Marx's system have become frequent recently. See, for example, Bródy [2], Morishima [8].

[2] See, for example, Lowenthal [5].

In the first case we have

$$\mathbf{p} = \mathbf{a}_n (\mathbf{I} - \mathbf{A})^{-1} w^* \qquad \text{(V.A.2)}$$

$$p_i = 1 \qquad \text{(V.A.3)}$$

where the exchange ratios prove to be proportional to the quantities $\mathbf{a}_n(\mathbf{I} - \mathbf{A})^{-1}$, which represent the vertically integrated labor coefficients, or quantities of labor "embodied" in the corresponding commodities.[3] In the second case, explicitly denoting the solution vector by $\mathbf{v}$, we have

$$w^* = 1 \qquad \text{(V.A.4)}$$

$$\mathbf{v} = \mathbf{a}_n (\mathbf{I} - \mathbf{A})^{-1} \qquad \text{(V.A.5)}$$

The exchange ratios become exactly *equal* to the physical quantities of embodied labor. It is precisely these quantities of embodied labor that Marx calls "values."

It should be noted that system (V.A.4), (V.A.5) has the property of making "labor embodied" coincide with "labour commanded." Each commodity i, evaluated at the corresponding v_i, $i = 1, 2, \ldots, n - 1$, can purchase in the economic system a quantity of labor ("labor commanded") exactly equal to the labor embodied in it.

3. *The "value system."* Marx carries out his analysis in terms of "values," defined here by (V.A.5), but focuses his attention on what is for him a fundamental distortion that occurs in a capitalist society. The owners of the means of production (the "capitalists") find themselves in a privileged position, which allows them not to pay the "complete" wage rate w^*.

Suppose that we can define in physical terms, i.e., as a bundle of heterogeneous commodities, a set of h quantities $d_1, d_2, \ldots, d_h$, which together constitute the subsistence real wage, which we shall denote by the column vector

$$\mathbf{d} = \begin{bmatrix} d_1 \\ d_2 \\ \vdots \\ d_h \\ 0 \\ \vdots \\ 0 \end{bmatrix} \qquad \text{(V.A.6)}$$

[3] See pp. 76.

(It will be assumed that the matrix $\mathbf{A}$ is so ordered that its first h rows and h columns refer to the h subsistence commodities and industries.) Of course, $h < n - 1$.[4] Marx argues that

$$\mathbf{vd} = \delta w^* \qquad \text{where } \delta < 1 \tag{V.A.7}$$

That is, the capitalists pay the workers only the subsistence wage $\mathbf{vd}$, which represents a fraction $\delta < 1$ of the "complete" wage w^*. What remains, i.e., the fraction $(1 - \delta)$ of w^*, represents the "unpaid wage" or "surplus value," which is appropriated by the capitalists.

Using the solutions (V.A.4) and (V.A.5), in which $w^* = 1$, and substituting (V.A.7) therein, we can rewrite (V.A.1) as

$$\mathbf{vA} + \frac{1}{\delta}\mathbf{vda}_n = \mathbf{v} \tag{V.A.8}$$

or

$$\mathbf{vA} + \mathbf{vda}_n + \frac{1 - \delta}{\delta}\mathbf{vda}_n = \mathbf{v} \tag{V.A.9}$$

It may now be noted that the ratio $(1 - \delta)/\delta$, which we shall call σ, so that

$$\sigma = \frac{1 - \delta}{\delta} = \frac{1}{\delta} - 1 \tag{V.A.10}$$

represents what Marx calls the "rate of surplus value," i.e., the unpaid part of w^* expressed as a percentage fraction of the part which is paid. Or, as it is also said (all the quantities involved being expressed in terms of physical quantities of embodied labor), σ represents the ratio of "surplus labor" to "necessary labor." Or again, $(1 - \delta)$ also represents the fraction of the working day (or of the "working year" if a "year" is the unit of time) in which the worker works for the capitalist, and δ represents the fraction in which he works for himself. This was Marx's reason for calling their ratio σ not only the "rate of surplus value" but also the "rate of exploitation."

It may also be noted that, since the subsistence wage (V.A.7) is assumed to be the same for all workers, the rate of surplus value (or of exploitation) σ proves to be the same in all industries. In fact, (V.A.9) can be rewritten

$$\mathbf{vA} - \mathbf{vda}_n + \sigma\mathbf{vda}_n = \mathbf{v} \tag{V.A.11}$$

or

$$\mathbf{vA} + \mathbf{vda}_n(1 + \sigma) = \mathbf{v} \tag{V.A.12}$$

---

[4] Notice that, as a consequence of the hypothesis that all commodities require labor, directly or indirectly, to be produced, wage goods are necessarily basic commodities.

where σ is indeed the same in all industries. The solutions for $\mathbf{v}$ and σ (and δ) are, of course, still those obtained from (V.A.4), (V.A.5), together with (V.A.7), (V.A.10).

The same solutions for $\mathbf{v}$ and σ can, however, be obtained in an alternative way directly from (V.A.12), if one adds the equation

$$\mathbf{vd}(1 + \sigma) = w^* = 1 \qquad \text{(V.A.13)}$$

which defines a unit of embodied labor to be the *numéraire* for the "values." The method of solution is by now familiar to us. Expression (V.A.12) is a system of linear and homogeneous equations in the "values." A necessary condition for the existence of nonzero solutions is that

$$\det[\mathbf{I} - \mathbf{A} - (1 + \sigma)\mathbf{da}_n] = 0 \qquad \text{(V.A.14)}$$

Solving this equation, we obtain the value of σ, which, when substituted into (V.A.12), (V.A.13), enables us to determine the $n - 1$ elements of $\mathbf{v}$ (from $n - 1$ independent equations).[5]

As emerges clearly from (V.A.11), the "value" of each commodity may be regarded as the sum of three components: (i) replacement of the means of production, or "constant capital" (each element of the vector $\mathbf{vA}$); (ii) replacement of the capital advanced by the capitalists as wages, or "variable capital" (each element of the vector $\mathbf{vda}_n$); and (iii) "surplus value" (each element of the vector $\sigma\mathbf{vda}_n$). In the same way, if $\bar{\mathbf{Q}}$ is the (column) vector of the physical quantities of all commodities produced in a given economic system, the total gross product $\mathbf{v}\bar{\mathbf{Q}}$ may be expressed as the sum of three components:

$$\mathbf{vA}\bar{\mathbf{Q}} + \mathbf{vda}_n\bar{\mathbf{Q}} + \sigma\mathbf{vda}_n\bar{\mathbf{Q}} = \mathbf{v}\bar{\mathbf{Q}} \qquad \text{(V.A.15)}$$

---

[5] It may be interesting to note that, from an analytical point of view, (V.A.14) is much simpler than the corresponding equation in the price system, i.e., (V.A.22), which will be obtained in the following section. For matrix $\mathbf{da}_n$ is the product of two vectors and therefore has rank 1, i.e., cannot contain more than one linearly independent vector (see *Mathematical Appendix*, Theorem (i), p. 251). This means that σ will have at most one nonzero solution, by contrast with π in (V.A.22), which may have up to $(n - 1)$ nonzero solutions.

Alternatively, (V.A.14) may be written

$$\det[\mathbf{I} - (1 + \sigma)\mathbf{da}_n(\mathbf{I} - \mathbf{A})^{-1}] = 0 \qquad \text{(V.A.14a)}$$

which is an expression formally of the same type as (V.A.22) of the following section, but precisely with the simplification that σ emerges as having at most one nonzero solution, owing to $\mathbf{da}_n$, and therefore also $\mathbf{da}_n(\mathbf{I} - \mathbf{A})^{-1}$, both being matrices of rank 1 (see *Mathematical Appendix*, p. 258). It may also be interesting to point out that the elements of matrix $\mathbf{da}_n(\mathbf{I} - \mathbf{A})^{-1}$ have a precise economic meaning, i.e., that of vertically integrated subsistence consumption coefficients, as may be realized from an analysis of the type developed in Pasinetti [9].

which represent the constant capital, the variable capital, and the total surplus value, respectively, for the whole economy. All the physical quantities, being multiplied by **v**, come to be expressed in terms of "values" or quantities of embodied labor.[6]

It follows that the rate of surplus value can also be derived as the ratio between the two aggregates which are shown as the second and third terms, respectively, in the sum on the left side of (V.A.15). On the other hand, contrary to what was thought by Marx,[7] it does not follow that the rate of profit for the system as a whole should be obtained as the ratio between the third term (total surplus value) and the sum of the first two terms (total capital) of (V.A.15). To obtain the rate of profit, one must turn to a completely different system of equations.

4. *The "price-of-production system."* The system of equations of the previous section, which may be called "the value system," cannot, however, be observed in practice because, in a capitalist economy, that part of the net product which is not paid in wages is distributed in the form of profits. And profits are distributed in proportion to total capital, not in proportion to total wages (as, by definition, surplus value would be).

This implies that the exchange ratios, or "prices of production," which can be observed in a capitalist system will differ from the "values." Now, if we assume that wages are advanced by the capitalists at the beginning of the production period, and hence that the wages fund is itself part of capital, the "prices of production" will be given by the system of equations

$$(\mathbf{pA} + w\mathbf{a}_n)(1 + \pi) = \mathbf{p} \tag{V.A.16}$$

Moreover, if we assume, as in the previous section, that the wage rate can be specified in physical terms as **d**, defined by (V.A.6), and thus that

$$w = \mathbf{pd} \tag{V.A.17}$$

we obtain, after substitution in (V.A.16)

$$(\mathbf{pA} + \mathbf{pda}_n)(1 + \pi) = \mathbf{p} \tag{V.A.18}$$

That is,

$$\mathbf{p}[\mathbf{I} - (1 + \pi)(\mathbf{A} + \mathbf{da}_n)] = \mathbf{0} \tag{V.A.19}$$

---

[6] Note that expressions (V.A.11) for the single industries and (V.A.15) for the whole economy are a generalization of Marx's own expressions considered in Section 4.1 of Chapter I.

[7] See for example Marx [1, p. 42]. See also pp. 21–22 above.

The matrix $(\mathbf{A} + \mathbf{da}_n)$, which may be called $\mathbf{A}^{(+)}$, that is,

$$\mathbf{A}^{(+)} = \mathbf{A} + \mathbf{da}_n \qquad\qquad\qquad\qquad (V.A.20)$$

is a matrix of interindustry coefficients which is, so to speak, "augmented" by the consumption coefficients needed for the maintenance of the workers. We have already referred to this matrix several times[8] but without ever having had to distinguish it explicitly from the matrix $\mathbf{A}$ (our analysis being exactly the same, in formal terms, whether the interindustry coefficients matrix was interpreted as including the subsistence consumption coefficients or as excluding them). But the distinction has now become necessary.

Using (V.A.20), we can rewrite (V.A.19) as

$$\mathbf{p}[\mathbf{I} - (1 + \pi)\mathbf{A}^{(+)}] = \mathbf{0} \qquad\qquad\qquad\qquad (V.A.21)$$

We thus obtain a system of linear and homogeneous equations of a kind which we have already considered several times. We know that a necessary condition for the system to have economically meaningful solutions is that

$$\det[\mathbf{I} - (1 + \pi)\mathbf{A}^{(+)}] = 0 \qquad\qquad\qquad\qquad (V.A.22)$$

Furthermore, we know that the rate of profit satisfying the characteristic equation (V.A.22), to be denoted by $\Pi^{(A+)}$, is non-negative if the maximum eigenvalue of $\mathbf{A}^{(+)}$ is less than or equal to unity, which we shall of course assume. In symbols, we assume that

$$\lambda_m^{(A+)} \leq 1 \qquad \text{which implies} \qquad \Pi^{(A+)} \geq 0 \qquad\qquad (V.A.23)$$

where $\Pi^{(A+)}$ is derived from (V.5.11), in correspondence to $\lambda_m^{(A+)}$. After substituting this rate of profit into (V.A.21) and adding whatever further equation we choose in order to define a *numéraire* for the price system, we can determine all the "prices of production" in terms of the chosen *numéraire*.

5. *A comparison.* It is not difficult now to understand why the "value system" (V.A.12) differs from the "price-of-production system" (V.A.19). The fundamental diversity lies in the different ways in which that part of the net product which is not paid as wages is distributed among the various industries. In the "value system" it is distributed (as "surplus value") in proportion to the wages advanced to the workers (or "variable capital"); in the "price-of-production system" it is distributed (as profits) in proportion to the sum of "variable capital" and "constant capital." The rate of profit will therefore be *less than* (or, in the limiting case in which there is no constant capital, equal to) the rate

[8] See pp. 74 and 76n.

of surplus value, simply because the same physical quantities, of which both surplus value and profits are made up, must in the case of profits, be spread over a larger amount of capital (total capital, and not merely variable capital).

Rigorous confirmation of this intuitive[9] argument can be found in the fact that the rate of surplus value and the rate of profit are the solutions of the characteristic equations (V.A.14) and (V.A.22), respectively. Straightforward comparison of these two equations provides immediate confirmation of Marx's three propositions already mentioned in Section 4.2 of Chapter I, namely, that: (i) $\pi > 0$ if and only if $\sigma > 0$[10]; (ii) $\pi < \sigma$, except in the limiting case of $\mathbf{A} = \mathbf{O}$, when π and σ become equal; (iii) π is a monotonically increasing function of σ and *vice versa*.[11]

It may be of interest to note that, from the standpoint of the formulations of Chapter V, Section 5.1, the "value system" and the "price-of-production system" correspond to the two extreme (opposite) cases considered there for the exogenous determination of the

---

[9] The argument is "intuitive" because of the analytical complication that, although the physical quantities which constitute both total surplus value and total profits are the same, their evaluation is different according as it is made at the "values" or at the "prices of production."

[10] Morishima [8] calls this proposition "the fundamental Marxian theorem."

[11] Equations (V.A.14) and (V.A.22) may also be written

$$\det\left[\frac{1}{1+\sigma}\mathbf{I} - \left(\frac{1}{1+\sigma}\mathbf{A} + \mathbf{da}_n\right)\right] = 0 \qquad\qquad (\text{V.A.14b})$$

$$\det\left[\frac{1}{1+\pi}\mathbf{I} - (\mathbf{A} + \mathbf{da}_n)\right] = 0 \qquad\qquad (\text{V.A.22a})$$

As is easily seen, these two equations coincide only in the two particular cases in which $\mathbf{A} = \mathbf{O}$ (no constant capital) and in which $\mathbf{A}$ and $\mathbf{d}$ are such as to yield the solution $\sigma = 0$, which also implies $\pi = 0$. In all other cases (where both $\sigma > 0$ and $\pi > 0$), it must be the case that $\pi < \sigma$. For

$$\frac{1}{1+\sigma}\mathbf{A} < \mathbf{A}$$

and therefore

$$\frac{1}{1+\sigma} < \frac{1}{1+\pi}$$

or $\sigma > \pi$, owing to the Perron-Frobenius theorems (see *Mathematical Appendix*, Theorems 3 and 3a, p. 272 and p. 275. Since both σ and π are decreasing monotonic functions of each single element of the corresponding inverse matrix, and since $\sigma > \pi$ at any of their positive values, the rate of profit proves to be an increasing monotonic function of the rate of surplus value, and conversely.

distributive variable, but with respect to two different coefficients matrices. "Values" are derived by setting the rate of profit equal to zero in a system involving the matrix $\mathbf{A}$, while "prices of production" are derived by setting the (surplus) wage rate equal to zero in a system involving the matrix $\mathbf{A}^{(+)}$. These are two completely different systems of equations.[12] It is hardly surprising, then, that they should have different solutions. Hence, in general, $\mathbf{v} \neq \mathbf{p}$.

It follows, for example, that for any total output, given in physical terms by the (column) vector $\bar{\mathbf{Q}}$, the valuation of this output will differ accordingly as it is done in terms of "values" or in terms of "prices of production"; thus, in general,

$$\mathbf{v}\bar{\mathbf{Q}} \neq \mathbf{p}\bar{\mathbf{Q}} \tag{V.A.24}$$

[12] One can thus understand why Samuelson may have got impatient to the point of making the sarcastic remark: ".... the 'transformation algorithm' is precisely of the following form: 'contemplate two alternative and discordant systems. Write down one. Now transform by taking an eraser and rubbing it out. Then fill in the other one. *Voila!* You have completed your transformation algorithm.' " (Samuelson [10, p. 400].)

But one must beware of superficial impressions. Although matrices $\mathbf{A}$ and $\mathbf{A}^{(+)}$ are different from each other, they do not differ in an arbitrary way. All their differences reduce to the specific matrix $\mathbf{da}_n$ which has the important property of distributing subsistence goods over the columns of $\mathbf{A}^{(+)}$ in proportion to the labor coefficients. Hence it would be a mistake to think – from a superficial look at (V.A.21) – that proportionality of profits to capital is the sole criterion adopted there for the distribution of the net output. This is not so, because that part of the net output which refers to subsistence goods has already been distributed, within matrix $\mathbf{A}^{(+)}$, in proportion to the labor coefficients. Actually one can see that, as $\mathbf{d}$ is increasing, the "prices of production" (V.A.21) tend to the "values," until eventually they coincide with them at the extreme point at which $\mathbf{d}$ has absorbed all the net product and nothing is left over for profits. Let us consider this extreme case. If, *ex hypothesi*, the maximum eigenvalue of $\mathbf{A}^{(+)}$ is 1, which means $\Pi^{(A+)} = 0$, then (V.A.19) becomes

$$\mathbf{p}(\mathbf{I} - \mathbf{A} - \mathbf{da}_n) = 0$$

And, if the wage rate is set equal to 1, i.e.,

$$\mathbf{pd} = 1$$

we obtain after substitution

$$\mathbf{p} = \mathbf{pA} + \mathbf{a}_n$$

and thus

$$\mathbf{p} = \mathbf{a}_n(\mathbf{I} - \mathbf{A})^{-1} = \mathbf{v}$$

This is precisely expression (V.A.5) defining the "values." In other words, when $\Pi^{(A+)} = 0$, the "prices of production" (V.A.19) coincide with the "values" (V.A.5), simply because profits are zero and all the net product (relative to matrix $\mathbf{A}$) has already been distributed within the columns of matrix $\mathbf{A}^{(+)}$ in proportion to the quantities of labor.

Moreover, the ratio of total surplus value to total capital, expressed in "values," will differ from the rate of profit for the system as a whole; thus, in general,

$$\frac{\sigma \mathbf{v da}_n \bar{\mathbf{Q}}}{\mathbf{v}(\mathbf{A} + \mathbf{da}_n)\bar{\mathbf{Q}}} \neq \frac{\Pi^{(A+)}\mathbf{p}(\mathbf{A} + \mathbf{da}_n)\bar{\mathbf{Q}}}{\mathbf{p}(\mathbf{A} + \mathbf{da}_n)\bar{\mathbf{Q}}} \tag{V.A.25}$$

Finally, total surplus value will be different from total profits; thus, in general,

$$\sigma \mathbf{v da}_n \bar{\mathbf{Q}} \neq \Pi^{(A+)}\mathbf{p}(\mathbf{A} + \mathbf{da}_n)\bar{\mathbf{Q}} \tag{V.A.26}$$

As is well known, Marx thought (incorrectly) that all three of these expressions would be equalities.[13] That cannot be so, except in very special cases.[14]

6. *The "standard system" as a special case.* Before proceeding further, it may be of interest to open a digression and consider the special case of a hypothetical economic system which happens to realize the proportions of Sraffa's standard system. We must, however, distinguish between a standard system defined with respect to the matrix $\mathbf{A}$, and a standard system defined with respect to the matrix $\mathbf{A}^{(+)}$, since these two matrices are here explicitly distinguished from each other.

Consider first the standard system defined with reference to matrix $\mathbf{A}$. As we know, a standard system of this kind is defined by the vector of quantities $\mathbf{Q}^*$ which is the solution to the system of equations

$$[\mathbf{I} - (1 + R)\mathbf{A}]\mathbf{Q}^* = \mathbf{0} \tag{V.12.4}$$

$$\mathbf{a}_n \mathbf{Q}^* = 1 \tag{V.12.5}$$

where

$$\det[\mathbf{I} - (1 + R)\mathbf{A}] = 0$$

Taking the standard net product as the *numéraire*, the "prices of production" for such an economic system will be given by

$$\mathbf{p}[\mathbf{I} - (1 + \Pi^{(A+)})(\mathbf{A} + \mathbf{d}^*\mathbf{a}_n)] = \mathbf{0} \tag{V.A.27}$$

$$\mathbf{p}(\mathbf{I} - \mathbf{A})\mathbf{Q}^* = 1 \tag{V.A.28}$$

where we explicitly assume that $\mathbf{d}^*$, the actual wage rate in physical terms, has the same composition as the standard commodity. The

---

[13] See, for example, Marx [1, pp. 42, 157, 164].

[14] At most, one could take advantage of the degree of freedom in the price system and choose such a *numéraire* as to reduce one inequality to an equality (see also Section 7 below). The other two, however, would inevitably remain inequalities.

corresponding system of "values" will of course be different:

$$\mathbf{vA} + \mathbf{vd}^*\mathbf{a}_n(1 + \sigma) = \mathbf{v} \qquad\qquad \text{(V.A.29)}$$

It will be noted that, the total quantity of labor having been set equal to unity, (V.12.5) can be rewritten as:

$$\mathbf{a}_n(\mathbf{I} - \mathbf{A})^{-1}(\mathbf{I} - \mathbf{A})\mathbf{Q}^* = 1 \qquad\qquad \text{(V.A.30)}$$

which, from (V.A.5), becomes

$$\mathbf{v}(\mathbf{I} - \mathbf{A})\mathbf{Q}^* = 1 \qquad\qquad \text{(V.A.31)}$$

That is, the quantity of labor embodied in the net product of the system is equal to unity. Thus, owing to the normalization adopted, the net product comes to be equal to unity whether it is evaluated at prices of production – equation (V.A.28) – or at "values" – equation (V.A.31).

It also follows that thinking of fractions of the *standard* net product in terms of prices always comes to be the same thing as thinking of them in terms of "values" (i.e., of quantities of embodied labor). Hence, if wages are actually paid in standard commodity, i.e., in fractions of the standard net product, as we have assumed, the wage rate w, which in the normalized standard system also represents the fraction of the net product which goes to wages, comes to represent also the fraction of the total labor which is embodied in wages (or the fraction of the working "year" in which the worker works for himself), which we previously called δ (Section 3). This implies that w can be replaced by δ in the remarkable relation (V.12.9) derived by Sraffa for the standard system.

However, the system of prices of production (V.A.27) is slightly different from Sraffa's price system, since profits are also reckoned on wages. (That is, Marx assumes that wages are advanced to the workers at the beginning of the production period, while Sraffa assumes them to be paid at the end.) We must therefore derive the relation between π and w, which is analogous to Sraffa's relation (V.12.9), for the case in which wages are paid at the beginning of the year. By going through the steps of our earlier argument, (V.12.2)–(V.12.9), with the sole difference that the vector of wages $\mathbf{a}_n w$ is now multiplied by $(1 + \pi)$, we arrive at the new relation

$$\pi = \frac{R}{1 + Rw}(1 - w) \qquad\qquad \text{(V.A.32)}$$

in place of Sraffa's (V.12.9). As will be seen, we still obtain a relation between π and w which is very simple, is independent of prices, and has intercepts: $\pi = R$ and $w = 1$. However, (V.A.32) is no longer a linear function but rather a hyperbolic one, with asymptotes $w = -1/R$ and $\pi = -1$. (See Fig. V.A.1.)

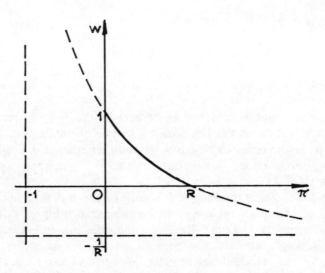

FIG. V.A.1. Standard system relation between w and π when wages are advanced

Thus, returning to the preceding argument, it may be concluded that in a standard system in which wages actually consisted of standard commodity, (V.A.32) could be rewritten

$$\pi = \frac{R}{1 + R\delta}(1 - \delta) \tag{V.A.33}$$

from which, using (V.A.10), one can also derive the relation between the rate of profit and the rate of surplus value:

$$\pi = R \frac{\sigma}{1 + \sigma + R} \tag{V.A.34}$$

$$\sigma = \pi \frac{1 + R}{R - \pi} \tag{V.A.35}$$

These two expressions, incidentally, provide a confirmation of the three propositions concerning the relations between π and σ[15] stated in the previous section.

It is now interesting to check what happens to the three inequalities (V.A.24), (V.A.25), (V.A.26). First of all, total gross output, given by the vector $\mathbf{Q}^*$, is a scalar multiple of the standard net product, i.e., of the vector $(\mathbf{I} - \mathbf{A})\mathbf{Q}^*$. And, since $\mathbf{p}(\mathbf{I} - \mathbf{A})\mathbf{Q}^* = \mathbf{v}(\mathbf{I} - \mathbf{A})\mathbf{Q}^*$, it must also be true that $\mathbf{p}\mathbf{Q}^* = \mathbf{v}\mathbf{Q}^*$. Secondly, with wages being paid in standard commodity, all that remains after the payment of wages – surplus value, if evaluated at "values"; or profits, if evaluated at prices – will also consist of standard commodity and will therefore be a scalar multiple of the net product. This means that total surplus value will be equal to total profits. Finally, the rate of profit, by being a ratio between two scalar multiples of the same standard net product, will remain the same, whether evaluated at "values" or at prices. In other words, all three inequalities (V.A.24), (V.A.25), (V.A.26) become equalities in the present case.

But let us now consider the standard system defined with respect to the matrix $\mathbf{A}^{(+)} = \mathbf{A} + \mathbf{d}\mathbf{a}_n$. Its solution will here be denoted by $\mathbf{Q}^{**}$. In formal terms this new standard system is represented by the same

---

[15] In the case of wages being paid at the end of the production period (as in Sraffa's model) the three relations (V.A.33), (V.A.34), (V.A.35) would become much simpler; i.e., in the same order,

$$\pi = R(1 - \delta) \tag{V.A.36}$$

$$\pi = R\frac{\sigma}{\sigma + 1} \tag{V.A.37}$$

$$\sigma = \frac{\pi}{R - \pi} \tag{V.A.38}$$

From the standpoint of Marxian analysis, these expressions have the drawback of not making the rate of profit necessarily smaller than the rate of surplus value, the reason being that in Sraffa's prices the rate of profit is proportional to "constant capital" only, and not to the sum of "constant" plus "variable" capital, as in Marx's "prices of production."

John Eatwell [4] who proposed expressions (V.A.36), (V.A.37), (V.A.38), also claimed that these expressions are valid in general, and not only with reference to the "standard system," with the one proviso that the wage rate be expressed in terms of the standard commodity (in the same way as Sraffa's (V.12.9) is valid in general, if the wage rate is expressed in standard commodity). This claim, however, seems to me rather weak. For in Marx's analysis the wage rate is not something that can indifferently be expressed in terms of any *numéraire*. It is a well-defined set of commodities, and therefore of embodied labor. And this embodied labor would obey relations (V.A.33) – (V.A.38) only if the wage rate were actually paid in standard commodity.

equations as considered above – (V.12.4), (V.12.5) – except that the matrix $\mathbf{A}$ must be replaced by the matrix $\mathbf{A}^{(+)}$. However, we have to distinguish two cases: (i) the case in which the real wage $\mathbf{d}$ is of the same composition as the standard commodity, so that $\mathbf{d} = \mathbf{d}^*$, and (ii) the case in which the real wage $\mathbf{d}$ has a composition different from that of the standard commodity. In case (i) it will be clear that $\mathbf{Q}^* = \mathbf{Q}^{**}$, and hence that one returns to the standard commodity defined with respect to the matrix $\mathbf{A}$ (i.e., the two standard systems come to coincide). In case (ii), by contrast, $\mathbf{Q}^* \neq \mathbf{Q}^{**}$. The standard system defined with respect to the matrix $\mathbf{A}$ differs from that defined with respect to the matrix $\mathbf{A}^{(+)}$. With this new standard system it is no longer possible to use the normalization of the price system suggested by Sraffa. For (V.12.5), which now becomes $\mathbf{a}_n \mathbf{Q}^{**} = 1$, always implies that the net product of the system, wages plus profits, is equal to unity when evaluated at "values." But the expression $\mathbf{p}(\mathbf{I} - \mathbf{A}^{(+)})\mathbf{Q}^{**}$ no longer represents the net product of the system but rather a "net product" which does not include wages; i.e., it represents only profits. (This is the Classical notion of "net product.") If one wishes to maintain direct comparability between "values" and "prices of production," this "net product," evaluated at "prices of production," must be set equal to the quantity of labor embodied in it; hence the price system must be closed, not by equation $\mathbf{p}(\mathbf{I} - \mathbf{A}^{(+)})\mathbf{Q}^{**} = 1$, but rather by the equation

$$\mathbf{p}(\mathbf{I} - \mathbf{A}^{(+)})\mathbf{Q}^{**} = \mathbf{v}(\mathbf{I} - \mathbf{A}^{(+)})\mathbf{Q}^{**} \qquad (\text{V.A.39})$$

in which both sides will, of course, be *less than* unity. (It also follows that the sum of wages and profits, which has a "value" equal to unity, will no longer necessarily be equal to unity if evaluated at "prices of production.")

Nevertheless, even with this normalization, the three inequalities (V.A.24), (V.A.25), (V.A.26) become equalities in this new standard system. Total surplus value and total profits are equal to each other owing to (V.A.39). Moreover, $\mathbf{pQ}^{**} = \mathbf{vQ}^{**}$, because each side of this equality is the same scalar multiple of the corresponding term in (V.A.39). Finally, as in all standard systems, the rate of profit is a physical notion and is therefore independent of both "values" and prices.

7. *The "transformation of values into prices of production."* But let us return to the general case in order to face explicitly the "problem of the transformation of values into prices of production." By defining $\hat{\mathbf{v}}$ to be the diagonal matrix, of order $(n - 1)$, which has the $(n - 1)$ "values" as its principal diagonal elements, we can post-multiply the

"value system" (V.A.12) throughout by $\hat{\mathbf{v}}^{-1}$ and rewrite it as

$$\mathbf{1}(\hat{\mathbf{v}}\mathbf{A}\hat{\mathbf{v}}^{-1}) + \mathbf{1}(\hat{\mathbf{v}}\mathbf{da}_n\hat{\mathbf{v}}^{-1})(1 + \sigma) = \mathbf{1} \qquad \text{(V.A.40)}$$

where $\mathbf{1}$ is a row vector with every element equal to unity. This system is, of course, closed by the same equation as before, namely

$$\mathbf{vd}(1 + \sigma) = w^* = 1 \qquad \text{(V.A.13)}$$

which sets a unit of embodied labor to be the unit of measurement for "values".

Written in this way, system (V.A.40) is a "value system" which has, so to speak, been transformed with respect to the physical quantities. The physical quantities of commodities are no longer expressed in their conventional units of measurement (tons, meters, liters, etc.) but have instead been reexpressed in terms of physical quantities of embodied labor. As will be realized, the term $\hat{\mathbf{v}}\mathbf{A}$ reexpresses all the interindustry coefficients in terms of embodied labor, while the post-multiplication by $\hat{\mathbf{v}}^{-1}$ (i.e., the division of each column of the matrix by the quantity of labor embodied in each unit of the corresponding commodity produced) means that each interindustry coefficient is now referred to the corresponding commodity output measured in units of embodied labor. In the same way, $\hat{\mathbf{v}}\mathbf{d}$ reexpresses the physical wage rate in terms of quantities of embodied labor, while the vector $\mathbf{a}_n\hat{\mathbf{v}}^{-1}$ reexpresses the direct labor coefficients, so that each of them refers to an output embodying one unit of labor. And since the "value" of each physical unit of embodied labor is clearly unity, by definition, the new transformed vector of "values" is simply the vector $\mathbf{1}$ (a vector with every component equal to unity). From another point of view we could say that we have redefined all the physical units of measurement in such a way that the physical unit of *any* commodity has a "value" equal to unity.

Reconsider now the system of "prices of production":

$$(\mathbf{pA} + \mathbf{pda}_n)(1 + \pi) = \mathbf{p} \qquad \text{(V.A.16)}$$

to which must be added an equation defining the *numéraire* for the system. To preserve symmetry with (V.A.13), the logical step seems to be to set

$$\mathbf{pd}(1 + \sigma) = 1 \qquad \text{(V.A.41)}$$

Thus the "complete" wage rate, or per-worker net product in terms of wage goods, is set equal to unity, when evaluated at "prices of production", in the same way as it is set equal to unity when evaluated at "values."

We now define a new row vector $\mathbf{x}$, which shows the ratios of the "prices of production" to the corresponding "values":

$$\mathbf{x} = \mathbf{p}\hat{\mathbf{v}}^{-1} \tag{V.A.42}$$

and, conversely,

$$\mathbf{p} = \mathbf{x}\hat{\mathbf{v}} \tag{V.A.43}$$

Post-multiplying (V.A.16) by $\hat{\mathbf{v}}^{-1}$ and substituting from (V.A.43), we obtain

$$\mathbf{x}(\hat{\mathbf{v}}\mathbf{A}\hat{\mathbf{v}}^{-1} + \hat{\mathbf{v}}\mathbf{da}_n\hat{\mathbf{v}}^{-1})(1 + \pi) = \mathbf{x} \tag{V.A.44}$$

where the vector $\mathbf{x}$ is itself a vector of prices of production, these prices being expressed, however, relative to the "values."

This system of equations is the same as the "prices-of-production system" in Section 4, except that it is now so written as to single out explicitly the "values" as the magnitudes from which to start. Hence its "solution" is equivalent to a "transformation" of the "transformed values" $\mathbf{1}$ into the "transformed prices" $\mathbf{x}$ and thus to a "transformation" of the "values" $\mathbf{v}$ into the "prices of production," $\mathbf{p}$.

It goes without saying that, in general, $\mathbf{x} \neq \mathbf{1}$ and thus $\mathbf{p} \neq \mathbf{v}$. Prices and "values" will diverge. These divergences will depend *mainly* on the "organic composition of capital" in each industry as compared with that in the industry producing the commodity which is taken as the *numéraire*, but also on the intricate network of relations between rate of profit and prices in the whole economic system. We have examined this problem in Section 5.7 of Chapter V, with reference to the divergences between any two sets of prices. "Values" and "prices of production" are clearly a particular case of that same problem. And we know we cannot state a general rule, i.e., a rule valid for absolutely all cases. We can say that *in most cases* those ratios, in $\mathbf{x}$, referring to commodities with an "organic composition of capital" greater than that of the composite commodity $\mathbf{d}$ will turn out to be greater than unity (and the respective prices greater than the corresponding "values"); and those ratios relating to commodities with an "organic composition of capital" smaller than that of the composite commodity $\mathbf{d}$ will turn out to be less than unity (and the respective prices smaller than the corresponding "values"). There may always be some prices, however, which do not follow this rule.

The choice of the composite commodity $\mathbf{d}(1 + \sigma)$ as *numéraire* (and hence of its price as the "watershed" between prices which are greater and prices which are smaller than the corresponding values) is, of course, arbitrary. Other choices could equally be made. And, indeed, in the economic literature on the transformation problem, various alternative suggestions have been made in this connection,[16] all of which reduce to the choice of a particular commodity, or composite commodity, the "value" of which remains invariant when it is transformed into a "price of production."[17] In our example this choice was made in (V.A.41) and is equivalent to setting

$$\mathbf{vd} = \mathbf{pd} \tag{V.A.45}$$

i.e., to choosing the composite wage commodity as the commodity whose "value" and "price of production" remain invariant in the transformation process. It is to be noted that the criterion used in this choice is simply one of logical symmetry.[18] Definition (V.A.41), for the unit of measurement of "prices of production," is logically symmetrical to definition (V.A.13) for the unit of measurement of "values."

In any event, whatever may be the commodity, or composite commodity, whose "value" and "price of production" are chosen to remain invariant, it can be concluded that the Marxian process of the "transformation of values into prices of production" may be expressed, in analytical terms, by the solution of a system of linear equations. It thus consists of the search for a linear operator which will "transform" a certain vector $\mathbf{v}$ into another vector $\mathbf{p}$ (or into some scalar multiple thereof).

8. *Uniform "organic composition of capital," another special case.* The above-mentioned problem of finding a linear operator which effects the "transformation of values into prices of production" is not an analytically simple one, and Marx found it convenient to leave it to the end of his analysis (without then ever managing to solve it correctly).

---

[16] The following alternative suggestions may be mentioned: $\mathbf{vQ} = \mathbf{pQ}$, total value equal to total of prices; $\mathbf{vda}_n\mathbf{Q}\sigma = \mathbf{pA}^{(+)}\mathbf{Q}\Pi^{(A+)}$, total surplus value equal to total profits; $\mathbf{v(I - A}^{(+)})\mathbf{Q}^{**} = \mathbf{p(I - A}^{(+)})\mathbf{Q}^{**}$, standard commodity, with reference to matrix $\mathbf{A}^{(+)}$, evaluated at the "values" equal to the same, evaluated at the "prices of production." The first and third of these alternative suggestions have been justified with reference to Marx's idea of a commodity with organic composition of capital equal to the "social average." The second, on the other hand, has been justified with reference to Marx's argument that capitalists redistribute surplus value among themselves under the form of profits. (See Winternitz [12], Meek [7], Seton [11], Medio [6]). In all these attempts to be faithful to Marx the difficulty is, of course, that Marx's own arguments are not always logically consistent and thus would seem to justify different postulates at different places.

[17] The "transformation problem" therefore also entails the choice of an "invariance postulate," as it has been called by Seton [11].

[18] Yet it is interesting to find that Marx himself thought of the wage-goods industries as those with an "organic composition of capital" which is near the average for the whole economy. See Dobb [3, pp. 46, 72–73], Meek [7, p. 96]. In fact, the choice of the composite commodity $\mathbf{d}$ is not without a justification, as will be seen in Section 10 below.

As already mentioned,[19] in Volumes I and II of *Capital*, Marx carried out his analysis *as if* the "organic composition of capital" were the same for all industries. This device allowed him to avoid the "transformation" problem altogether. It may be worthwhile to reconsider briefly this Marxian device by using the notation of the preceding section, where all the physical quantities were expressed in terms of embodied labor.

Consider an economic system in which the "constant capital" in each industry is exactly the same proportion, γ, of the "variable capital" (both kinds of capital being expressed in terms of quantities of embodied labour), so that

$$\mathbf{1}\hat{\mathbf{v}}\mathbf{A}\hat{\mathbf{v}}^{-1} = \gamma\mathbf{1}\hat{\mathbf{v}}\mathbf{da}_n\hat{\mathbf{v}}^{-1}$$

where $\gamma \geq 0$ denotes the "organic composition of capital" (which is the same for all industries).

Note now that, for the definition of uniform "organic composition of capital" to be consistent with all possible income distributions, it must in fact also be true that

$$\hat{\mathbf{v}}\mathbf{A}\hat{\mathbf{v}}^{-1} = \gamma\hat{\mathbf{v}}\mathbf{da}_n\hat{\mathbf{v}}^{-1} \qquad\qquad (\text{V.A.46})$$

Substituting into (V.A.44), we obtain

$$\mathbf{x}\hat{\mathbf{v}}\mathbf{A}\hat{\mathbf{v}}^{-1} + \pi\gamma\mathbf{x}\hat{\mathbf{v}}\mathbf{da}_n\hat{\mathbf{v}}^{-1} + \mathbf{x}\hat{\mathbf{v}}\mathbf{da}_n\hat{\mathbf{v}}^{-1}(1 + \pi) = \mathbf{x}$$

or

$$\mathbf{x}(\hat{\mathbf{v}}\mathbf{A}\hat{\mathbf{v}}^{-1}) + \mathbf{x}(\hat{\mathbf{v}}\mathbf{da}_n\hat{\mathbf{v}}^{-1})(1 + \pi\gamma + \pi) = \mathbf{x} \qquad\qquad (\text{V.A.47})$$

from which, calling

$$\sigma = \gamma\pi + \pi \qquad\qquad (\text{V.A.48})$$

which implies

$$\pi = \frac{\sigma}{1 + \gamma} \qquad\qquad (\text{V.A.49})$$

it can be seen that the equation system (V.A.47) comes to coincide exactly with equation system (V.A.40). The solutions of the two systems must therefore be the same; i.e., it must be true in the present case that

$$\mathbf{x} = \mathbf{1} \qquad\qquad (\text{V.A.50})$$

---

[19] See pp. 21–22 above.

which implies[20]:

$$\mathbf{p} = \mathbf{v} \qquad\qquad\qquad (V.A.51)$$

We obtain thereby a confirmation of the proposition that, in the special case of a uniform "organic composition of capital" throughout the system, "values" are equal to "prices of production," and the transformation problem does not arise.[21] This is, however, a very special case which can in no way replace the general case.

[20] An alternative proof may be given in the following way. Start from

$$\hat{\mathbf{v}}\mathbf{A}\hat{\mathbf{v}}^{-1} = \gamma\hat{\mathbf{v}}\mathbf{d}\mathbf{a}_n\hat{\mathbf{v}}^{-1} \qquad\qquad (V.A.46)$$

and pre-multiply by $\mathbf{a}_n\hat{\mathbf{v}}^{-1}$. We obtain

$$\mathbf{a}_n\hat{\mathbf{v}}^{-1}\hat{\mathbf{v}}\mathbf{A}\hat{\mathbf{v}}^{-1} = (\gamma\mathbf{a}_n\hat{\mathbf{v}}^{-1}\hat{\mathbf{v}}\mathbf{d})\mathbf{a}_n\hat{\mathbf{v}}^{-1}$$

We may note now that the whole expression within brackets is a scalar. Call it $\lambda = (\gamma\mathbf{a}_n\hat{\mathbf{v}}^{-1}\hat{\mathbf{v}}\mathbf{d})$, and we have

$$(\mathbf{a}_n\hat{\mathbf{v}}^{-1})(\hat{\mathbf{v}}\mathbf{A}\hat{\mathbf{v}}^{-1}) = \lambda\mathbf{a}_n\hat{\mathbf{v}}^{-1}$$

Thus $\mathbf{a}_n\hat{\mathbf{v}}^{-1}$ turns out to be an eigenvector of matrix $\hat{\mathbf{v}}\mathbf{A}\hat{\mathbf{v}}^{-1}$. Since $\mathbf{a}_n\hat{\mathbf{v}}^{-1}$ is a vector of direct labor coefficients, and $\hat{\mathbf{v}}\mathbf{A}\hat{\mathbf{v}}^{-1}$ is an interindustry coefficient matrix, expressed in terms of physical units of embodied labor, it follows that all prices will always remain the same at all possible levels of the rate of profit (see footnote 9 on p. 79 and footnote 17 on p. 87). In the present context this means that the "prices of production" always coincide with the "values."

[21] The argument carried out in the text can also be reversed. Call

$$\gamma_j = \frac{\sum\limits_i v_i a_{ij}}{a_{nj}\sum\limits_i v_i d_i} \qquad\qquad j = 1, 2, \ldots, n-1$$

("organic composition of capital" in each industry), and

$$\pi_j = \frac{\sigma a_{nj}\sum\limits_i v_i' d_i}{\sum\limits_i v_i a_{ij} + a_{nj}\sum\limits_i v_i d_i} \qquad\qquad j = 1, 2, \ldots, n-1$$

(rate of profit in each industry if exchanges took place according to "values"). Following the same formulation and the same steps as in the text yields

$$\sigma = \gamma_j\pi_j + \pi_j \qquad\qquad (V.A.52)$$

and thus

$$\pi_j = \frac{\sigma}{1 + \gamma_j} \qquad\qquad j = 1, 2, \ldots, n-1 \qquad\qquad (V.A.53)$$

It necessarily follows that rates of surplus value and rates of profit can simultaneously be uniform in the whole economic system (this also implies surplus value equal to profits and "value" equal to "price of production" in each single industry) if and only if the "organic composition of capital" is exactly the same in all industries.

9. *The linear operator which effects the "transformation"*. The linear operator which "transforms" the values **v** into prices of production **p** can, nevertheless, be found very quickly by using our own formulations.

It will prove helpful to start by provisionally adopting as *numéraire* the wage rate which is actually paid, a procedure used frequently in Chapter V. If we set

$$w = \mathbf{pd} = 1 \qquad \text{(V.A.54)}$$

all prices come to be expressed in terms of "labor commanded," i.e., in terms of the quantity of labor which any particular commodity can purchase in the economic system. Relation (V.A.16) then becomes

$$\mathbf{pA}(1 + \pi) + \mathbf{a}_n(1 + \pi) = \mathbf{p} \qquad \text{(V.A.55)}$$

and can be rewritten in the following ways:

$$\mathbf{p}(\mathbf{I} - \mathbf{A}) = \pi\mathbf{pA} + (1 + \pi)\mathbf{a}_n$$
$$\mathbf{p} = \pi\mathbf{pA}(\mathbf{I} - \mathbf{A})^{-1} + (1 + \pi)\mathbf{a}_n(\mathbf{I} - \mathbf{A})^{-1}$$
$$\mathbf{p}[\mathbf{I} - \pi\mathbf{A}(\mathbf{I} - \mathbf{A})^{-1}] = (1 + \pi)\mathbf{a}_n(\mathbf{I} - \mathbf{A})^{-1} \qquad \text{(V.A.56)}$$

The right side of (V.A.56) is simply $(1 + \pi)\mathbf{v}$, as may be seen from (V.A.5), so that (V.A.56) can be written

$$\mathbf{p} = \mathbf{v}[\mathbf{I} - \pi\mathbf{A}(\mathbf{I} - \mathbf{A})^{-1}]^{-1}(1 + \pi) \qquad \text{(V.A.57)}$$

In a sense our problem is already solved. The matrix $[\mathbf{I} - \pi\mathbf{A}(\mathbf{I} - \mathbf{A})^{-1}]^{-1}(1 + \pi)$ is the linear operator which, for any given rate of profit, π, transforms the "values" **v** into the "prices of production," **p**. In the present context one must, of course, set $\pi = \Pi^{(A+)}$, where $\Pi^{(A+)}$ denotes the economically meaningful solution of the characteristic equation (V.A.22).

As may be verified by inspection, the "prices of production" in (V.A.57) will *always* be greater than the corresponding "values," except in the limiting case in which $\pi = 0$ and thus $\mathbf{p} = \mathbf{v}$. The reason for this is that, whereas the "values" are by definition expressed in terms of "embodied labor," the prices of production are expressed here in terms of "labor commanded." These two types of quantities of labor will indeed coincide in the limiting case of a zero rate of profit. But, as soon as the rate of profit is positive, each commodity can purchase, in the economic system, a quantity of labor ("labor commanded") greater than the quantity of labor embodied in it.[22]

This formulation might therefore be objected to on the grounds that the "values" and the "prices of production" are expressed in terms of two different kinds of quantities of labor and that the comparison between the two is not an immediate one (having to be made via the relation between "labor commanded" and "labor embodied").

This objection can be overcome by abandoning the *numéraire* (V.A.54) and returning to the formulation of Section 7, where the price-of-production system was closed with the equation

$$\mathbf{pd}(1 + \sigma) = 1 \qquad\qquad\qquad \text{(V.A.41)}$$

which is symmetrical to

$$\mathbf{vd}(1 + \sigma) = 1 \qquad\qquad\qquad \text{(V.A.13)}$$

and is equivalent to expressing the prices, as well as the "values," in terms of the "complete" wage rate, or per worker net product. Thanks to (V.A.41), the price of each commodity is being expressed in terms of that wage rate which could purchase a quantity of labor ("labor commanded") exactly equal to the labor embodied in it.

Substituting (V.A.41) into the system (V.A.16), (V.A.17), and setting the rate of profit in that system equal to $\Pi^{(A+)}$, we obtain the new expression

$$\mathbf{p} = \mathbf{v}[\mathbf{I} - \Pi^{(A+)}\mathbf{A}(\mathbf{I} - \mathbf{A})^{-1}]^{-1}\frac{1 + \Pi^{(A+)}}{1 + \sigma} \qquad\qquad \text{(V.A.58)}$$

where σ is the solution of the algebraic equation

$$\det[\mathbf{I} - \mathbf{A} - (1 + \sigma)\mathbf{da}_n] = 0 \qquad\qquad \text{(V.A.14)}$$

---

[22] Whereas "labor embodied" is physically determined by the technique of production, the amount of labor which any commodity can "command" varies with the level of the rate of profit (it decreases as the rate of profit increases or – which is the same – as the *real* wage rate decreases). This can be seen from (V.A.57) where, owing to $\mathbf{A}$ and $(\mathbf{I} - \mathbf{A})^{-1}$ and consequently to $\mathbf{A}(\mathbf{I} - \mathbf{A})^{-1}$ all being non-negative matrices – each of the nonzero elements of the inverse matrix within square brackets increases as π increases (Perron-Frobenius Theorems 3 and 3a. See *Mathematical Appendix*, pp. 272, 275). All prices are therefore an increasing, monotonic function of π.

It may also be of interest to point out that the columns of matrix $\mathbf{A}(\mathbf{I} - \mathbf{A})^{-1}$ have a well-defined economic meaning. They represent the vertically integrated units of productive capacities. See Pasinetti [9].

and $\Pi^{(A+)}$ is the economically meaningful solution of the characteristic equation

$$\det\left[\mathbf{I} - (1 + \pi)(\mathbf{A} + \mathbf{da}_n)\right] = 0 \qquad\qquad (\text{V.A.22})$$

The expression (V.A.58) gives us precisely the linear operator we have been looking for. It gives an explicit solution to the Marxian problem of the "transformation of values into prices of production." The matrix

$$[\mathbf{I} - \Pi^{(A+)}\mathbf{A}(\mathbf{I} - \mathbf{A})^{-1}]^{-1}\frac{1 + \Pi^{(A+)}}{1 + \sigma}$$

is the linear operator which transforms the "values" $\mathbf{v}$ into the prices of production, $\mathbf{p}$, both being expressed in terms of the same "complete" wage rate $\mathbf{d}(1 + \sigma)$. It should be noticed that this is a one-to-one transformation. The inverse of the matrix above, i.e.,

$$[\mathbf{I} - \Pi^{(A+)}\mathbf{A}(\mathbf{I} - \mathbf{A})^{-1}]\frac{1 + \sigma}{1 + \Pi^{(A+)}}$$

is the linear operator which effects the inverse transformation of the "prices of production," $\mathbf{p}$ into the values $\mathbf{v}$.

By contrast with the prices (V.A.57), the prices (V.A.58) are no longer unilaterally greater than the corresponding "values." Some prices will prove to be greater than, while others will prove to be smaller than, the corresponding "values," the borderline case being provided by the composite commodity $\mathbf{d}(1 + \sigma)$, which has both a price and a value of unity.

10. *Price system and rate of surplus value.* We may look at expressions (V.A.57) and (V.A.58) a little more closely. Of course, in the particular case in which the rate of profit (and thus the rate of surplus value) is zero, prices (V.A.57) and prices (V.A.58) coincide with each other, and both of them coincide with the "values" $\mathbf{v}$. But as soon as $\pi > 0$ (and thus also $\sigma > 0$), they all become different. Prices and "values" will in general differ in a very complicated way, as shown by the expressions above. Prices (V.A.57) and prices (V.A.58) will obviously only differ by a scalar multiple. The interesting thing to note is that this scalar multiple happens to be $(1 + \sigma)$, i.e., the same scalar multiple by which "necessary labor" differs from the sum of "necessary labor" and "surplus labor."[23] This circumstance deserves further investigation.

Prices (V.A.57) and prices (V.A.58) represent the same price structure; they differ only as to the *numéraire*. The former are expressed in

[23] See p. 124 above.

terms of the actual wage rate; they represent "labor commanded." The latter are expressed in terms of the "ideal" wage rate (or per worker net product) on the assumption that its composition is the same as that of the actual wage. These prices do not, of course, represent labor embodied in the corresponding commodities (for, by definition, it is the "values" that represent labor embodied). They "distort" labor embodied, so to speak, around the "values" (some prices turning out to be greater, and others smaller, than the corresponding "values," or quantities of embodied labor); but they "distort" it in such a way as to cancel out for the composite commodity representing the real wage. We might say that they represent labor embodied "on the average," if we could conventionally take the real wage as the "average" commodity. They have the property of giving us the total amount of labor embodied in the net product of the economic system if we use them to evaluate the particular net product that has the same physical composition as the real wage. This is an important property. We know that total labor embodied in the net product of an economic system is always the same irrespective of composition. Having now found a particular composition of the net product which, *at current prices*, reproduces total labor embodied, we may obviously use it for a more general purpose, by adopting it as the *numéraire* of the price system. This is precisely what is implied by *numéraire* (V.A.41).

Thanks to (V.A.41), prices (V.A.58) yield the relation

$$w(1 + \sigma) = w^* = 1 \qquad\qquad (V.A.59)$$

or

$$\sigma = \frac{1}{w} - 1 \qquad\qquad (V.A.60)$$

This is a remarkable expression. It reproduces the same relation given by (V.A.10), between σ and δ, i.e., a relation in terms of physical quantities of embodied labor, although w is here the wage rate that emerges from the price-of-production system. In other words, owing to the particular *numéraire* used, we have been able to obtain the relation between rate of surplus value and labor embodied in the real wage (or "necessary labor") by simply using the wage rate as it emerges from the price-of-production system. In this price system, w and δ have become interchangeable, precisely as in Sraffa's standard system (see Section 6)[24].

---

[24] There is, however, an important difference. In the analysis of Section 6 it was necessary to assume a real wage **d*** having the same composition as the standard commodity. No such restriction is necessary here. The real wage is taken for whatever it is. On the other hand, by using the present *numéraire* the (V.A.24), (V.A.25), and (V.A.26) will in general remain inequalities. Only in the very special case in which total profits were to be spent on commodities having the same composition as the real wage would those inequalities become equalities.

What generates this remarkable result is that the rate of surplus value, as it may now be realized, does not depend on the composition of that part of the net product that goes to the capitalists; it depends only on the physical composition, and on the magnitude, of the real wage. This is what confers upon the composite commodity (V.A.6), the real wage, a relevance that goes beyond, and has nothing to do with, the circumstance of whether it is or is not an "average" commodity.[25] Relation (V.A.60) holds for the general case.

To conclude, in any actual economic system (and not only in an economic system in which the net product has the same composition as the real wage), there exists a particular composite commodity (the per worker net product with the same composition as the real wage) which, if used as the *numéraire* of the price system, makes the wage rate w acquire the meaning of fraction of "necessary labor" out of total labor (this was denoted by δ in Section 3). It follows that, in such a price system, the rate of surplus value, or "rate of exploitation" in Marxian terminology, can be obtained directly from the price-of-production system as the reciprocal of the wage rate minus one.

11. *Numerical example.* The concepts introduced above can be illustrated with the aid of the numerical example, with three commodities and industries (wheat, iron, turkeys), introduced in Chapter II and subsequently used several times.

Given the matrix of interindustry coefficients and the vector of direct labor coefficients:

$$\mathbf{A} = \begin{bmatrix} \dfrac{186}{450} & \dfrac{54}{21} & \dfrac{30}{60} \\[2ex] \dfrac{12}{450} & \dfrac{6}{21} & \dfrac{3}{60} \\[2ex] \dfrac{9}{450} & \dfrac{6}{21} & \dfrac{15}{60} \end{bmatrix}$$

$$\mathbf{a}_n = \begin{bmatrix} \dfrac{18}{450} & \dfrac{12}{21} & \dfrac{30}{60} \end{bmatrix}$$

the quantities of labor embodied in a unit of each of the three commodities, which Marx calls "values," will be given by

$$\mathbf{v} = \mathbf{a}_n(\mathbf{I} - \mathbf{A})^{-1} \simeq [0.1818 \quad 1.81818 \quad 0.90909] \qquad \text{(V.A.61)}$$

---

[25] Marx obviously sensed the importance of the wage commodity in value-price relations, but did so only intuitively. See footnote 18 on p. 137.

The net product of the system (180 tons of wheat and 30 gross of turkeys) therefore has a "value" of

$$180 \times 0.1818 + 30 \times 0.90909 = 60$$

i.e., a "value" equal to the number of workers in the economic system.

If the entire net product were distributed as wages, each worker would receive 3 tons of wheat and $\frac{1}{2}$ gross of turkeys, i.e., a wage, expressed in "values," of

$$3 \times 0.1818 + \tfrac{1}{2} \times 0.90909 = 1$$

which is, by definition, the "complete" wage rate, $w^* = 1$.

We assume, however, that we are considering a capitalist economy in which the "capitalists" pay the workers the equivalent of an annual subsistence wage:

$$\mathbf{d} = \begin{bmatrix} 2 \\ 0 \\ 0.16666 \end{bmatrix}$$

i.e., a wage of 2 tons of wheat and 0.16666 gross (i.e., 2 dozens) of turkeys. In such an economic system the net product will be distributed as follows: 120 tons of wheat and 10 gross of turkeys will go to the workers (as subsistence wages); the remaining 60 tons of wheat and 20 gross of turkeys will go to the capitalists (as "surplus value").

The "value" of, or quantity of labor embodied in, the subsistence wage is given by

$$\mathbf{vd} = [0.1818 \quad 1.81818 \quad 0.90909] \begin{bmatrix} 2 \\ 0 \\ 0.16666 \end{bmatrix} \approx 0.515$$

(V.A.62)

Since $w^* = 1$, we therefore have

$$\delta \approx 0.515$$

This means that each worker works for himself for just over half his working time (to produce 2 tons of wheat and 2 dozens of turkeys), while for the rest of his working time, i.e., for just under half, he works for the capitalist (to produce the remaining output: 1 ton of wheat and 4 dozens of turkeys). The "rate of surplus value" will be

$$\sigma = \frac{1 - \delta}{\delta} = \frac{1}{\delta} - 1 \approx 94.11\%$$

One can obtain the same result by finding the root σ of the algebraic equation $\det[\mathbf{I} - \mathbf{A} - (1 + \sigma)\mathbf{da}_n] = 0$, which in the present example has the unique solution

$$\sigma \simeq 94.11\%$$

The rate of profit is determined as the economically meaningful solution of the parallel characteristic equation

$$\det[\mathbf{I} - (1 + \pi)(\mathbf{A} + \mathbf{da}_n)] = 0,$$

where $\mathbf{A}$ is the matrix specified above and $\mathbf{da}_n$ is

$$\mathbf{da}_n = \begin{bmatrix} 2 \\ 0 \\ 0.16666 \end{bmatrix} \begin{bmatrix} \dfrac{18}{450} & \dfrac{12}{21} & \dfrac{30}{60} \end{bmatrix} = \begin{bmatrix} \dfrac{36}{450} & \dfrac{24}{21} & \dfrac{60}{60} \\ 0 & 0 & 0 \\ \dfrac{3}{450} & \dfrac{2}{21} & \dfrac{5}{60} \end{bmatrix}$$

The maximum eigenvalue of

$$\mathbf{A} + \mathbf{da}_n = \mathbf{A}^{(+)} = \begin{bmatrix} \dfrac{222}{450} & \dfrac{78}{21} & \dfrac{90}{60} \\ \dfrac{12}{450} & \dfrac{6}{21} & \dfrac{3}{60} \\ \dfrac{12}{450} & \dfrac{8}{21} & \dfrac{20}{60} \end{bmatrix}$$

is

$$\lambda_m^{(A+)} \simeq 0.84361$$

and thus

$$\Pi^{(A+)} = \frac{1}{\lambda_m^{(A+)}} - 1 \simeq 18.54\%$$

As expected, the rate of profit (18.54%) turns out to be smaller than the corresponding rate of surplus value (94.11%).

On substituting this rate of profit for π in the equation system $\mathbf{p}[\mathbf{I} - (1 + \pi)\mathbf{A}^{(+)}] = \mathbf{0}$, we find the relative prices

$$p_2 \simeq 9.286 p_1 \tag{V.A.63}$$

$$p_3 \simeq 3.849 p_1 \tag{V.A.64}$$

It only remains to add a further equation which defines the *numéraire* for the price system. The choice made in previous sections is

$$[p_1\, p_2\, p_3] \begin{bmatrix} 2 \\ 0 \\ 0.1666 \end{bmatrix} (1 + 94.11\%) = 1 \qquad (V.A.65)$$

That is, we have defined a composite commodity which has the same composition as the real wage but has the magnitude of the per-worker net product. This composite commodity is

$$\begin{bmatrix} 2 \\ 0 \\ 0.1666 \end{bmatrix} (1 + 94.11\%) = \begin{bmatrix} 3.8822 \\ 0 \\ 0.3235 \end{bmatrix} \qquad (V.A.66)$$

and its price is being set equal to one.

The three equations (V.A.63), (V.A.64), (V.A.65) now yield the solution

$$\mathbf{p} = [0.1950 \quad 1.8109 \quad 0.7507]$$

expressing a vector of "prices of production" which definition (V.A.65) has made directly comparable with the corresponding vector of "values" (V.A.61). Price p_1 turns out to be greater than the corresponding value ($0.1950 > 0.1818$), while the prices p_2 and p_3 turn out to be smaller than the corresponding values ($1.8109 < 1.818$ and $0.7507 < 0.909$). On the average, however, they give the same result, in the sense that both prices and "values" make the price of the composite commodity (V.A.66) equal to one, i.e., equal to the quantity of labor embodied in it.

Note, moreover, that the actual wage rate turns out to be

$$w = \mathbf{pd} \simeq 0.515$$

which is precisely equal to δ, as emerges from (V.A.62). So that, directly from the price system, we can obtain

$$\sigma = \frac{1}{w} - 1 \simeq 94.11\%$$

the rate of surplus value.

We could of course reexpress the physical quantities of wheat, iron, and turkeys in terms of physical units of embodied labor rather than in terms of tons and gross, respectively, as done so far. If this were done, the vector of "values" would, by definition, become

$$[1 \quad 1 \quad 1]$$

and the corresponding vector of "prices of production" would be

$$\hat{\mathbf{v}}^{-1}\mathbf{p} = [1.0726 \quad 0.9960 \quad 0.8258]$$

Thus the price of wheat would be greater than, and the prices of iron and turkeys would be less than, unity (i.e., than the corresponding "values").

On the basis of a rule which is valid in most cases (though not in all cases, as pointed out in Section 7 above), we might infer that commodity 1 (wheat) will probably have an "organic composition of capital" greater than that of the composite wage commodity, which is used as the *numéraire* for both the price and the value systems; and that commodities 2 and 3 (iron and turkeys), by contrast, will probably have "organic compositions of capital" lower than that of the composite wage commodity. We can check this inference by computing the value of "constant capital" in the three industries:

$$\mathbf{vA} = [0.1248 \quad 1.0649 \quad 0.40909]$$

and the value of "variable capital" in the same industries

$$\mathbf{vda}_n = [0.0206 \quad 0.29437 \quad 0.25757]$$

Dividing each element of the first vector by the corresponding element of the second vector, we obtain the organic compositions of capital in the three industries, namely,

$$\gamma_1 = 6.0588$$

$$\gamma_2 = 3.6176$$

$$\gamma_3 = 1.5882$$

The "organic composition of capital" in the hypothetical, composite industry producing the wage commodity $\mathbf{d}$, denoted by γ^d, is given by

$$\gamma^d = \frac{2 \times 0.1248 + 0.1666 \times 0.40909}{2 \times 0.0206 + 0.1666 \times 0.25757} = 3.777$$

It can now be seen that $\gamma_1 > \gamma^d$, $\gamma_2 < \gamma^d$, $\gamma_3 < \gamma^d$, just according to the mentioned rule.

Summarizing our numerical example, then, the market mechanism "transforms" a rate of surplus value of 94.11% into a rate of profit of 18.45%; and the "values," [0.1818 1.81818 0.90909], into the "prices of production," [0.1951 1.8109 0.7507]; or, if the physical quantities were expressed in terms of embodied labor, the "values" [1 1 1] into the prices of production, [1.0726 0.9960 0.8258].

12. *Concluding remarks*. It may be concluded that the Marxian problem of the "transformation of values into prices of production," which has given rise to so much controversy in the economic literature, is expressed, in analytical terms, by an algebraic operation of linear transformation. A certain vector, representing the "values," is transformed into another vector, representing the "prices of production," on being multiplied by a matrix which represents the logical process of solving a system of equations. And the inverse of this matrix effects the inverse transformation of "prices of production" into "values." There is therefore a one-to-one correspondence between "values" and "prices of production". This is a conclusion which should no longer be open to dispute.

Discussion seems destined to continue, on the other hand, over the social meaning and interpretation of such "transformations." According to Marx, the "transformation of values into prices of production" is not merely an analytical, algebraic operation; it also reflects a real historical process.[26] It is the system of "values" which is conceived by Marx as correctly representing the relations between the people who take part in the productive process. The system of prices of production by contrast is conceived as a superstructure of capitalist societies, which have distorted the original exchange ratios and have made them conform to their own inner need for uniformity of the rates of profit.

Critics of Marx reject this interpretation and take the opposite view. Marxian accounting in terms of "values" appears to many of them to be a useless duplication of market accounting in terms of prices. They point out that, *on a strictly analytical ground*, there is no justification whatever for giving any sort of logical priority to either "values" over prices or to prices over "values." Each of them can be derived from the other; and both of them can be obtained from the interindustry relations expressed in terms of physical quantities of commodities. They go on to point out that the only system of exchange ratios which can be observed empirically is the system of prices. The "value" system is therefore regarded as a Marxist superstructure, something which, so to speak, belongs to Marxist ideology and has no empirical correlate.

It does not fall within the aims of this work to enter into controversies of this nature, which, incidentally, no mathematical elaboration

---

[26] In Marx's own words: "...it is quite appropriate to regard the values of commodities as not only theoretically but also historically *prius* to the prices of production." (Marx [1, p. 177].)

could ever settle. The objective of these notes has been to clarify the logico-mathematical aspects of the problem, a task which is always the essential and necessary preliminary to any discussion of greater scope.

References

[1] Marx, Karl, *Capital*, Vol. III, London: Lawrence and Wishart, 1959 (first published in German in 1894).

[2] Bródy, András, *Proportions, Prices and Planning—A Mathematical Restatement of the Labour Theory of Value*, Budapest: Akadémiai Kiadó, and Amsterdam: North Holland Publishing Co., 1970.

[3] Dobb, Maurice, *Political Economy and Capitalism*, London: Routledge and Kegan Paul, 1940.

[4] Eatwell, John, "Mr. Sraffa's Standard Commodity and the Rate of Exploitation," *Quarterly Journal of Economics*, 1975, p. 543–555.

[5] Lowenthal, Ester, *The Ricardian Socialists*, New York: Columbia University Press, 1911.

[6] Medio, Alfredo, "Profits and Surplus-Value: Appearance and Reality in Capitalist Production," in *A Critique of Economic Theory*, ed. by E. K. Hunt and J. G. Schwartz, Harmandsworth: Penguin Books, 1972.

[7] Meek, Ronald, "Some Notes on the Transformation Problem" *Economic Journal*, 1956, pp. 94–107.

[8] Morishima, Michio, *Marx's Economics*, Cambridge: Cambridge University Press, 1973.

[9] Pasinetti, Luigi L., "The Notion of Vertical Integration in Economic Analysis," *Metroeconomica*, 1973, pp. 1–29.

[10] Samuelson, Paul A., "Understanding the Marxian Notion of Exploitation: A Summary of the So-called Transformation Problem between Marxian Values and Competitive Prices," *Journal of Economic Literature*, 1971, pp. 399–431.

[11] Seton, Francis, "The Transformation Problem," *Review of Economic Studies*, 1956–1957, pp. 149–60.

[12] Winternitz, J., "Value and Prices: a Solution of the So-called Transformation Problem," *Economic Journal*, 1948, pp. 276–280.

CHAPTER SIX

The Choice of Technique

1 A Multiplicity of Methods of Production

IN this chapter we continue our examination of an economic system in which each industry produces only one commodity and in which all the production processes exhibit constant returns to scale. But we extend the scope of our enquiry to give explicit consideration to the choice of the methods of production.

In earlier chapters our analysis was confined to considering the technique of production for the economic system as a whole, represented by the interindustry matrix $\mathbf{A}$ and the vector of labor coefficients $\mathbf{a}_n$, which was actually observed. Such technique of production, however, might have been chosen from a wider range of technological possibilities. Thus, calling the set of all the alternative methods of production known at a given point in time the *technology* of the economic system, we can suppose these methods of production to be grouped together in a series of alternative techniques, each of which is represented by its own matrix of interindustry coefficients and by its own vector of labor coefficients. Of all these alternative techniques only one is actually chosen and is then the only one that can be observed.

This means that, behind the scenes as it were, a process of technological choice generally takes place which has been taken for granted in our previous analysis, but which will now be investigated explicitly.

2 The Criterion of Profitability

2.1. *Minimum cost.* In order to make a choice between alternative possibilities we must adopt a *criterion of choice*. It is assumed throughout this chapter that the criterion chosen is that of *profitability*. It is usually maintained that this is precisely the criterion which is automatically imposed upon producers who operate within a competitive system. For our purposes, however, it is unnecessary to make any particular assumption about the institutional characteristics of the economic system. It is simply assumed that, whatever those institutional characteristics may be, when there is more than one technical method available for the production of a given commodity, the method involving the minimum cost will be chosen.

2.2. *Dependence on technology and on income distribution.* It should be noted that the problem appears differently according as it is posed at the level of a single industry or at the level of the economic system as a whole. At the level of any single industry each price p_j ($j = 1, 2, \ldots, n - 1$) appears to depend on the technical coefficients of the jth industry, the prices of the means of production obtained from other industries, the wage rate, and the rate of profit. But in the economic system as a whole the prices of the means of production depend, in turn, on the production coefficients of the industries which produce them and on the prices of their means of production (as well as on the wage rate and the rate of profit). Thus proceeding "backwards," or rather proceeding, analytically, from equation system (V.3.1) to its "solution" (V.5.18), the prices of the other commodities turn out after all to be intermediate variables which are eliminated from the right side and are replaced by the corresponding technical coefficients. Technological choices therefore depend, in general, on the technical coefficients of the economic system as a whole.

An important property of the solution (V.5.18) is immediately apparent, however. Not all of the economic variables are found to be completely eliminated from the solution. In order to determine the system of prices, one must know, besides the technical coefficients, also one of the two distributive variables: the wage rate or the rate of profit.

The conclusion is that, even when considered at the level of the economic system as a whole, the profitability criterion is not an exclusively technical criterion. The choice of the technique which minimizes the costs of production depends not only on the technology of the economic system but also on the distribution of income between profits and wages.

3   The Choice of Technique for Non-basic Commodities

3.1. *A choice made at the level of the single non-basic industry.* It is useful to consider first the simpler problem of the choice of technique for non-basic commodities, which can in fact be solved at the level of the single industry (in contrast to what happens for the general case, as will be seen shortly).

Suppose that, in the economic system under consideration, the qth commodity is a non-basic commodity. And suppose, for simplicity, that it is not used in the production of any non-basic commodity. If three alternative methods of production, which we shall call δ, ε, τ,[1] are available for the production of commodity q, these methods may be represented by three (partitioned) column vectors:

$$\begin{bmatrix} \mathbf{a}_{1q}^{(\delta)} \\ \mathbf{0} \\ a_{nq}^{(\delta)} \end{bmatrix} \qquad \begin{bmatrix} \mathbf{a}_{1q}^{(\varepsilon)} \\ \mathbf{0} \\ a_{nq}^{(\varepsilon)} \end{bmatrix} \qquad \begin{bmatrix} \mathbf{a}_{1q}^{(\gamma)} \\ \mathbf{0} \\ a_{nq}^{(\tau)} \end{bmatrix}$$

where the $\mathbf{a}_{1q}^{(\delta)}$, $\mathbf{a}_{1q}^{(\varepsilon)}$, $\mathbf{a}_{1q}^{(\tau)}$ are the three alternative k-component vectors of basic-inputs coefficients (k being the number of basic commodities), $\mathbf{0}$ is an $(n - 1 - k)$-component zero vector, and $a_{nq}^{(\delta)}$, $a_{nq}^{(\varepsilon)}$, $a_{nq}^{(\tau)}$ are the three alternative labor-input coefficients. The use of any one of these alternative methods of production will entail one of three alternative costs of production for commodity q, i.e., one of the three alternative equilibrium prices:

$$p_q^{(\delta)} = \mathbf{p}_1\mathbf{a}_{1q}^{(\delta)}(1 + \pi) + a_{nq}^{(\delta)}w$$

$$p_q^{(\varepsilon)} = \mathbf{p}_1\mathbf{a}_{1q}^{(\varepsilon)}(1 + \pi) + a_{nq}^{(\varepsilon)}w \qquad\qquad \text{(VI.3.1)}$$

$$p_q^{(\tau)} = \mathbf{p}_1\mathbf{a}_{1q}^{(\tau)}(1 + \pi) + a_{nq}^{(\tau)}w$$

where, as usual, π denotes the (uniform) rate of profit, w the (uniform) wage rate in terms of any basic commodity, and $\mathbf{p}_1$ is the k-component (row) vector of the prices of the basic commodities.

The interesting feature of expressions (VI.3.1) is that *all* the magnitudes on the right sides are already *given* with respect to the price of commodity q. For $\mathbf{p}_1$, the prices of the basic commodities, and w, the wage rate in terms of a basic commodity, are already determined by the rest of the price system, quite independently of the prices of any non-basic commodity (see Section 10.3 of Chapter V). Thus for any given rate of profit the problem of the choice of technique for commodity q is reduced to a simple comparison of the three prices – i.e., costs – (VI.3.1) at the level of the qth industry, and to the choice of the method which entails the minimum cost.

This choice is, of course, relative to a given rate of profit. It would change if the rate of profit were to be fixed at a different level. In other words, given all the alternative methods of production, the choice is a function of the rate of profit. Suppose, for example, that in the

---

[1]Following a widespread convention in recent economic literature, Greek letters are being used here to denote alternative production methods. The warning must be added, however, that this is being done independently of the meaning that some of the same Greek letters may have in other chapters.

economically meaningful range of variation of the rate of profit π (i.e., in $0 \leq \pi \leq \Pi$), the three alternative prices (VI.3.1) trace out the three curves shown in Fig. VI.1. Method δ is clearly obsolete and will never be chosen. It involves a cost for commodity q greater than that of some other method of production for all relevant rates of profit. By contrast, neither of the methods ε or τ can be said to be superior to the other. The choice between them depends on the level of the rate of profit. For all rates of profit lying between zero and π_1, we have $p_q^{(\tau)} < p_q^{(\varepsilon)}$, and hence τ is found to be the more profitable technical method. But for all rates of profit lying between π_1 and π_2, we have $p_q^{(\varepsilon)} < p_q^{(\tau)}$, and thus ε becomes the more profitable method. Finally, for $\pi_2 < \pi < \Pi$, we have $p_q^{(\tau)} < p_q^{(\varepsilon)}$ again, and hence τ is the more profitable technical method once again. The two particular rates of profit π_1 and π_2 represent points at which a switch of techniques occurs or, more simply, *switch points*. At these two particular rates of profit, $p_q^{(\tau)} = p_q^{(\varepsilon)}$, and hence the two methods ε and τ are equally profitable. To conclude, even though, in general, one method will be the more profitable one, there are particular points, such as π_1 and π_2 in Fig. VI.1, at which two different methods can coexist.

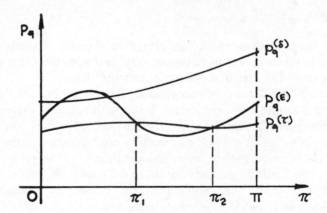

FIG. VI.1. Comparison of 3 methods for the production of a non-basic commodity

It will be realized immediately that the argument set out above is independent of the type of *numéraire* used for the price system. For, given any rate of profit $\bar{\pi}$, changing the commodity in terms of which prices are expressed simply means dividing both sides of each of the three equalities (VI.3.1) by the same number (i.e., by the price of the new *numéraire*). This leaves unchanged the ordering yielded by the comparison of the three prices. It follows that, although a change of *numéraire* changes the form of all the curves in Fig. VI.1, the switch points (and hence the ordering by profitability of the three methods at any point) remain unchanged.[2]

3.2. *Limited effects of the choice.* It may be of interest to draw attention to the limited significance, for the system as a whole, of the technical choices for non-basic commodities. The effects of such choices are confined entirely within the sphere of price variations for the commodity in question (or at most for other non-basic commodities that might be required for its production). These choices have no effect whatever on the rest of the economic system. All the other prices remain unchanged, as indeed do the maximum rate of profit; the standard commodity; the standard net product of the economic system; and, for any predetermined rate of profit, the wage rate in terms of the standard commodity, or in terms of any basic commodity, or even in terms of any non-basic commodity which does not use, as a means of production, the commodity whose process of production is under consideration. This means that any change in the technical coefficients (and therefore any technical progress) that might occur in the processes of production for non-basic commodities yields benefits only to the consumers of those commodities.

4   The Choice of Technique for Basic Commodities

4.1. *A choice involving the economic system as a whole.* We can now consider the more complex case of the choice of technique for basic commodities. Suppose that commodity h is a basic commodity and that, as above, three alternative technical methods are available for its production, these methods being labeled α, β, γ. Suppose furthermore that method γ is the one actually used, so that all the prices (and the wage rate) that can be observed are those corresponding to an economic system in which commodity h is produced by method γ.

As in the previous case, at the level of industry h one could compare the three alternative costs, or equilibrium prices, $p_h^{(\alpha)}$, $p_h^{(\beta)}$, $p_h^{(\gamma)}$, i.e.,

$$p_h^{(\alpha)} = \mathbf{p}^{(\gamma)}\mathbf{a}_h^{(\alpha)}(1 + \pi) + a_{nh}^{(\alpha)}w^{(\gamma)}$$

$$p_h^{(\beta)} = \mathbf{p}^{(\gamma)}\mathbf{a}_h^{(\beta)}(1 + \pi) + a_{nh}^{(\beta)}w^{(\gamma)} \qquad \text{(VI.4.1)}$$

$$p_h^{(\gamma)} = \mathbf{p}^{(\gamma)}\mathbf{a}_h^{(\gamma)}(1 + \pi) + a_{nh}^{(\gamma)}w^{(\gamma)}$$

---

[2] The case of a non-basic commodity which is required as a means of production for other non-basic commodities will not be considered explicitly here, owing to its simplicity. The only modification to the conclusions reached above would be that the price of such a non-basic commodity would also vary in the same direction as p_q, as the one or the other method of production is chosen. The general case is investigated, in any case, in Section 5 of this chapter.

where the symbols have the same meaning as in (VI.3.1), all prices and the wage rate on the right side being those corresponding to technique γ, and all being expressed in terms of *any* basic commodity.

In the present context, however, the comparison could not be but a provisional one. For, if the comparison were to lead to a change of production method, and thus of the price p_h, then since that price enters into the formation of all the other prices a change would take place also in the prices on the right sides of all three equalities (VI.4.1). These changes, in turn, would give rise to a further change in the price p_h, and that would lead to a second round of changes in all prices. And so on, via an infinite but convergent[3] process, toward a completely new system of prices.

Thus in the case of basic commodities, since they are themselves used in the production of all commodities, changing a method of production in a single industry has effects throughout the whole economic system. (Technical progress in any single industry thus yields benefits for all consumers.) In analytical terms this means that the choice of technique for basic commodities cannot be based on a simple comparison of the three alternative prices (VI.4.1) and thus on a diagram similar to that of Fig. VI.1. The solution to the problem of choice of technique can only be sought with reference to the economic system as a whole.

4.2. *The technological frontier of income distribution possibilities.* Let us begin by considering the case in which, whereas the three alternative methods (VI.4.1) are known for the production of commodity h, only one method of production is available for each of the other commodities. The technology for the economic system as a whole will therefore simply be represented by the three alternative techniques

$$\begin{bmatrix} \mathbf{A}^{(\alpha)} \\ \mathbf{a}_n^{(\alpha)} \end{bmatrix} \qquad \begin{bmatrix} \mathbf{A}^{(\beta)} \\ \mathbf{a}_n^{(\beta)} \end{bmatrix} \qquad \begin{bmatrix} \mathbf{A}^{(\gamma)} \\ \mathbf{a}_n^{(\gamma)} \end{bmatrix} \qquad \text{(VI.4.2)}$$

i.e., by three matrices which are the same in all columns *except* in column h, which is different for each of the three matrices. We shall suppose, moreover, that *all* coefficients are independent of scale (constant returns to scale).

Even though the three matrices (VI.4.2) differ only with respect to one column, they involve three completely different systems of prices. It might seem, at first sight, that they cannot be compared with one another. But that is not so.

---

[3] Convergence is assured by the fact that the new matrix $\mathbf{A}$ is necessarily a convergent matrix. If it were not, the economic system would not be a viable one and would fall outside the relevant field for our investigation.

We can use as the *numéraire* a commodity – commodity 1, say – which is produced in all three alternative systems, and then find the solution for the wage rate, in terms of commodity 1, in each of the three alternative systems of price equations. As we know, through this process we can eliminate all the prices and obtain three polynomial equations, such as (V.6.8), each of which expresses, for the corresponding alternative system, the wage rate as a function of the rate of profit. We thus obtain for each alternative system a particular relationship between the wage rate, in terms of commodity 1, and the rate of profit. And, since the wage rate is expressed in terms of the same commodity in all of the three price systems, those three relationships can be compared. They can even be shown on the same diagram (see Fig. VI.2). If the number of basic commodities produced in all three alternative systems is k, each of the three polynomial equations will be of degree k; and this implies that, taken two at a time, the curves representing these polynomial equations can intersect up to k times. For our purposes, of course, only intersections lying in the positive quadrant are of interest.

Suppose then that, in terms of commodity 1, the three alternative polynomial relationships between $w^{(1)}$ and π for the three techniques α, β, γ are as shown in Fig. VI.2.

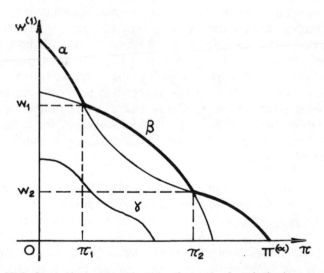

FIG. VI.2. Comparison of 3 methods for the production of a basic commodity

It will be seen immediately that γ is an obsolete technique, since it yields an outcome inferior to that of some other techniques at all possible levels of the rate of profit. Techniques α and β, by contrast, are both eligible for use, depending on the rate of profit.

It now becomes clear that the profitability criterion, while manifesting itself at the level of a single industry as the criterion leading to the choice associated with the minimum cost, manifests itself at the level of the economic system as a whole as the criterion leading to the choice of the technique which, for any given rate of profit, yields the highest wage rate, or – which is the same thing – for any given wage rate, yields the highest rate of profit.

In our example, for any rate of profit π lying in the interval $0 < \pi < \pi_1$ or $\pi_2 < \pi < \Pi^{(\alpha)}$, technique α is the most profitable one (being that which yields the highest wage rate for any predetermined rate of profit, or the highest rate of profit for any predetermined wage rate). And for every rate of profit in the interval $\pi_1 < \pi < \pi_2$, β becomes the most profitable technique. The singular points π_1 and π_2 (there are two such points in Fig. VI.2, but there could be as many as k) are points at which a switch of technique occurs (*switch points*). They represent the singular points at which the two alternative techniques α and β yield exactly the same rate of profit and the same wage rate. At such singular points either of the two techniques α and β, or any linear combination of them, is equally profitable.

Thus, considering all the possible choices over the whole economically meaningful range of variation of the rate of profit, it can be said that the profitability criterion will lead the economic system to a point lying on one of the outermost segments (or to one of the outermost points) of the curves shown in Fig. VI.2, i.e., to a point on the envelope of all the curves showing the alternative relationships between $w^{(1)}$ and π. This envelope is shown in heavy type in Fig. VI.2. It represents what we may call the *technological frontier of possible distributions of income between profits and wages*, or the technological frontier of income distribution possibilities, or, more simply still, the technological frontier.

4.3. *Analytical properties of the technological frontier.* The technological frontier of income distribution possibilities has the following remarkable properties, which we shall call propositions (i), (ii), (iii), (iv).

(i) At the switch points between techniques α and β, each commodity has the same price irrespective of whether it is produced by technique α, or by technique β, or by any linear combination of the two. In other words at points π_1 and π_2 we have $\mathbf{p}^{(\alpha)} = \mathbf{p}^{(\beta)}$.

(ii) If, at a certain rate of profit, one of the two techniques is more profitable than the other, it will yield prices, in terms of the wage rate, that are strictly *lower* than those yielded by the other technique; this being so for *all* commodities (and not just for commodity h). In our example, in the two intervals $0 \leq \pi \leq \pi_1$ and $\pi_2 \leq \pi \leq \Pi^{(\alpha)}$, we shall have $\mathbf{p}^{(\alpha)} < \mathbf{p}^{(\beta)}$, while in the interval $\pi_1 \leq \pi \leq \pi_2$, we shall have $\mathbf{p}^{(\alpha)} > \mathbf{p}^{(\beta)}$, all these prices being in terms of the wage rate.

(iii) Comparisons in terms of the w-π relations are independent of the *numéraire* used for the price system. In other words, while a change of *numéraire* will certainly change the shape of all alternative relations between w and π (as was seen in Section 6.3 of Chapter V), and therefore of the entire technological frontier, it will nevertheless leave the switch points unchanged, i.e., will leave unaltered the ordering of the various techniques on the technological frontier.

(iv) The technological frontier of the income distribution possibilities is strictly decreasing as the rate of profit increases.

These four propositions can easily be proved.

Proof of proposition (*i*). At any switch point it must necessarily be true that $p_h^{(\alpha)} = p_h^{(\beta)}$. (If $p_h^{(\alpha)} \neq p_h^{(\beta)}$ were to hold, then one of the two techniques would be more profitable than the other, contrary to the hypothesis that we are at a switch point). Since all the other industries have the same coefficients, whether for α or for β, then all the other prices must also be the same.

Proof of proposition (*ii*). For the purposes of this proof we must set $w = 1$, i.e., adopt the wage rate as *numéraire* for the price system. Suppose that technique β is in use but that, at the ruling rate of profit $\bar{\pi}$ and the prices $\mathbf{p}^{(\beta)}$, it is found that $p_h^{(\alpha)} < p_h^{(\beta)}$. Method α will then be substituted for method β. *Ex hypothesi*, the price of commodity h will strictly decrease immediately as this switch is made. But, since this price enters into the formation of all the other prices, all these other prices will also decrease. This will cause a further lowering of the price of commodity h and thus a second round of reductions in all the other prices. And so on, through an infinite but convergent series of successive rounds, as already noted in Section 4.1. Since *all* the prices are strictly decreasing in every round, the final outcome must inevitably be that *all* prices are strictly lower in terms of the wage rate. A similar proof can be given for the case in which the rate of profit is such as to render technique β more profitable than technique α.

Proof of proposition (*iii*). It has just been found that, at any given rate of profit other than at a switch point, all the prices for the chosen technique, in terms of the wage rate, are *strictly lower* than those associated with the other technique. But this implies that the wage rate for the chosen technique will be strictly greater than that associated with the other technique in terms of all commodities, i.e., *in terms of any numéraire*.

Proof of proposition (*iv*). It was seen in Section 6.3 of Chapter V that each relation between w and π is strictly decreasing as π increases (at least in the case of single-product industries). The technological frontier is made up of segments of such relations. And, if each segment is strictly decreasing, the entire frontier will necessarily be strictly decreasing.

5   The Choice of Technique in General

5.1. *The problem stated*. We can now formulate the problem of choice of technique in general terms for basic and for non-basic commodities with no restrictions as to the number of methods of production available. In general, if for each industry j ($j = 1, 2, \ldots, n - 1$), s_j alternative technical methods are available for the production of the corresponding commodity, the technology of the economic system as a whole will be represented by a whole series of alternative techniques obtained from all the possible combinations of technical methods available for the production of the $(n - 1)$ commodities. Thus relabeling these alternative techniques with the letters $\alpha, \beta, \gamma, \ldots, \omega$, the technology of the system will be represented by a series of matrices:

$$\begin{bmatrix} \mathbf{A}^{(\alpha)} \\ \mathbf{a}_n^{(\alpha)} \end{bmatrix} \quad \begin{bmatrix} \mathbf{A}^{(\beta)} \\ \mathbf{a}_n^{(\beta)} \end{bmatrix} \quad \ldots \quad \begin{bmatrix} \mathbf{A}^{(\omega)} \\ \mathbf{a}_n^{(\omega)} \end{bmatrix} \qquad \text{(VI.5.1)}$$

each of which will yield a particular system of prices, a particular maximum rate of profit, and a particular relation between w and π. Again we shall assume that all coefficients are independent of scale.

Expressing the wage rate and all prices in terms of a commodity produced in all the alternative systems, we obtain ω relations between w and π which can be shown and compared on the same diagram. We might, for example, obtain Fig. VI.3, where the wage rate has been expressed in terms of commodity 1, chosen from among the basic commodities.

We shall assume that all the techniques which are not shown in Fig. VI.3 are techniques such as δ, i.e., techniques which never appear on the outermost frontier. These techniques (in practice, the majority!) are clearly irrelevant for the problem of technical choice, either because they are technically inferior or because they embody particularly inefficient combinations of production processes.

The only techniques relevant to technical choice are those which contribute to the outermost envelope of all the relations between w and π, namely, in our example, techniques: α, β, γ, τ. These techniques follow one another in order as the rate of profit rises and gets across the switch points π_1, π_2, π_3. At a final switch point, however, there is a reswitch of technique. Technique α comes back to become the most profitable technique associated with the highest rate of profit. Thus in our example the technological frontier exhibits one reswitching of technique. (In general, of course, there could be many such reswitchings; more precisely, for any pair of techniques the number of switches and reswitches could be any number up to the degree of the polynomial obtained by equating the two corresponding relations between w and π.)

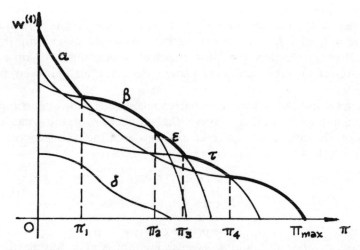

FIG. VI.3. The technological frontier of the income distribution possibilities

In Fig. VI.3, too, the segments of the various curves which appear on the outer envelope are shown in heavy type. This envelope represents, for the economic system as a whole, what we have called the technological frontier of income distribution possibilities.

5.2. *Logical priority of the choice of technique for basic commodities.* It is to be noted that the alternative techniques which appear in Fig. VI.3 refer to basic commodities only. In fact, if two techniques were to differ only with respect to the method of production for a non-basic commodity, they would appear in Fig. VI.3 as if they were the same technique. There is only one exception to this rule, namely, the case in which the non-basic commodity produced by the two alternative methods is actually used as the *numéraire* for the price system. Even then, however, all the other non-basic commodities (provided, of course, that they do not enter into the production of the non-basic commodity used as the *numéraire*) would continue to be entirely irrelevant to the technological frontier of Fig. VI.3. In order to avoid exceptional cases the *numéraire*-commodity has therefore been assumed to be a basic commodity.

The meaning of all this is, quite simply, that the choice of technique for basic commodities is logically prior to the choice of the methods of production for non-basic commodities. The technical choices for the latter commodities can be made at a (logically) subsequent stage, according to the procedure explained in Section 3.1 above, after the technique for the basic commodities has already been chosen.

5.3. *Multiplicity of methods of production in all industries.* It must now be considered whether, and to what extent, the results obtained in Section 4.3, with respect to two techniques which differ only in one method of production (i.e., for matrices which differ in only one column), can be extended to the general case. We shall proceed in two stages.

Suppose first that all the alternative techniques which contribute to the technological frontier involve the production of the same commodities. In this case the matrices representing the economically relevant techniques, in our example

$$\begin{bmatrix} \mathbf{A}^{(\alpha)} \\ \mathbf{a}_n^{(\alpha)} \end{bmatrix} \qquad \begin{bmatrix} \mathbf{A}^{(\beta)} \\ \mathbf{a}_n^{(\beta)} \end{bmatrix} \qquad \begin{bmatrix} \mathbf{A}^{(\varepsilon)} \\ \mathbf{a}_n^{(\varepsilon)} \end{bmatrix} \qquad \begin{bmatrix} \mathbf{A}^{(\tau)} \\ \mathbf{a}_n^{(\tau)} \end{bmatrix} \qquad\qquad \text{(VI.5.2)}$$

and hence also the alternative price vectors $\mathbf{p}^{(\alpha)}$, $\mathbf{p}^{(\beta)}$, $\mathbf{p}^{(\varepsilon)}$, $\mathbf{p}^{(\tau)}$ all have the same *number* of columns, even though, of course, the matrices of technical coefficients can differ in more than one column.

It may now be noted that, if a technique is to be on the technological frontier, no price associated with it can be greater, in terms of the wage rate, than the corresponding price obtainable with any other technique. For, if that were not so, i.e., if even only one price obtainable with another technique were lower, the method of production for the corresponding commodity would prove more profitable and would be adopted in preference to the original method; which contradicts the initial assumption that the technique considered is on the technological frontier. Hence, at all rates of profit for which α is the most profitable technique, in terms of the wage rate,

$$\mathbf{p}^{(\alpha)} \le \mathbf{p}^{(x)}, \qquad\qquad x = \beta, \varepsilon, \tau \qquad\qquad \text{(VI.5.3)}$$

Similar propositions hold for each of the other techniques, at the rates of profit for which each of them is the most profitable technique.

It follows, by exactly the same argument, that at every switch point the two techniques concerned must yield exactly the same prices for *all* commodities (and not merely the same wage rate and the same rate of profit). This means, in our example, that

$$\mathbf{p}^{(\alpha)} = \mathbf{p}^{(\beta)} \qquad \text{at switch point } \pi_1$$

$$\mathbf{p}^{(\beta)} = \mathbf{p}^{(\varepsilon)} \qquad \text{at switch point } \pi_2$$

$$\mathbf{p}^{(\varepsilon)^{\cdot}} = \mathbf{p}^{(\tau)} \qquad \text{at switch point } \pi_3 \qquad\qquad\text{(VI.5.4)}$$

$$\mathbf{p}^{(\tau)} = \mathbf{p}^{(\alpha)} \qquad \text{at switch point } \pi_4$$

in terms of *any numéraire*.

A further result may now be noted. As pointed out in Chapter V, Section 3, each price vector is the solution of a system of $(n - 1)$ equations in which, after one price has been fixed arbitrarily, there remains only one degree of freedom. This implies that if at profit rate π_1 the two alternative systems α and β (adjacent to each other on the technological frontier) are to yield exactly the same solution for all prices, they can, in general, differ in only one equation (except for the peculiar cases of equation systems with the rare coincidence of having identical solutions). In other words, each of the two alternative price systems can be made determinate by the addition of one single equation (which could come from the other system). This would determine the rate of profit at which the two systems become equally profitable (i.e., have the same solutions). The implication is that the two alternative matrices

$$\begin{bmatrix} \mathbf{A}^{(\alpha)} \\ \mathbf{a}_n^{(\alpha)} \end{bmatrix}, \quad \begin{bmatrix} \mathbf{A}^{(\beta)} \\ \mathbf{a}_n^{(\beta)} \end{bmatrix}$$

differ, in general, in *only one* column (leaving aside the peculiar case just mentioned). By precisely the same argument the two matrices

$$\begin{bmatrix} \mathbf{A}^{(\beta)} \\ \mathbf{a}_n^{(\beta)} \end{bmatrix}, \quad \begin{bmatrix} \mathbf{A}^{(\varepsilon)} \\ \mathbf{a}_n^{(\varepsilon)} \end{bmatrix}$$

will also differ, in general, in only one column. And so will the two matrices

$$\begin{bmatrix} \mathbf{A}^{(\varepsilon)} \\ \mathbf{a}_n^{(\varepsilon)} \end{bmatrix}, \quad \begin{bmatrix} \mathbf{A}^{(\tau)} \\ \mathbf{a}_n^{(\tau)} \end{bmatrix} \quad \text{and the two matrices} \quad \begin{bmatrix} \mathbf{A}^{(\tau)} \\ \mathbf{a}_n^{(\tau)} \end{bmatrix}, \quad \begin{bmatrix} \mathbf{A}^{(\alpha)} \\ \mathbf{a}_n^{(\alpha)} \end{bmatrix}$$

The conclusion to be drawn is that, on the technological frontier, although the various techniques may differ in more than one method of production (and the corresponding matrices in more than one column), those techniques which are adjacent at a switch point will differ, in general, in only one method of production (and the corresponding matrices will differ in only one column). In other words, as one gradually moves along the technological frontier, the methods of production will change, in general, one at a time: only one method of production will change at each switch point.

There remains, of course, the exceptional case of coincidental solutions. This corresponds to the very special case in which more than two curves happen to intersect at exactly the same point (as shown in Fig. VI.4).   Even in this very special case, however, the various curves which intersect at exactly the same point (yielding, at this point, exactly the same price) can, in general, be so ordered as to make only one method of production change between adjacent curves. Hence the necessary comparison can always be made between matrices which differ in only one column.

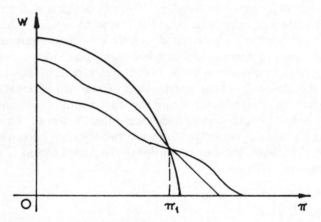

Fig. VI.4. Exceptional case of 3 technical methods which are equi-profitable at the same rate of profit π_1

The remarkable upshot of this analysis is that, on the technological frontier, one is always led back to the comparison of two techniques which differ in only one method of production (two interindustry matrices **A** and two labor vectors $\mathbf{a}_n$ which differ in only one column). And this means that one is always led back to the case considered in Section 4.3 above. The conclusion is thus that all the propositions stated in Section 4.3 for the particular case in which alternative methods of production are available in only one industry are valid for the more general case in which no restrictions are placed on either the number of known methods of production or the number of industries with alternative methods of production.

5.4. *The case of different commodities being required by different techniques.* It was assumed in the preceding section that all the alternative techniques produce exactly the same commodities. But this might not be so. Two alternative methods for the production of the same consumption good, for example, might use completely different capital goods.

Suppose then that technique α produces m commodities and that, of these m commodities, q are specific to technique α and $(m - q)$ are common to technique α and technique β. In the same way suppose that technique β produces $(m - q + g)$ commodities, where g is the number of commodities specific to technique β (and thus not produced with technique α). The matrix $\mathbf{A}^{(\alpha)}$ thus has m columns and the matrix $\mathbf{A}^{(\beta)}$ has $(m - q + g)$ columns. The two matrices are not directly comparable.

It may be noted, however, that in order to obtain and compare the relations between w and π it is not necessary that the corresponding matrices have the same number of rows and columns. To make a comparison, as in Fig. VI.3, all that is required is that the wage rate be expressed in terms of a commodity which is common to all the alternative systems which are to be compared. The only effect on the analysis presented above is that any comparison of alternative prices must of course, be confined to the prices of those commodities which are common to the systems being compared.[4]

We can, however, adopt an analytically more elegant procedure.[5] In the case of the two techniques α and β just referred to, one can augment the matrix $\mathbf{A}^{(\alpha)}$ with g extra columns and rows corresponding to the methods of production for the g commodities produced only by technique β; and in the same way one can augment the matrix $\mathbf{A}^{(\beta)}$ with q extra columns and rows relating to the methods of production for the q commodities produced only by technique α. One thus obtains two augmented matrices, which may provisionally be called $\mathbf{A}^{(\alpha+)}$ and $\mathbf{A}^{(\beta+)}$, which are of the same order, i.e., which have the same number of rows and columns. One must naturally adopt an analogous procedure for the vectors of labor coefficients, obtaining two (row) vectors $\mathbf{a}_n^{(\alpha+)}$ and $\mathbf{a}_n^{(\beta+)}$, which also have the same number of columns.

---

[4] It may be useful to point out that this is precisely the case of the simple example, so widely used in recent economic literature, of two alternative economic systems, each of which is composed of two industries, producing respectively a consumption good (which is the same for both systems) and a capital good (which is different in the two systems). See, for example, Hicks [7], Morishima [13], Spaventa [25], [26]. In such an example, the alternative prices that can be compared are *only* those of the consumption good (the only one that is common to both systems).

[5] This procedure was suggested by Sraffa [27, pp. 82–83], and followed by Bharadwaj [1].

The economic meaning of this formal procedure is that the g commodities produced only in system β – which will, in general, be basic commodities in that system – are introduced into the system α^+ as non-basic commodities, since they are not used in the production of the other commodities. And this can always be done. (As has been seen, non-basic commodities have no influence whatever on the relation between w and π.) In the same way the q commodities produced only in system α are introduced as non-basic commodities in system β^+. It follows that the two alternative matrices

$$\begin{bmatrix} \mathbf{A}^{(\alpha+)} \\ \mathbf{a}_n^{(\alpha+)} \end{bmatrix} \qquad \begin{bmatrix} \mathbf{A}^{(\beta+)} \\ \mathbf{a}_n^{(\beta+)} \end{bmatrix}$$

(after appropriate rearrangement of their rows and columns) now give rise to two price vectors which have exactly the same *number* of components and which refer to exactly the same commodities.

It actually becomes quite unnecessary, at this point, to use any special terminology or symbols. Given that one can always adopt the analytical device of augmenting the various matrices, one can simply reinterpret the original matrices (VI.5.2) as matrices which have already been augmented, whenever that is necessary. When this procedure is adopted, there is no longer any need to distinguish between the case in which each commodity is produced in every alternative system and the case in which some commodities are common to all the systems, while others are specific to a particular system. Using this analytical device, we can always write the matrices (VI.5.2), for the general case, in such a way that they are all of the same order, i.e., having the same number of rows and columns. They will thus give rise to a series of alternative price vectors $\mathbf{p}^{(\alpha)}$, $\mathbf{p}^{(\beta)}$, $\mathbf{p}^{(\varepsilon)}$, $\mathbf{p}^{(\tau)}$ which will necessarily refer to exactly the same commodities.

We are therefore led back to the case examined in the previous section and, through it in turn, to the even simpler case considered in Section 4.3.

5.5. *A synthesis.* The remarkable implication of the preceding analysis is that the four propositions set out at the end of Section 4.3, although derived for the simplified case of two techniques which differ in only one method of production, are in fact valid for the far more general case in which no restriction is placed on the number of methods of production or the number and the kinds of commodities produced with the various techniques.

To conclude, the following propositions continue to hold for the general case: (i) at each switch point between two alternative techniques which are adjacent on the technological frontier, these two alternative techniques yield exactly the same prices for every commodity; (ii) at any rate of profit at which there is a single most profitable technique, that technique will yield prices, in terms of the wage rate, which are strictly lower than those associated with any other technique, for *all* commodities (provided only that there is at least one basic commodity common to all the alternative techniques); (iii) comparisons in terms of the w-π relations are independent of the *numéraire* used for the price system; (iv) the technological frontier of income distribution possibilities is strictly decreasing as the rate of profit increases.

For rigor's sake it is necessary to add that these results do depend on the assumptions of no joint production and constant coefficients. If these assumptions were not satisfied, the analysis would become more complicated. We shall come back to this point any time that it becomes relevant to the discussion that follows.

6 "Nonsubstitution"

6.1. *Introductory remarks.* The analysis of the switching of technique as the rate of profit is changed, which has been discussed above, has had some quite upsetting effects upon traditional economic theory. For all its simplicity, it has revealed that some of the most deep-rooted convictions of traditional theory are devoid of any foundation.

6.2. *"Nonsubstitution theorems."* The first result that may be brought out is that technical choices are far less dependent on economic variables than traditional theory had led us to suppose. The only economic variable that proves to be relevant in this connection is the rate of profit. Indeed, as has been seen, once the technology is given and the rate of profit is fixed, the price structure is determined.

This simple result came as a surprise to many economists. For traditional economic theory had always maintained that the choice of technique depends on initial endowments and on the composition of demand. More specifically, it had maintained that if, for example, demand rose for a consumer good produced by methods which are highly capital intensive, while, at the same time, demand fell for a consumer good produced by methods which are low capital intensive that would have caused a substitution of less capital intensive methods for more capital intensive methods, causing all prices to change. But one can verify immediately that, in the new equilibrium position, that will not occur at all. Given the rate of profit, the technique proves to be determined. Thus all prices are found to be determined, independently of the composition of demand and of the total amount of capital per worker. In other words, a change in the composition of demand induces no substitution among the inputs.

This result, which has been presented in various ways,[6] has become well known in the recent economic literature by the rather pompous name of the *nonsubstitution theorem* (or also, to compound the confusion, as the *substitution theorem*).

6.3. *Theoretical irrelevance of changes in the input proportions, and thus of substitution, in the general case.* The basis on which the traditional claim on substitution was made will be examined in detail in the *Appendix* to this chapter.

Here we can take a further step and point out how the title itself, the "nonsubstitution theorem," is inevitably misleading. When one talks of a "nonsubstitution theorem" or, even worse, of a "substitution theorem" (meaning by that a situation of zero substitution), one somehow conveys the idea that substitution is to be taken for granted, as the normal rule. So that, if one ever encounters a case of nonsubstitution, one immediately tends to associate it with an extreme situation, or a freak case; and one begins to look for the special assumptions that must lie behind it.

In our analysis of the switching of technique we have seen that the four propositions of Sections 4.3 and 5.5 have been reached on the assumptions of no joint production and constant coefficients. It has thus appeared normal to attribute the phenomenon of nonsubstitution to these two "very special" assumptions.

But this has been a logical *non-sequitur*. When there is joint production and/or nonconstant coefficients, the problem of choice of technique becomes more complicated, but this does not mean that we should go back to the traditional concept of "substitution". We are moving here in a theoretical world of production of commodities by means of commodities, which is different from the traditional world of given scarce resources.

Of course, with joint production and/or nonconstant coefficients, a change in the composition of demand may indeed require a change of technique. However, nothing can be said *a priori* about the direction in which the input proportions will change. Replacing one technique with another means changing a whole series of inputs (a vector of inputs) and, with joint production, even a whole vector of outputs. This means that we have no way of stating anything *a priori* about how any single input will change when the technique changes. It may change in one direction or in the opposite direction; it may even disappear altogether or appear anew. More specifically, the *direction of change* of the input

---

[6] Statements and proofs of the "nonsubstitution theorem," i.e. essentially of propositions (i), (ii), (iii), (iv) of Sections 4.3 and 5.5, are contained in Samuelson [18], [19], Morishima [11], Mirrlees [10], Levhari [8]. See also Goodwin [6].

proportions is something that cannot be related unambiguously to the change of technique and, most of all, something that cannot be related unambiguously to the changes of prices.

This is a crucial point. The whole traditional theory had maintained precisely the contrary. We had been accustomed to think of changes of technique and changes of input proportions as if they were the same thing. For we had been accustomed to expect that a change in a specific direction of the input proportions is always and necessarily associated with a change in the opposite direction of the corresponding relative prices. This traditional belief is false.

The choice of technique is *not* a choice of input proportions (which move in their own unpredictable way); the two must not be confused with each other. More precisely, a change of technique will indeed entail a change of prices, but there is no unidirectional way in which we may relate, to this change of prices, changes in the corresponding input proportions. In this context, therefore, the very idea of "substitution among the production inputs," so central to the traditional theory, loses all conceptual sense.[7]

To conclude, in general (and not only in the special case of no joint production and constant coefficients), the traditional notion of "substitution" becomes useless or irrelevant. Change in the input proportions with which the notion of substitution had been associated have no theoretical role to play; they provide no guide to saying anything on the direction of change of the technique of production or on the direction of change of relative prices.

7   Reswitching of Technique and Traditional Capital Theory

7.1. *Samuelson's "surrogate production function."* The worst surprises for advocates of the traditional theory have, however, come in the field of capital theory. Even those economists who had admitted nonsubstitution, when the rate of profit is given, continued to maintain nevertheless that substitution between capital and labor would inevitably have to take place, in any case, as the rate of profit *varied*, in accordance with the orthodox idea of a production function.

As seen in Chapter I, this function, which has been a major feature of the marginal theory of production since the beginning of this century, expresses the net product as a given technological function of

---

[7] A way to conceal the problem might, of course, be to call "perverse substitution" those changes in the input proportions that are in the opposite direction to the one which traditional theory claimed to be the case. But that would obviously only be a verbose and complicated way of admitting that the systematic relation, traditionally taken for granted, does not exist.

two factors of production, labor and capital, in such a way that, as the factor proportions vary (i.e., as one factor is "substituted" for the other), the ratio between the wage rate and the rate of profit varies in the opposite direction. In this way the wage rate and the rate of profit are presented as the "prices of the productive factors." They appear to play the typical role of any other price in traditional theory, namely, that of being related to the corresponding physical quantity by an inverse, monotonic relation and thus of representing, in a sense, an "index of scarcity." Professor Samuelson gave a most vivid picture of this traditional concept with his "surrogate production function," a construction derived from a multisector multitechnique linear model, and yet evincing all the basic features of an orthodox production function.[8]

Here again, however, it is not difficult to verify, from the very analysis of the previous pages, that traditional theory had led us astray.

[8] Briefly, Samuelson [20] proposed the following "model." Suppose an infinite number of techniques, each of which is represented by a *linear* relation between w and π. (See Fig. V1.5). Then the envelope of the family of straight lines thereby obtained, i.e. the technological frontier of the income distribution possibilities, shows all the properties of an isoquant of a traditional production function (see pp. 27–32). By moving along the technological frontier (as the rate of profit decreases and the wage rate increases) one goes over to techniques which can unambiguously be said to be increasingly capital intensive, as they require an increasing capital/output ratio and an increasing capital/labor ratio. Consistently, Samuelson called this technological frontier the "factor price frontier."

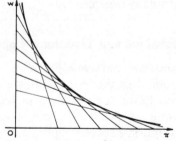

FIG. VI.5. Samuelson's "surrogate production function"

Unfortunately, the hypothesis of linear w-π relationships is extremely restrictive. As we have seen already (pp. 86–87), it restricts the analysis to the purely hypothetical case in which all technical methods of production happen to require exactly the same capital intensity. The curious thing about this hypothesis is that it is precisely the same restrictive hypothesis which led both Ricardo and Marx into difficulties and prevented them from extending their theories of value to the general case. Samuelson has fallen into the same trap. It should be noted that the uniform-capital-intensity hypothesis crucially entails constant prices as income distribution varies. In analytical terms this makes it equivalent to the assumption of a one-commodity world. See Garegnani [4], [5], Spaventa [25], Pasinetti [15].

7.2. *Nonexistence in general of a monotonic relation between rate of profit and capital/output (and capital/labor) ratios.* A close examination of the results already obtained shows without any doubt that the traditional belief in the existence of an inverse, monotonic relation between the rate of profit and the total quantity of capital per worker (and between the rate of profit and net product per worker) is entirely devoid of any foundation.

This results from the simple fact, which has become well known as the "reswitching of techniques" phenomenon, that the w-π curves corresponding to alternative techniques can intersect more than once.[9] As already pointed out (Sections 4.2 and 5.1 in this chapter and Chapter V, Section 6.3), the relations between w and π are polynomial equations of degree k (where k is the number of basic commodities). Taken two at a time, they can therefore intersect up to k times. This implies that a given technique, after having been discarded, can return to the technological frontier many times as the rate of profit increases. The significance of these switches and reswitches can be shown by using the same diagrams as above. Reconsider techniques α and β in Fig. VI.2 and suppose, for simplicity, that the economic system is in a stationary state. One can read off the net product per worker associated with technique α (in terms of commodity 1) as the intercept of curve α on the vertical axis (since the net product per worker equals the wage rate when $\pi = 0$); in the same way, one can read off the net product per worker associated with technique β as the intercept of curve β on the vertical axis. Now, at switch point π_1, the profit per worker for each technique can be read off from the vertical axis as the difference between the intercept of the corresponding curve and the point w_1. And, since the rate of profit is the same for both techniques, it follows that technique α, which yields a higher profit per

[9] Well aware of the crucial importance, for the validity of the "surrogate production function," of the assumption that any two w-π curves intersect each other only once, Samuelson suggested, and a pupil of his, Levhari [8], thought he had proved, a "non-switching theorem." This theorem stated that, even in the case of nonlinear relations, any two w-π curves could not intersect more than once. But the nonswitching theorem was proved false by the author of the present notes, in a short paper presented at the first World Congress of the Econometric Society (Rome, September 1965), then enlarged and published as [15]. That paper stimulated a whole series of other papers which, although written later, were published together (Levhari and Samuelson [9], Morishima [12], Bruno, Burmeister, and Sheshinski [2]). The question debated in these papers was whether an irreducible, rather than a reducible, interindustry matrix could affect any of the reswitching conclusions. But all the authors had to conclude that the reswitching possibilities would not be affected at all. To this discussion Garegnani added his own, independent, contribution [4]. After the publication of these articles, the generality of the reswitching of technique phenomenon has become a well-acknowledged result.

worker than technique β, must also have a higher total amount of capital per worker. The same can be said of switch point π_2. Thus at point π_1 an increase in the rate of profit involves the transition to a technique with a *lower* amount of capital per worker (and with a lower net product per worker), while at switch point π_2 an increase in the rate of profit involves the transition to a technique with a *higher* amount of capital per worker (and with a higher net output per worker).[10] This invalidates, in a conclusive way, the inverse, monotonic relations which traditional theory assumed to exist between the rate of profit and the "quantity" of capital and between the rate of profit and net output per worker. (Cf. Chapter I, Section 5.3.)

Further theoretical studies on reswitching of techniques have shown that nonmonotonic relations between the rate of profit and the amount of capital, and between the rate of profit and net output per man, can occur even in the absence of any "reswitching" of technique on the technological frontier.[11] This means that "reswitching" is not even a necessary condition for the invalidation of a conviction which the traditional theory of capital took absolutely for granted and as completely self-evident.

It is important to emphasize that, unlike the "nonsubstitution theorem," none of these propositions is at all dependent on the assumption of constant technical coefficients or of no joint production.

The truly remarkable and general conclusion is that, contrary to what was thought until recently, one can say nothing *a priori* about the direction of changes in the capital/labor ratio and in the net output/labor ratio as the rate of profit is changed.

7.3. *The marginal theories of capital and income distribution called into question.* The nonexistence in general of an inverse, monotonic relation between the rate of profit and the ratios of capital to labor and net output to labor carries with it a whole series of negative implications of a rather remarkable character.

[10] Note that these propositions are valid whatever the convention for measuring the "quantity" of capital may be.

[11] This can be seen from Fig. VI.3 by taking advantage of the device used at the beginning of this section with reference to Fig. VI.2. By supposing a stationary economic system one can see immediately from Fig. VI.3 that technique β, though reaching the technological frontier before technique ε, entails a net output per worker lower than that of technique ε. Confining our analysis to techniques α, β, ε only, we can see that at switch point π_1, an increase in the rate of profit makes the system switch to a technique with a lower capital/labor ratio; and at switch point π_2 an increase in the rate of profit makes the system switch to a technique with a higher capital/labor ratio. The rate of profit and the capital/labor ratio are therefore not related in a monotonic way, although the three techniques α, β, ε appear in succession and without any reswitching on the technological frontier. For further details see Pasinetti [15, p. 516n], Spaventa [25].

First of all, it destroys for ever the fundamental idea of traditional capital theory – as developed by Böhm-Bawerk, Wicksell, John Bates Clark, and a whole school of marginal economists – that the existing techniques of production could be synthetically expressed by a production function, which would relate the "factors" capital and labor to the net product in such a way as to establish a well-defined relation between variations in the distribution of income between profits and wages and variations in capital per worker and net output per worker. Such a production function, although widespread in the economic literature for more than half a century, is revealed to be an illusion. Very simply, it does not exist. It is impossible to construct, for heterogeneous capital goods, any single, equivalent "quantity" an increase in which could be systematically associated with its falling "marginal productivity."

Furthermore, the finding that, as the rate of profit falls, techniques of production do not succeed one another in order of increasing capital intensity deprives of all meaning the other fundamental idea of traditional capital theory, namely, the idea that, given the technology, a process of *substitution between capital and labor* must take place, as the ratio between the rate of profit and the wage rate varies in the opposite direction. All this does not, of course, mean that one should ignore the existence of processes of substitution between capital and labor; quite the contrary! Such processes are indeed of great importance in any industrial system and are characteristic of all growing economies. What all this merely means is that we have been mistaken in the past in attributing the process of substitution of capital for labor to changes in the rate of profit. An explanation of the phenomenon must be sought in other directions.[12]

Finally, the outcomes relating to the "reswitching of technique" have also put into question the traditional idea that the rate of profit represents the "price" of, and hence an optimal means of rationing, "capital" as a factor of production. Thus a critical reexamination has also become necessary in relation to this idea, which had appeared for a long time to be one of the most interesting aspects of the marginal theory of capital. It should be added that, along with the marginal theory of capital, the entire structure of the marginal theory of income distribution – as proposed by Wicksteed, John Bates Clark, Wicksell, and a long train of other marginal economists who believed profits and wages to be governed by the "marginal productivities" of the factors "capital" and "labor" – is found as a consequence to rest on nonexistent or illusory foundations.

[12] In [14], for instance, the process of substitution of capital for labor is explained entirely as a consequence of technical progress.

8 Misconceptions Concerning an Accounting Expression

8.1. *Solow's "rate of return."* The debate on the reswitching of technique has had a polemical sequel concerning an accounting expression for the rate of profit, which has given new life to the illusion that, at least in a certain sense, there exists a marginal productivity of capital for society as a whole.

In any linear production model, whenever two economic systems α and β happen to have both a common wage rate and common prices at a given rate of profit (although they may differ with respect to both the total quantity of capital per worker and net output per worker), the common rate of profit, $\pi^\dagger$, can be equally well expressed by any one of the following accounting expressions:

$$\pi^\dagger = \pi_\alpha = \pi_\beta = \frac{\mathbf{p}^\dagger \mathbf{y}_\alpha - w^\dagger}{\mathbf{p}^\dagger \mathbf{k}_\alpha} = \frac{\mathbf{p}^\dagger \mathbf{y}_\beta - w^\dagger}{\mathbf{p}^\dagger \mathbf{k}_\beta} = \frac{\mathbf{p}^\dagger(\mathbf{y}_\beta - \mathbf{y}_\alpha)}{\mathbf{p}^\dagger(\mathbf{k}_\beta - \mathbf{k}_\alpha)}$$

(VI.8.1)

where $\mathbf{p}^\dagger$ denotes the (row) vector of prices common to systems α and β; $w^\dagger$ denotes the wage rate common to the two systems; $\mathbf{y}_\alpha$ and $\mathbf{y}_\beta$ denote the (column) vectors of the quantities of commodities making up the per capita net outputs of systems α and β, respectively; and $\mathbf{k}_\alpha$ and $\mathbf{k}_\beta$ denote the (column) vectors of the quantities of commodities making up the per capita capital for systems α and β, respectively.

Systems α and β might be two economic systems which use two different techniques but which are at a switch point (and thus prove to be equally profitable), or they might be two economic systems which use exactly the same technique but produce net outputs of two different compositions (and thus require, at prices $\mathbf{p}^\dagger$, two different total amounts of capital).

The last of expressions (VI.8.1) has been the misleading one. Solow,[13] by harking back to Irving Fisher,[14] believed that

$$\pi^\dagger = \frac{\mathbf{p}^\dagger(\mathbf{y}_\beta - \mathbf{y}_\alpha)}{\mathbf{p}^\dagger(\mathbf{k}_\beta - \mathbf{k}_\alpha)}$$

(VI.8.2)

could be interpreted by saying that the rate of profit $\pi^\dagger$ measures "the social rate of return to saving" on a transition from the system with a lower, to the system with a higher quantity of capital. The basic

[13] Solow [22], [23].

[14] Fisher [3].

argument has been that society, by abstaining from current consumption of amount $\mathbf{p}^{\dagger}(\mathbf{k}_{\alpha} - \mathbf{k}_{\beta})$, which might be expressed in terms of corn for example, and by adding it to the means of production, could obtain in perpetuity an increase in net output, and thus in possible consumption, of $\mathbf{p}^{\dagger}(\mathbf{y}_{\alpha} - \mathbf{y}_{\beta})$, which could also be expressed in terms of corn. Looking at the whole thing in terms of "abstentions" from consumption, or current "sacrifices," and future "gains" of consumption, it was thus thought possible to see in (VI.8.2) a "technocratic notion"[15] and to assert that the "market rate [of interest] measures the 'net productivity of capital.' "[16]

8.2. *An alternative verbal expression for* "*rate of profit.*" It may be noted immediately that the denominator of an expression for the rate of profit (or for the rate of interest) can always be called "today's abstention from consumption," while the numerator can always be called the "perpetual future increase in consumption." In fact it can always be said that someone abstains from consumption when he deposits $100 in the bank, and that he can then increase his consumption every time that he receives, at the end of the year, $5 as interest at 5%. In saying that, one does nothing more than simply give a definition of what the rate of interest is, without, however, giving any explanation of it whatsoever.

In the same way, by calling the denominator of (VI.8.2) "today's abstention from consumption" and the numerator "future increase in consumption," one does no more than define that rate of profit at which the two techniques α and β are equally profitable. One thereby obtains no concept which is new or independent of the rate of profit, since what appears on the left side of the equality sign is not different from what appears on its right side, even if the latter is written in a more complicated way.

For (VI.8.2) to provide a "technocratic notion," i.e., a concept which is distinct from, and can serve to explain, the rate of profit, the denominator of (VI.8.2) would have to represent unambiguously an "increment of capital in the economic system as a whole," and its numerator would have to represent unambiguously an "increment of total net product." Only then could (IV.8.2) be likened to the traditional notion of the "marginal productivity of capital," which is, by definition, a *physical concept*. But this is obviously not the case in (VI.8.2). This expression involves an *evaluation* of both the "abstention from consumption" and the "gain in consumption" in terms of a

---

[15] Solow [22, p. 17].

[16] Samuelson [21, p. 580]. See also Bruno, Burmeister, and Sheshinski [2, pp. 551–552].

complete system of prices. It therefore cannot have an unambiguous meaning for society as a whole.[17,18]

More precisely, as we know from the reswitching of technique analysis, when α and β are two economic systems which use two different techniques for the same physical change from α to β, there can be up to k price systems and hence up to k rates of profit which satisfy expression (VI.8.2).[19] When, moreover, α and β are two economic systems using the same technique to produce two net outputs of different compositions, there is not even a finite but an infinitely large family of price systems and rates of profit which satisfy (VI.8.2). In that case, in fact, *every* rate of profit can be expressed by (VI.8.2). The notion of the "rate of return for society as a whole," which has been associated with (VI.8.2), could hardly turn out to be more vacuous. It is a concept which is totally devoid of any autonomous content, being simply an alternative verbal expression to denote a particular rate of profit.[20]

[17] It appears therefore to be one of the various "spurious" versions (as Sraffa called them [27, p. vi]), of the notion of marginal productivity.

[18] Solow [23], [24] claimed that, in any linear model in which there is only one consumption good but many capital goods, his notion of "social rate of return to saving" has the remarkable property of expressing abstentions from, and gains of, consumption in physical terms. But we may remark: (i) if there is one single consumption good, *ex hypothesi*, then "abstentions" from, and "gains" of, consumption cannot indeed but refer to the same consumption good, by definition; (ii) yet that does not imply at all that "if there is only one consumption good, the rate of return is a 'physical' concept" [24, p. 425]. This proposition of Solow's is false. For at each switch point between any two techniques α and β the whole price structure is different, although the physical change of technique is the same. This means that we obtain a different "rate of return," i.e., different "abstentions" from, and "gains" of, consumptions, in terms of the same consumption good, at each one of the various switch points. And clearly if, *for the same physical change* of technique, there can be many rates of return, the "rate of return" cannot be a "physical concept." (See, for details, Pasinetti [17]).

[19] We may note that, for expression (V1.8.2) to be used, the switch point between any two techniques α and β need not even be on the technological frontier! For instance,

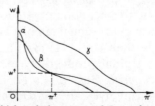

FIG. VI.6. Case in which techniques α and β are dominated by technique γ

consider a case such as that represented in Fig. V1.6. Switch point $\pi\dagger$, between α and β, is dominated by technique γ. Yet such a switch point $(w\dagger, \pi\dagger)$ is characterized by a system of prices at which the two techniques α and β are equally profitable; and at such prices the rate of profit $\pi\dagger$ can be represented by expression (VI.8.2).

[20] A detailed analysis may be found in [16].

9 Concluding Remarks

It has not often happened in economic theory that an analysis as simple as that concerning the switches of technique has had such disastrous effects on the notions of traditional theory.

Keynesian analysis had made us aware, for some time, of the exaggerated importance which traditional theory attributed to the rate of interest as a regulator of savings. Another sharp warning has now been sounded. The importance attributed to the rate of profit (and in equilibrium to the market rate of interest) as a regulator of the capital intensity of investment has also been shown to be exaggerated.

It follows that a series of critical reexaminations and validations of basic ideas has now become essential. Ideas which, for more than half a century, appeared to be fundamental to economic theory, such as that of "capital" as a factor of production, of the rate of profit as the "price" and hence the optimal rationer of the factor "capital," of the production function in terms of capital and labour, of the marginal productivity of capital, etc., have been shown to have defective or even nonexistent foundations. Unfortunately, current economic literature is full of these concepts, and it will not be easy to rid it of them quickly.

Indeed it seems that, for some time to come, progress in the theory of capital and income distribution will only be possible – to use an expression coined by Samuelson in another context[21] – "by the negative act of dumping ballast."

References

[1] Bharadwaj, Krishna, "On the Maximum Number of Switches between Two Production Systems," *Schweizerische Zeitschrift für Volkswirtschaft und Statistik*, 1970, pp. 409–429.

[2] Bruno, Michael, Burmeister, Edwin, and Sheshinski, Etyan, "The Nature and Implications of the Reswitching of Techniques," *Quarterly Journal of Economics*, 1966, pp. 526–553.

[3] Fisher, Irving, *The Theory of Interest*, New York: Macmillan, 1930.

[4] Garegnani, Pierangelo, "Switching of Techniques," *Quarterly Journal of Economics*, 1966, pp. 555–567.

[5] ———, "Heterogeneous Capital, the Production Function and the Theory of Distribution," *Review of Economic Studies*, 1970, pp. 407–438.

[6] Goodwin, Richard M., *Elementary Economics from the Higher Standpoint*, Cambridge: Cambridge University Press, 1970.

[21] P. A. Samuelson, *Collected Scientific Papers*, Cambridge, Mass.: MIT Press, 1972, Vol. III, p. 19.

[7] Hicks, John R., *Capital and Growth*, Oxford: Clarendon Press, 1965.

[8] Levhari, David, "A Nonsubstitution Theorem and Switching of Techniques," *Quarterly Journal of Economics*, 1965, pp. 98–105.

[9] Levhari, David, and Samuelson, Paul A., "The Nonswitching Theorem Is False," *Quarterly Journal of Economics*, 1966, pp. 518–519.

[10] Mirrlees, James A., "The Dynamic Nonsubstitution Theorem," *Review of Economic Studies*, 1969, pp. 67–76.

[11] Morishima, Michio, *Equilibrium Stability and Growth*, Oxford: Clarendon Press, 1964.

[12] ———, "Refutation of the Nonswitching Theorem," *Quarterly Journal of Economics*, 1966, pp. 520–525.

[13] ———, *Theory of Economic Growth*, Oxford: Clarendon Press, 1969.

[14] Pasinetti, Luigi, "A New Theoretical Approach to the Problems of Economic Growth," *Pontificiae Academiae Scientiarum Scripta Varia*, No. 28, Vatican City: 1965, pp. 571–696. (Republished in *The Econometric Approach to Development Planning*, Amsterdam, North-Holland Publ. Co., 1965).

[15] ———, "Changes in the Rate of Profit and Switches of Techniques," *Quarterly Journal of Economics*, 1966, pp. 503–517.

[16] ———, "Switches of Techniques and the 'Rate of Return' in Capital Theory," *Economic Journal*, 1969, pp. 508–531.

[17] ———, "Again on Capital Theory and Solow's 'Rate to Return,'" *Economic Journal*, 1970, pp. 428–431.

[18] Samuelson, Paul A., "Abstract of a Theorem Concerning Substitutability in Open Leontief Models," in *Activity Analysis of Production and Allocation*, ed. by T. C. Koopmans, New York: John Wiley and Sons, 1951, pp. 142–146.

[19] ———, "A New Theorem on Nonsubstitution," in *Money Growth and Methodology and Other Essays in Economics, in honor of J. Åkerman*, ed. by Hugo Hegeland, Lund: CWK Gleerup, 1961.

[20] ———, "Parable and Realism in Capital Theory: The Surrogate Production Function," *Review of Economic Studies*, 1962, pp. 193–206.

[21] ———, "A Summing Up," *Quarterly Journal of Economics*, 1966, pp. 568–583.

[22] Solow, Robert M., *Capital Theory and the Rate of Return*, Amsterdam: North Holland Publishing Co., 1963.

[23] ———, "The Interest Rate and Transition between Techniques," in *Socialism, Capitalism and Economic Growth, in honour of*

Maurice Dobb, ed. by C. H. Feinstein, Cambridge: Cambridge University Press, 1967, pp. 30–39.

[24] ———, "On the Rate of Return: Reply to Pasinetti," *Economic Journal*, 1970, pp. 423–428.

[25] Spaventa, Luigi, "Realism without Parables in Capital Theory," in *Recherches récentes sur la fonction de production*, Facultés universitaires N.-D. de la Paix, Namur, 1968, pp. 15–45.

[26] ———, "Rate of Profit, Rate of Growth and Capital Intensity in a Simple Production Model," *Oxford Economic Papers*, 1970, pp. 129–147.

[27] Sraffa, Piero, *Production of Commodities by Means of Commodities*, Cambridge: Cambridge University Press, 1960.

APPENDIX TO CHAPTER SIX

Linear Programming, Substitution, and the Meaning of the Price System

1. *Introductory remark.* At this point we are in a position to compare the approach to the choice of technique developed in the preceding pages with the approach to the same problem which is typical of traditional economic theory.

2. *Linear programming.* For linear models, the traditional approach is best expressed by an application of linear programming.[1] As is well known, linear programming is a mathematical technique for the solution of maximum (or minimum) problems when the functions concerned are linear. As a mathematical technique it is neutral with respect to any particular theory.[2] But, when considering the choice of technique, it has been applied to a typically traditional problem (the optimum allocation of given resources), and has thereby made traditional concepts reemerge in a linear context.[3]

When many alternative techniques exist, the application of linear programming consists in taking all commodities inherited from the past as given. If we are at time t, we may denote those commodities by $\bar{Q}_1(t-1), \bar{Q}_2(t-1), \ldots, \bar{Q}_{n-1}(t-1)$ and add to them the labor force

---

[1] See, for example, Koopmans [3], [4, Essay I]; Dorfman [1], Dorfman, Samuelson, Solow [2].

[2] This point is worth stressing, as the still prevalent conviction is that linear programming and marginal economic analysis are the same thing. Compare, for example, the following (misleading) statement by Dorfman, Samuelson, and Solow: "Linear programming *is* marginal analysis, appropriately tailored to the case of a finite number of activities. 'Traditional' marginal analysis is tailored to the case of a differentiable production function" [2, p. 133 n].

[3] In other words, it is the common problem investigated (the optimum allocation of given resources) that accounts for the similarity of the results, not the mathematical technique, which as such has nothing to do with marginal economic theory. In fact, our own analysis of the choice of technique in Chapter VI could well be alternatively framed in terms of linear programming.

$\bar{Q}_n(t - 1)$ to form the column vector

$$\bar{\mathbf{Q}}(t - 1) = [\bar{Q}_1(t - 1), \bar{Q}_2(t - 1), \ldots, \bar{Q}_{n-1}(t - 1), \bar{Q}_n(t - 1)]'$$

$$(\text{VI.A.1})$$

This is the vector of the "given resources" at the beginning of period t (commodities and labor are all "resources" treated as "given" in the same way). The technology of the system is then normally represented by adjoining all the coefficient vectors representing all the alternative technical methods that are known for the production of each commodity. Thereby a large rectangular matrix $\tilde{\mathbf{A}}$ is obtained with n rows and as many columns–which we may take in general to be $(n - 1) \times \omega$ – as the number of all the known technical methods:

$\tilde{\mathbf{A}} =$

$$\begin{bmatrix} a_{11}^{(\alpha)} & \cdots & a_{11}^{(\omega)} & a_{12}^{(\alpha)} & \cdots & a_{12}^{(\omega)} & \cdots & a_{1,n-1}^{(\alpha)} & \cdots & a_{1,n-1}^{(\omega)} \\ a_{21}^{(\alpha)} & \cdots & a_{21}^{(\omega)} & a_{22}^{(\alpha)} & \cdots & a_{22}^{(\omega)} & \cdots & a_{2,n-1}^{(\alpha)} & \cdots & a_{2,n-1}^{(\omega)} \\ \vdots & & \vdots & \vdots & & \vdots & & \vdots & & \vdots \\ a_{n-1,1}^{(\alpha)} & \cdots & a_{n-1,1}^{(\omega)} & a_{n-1,2}^{(\alpha)} & \cdots & a_{n-1,2}^{(\omega)} & \cdots & a_{n-1,n-1}^{(\alpha)} & \cdots & a_{n-1,n-1}^{(\omega)} \\ a_{n1}^{(\alpha)} & \cdots & a_{n1}^{(\omega)} & a_{n2}^{(\alpha)} & \cdots & a_{n2}^{(\omega)} & \cdots & a_{n,n-1}^{(\alpha)} & \cdots & a_{n,n-1}^{(\omega)} \end{bmatrix}$$

$$(\text{VI.A.2})$$

The following linear program can then be formulated:

$$\text{Maximize} \quad \bar{\mathbf{p}}\mathbf{x} \qquad (\text{VI.A.3})$$

$$\text{subject to} \quad \tilde{\mathbf{A}}\mathbf{x} \le \bar{\mathbf{Q}}(t - 1) \qquad (\text{VI.A.4})$$

$$\mathbf{x} \ge \mathbf{0} \qquad (\text{VI.A.5})$$

where $\bar{\mathbf{p}}$ is a given (row) vector of prices of the final commodities and $\mathbf{x}$ is the unknown (column) vector of the (output) activity levels of the $(n - 1) \times \omega$ methods of production. Both vectors have $(n - 1) \times \omega$ components, the same price being repeated ω times for each of the ω alternative methods for the same commodity.

Note that in this problem not only technology $\tilde{\mathbf{A}}$ but also resources $\bar{\mathbf{Q}}(t - 1)$ and prices $\bar{\mathbf{p}}$ are taken as given. The unknowns are the components of vector $\mathbf{x}$. Let us call the solution vector $\mathbf{x}^*$. Its components will turn out to be positive for the methods chosen, and zero for the methods discarded. This is how the choice of technique is arrived at. The chosen technique is called optimum in the sense that it maximizes total revenue (the objective functions $\bar{\mathbf{p}}\mathbf{x}$) subject to the requirement that, for each single "resource," no more of it can be used than the existing quantity. In general, for any particular commodity which is actually produced, the corresponding components of $\mathbf{x}^*$ will all be zero, except one (referring to the chosen method of production), but there might of course be cases in which two such components are positive (two methods for the same commodity being equally profitable).

It should also be noted that absolutely no reference to actual costs is made in this program. The existing "resources" are simply taken as *given* (as if they were all coming from nature). If, in the past, they happened to have a cost of production, it is considered irrelevant.

3. *A "dual" linear program.* The same problem of choice of technique may be reconsidered from another (dual) point of view by formulating the following alternative linear program (which is said to be the "dual" to the previous one, called in turn the "primal"):

$$\text{Minimize} \qquad \mathbf{r}\bar{\mathbf{Q}}(t - 1) \qquad\qquad\qquad (\text{VI.A.6})$$

$$\text{subject to} \qquad \mathbf{r}\tilde{\mathbf{A}} \geq \bar{\mathbf{p}} \qquad\qquad\qquad (\text{VI.A.7})$$

$$\mathbf{r} \geq \mathbf{0} \qquad\qquad\qquad (\text{VI.A.8})$$

where $\mathbf{r}$ is the n-component (row) vector of imputed prices (or rent-prices) of the existing "resources." The data of the problem are the same as before, namely, technology $\tilde{\mathbf{A}}$, the endowment of "resources" $\bar{\mathbf{Q}}(t - 1)$, and the final prices $\bar{\mathbf{p}}$. But the solution is now represented by that vector of imputed rent-prices $\mathbf{r}^*$ that minimize total "cost" (the objective function $\mathbf{r}\bar{\mathbf{Q}}(t - 1)$), subject to the constraint that "costs" may not be lower than the corresponding prices. Obviously only those methods for which "costs" are exactly equal to the corresponding prices will be chosen. The components of vector $\mathbf{r}^*$, i.e. the imputed rent-prices, will turn out to be either zero (and the corresponding resources will be called *free goods*) or positive (and the corresponding resources will be called *scarce goods*).

It should be noted that a whole system of prices for the given resources has thereby come into being. However, this is a system of prices that has absolutely no reference to costs of production. All such prices are *rent*-prices; they are *imputed* to the corresponding "resources" as a consequence of the minimization process on the basis of the final prices and the relative scarcities of existing "resources." The sense in which one refers to the left side of (VI.A.7) as "costs" and to (VI.A.6) as "total cost" is therefore that of *imputed* costs, not that of costs of production.

4. *Relations between the "primal" and the "dual" programs.* The "primal" and the "dual" linear programs are clearly related to each

other. Pre-multiplying (VI.A.4) by $\mathbf{r}$, we obtain

$$\mathbf{r}\tilde{\mathbf{A}}\mathbf{x} \leq \mathbf{r}\bar{\mathbf{Q}}(t-1) \tag{VI.A.9}$$

and, post-multiplying (VI.A.7) by $\mathbf{x}$, we obtain

$$\mathbf{r}\tilde{\mathbf{A}}\mathbf{x} \geq \bar{\mathbf{p}}\mathbf{x} \tag{VI.A.10}$$

from which it follows that the solution to (VI.A.3) and the solution to (VI.A.6) – i.e., $\mathbf{x}^*$ and $\mathbf{r}^*$, respectively – must satisfy the exact equality

$$\mathbf{r}^*\bar{\mathbf{Q}}(t-1) = \mathbf{r}^*\tilde{\mathbf{A}}\mathbf{x}^* = \bar{\mathbf{p}}\mathbf{x}^* \tag{VI.A.11}$$

In other words, the solution to the "primal" problem and the solution to the "dual" problem, when they exist, make the two objective functions coincide. The common solution is in fact the saddle point of a minimax problem.

From this it easily follows[4] that the zero components of vector $\mathbf{r}^*$ (the zero rent-prices in the "dual" problem) correspond to those "resources" which in the "primal" program turn out to be redundant (the free resources). And the positive components of vector $\mathbf{r}^*$ (the positive rent-prices) correspond to those "resources" which, in the "primal" program, are fully utilized (the *scarce* resources). Symmetrically the positive components of vector $\mathbf{x}^*$ (the technical methods that in the "primal" program turn out to be the chosen ones) correspond to those methods for which, in the "dual," imputed costs exactly cover prices. And the zero components of vector $\mathbf{x}^*$ (discarded methods) correspond to those methods for which, in the "dual," imputed costs are higher than prices (inefficient methods).[5]

It can also be shown[6] that, if one takes the partial derivative of the objective funtion $\mathbf{p}\mathbf{x}$ with respect to each physical quantity $Q_i(t-1)$, $i = 1, 2, \ldots, n$, this derivative will either coincide with the corresponding r_i^*, or, if it does not, it will take up two different values on either side of r_i^*, according to whether the solution point is approached from the left, i.e., whether it is a left-hand side derivative, which we may denote by $[\partial(\mathbf{p}\mathbf{x})/\partial Q_i]^-$, or it is approached from the right – i.e., it is a right-hand side derivative, which we may denote by $[\partial(\mathbf{p}\mathbf{x})/\partial Q_i]^+$. More precisely,

$$\left[\frac{\partial(\mathbf{p}\mathbf{x})}{\partial Q_i}\right]^- \geq r_i^* \geq \left[\frac{\partial(\mathbf{p}\mathbf{x})}{\partial Q_i}\right]^+, \qquad i = 1, 2, \ldots, n-1 \tag{VI.A.12}$$

---

[4] See the references cited in footnote 1 above.

[5] We neglect, for simplicity's sake, the extreme case of a boundary solution. In such a case a zero price might be associated with a binding constraint, i.e., with a "resource" which is fully utilized.

[6] See, for example, Koopmans [4, p. 93].

This has been seen as a generalization of the traditional conditions of equality between marginal productivities and the imputed rewards of the corresponding factor inputs.

5. *The phenomenon of substitution.* We have reached a sufficient number of results to be able to draw the conclusions relevant for our comparisons.

To begin with, we can see clearly that the "primal" and the "dual" programs formulated above express a typical problem of optimum allocation of given resources. And the results are as would be expected. The technique that is chosen depends on the endowment of the "resources," $\bar{\mathbf{Q}}(t - 1)$, i.e., on supply, and on the final prices $\bar{\mathbf{p}}$, which might here be taken as an expression of demand. Actually, when framed in this way, the whole theoretical setup cries out for the development of a theory of demand, which is what traditional theory goes on to do.

But we do not need go into a detailed theory of demand to perceive what happens when changes take place. Suppose, for example, that, from a situation $[\bar{\mathbf{Q}}(t - 1), \bar{\mathbf{p}}]$, we go over to a situation in which endowments and final prices (call them $\bar{\bar{\mathbf{Q}}}(t - 1)$ and $\bar{\bar{\mathbf{p}}}$) are exactly the same as previously, except that $\bar{\bar{Q}}_k(t - 1) < \bar{Q}_k(t - 1)$; i.e., one single component of the resource endowment is smaller than before. And suppose also that $\bar{Q}_k(t - 1)$ was redundant in the previous situation (with a zero rent-price), while $\bar{\bar{Q}}_k(t - 1)$ is no longer redundant in the new situation, so that the price of resource k has become positive. The rent-price structure has changed, and in particular the price of resource k (which has become scarce) has obviously increased. In general, both solutions $\mathbf{x}^*$ and $\mathbf{r}^*$ will change. Now, if, as will normally be the case when the techniques are many, the optimum technique also changes, it will change in such a way as to make the input proportions vary in the direction of making the chosen technique *less* resource k intensive. In other words, the change from the old to the new technique, consequent upon an increasing scarcity of resource k, will cause an increase in the price of k and a process of physical substitution of other resources for resource k.

The same concepts may be illustrated by a similar exercise on the price vector. Suppose that, from situation $[\bar{\bar{\mathbf{Q}}}(t - 1), \bar{\mathbf{p}}]$, we go to a new situation $[\bar{\bar{\mathbf{Q}}}(t - 1), \bar{\bar{\mathbf{p}}}]$, which is in all respects similar to the previous one except that $\bar{\bar{p}}_1 > \bar{p}_1$, i.e., the price of final commodity 1 has increased. And suppose that final commodity 1 is the most heavily resource j intensive of all. Again our two programs will lead to a new solution for the rent-prices in which the rent-price of resource j has increased; and to a new solution for the levels of activities, in which, if the chosen technique has changed at all, it has changed in the direction of being less resource j intensive. In other words, an increase in the price of a final commodity causes an increase in the rent-price of that particular resource (here called resource j) which is intensively required by that final commodity, and a process of physical substitution of other resources for resource j.

Summarizing, we may state the following proposition.

Traditional proposition (a). A change in final prices (relative to endowments) or a change in endowments (relative to final demand) entails, in general, a change of the chosen technique, and thus a change of the rent-prices and of the input proportions, in such a way that the input proportions change in the direction opposite to that of the corresponding rent-prices. One can say unambiguously that the change of prices entails a *process of physical substitution* among the various resources.

It should be noted that what allows us to talk of "substitution among the various resources" is the unambiguous direction of the changes in the input proportions. Resources that become relatively less scarce (and less expensive) are substituted for resources that become relatively more scarce (and more expensive). In this context, choice of technique and choice of the input proportions are interchangeable concepts. They may be regarded (and they have in fact been regarded) as expressing the same thing.

6. *The traditional meaning of prices*. A few further conclusions follow, from the "dual" program, on the meaning of the rent-prices. These prices, as already pointed out, have absolutely nothing to do with costs of production (even if there have been costs of production in the past). They simply emerge from a logical process of *imputation* inherent in the minimization-of-cost solution to the "dual" program. And it can be seen directly from (VI.A.12) that each rent-price (at given final prices) is inversely related to the physical quantity of the corresponding resource endowment. It represents a sort of index of its scarcity.

We may therefore state also another proposition.

Traditional proposition (b). The rent-prices that are imputed to the given resources appear to have the meaning of "indexes of scarcity." The utilization, or "allocation," of the various resources on the basis of these prices is therefore an allocation on the basis of their degrees of scarcity. Such an allocation is optimum (efficient) in the sense that it realizes the minimization of imputed costs.

7. *Nonsubstitution*. We have by now all the elements necessary for a comparison with the choice-of-technique analysis developed in Chapter VI.

It should be evident at this point that in Chapter VI we have been looking at the production process in a completely different way. We have been considering an economic system in which no commodity is "given"; all commodities are produced. What in Sections 2 through 6 of this Appendix have been taken as the "given resources," i.e., the physical quantities $\bar{Q}_1(t-1)$, $\bar{Q}_2(t-1)$, ..., $\bar{Q}_{n-1}(t-1)$, in Chapter VI have been considered as themselves the variables.[7] And our task is that of looking for the values that these variables must take (equilibrium values) in order that the production process may go on.

It follows immediately that, in a production context such as the one considered in Chapter VI, the traditional proposition (a) of Section 5 no longer applies. In fact, it makes no sense. It makes no sense to talk of "endowments" of given physical quantities if these physical quantities, to be carried over from one period to another, are the unknowns to be determined. It makes no sense to talk of "scarce" resources, if these resources can be produced in whatever quantities may be needed by the economic system.

We can therefore understand why in Chapter VI the conclusions reached about the choice of technique are in sharp contrast with the traditional ones. More specifically, we can understand why the choice of technique does not depend on the composition of demand.

When all inputs are themselves produced, a change in the composition of demand simply means that more of some inputs and less of other inputs will have to be produced, while the optimum technique remains the same. In other words, the process of adaptation to any given change in the composition of final demand is, in a production context, radically different from the one considered by traditional theory. Whereas, with given and fixed inputs (the traditional case), the only way to adapt is through a change of technique which may allow the substitution of some inputs for others, in a production context in which all inputs are themselves produced the obvious way to adapt is to produce the inputs which are needed and to cut down production of those which are no longer needed. There is no question of changing the technique. Input substitution, in a production context, has no role to play.

8. *On substitution as a short-run phenomenon.* A partial reconciliation with the traditional view has been attempted by trying to retain some relevance to the idea of substitution in the short run. The argument is that in the short run, if demand suddenly changes, entrepreneurs who are stuck with what they inherit from the previous period will try to substitute temporarily one input for the other, although in the long

[7] Only the labor force was taken as given.

run, when inputs are adapted to the new situation, they will go back to the old technique and substitution will be undone.

Yet this is a different sort of problem altogether. What happens in the short run in the face of a sudden change, i.e., what happens in a disequilibrium situation, is a much more complicated matter. One cannot, of course, exclude the possibility that some temporary substitution may play some useful role. But many other things may also happen in the short run. Most of all, much will depend on how long the entrepreneurs expect the temporary scarcity to last – a point that the traditional approach does not consider at all. This means that this approach, even if confined to the short run, is at best incomplete.

What is important to stress here in any case is that any process of substitution cannot but be presented, in a production context, as a passing and short-lived phenomenon, soon to be reversed. As far as the equilibrium situation is concerned, substitution turns out to have no relevance at all.

9. *Irrelevance of substitution in the general case.* Another route which has been pursued to minimize the importance of the new results, already pointed out in Section 6.3 of Chapter VI, consists in attributing the irrelevance of substitution to the "very special" case of no joint production and constant coefficients. But the inconsistency of this contention is here brought into sharp relief by the very analysis of the previous pages.

The assumptions of no joint production and constant coefficients have also been made in Sections 2 through 6 of this Appendix in order to illustrate the traditional idea of substitution. The fact that substitution occurs in the theoretical scheme considered in this Appendix and does not occur in the theoretical scheme considered in Chapter VI cannot therefore be due to those two assumptions (which are made in both cases!). It is obviously due to the specifically different features of the two theoretical schemes here compared.

As already pointed out in Section 6.3 of Chapter VI, the joint production and nonconstant coefficient case is more complicated than, but not basically different from, the case concerning single products and constant coefficients. The complication arises from the fact that a change of the composition of demand may entail a change of the optimum technique and of the price structure. However, this does not enable us to say anything about the *direction* in which the input proportions will change.

As we have seen in Section 5 of this Appendix, it is precisely the unambiguous direction in which relative prices and input proportions are related to each other that justifies talking of "substitution." But there is nothing of the sort in a production context. No general relation exists between the changes in the price structure and the changes in the input proportions. More specifically, no monotonic inverse relation exists, in general, between the variation of any price, relative to another price, and the variation of the proportions among the two inputs to which these two prices refer. When this is so, to talk of "substitution" among these inputs no longer makes any sense.

10. *On "marginal productivities."* At this point it may also be worth considering briefly what happens, in a production context, to the partial derivatives (which have been associated with the notions of "marginal productivities") that appear in the equalities/inequalities (VI.A.12). Any such partial derivative clearly has a sense when it is possible to go from one technical method to another by simply varying the quantity of one single input (with respect to which the derivative is taken), while leaving all the others unchanged. Cases in which this is possible may of course exist, but they must clearly be considered as representing very special and limited cases indeed.

In the general case, as we have seen, a change of a method of production means a change of *a whole series* (a vector) of physical inputs. And then taking a partial derivative makes very little sense. Adding any physical quantity of any input will make that input redundant without making any difference to production. And, conversely, taking away any quantity of any single physical input will cause a bottleneck, i.e., a reduction of final production because of insufficiency of just one physical input, while causing all the others to become redundant (complementarity of all inputs). In both cases the partial derivative of total revenue with respect to any particular physical input, i.e., the traditional notion of "marginal productivity," becomes an entirely useless and irrelevant concept. Thus, even if one insists in taking the partial derivatives on the two sides of any price (the left-side partial derivative and the right-side partial derivative), these derivatives will in general turn out to be so far apart from each other as to have no relation with the price concerned and therefore to serve no useful purpose.

The important aspect of this conclusion is that it is reached here with reference to the general case of multiplicity of techniques of production and not (as the traditional economic literature has always insisted on claiming) with reference to the case of one single technique. In other words, complementarity among the physical inputs, and thus the irrelevance of "marginal productivities," turn out to be much more general and widespread phenomena than they have normally been supposed to be. They concern a world of multiple alternative techniques of production, and not only the special case of a single technique.[8]

11. *Nonscarce goods with positive prices.* The other traditional proposition, proposition (b) of Section 6, may be dealt with more quickly.

In a theoretical schema of production of commodities by means of commodities, *all* goods are produced, i.e., are nonscarce. Therefore their prices cannot possibly represent relative scarcities. Hence traditional proposition (b) also no longer applies—or rather makes no sense.

The diversity of approach is here revealed to be even sharper than in the case of traditional proposition (a), as some of the attributes traditionally attached to prices and commodities are revealed to founder. In the traditional context any nonscarce good is a free good and has a zero price. But in a production context all goods are nonscarce and yet their prices are positive (and not zero!). Nonscarce commodities are not the same thing as free goods.

12. *The meaning of production prices.* To grasp the meaning of prices in a production context, one only needs to go back to the analysis carried out in Chapter V. Consider expression (V.7.4); all prices are shown to be eventually reducible to dated quantities of labor. At least for single-product industries, there can be no doubt whatever on this point. Production prices are physical quantities of labor, weighted with the compounded rate of profit appropriate to their conceptual dates of application.

References

[1] Dorfman, Robert, *Application of Linear Programming to the Theory of the Firm*, Berkeley: University of California Press, 1951.
[2] Dorfman, R., Samuelson, P. A., and Solow, R. M., *Linear Programming and Economic Analysis*, New York: McGraw-Hill Book Co., 1958.

[8] To put the same point in another way, we may say that an unwarranted and confusing association has been made between the case of "fixed coefficients" and the special case of a single technique. There is absolutely no justification for such an association. We might well have an enormously large number of alternative techniques and yet be justified in saying that each technique is characterized by fixed coefficients. What will normally happen in such a situation is that, when a change of technique takes place, it entails a change of many or even of *all* the technical coefficients at the same time. It is therefore the traditional conception itself of change of technique that is revealed to be too restrictive. A change of technique may well mean a discrete change in all coefficients rather than an infinitesimal change in any one coefficient at a time.

[3] Koopmans, Tjalling C., "Analysis of Production as an Efficient Combination of Activities," in *Activity Analysis of Production and Allocation*, ed. by T. C. Koopmans, New York: John Wiley and Sons, 1951, pp. 31–97.

[4] ———, *Three Essays on the State of Economic Science*, New York: McGraw-Hill Book Co., 1957.

CHAPTER SEVEN

An Introduction to Dynamic Production Models

1 Population Growth and Constant Technical Coefficients

THE theoretical schemata considered thus far have been developed with reference to stationary economic systems, i.e., to economic systems in which population, technology, and consumers' preferences have not only been thought of as exogenously given but as actually being constant through time. In reality, one hardly ever observes economic systems which undergo no changes. Population, technical knowledge, and consumers' preferences are in constant movement in any industrialized economic system.

The natural step to take at this point ought, therefore, to be that of continuing our study with reference to economic systems which are no longer stationary but growing. However, theoretical economists have not yet elaborated dynamic models of production which can be considered satisfactory. The only magnitude whose growth it has been found easy to incorporate into a production model is the labor force (and thus population). Changes in the other two magnitudes (technology and consumers' preferences) have, by contrast, proved to be far less amenable to theoretical treatment.

The following pages are concerned with the problems which arise in an economic system undergoing a growth of population (and of the labor force). The assumption is maintained, however, that technical knowledge and consumers' preferences remain unchanged. Strictly speaking, an economic system of this kind cannot be considered a truly "dynamic" one (and it has indeed been called "quasi-dynamic" or, from another point of view, "quasi-stationary"). For, although it embodies those dynamic aspects which are inherent in the growth of the labor force, and of the system of physical quantities, it continues to exhibit features which are typical of stationary systems: constancy of the structures of prices, of production, and of consumption. Such a system gives rise to a type of dynamics in which all sections of the economy grow at the same percentage rate as the rate of population growth, while keeping all proportions constant. This is obviously a simplified type of dynamics, which we may call *proportional dynamics*:

growth concerns the total quantities alone, while per capita quantities remain absolutely constant.[1]

2   Physical Growth and the Price System

2.1. *Constant coefficients and growth of the labor force.* We consider now an economic system which, as far as our data are concerned, is the same in all respects as the system considered in earlier chapters, except that population grows through time.

More precisely, we assume, as in the two preceding chapters, that the technique for the system as a whole is represented by $(n - 1)$ single-product production methods (or industries):

$$\begin{bmatrix} \mathbf{A} \\ \mathbf{a}_n \end{bmatrix} \tag{VII.2.1}$$

This technique has been chosen from a wider range of alternative techniques, i.e., from a technology:

$$\begin{bmatrix} \mathbf{A}^{(\alpha)} \\ \mathbf{a}_n^{(\alpha)} \end{bmatrix}, \quad \begin{bmatrix} \mathbf{A}^{(\beta)} \\ \mathbf{a}_n^{(\beta)} \end{bmatrix}, \quad \cdots \quad \begin{bmatrix} \mathbf{A}^{(\omega)} \\ \mathbf{a}_n^{(\omega)} \end{bmatrix} \tag{VII.2.2}$$

which remains constant through time.

Population N, by contrast, increases at a given percentage rate *per annum* $\bar{g} \geq 0$ (so that our previous analysis constitutes the particular case in which $\bar{g} = 0$).[2] Denoting time by t, we can write

$$N(t) = N(0)[1 + \bar{g}]^t \tag{VII.2.3}$$

Assuming that the total labor force Q_n is proportional to total population, we have

$$Q_n(t) = \mu N(t) \tag{VII.2.4}$$

where μ denotes the (constant) proportion of the total population which is active in the process of production. Hence

$$Q_n(t) = \mu N(t) = Q_n(0)[1 + \bar{g}]^t \tag{VII.2.5}$$

Now our task is to look for those relations which must hold in order that the economic system, which we assume to be in equilibrium at time zero (by which we mean with full employment of the labor force and full utilization of productive capacity), may remain in dynamic equilibrium (i.e., may maintain full employment and full capacity utilization) through time.

---

[1] Almost all the mathematical models of growth presented in the recent economic literature refer to economic systems with proportional dynamics (or with a slight variation of it). But there are exceptions, as for instance [11].

[2] The letter g therefore denotes a *percentage* annual rate of growth. For brevity, whenever no misunderstanding is possible, we shall simply call it "rate of growth."

2.2. *Growth of the physical quantities.* All the physical quantities will obviously have to grow. We denote them by the symbols used previously with the addition of the suffix t to indicate that they refer to the time period ("year") t. Hence

$$\mathbf{Q}(t) = \begin{bmatrix} Q_1(t) \\ Q_2(t) \\ \vdots \\ Q_{n-1}(t) \end{bmatrix}, \qquad \mathbf{Y}(t) = \begin{bmatrix} Y_1(t) \\ Y_2(t) \\ \vdots \\ Y_{n-1}(t) \end{bmatrix} \qquad \text{(VII.2.6)}$$

where $\mathbf{Q}(t)$ is the (column) vector of the total physical quantities of commodities $1, 2, \ldots, n - 1$, in year t; and $\mathbf{Y}(t)$ is the (column) vector of the physical quantities of the same commodities which, in the same year, make up the net product, or surplus, or net national income, of the economic system as a whole.

The complete system of physical quantities can be represented, in a manner analogous to that used previously, by the system of equations

$$\mathbf{Q}(t) - \mathbf{A}\mathbf{Q}(t) = \mathbf{Y}(t) \qquad \text{(VII.2.7)}$$

to which we must add the equation

$$\mathbf{a}_n \mathbf{Q}(t) = Q_n(t) = \mu N(t) \qquad \text{(VII.2.8)}$$

expressing the condition of full employment of the labor force.

Since $N(t)$ grows through time, according to (VII.2.3), we must now investigate how the other physical quantities should grow too.

2.3. *Net product divided between consumption and new investment.* We can say at once that, if the labor force is growing, it will be necessary to provide the new workers with new capital goods, i.e., with new productive capacity. This implies that at the end of each year it will no longer suffice, in a growing economic system, to set aside the quantities $\mathbf{A}\mathbf{Q}(t)$ as replacements of the means of production. It will also be necessary to set aside other quantities to permit the *expansion* of the means of production. In other words, the net product of the economic system, $\mathbf{Y}(t)$, can no longer be devoted entirely to consumption. A part of it must be devoted to new investment. We therefore define two new vectors

$$\mathbf{C}(t) = \begin{bmatrix} C_1(t) \\ C_2(t) \\ \vdots \\ C_{n-1}(t) \end{bmatrix}, \qquad \mathbf{J}(t) = \begin{bmatrix} J_1(t) \\ J_2(t) \\ \vdots \\ J_{n-1}(t) \end{bmatrix} \qquad \text{(VII.2.9)}$$

where $\mathbf{C}(t)$ denotes the (column) vector of the physical quantities of the commodities $1, 2, \ldots, (n - 1)$, which are devoted to consumption, and $\mathbf{J}(t)$ denotes the (column) vector of the physical quantities of the same commodities $1, 2, \ldots, (n - 1)$, which are set aside for new investment. By definition, of course,

$$\mathbf{Y}(t) = \mathbf{C}(t) + \mathbf{J}(t) \tag{VII.2.10}$$

Equation (VII.2.7) may now be rewritten

$$\mathbf{Q}(t) - \mathbf{A}\mathbf{Q}(t) - \mathbf{J}(t) = \mathbf{C}(t) \tag{VII.2.11}$$

This makes it necessary to seek the relation between $\mathbf{J}(t)$ and the preexisting means of production. But before doing this, we must specify how consumption $\mathbf{C}(t)$ evolves through time.

2.4. *Growth of total consumption and invariance of its composition.* The evolution of the components of $\mathbf{C}(t)$ through time is, in fact, very simple within the present model. Although there is a problem of choice over the *composition* of consumption, to which we shall return below, we can say immediately that, since consumers' preferences, technology, and the structure of prices are all assumed to be constant through time, the choice of the composition of consumption is made once for all.

This means that if we define a new column vector

$$\mathbf{c} = \begin{bmatrix} c_1 \\ c_2 \\ \cdot \\ \cdot \\ c_{n-1} \end{bmatrix} = \frac{1}{N(t)} \mathbf{C}(t) \tag{VII.2.12}$$

representing the per capita consumption of the commodities $1, 2, \ldots, n - 1$, this vector will remain constant in dynamic equilibrium. (We have therefore written it without the t suffix).

Hence we may write

$$\mathbf{C}(t) = \mathbf{c} N(t) = \mathbf{c} N(0) [1 + \bar{g}]^t \tag{VII.2.13}$$

in order to represent the evolution of the *demand* for consumer goods in dynamic equilibrium (i.e., the evolution of demand given that full employment is maintained). Equation (VII.2.13) states that the average individual always demands the same goods, so that the composition of demand remains constant through time. However, since the number of individuals increases, total demand for each consumption good increases at the same percentage growth rate of population ($\bar{g}$),

2.5. *New investments.* Let us now consider new investments. If the demand for each consumer good increases at the annual percentage rate $\bar{g}$, then a necessary condition for the corresponding production to take place without there being any unutilized productive capacity is that all the means of production increase at the same annual percentage rate $\bar{g}$. This condition gives us the expression for investments we have been looking for:

$$\mathbf{J}(t) = \bar{g}\mathbf{AQ}(t) \qquad\qquad (VII.2.14)$$

This means that, at the end of every year, all physical quantities making up the means of production $\mathbf{AQ}(t)$ will have to increase at exactly the same percentage rate.

2.6. *The dynamic-equilibrium solution.* Substituting (VII.2.14) and (VII.2.13) into (VII.2.11), we obtain the system of $(n - 1)$ equations:

$$\mathbf{Q}(t) - \mathbf{AQ}(t) - \bar{g}\mathbf{AQ}(t) = \mathbf{c}\,N(t) \qquad\qquad (VII.2.15)$$

We can solve it immediately and obtain

$$\mathbf{Q}(t) = [\mathbf{I} - (1 + \bar{g})\mathbf{A}]^{-1}\mathbf{c}N(t) \qquad\qquad (VII.2.16)$$

or, in greater detail, using (VII.2.3),

$$\mathbf{Q}(t) = [\mathbf{I} - (1 + \bar{g})\mathbf{A}]^{-1}\mathbf{c}\,N(0)\,[1 + \bar{g}]^{t} \qquad\qquad (VII.2.16a)$$

Since all the coefficients on the right side of (VII.2.16a) are constant through time, and since the only factor which varies is the exponential scalar function $(1 + \bar{g})^{t}$, it follows that (VII.2.16a) implies that each of the total physical quantities in $\mathbf{Q}(t)$ grows through time at exactly the same percentage rate of growth $\bar{g}$ as do the physical quantities in $\mathbf{C}(t)$.

The solution (VII.2.16a) defines, so to speak, a "dynamic path" along which productive capacity for each commodity is increased from year to year by exactly the amount required by the increase in the corresponding demand. Along such a dynamic path the growth of the system is perfectly balanced and proportional. Consumption $\mathbf{C}(t)$, net investment $\bar{g}\mathbf{AQ}(t)$, the means of production $\mathbf{AQ}(t)$, and hence the total physical quantities $\mathbf{Q}(t)$ all increase at the same percentage growth rate $\bar{g}$. All proportions remain constant through time.

We can see here in detail the meaning of the proportional dynamics of the economic system under consideration.

2.7. *The full-employment condition.* It will be noted that (VII.2.15) represents a dynamic version of the open Leontief model[3] (cf. Chapter IV, Section 4.2), and that its solution (VII.2.16) may be regarded as a

---

[3] Leontief attempted at the outset to go over to a dynamic version of his model by assuming the initial conditions to be given independently of technology. But he encountered numerous difficulties which were never solved completely. See Leontief [7] and Jorgenson [2].

generalization of (IV.5.2), which in its turn could now be looked upon as the special case of (VII.2.16) in which $\bar{g} = 0$.

For every given exponential evolution of consumption, $\mathbf{C}(t)$, through time, the solution (VII.2.16) gives the evolution of the total physical quantities $\mathbf{Q}(t)$ which are required – as direct, indirect, and, we might add, hyper-indirect requirements (meaning by this last the requirements for new investment) – to keep the economic system in dynamic equilibrium. The inverse matrix

$$[\mathbf{I} - (1 + g)\mathbf{A}]^{-1} \qquad\qquad (VII.2.17)$$

has in fact been called the "Leontief dynamic inverse matrix."[4]

It must also be pointed out, however, that the solution (VII.2.16) involves a well-determined evolution of labor requirements $L(t)$, namely

$$L(t) = \mathbf{a}_n \mathbf{Q}(t) = \mathbf{a}_n[\mathbf{I} - (1 + \bar{g})\mathbf{A}]^{-1}\mathbf{c}\, N(0)\, [1 + \bar{g}]^t \quad (VII.2.18)$$

Hence, if our dynamic equilibrium solution is to ensure not only full utilization of productive capacity but also full employment of the labor force, then we must impose the further condition:

$$L(t) = Q_n(t) \qquad\qquad (VII.2.19)$$

or, after substitution into (VII.2.18),

$$\mathbf{a}_n[\mathbf{I} - (1 + \bar{g})\mathbf{A}]^{-1}\mathbf{c}\, N(t) = Q_n(t) \qquad\qquad (VII.2.20)$$

The left and right sides of this equality condition are indeed compatible with one another, since *ex hypothesi* $N(t)$ and $Q_n(t)$ are growing at the same annual percentage rate $\bar{g}$. But this does not mean that the two sides will always automatically be equal to one another. This will be so only if the initial situation is an appropriate one.

2.8. *Implications for consumption choice.* Expression (VII.2.20) actually introduces a further restriction into the model, a restriction which is similar to the one we met in the case of the open Leontief system (cf. Chapter IV, Section 6).

The expression (VII.2.15) contains $(n - 1)$ equations and (VII.2.20) is a further equation; in total, therefore, we have n equations. Thus far, however, we have considered only $(n - 1)$ unknowns: the $(n - 1)$ physical quantities in the vector $\mathbf{Q}(t)$. Written in this form, the system is overdetermined. To make it determinate it is necessary to introduce another unknown; and this unknown cannot but be found within the vector of per capita consumption, $\mathbf{c}$.

---

[4] After Leontief [8].

Indeed, we are now in a position to understand better the meaning of the vector $\mathbf{c}$. We can say that its components $c_1, c_2, \ldots, c_{n-1}$ represent the choices of consumption which are open to the consumers in the economic system under consideration. These choices are naturally not unbounded. To begin with, no consumption coefficient can be negative:

$$c_i \geq 0, \qquad\qquad i = 1, 2, \ldots, n - 1 \qquad (VII.2.21)$$

Furthermore, given that (VII.2.21) is satisfied, the per capita consumption coefficients cannot all be chosen at will. This is precisely what the restriction (VII.2.20) expresses. At least one of the per capita consumption coefficients must be treated as an unknown, and thus be determined so as to satisfy (VII.2.15), (VII.2.20).

This is, after all, in conformity with common sense. The consumption possibilities available to the economic system as a whole are limited by its technical possibilities. On average, each consumer is free to determine the *proportions* in which he consumes the various commodities but not the absolute level of consumption. The latter depends on technology and on the growth rate of the economic system.

2.9. *Invariance of the price structure.* We have dealt so far with the movements through time of the physical quantities, and we now turn to prices. In a growing economic system in which technology remains constant and the only source of growth is the increase in population, the price system is much easier to deal with than the physical quantity system. In fact, it can simply be written as

$$\mathbf{p} = \mathbf{a}_n[\mathbf{I} - (1 + \bar{\pi})\mathbf{A}]^{-1}w \qquad (VII.2.22)$$

which is precisely the same expression as considered in Chapter V, Section 5.6, provided only that the same *numéraire* is kept through time, i.e., provided that we fix

$$w(t) = w(0) = 1 \qquad (VII.2.23)$$

or, alternatively,

$$p_j(t) = p_j(0) = 1 \qquad (VII.2.24)$$

where j is any one of the commodities $1, 2, \ldots, n - 1$ (or any linear combination of them). If the given rate of profit $\bar{\pi}$ does not change, the technique chosen will not change and thus all magnitudes which appear in (VII.2.22) will remain constant through time. It has clearly become unnecessary to use any time suffix t since all prices remain constant as time goes on.

With respect to prices there is therefore no difference whatever between a stationary system and a system with population growth, when the same *numéraire* is kept through time. All the expressions obtained for prices in a stationary system remain valid for an economic system with population growth and constant technical coefficients.

2.10. *A rate of inflation.* It should be noted, however, that our equations imply nothing about the *numéraire*, and therefore that there is no necessity that the *numéraire* remain the same through time, as is the case with (VII.2.23) or (VII.2.24). In fact, expression (VII.2.23) fixes something more than the *numéraire* of the price system; it states not only that *w* is equal to unity, but also that it remains equal to unity for *all* time. There clearly is no necessity that this should be so. (The same remark can be made with reference to (VII.2.24)). To put it from a different standpoint, what our system of equations leaves free to be fixed exogenously, when we consider movements through time, is the whole movement of the *numéraire* through time, and not merely the *numéraire* at any particular point in time.

Suppose, for example, that, instead of closing the price system with (VII.2.23), we were to close it with

$$w(t) = w(0)[1 + \bar{\rho}]^t = [1 + \bar{\rho}]^t \qquad (VII.2.25)$$

where $w(0) = 1$ and $\bar{\rho}$ is an (exogenously given) percentage rate of growth of the wage rate through time. We may simply call $\bar{\rho}$ the "rate of inflation" [and may obviously look at (VII.2.23) as the particular case in which $\bar{\rho} = 0$, i.e., the rate of inflation is zero]. Now, with (VII.2.25) the price system becomes

$$\mathbf{p}(t) = \mathbf{a}_n[\mathbf{I} - (1 + \bar{\pi})\mathbf{A}]^{-1} \cdot [1 + \bar{\rho}]^t \qquad (VII.2.26)$$

All prices now do need a time suffix t, since all of them are rising at the rate of inflation $\bar{\rho}$. This rate of inflation is, however, exactly the same for all prices, so that their structure remains absolutely constant as time goes on.

Observe that, from a formal point of view, expression (VII.2.26) for prices has now become almost "dual" to expression (VII.2.16a) for the physical quantities. An important difference remains. In (VII.2.16a) the rate of growth of population $\bar{g}$ appears both inside the inverse matrix and outside it as the factor that scales up the economic system proportionally as time goes on. By contrast, in (VII.2.26), what appears inside the inverse matrix is the rate of profit $\bar{\pi}$, while the factor that scales up the price system proportionally is the rate of inflation $\bar{\rho}$, which appears outside the inverse matrix. There clearly is no reason why the two should coincide. Though both exogenous to our system of equations, the rate of profit and the rate of inflation are two entirely different things and have entirely different determinants.

In the present analysis, for simplicity's sake, we shall make the assumption that the rate of inflation is zero, i.e., that the *numéraire*, whatever it may be, remains equal to unity for all time.

3 The Relation Between per Capita Consumption and the Rate of Growth

3.1. *The price system and the physical quantity system as dual to each other.* In spite of what has been said in the previous section, it is nevertheless possible, from a purely formal point of view, to express the price system and the physical quantity system as perfectly dual to each other and independently of time. This can be done by concentrating our attention on proportions, rather than on absolute levels, and therefore by "eliminating" both $\bar{g}$ and $\bar{\rho}$ as the scaling up factors of the physical quantity system and of the price system, respectively.

For the price system this means considering *relative prices*. This has already been done with (VII.2.22) plus either (VII.2.23) or (VII.2.24). More generally, by dividing through by $w(t) = [1 + \bar{\rho}]^t$, (VII.2.26) becomes

$$\mathbf{p} = \mathbf{a}_n[\mathbf{I} - (1 + \bar{\pi})\mathbf{A}]^{-1} \qquad (VII.3.1)$$

which expresses the structure of prices independently of time.

For the physical quantity system similar steps can be taken by considering *relative quantities*. Since all proportions remain constant, the physical quantities too may thereby be expressed independently of time. Let us define a new (column) vector $\mathbf{q}(t)$, with $n - 1$ components, which we shall call the vector of per capita physical quantities:

$$\mathbf{q}(t) = \begin{bmatrix} \dfrac{Q_1(t)}{N(t)} \\[2mm] \dfrac{Q_2(t)}{N(t)} \\[2mm] \vdots \\[2mm] \dfrac{Q_{n-1}(t)}{N(t)} \end{bmatrix} = \frac{1}{N(t)}\mathbf{Q}(t) \qquad (VII.3.2)$$

Thus, returning to (VII.2.15) and (VII.2.16a) and dividing through by $N(t) = N(0)[1 + \bar{g}]^t$, we can write

$$\mathbf{q} - \mathbf{Aq} - \bar{g}\mathbf{Aq} = \mathbf{c} \qquad \text{(VII.3.3)}$$

and

$$\mathbf{q} = [\mathbf{I} - (1 + \bar{g})\mathbf{A}]^{-1}\mathbf{c} \qquad \text{(VII.3.4)}$$

respectively, where it is no longer necessary to use the t suffix for the vector $\mathbf{q}$, since the latter remains invariant in dynamic equilibrium. Each of its components is a ratio $Q_i(t)/N(t)$, $i = 1, 2, \ldots, n - 1$, with a numerator and a denominator which increase at exactly the same percentage growth rate, so that each component remains completely invariant through time. It is of course also necessary to apply the same operation of dividing by $N(t)$ to (VII.2.20), which becomes

$$\frac{1}{\mu}\mathbf{a}_n\mathbf{q} = 1 \qquad \text{(VII.3.5)}$$

It is now clear that expression (VII.3.4), showing the system of relative physical quantities in an economic system in dynamic equilibrium, is exactly dual to expression (VII.3.1), showing the corresponding system of relative prices.

The system of physical quantities and the system of prices had remained slightly asymmetrical in the previous chapters, owing to the fact that the rate of growth $\bar{g}$ had not yet been introduced, but they have become perfectly symmetrical at this stage. As can be seen by comparing (VII.3.1) and (VII.3.4), the system of prices uses the columns of the matrix $\mathbf{A}$ multiplied by $(1 + \bar{\pi})$, and the system of physical quantities uses the corresponding rows multiplied by $(1 + \bar{g})$. In the former the columns are multiplied by the row vector $\mathbf{a}_n$, yielding the row vector $\mathbf{p}$; in the latter the rows are multiplied by the column vector $\mathbf{c}$, yielding the column vector $\mathbf{q}$. The duality is perfectly symmetrical.

3.2. *A strictly decreasing relationship between per capita consumption and rate of growth.* Expression (VII.3.4) provides the basis for a further exercise which is used here to illustrate the relation between the rate of growth and per capita consumption for any given technique of production.

Consider a hypothetical economic system in which per capita consumption consists of commodity 1. This is equivalent to having chosen to set equal to zero all the $(n - 2)$ per capita consumption levels which are open to choice and then considering c_1 as an unknown. The vector

c takes up the special form, which we shall denote by $c^{(1)}$:

$$c = c^{(1)} = \begin{bmatrix} c_1 \\ 0 \\ 0 \\ \vdots \\ 0 \end{bmatrix} \qquad\qquad \text{(VII.3.6)}$$

That is, commodity 1 is the only commodity produced for consumption. All the other commodities are therefore produced only in those quantities which are strictly necessary to replace, and to expand at the given rate of growth $\bar{g}$, the means of production required, directly and indirectly in the system as a whole, to obtain commodity 1 as the consumption good.

Substituting (VII.3.6) into (VII.3.4) and pre-multiplying by a_n, we obtain

$$a_n q = a_n[I - (1 + \bar{g})A]^{-1}c^{(1)} \qquad\qquad \text{(VII.3.7)}$$

But $a_n q = \mu$ from (VII.3.5). This means that (VII.3.7) is not a system of equations but a single equation. More simply; it can be written

$$1 = a_n[I - (1 + \bar{g})A]^{-1}c^{(1)}\mu^{-1} \qquad\qquad \text{(VII.3.8)}$$

that is, as an equation which determines the average per capita consumption c_1, which can be obtained in dynamic equilibrium with a given technique $[A, a_n]'$ and a given rate of growth $\bar{g}$.

Of course, per capita consumption will be different at different rates of growth. And it is just here that the interest of (VII.3.8) is found. It enables us to make a series of comparisons of the comparative dynamics type. We can think of (VII.3.8) as an implicit relation between g (the growth rate of the economic system) and c_1 (the equilibrium per capita consumption when all consumption is made up of commodity 1). This is clearly a polynomial relation of degree k (if k is the number of basic commodities and commodity 1 is a basic commodity).

The reader may now notice that we have already met this relation (in Chapter V, Section 6.3) in connection with the rate of profit π and the wage rate $w^{(1)}$, expressed in terms of commodity 1. The surprising result, however, is that (VII.3.8) is not merely a relation "similar" to (V.6.8); *it is exactly the same relation*, although between different variables. We have here the growth rate g taking the place of the profit rate π, and the consumption per worker in terms of physical commodity 1, $\mu^{-1}c_1$, taking the place of the wage rate $w^{(1)}$, also in terms of commodity 1.

This means that exactly the same polynomial equation expresses both the relation between π and $w^{(1)}$ and the comparative dynamics relationship between g and $\mu^{-1}c_1$. Such a polynomial relationship was drawn in Fig. V.3, with π on the horizontal axis and $w^{(1)}$ on the vertical axis. We can now redraw it with g on the horizontal axis and c_1 on the vertical axis, leaving aside the constant μ^{-1}, which does not make any qualitative difference (see Fig. VII.1). We know, from our previous analysis,[5] that this relation is strictly decreasing. And this ought to be intuitively obvious in the present context too. In equilibrium, given a particular technique $[\mathbf{A}, \mathbf{a}_n]'$, the higher the growth rate, the smaller will be the per capita consumption which the economic system can afford. The growth rate and the per capita consumption are thereby revealed to be inversely related to each other. It is important to note that these propositions are quite unambiguous, since relation (VII.3.8) is expressed in physical terms (in terms of physical commodity 1).

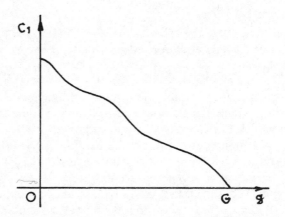

FIG. VII.1. Relation between per capita consumption and the rate of growth

We could of course repeat the entire exercise in terms of each of the other basic commodities to obtain similar relations between g and $\mu^{-1}c_2$, between g and $\mu^{-1}c_3, \ldots,$ between g and $\mu^{-1}c_k$ (or, which is the same thing apart from the constant μ^{-1}, between g and c_2, between g and $c_3, \ldots,$ between g and c_k). These relations are exactly the same relations as hold between π and $w^{(2)}$, between π and $w^{(3)}, \ldots,$ between π and $w^{(k)}$. As we saw in Chapter V, these relations are all different from one another; nevertheless they are all strictly decreasing and they all intersect the horizontal axis at the same point,

[5] See, pp. 88–89.

which we shall here call G (See Fig. VII.1). This point G is obviously the same as the point Π in Fig. V.3.

3.3. *The maximum rate of growth*. Looking at (VII.3.8), we may remark that for $g = 0$ (i.e., in a stationary system) there is associated with every technique $[\mathbf{A}, \mathbf{a}_n]'$ a maximum amount of per capita consumption, in terms of commodity 1, which can be read off as the intercept, on the vertical axis, of the curve shown in Fig. VII.1. A similar statement may be made with respect to commodities 2, 3, ..., k, to each of which there will correspond a curve similar to that of Fig. VII.1. Of course, each one of these curves will have its own intercept on the vertical axis. By contrast, on the horizontal axis, all curves will have exactly the same intercept. This means that for every technique $[\mathbf{A}, \mathbf{a}_n]'$ there is a unique (economically meaningful) maximum rate of growth G at which the economic system can grow.

We can find this maximum rate of growth at once by setting $\mathbf{c} = \mathbf{c}^{(1)} = \mathbf{0}$, and thus $g = G$, in (VII.3.3). We obtain

$$[\mathbf{I} - (1 + G)\mathbf{A}]\mathbf{q} = \mathbf{0} \tag{VII.3.9}$$

that is, a linear and homogeneous system which will have nonzero solutions only if

$$\det[\mathbf{I} - (1 + G)\mathbf{A}] = 0 \tag{VII.3.10}$$

This too is a condition which we have already encountered in Chapter V, Section 9.1, where we sought the value of η which satisfies the characteristic equation

$$\det(\eta\mathbf{I} - \mathbf{A}) = 0 \tag{VII.3.11}$$

We found that, $\mathbf{A}$ being a non-negative matrix, only its maximum eigenvalue η_m has an economic meaning (by a straightforward application of the Perron-Frobenius theorems, according to which only the eigenvector of physical quantities associated with η_m has all non-negative components).

It then follows that

$$\eta_m = \frac{1}{1 + G} \tag{VII.3.12}$$

and hence, from (V.9.2) and (V.9.5), that

$$G \equiv R \equiv \Pi \tag{VII.3.13}$$

We have thus discovered that the maximum eigenvalue of the matrix of interindustry coefficients $\mathbf{A}$ is related, by exactly the same function (VII.3.12), not only to the maximum rate of profit and the uniform rate of surplus, but also to the maximum rate at which the system can grow. Or, rather, the mathematical properties of the systems of equations which we have considered imply that three distinct economic concepts (the maximum rate of profit, the uniform rate of surplus, and the maximum growth rate of the system) are expressed by exactly the same number:

$$\frac{1}{\eta_m} - 1 \equiv R \equiv \Pi \equiv G \tag{VII.3.14}$$

This number must of course be greater than zero or

$$\eta_m < 1$$

for the economic system to be viable.

To conclude, a purely mathematical notion, the maximum eigenvalue of $\mathbf{A}$, has an economic meaning which can be expressed via relation (VII.3.14) in terms of either the maximum rate of profit (Π) or the uniform rate of surplus (R), or the maximum rate at which the economic system can grow (G).

3.4. *The particular cases of a linear relation.* It is worth stressing that the g-c_i relationship examined above is a relation between a percentage rate of growth and a physical quantity of commodity i ($i = 1$, $2, \ldots, n - 1$) – it is a relation in *physical terms*. Therefore, though of a shape as complicated as that of the corresponding relation between π and $w^{(i)}$ (as it is expressed by exactly the same function), it is free from any ambiguity.

Yet one may ask, if only as an exercise in logic, whether there are conditions that would make such a relation a linear function. And, of course, an implicit answer to this question is already contained in our earlier analysis of the conditions that make the π-w relation a linear function (since the two are in fact the same function). But it may be worth examining the same problems with explicit reference to consumption and growth.

Consider the general expression for the per capita net product $\mathbf{p}(\mathbf{I} - \mathbf{A})\mathbf{q}$, and call γ the proportion of it that is devoted to consumption and $(1 - \gamma)$ the proportion that is devoted to new investment ($0 \le \gamma \le 1$). The rate of growth of the economic system may therefore be expressed as[6]

$$g = (1 - \gamma)\frac{\mathbf{p}(\mathbf{I} - \mathbf{A})\mathbf{q}(g)}{\mathbf{p}\mathbf{A}\mathbf{q}(g)} \tag{VII.3.15}$$

---

[6] Note the symmetry between (VII.3.15) and (V.6.1) on p. 85. The former expresses the growth rate as depending both on the share of consumption in net national income and on the variation of the composition of output (due to variations of the division of net income between consumption and new investment); the latter expresses the rate of profit as depending both on the share of wages in net national income and on the variation of prices (due to variations of the distribution of net income between wages and profits).

where the vector of physical quantities has been written as $\mathbf{q}(g)$ to stress the fact that its composition does depend on the rate of growth itself. For, in general, the composition of consumption will be different from the composition of gross and net investments. Moreover, it will be different at different rates of growth (because of different absolute levels of per capita consumption).

It should now be noted that expression (VII.3.15) is in fact the relation between the rate of growth (g) and per capita consumption, though the latter is no longer expressed here in terms of one physical commodity, but as a proportion γ of a composite commodity (the per capita net product). When $\gamma = 1$, consumption is at its maximum, all net product is consumed, and $g = 0$. When $\gamma = 0$, consumption is nil, all net product is reinvested, and $g = G$. This relation appears therefore more complicated here than in earlier pages because the composite commodity, in terms of which consumption is expressed, is itself changing in composition with changes in the rate of growth.

Yet, in spite of the apparent complexity, expression (VII.3.15) shows immediately the conditions under which the relation between g and γ becomes linear. The necessary and sufficient condition clearly is that the ratio $[\mathbf{p(I - A)q/pAq}]$ remains constant at all possible levels of the rate of growth. This happens if, and only if, either or both of the following requirements are satisfied: (i) the composition of $\mathbf{q}$ remains constant at all possible levels of g within the interval $0 \le g \le G$, whatever the price system may be; (ii) the price system $\mathbf{p}$ is such as to yield the same ratio of value added to the means of production in all industries, whatever the composition of production may be.[7]

We already know the very few and very special cases that satisfy these requirements. First of all, we know that Sraffa's standard system, i.e., the particular (column) vector $\mathbf{q}^*$, defined as the right-hand eigenvector of matrix $\mathbf{A}$, satisfies requirement (i). If an economic system happened to be in the proportions of the standard system, then investment, consumption, the net product, and the means of production would all have exactly the same composition, so that, whatever the price system may be,

$$\frac{\mathbf{p(I - A)q}^*}{\mathbf{pAq}^*} = G \tag{VII.3.16}$$

at all levels of the growth rate within $0 \le g \le G$.

---

[7] Note again the symmetry with the two requirements under which expression (V.6.1) is linear: (i) that relative prices in $\mathbf{p}$ remain constant at all possible levels of π (case of uniform capital intensity); or (ii) that the composition of $\mathbf{q}$ be such as to yield the same rate of surplus for all commodities (case of the standard system).

Secondly, we also know that the particular prices that correspond to a zero wage rate (which in Chapter V, Section 5.5, we associated with a pure capital theory of value), i.e., the particular vector $\mathbf{p}^*$, which is the left-hand eigenvector of matrix $\mathbf{A}$, satisfies requirement (ii). At prices $\mathbf{p}^*$, all value added goes to profits. Therefore the ratio of value added to the means of production is the same in all industries, whatever their productions may be. It follows that the ratio of the total net product (all going to profits) to the total capital is always equal to Π, and thus to G, whatever the composition of production may be. That is,

$$\frac{\mathbf{p}^*(\mathbf{I} - \mathbf{A})\mathbf{q}}{\mathbf{p}^*\mathbf{A}\mathbf{q}} = G \tag{VII.3.17}$$

at all levels of g, $0 \le g \le G$, and for all compositions of $\mathbf{q}$.

Hence, both in the case of a standard system, i.e., when $\mathbf{q} = \mathbf{q}^*$, and in the case of a system with prices corresponding to the extreme case of $\pi = \Pi$, i.e., when $\mathbf{p} = \mathbf{p}^*$ (and of course *a fortiori* when both $\mathbf{q} = \mathbf{q}^*$ and $\mathbf{p} = \mathbf{p}^*$), the relationship (VII.3.15) between g and γ becomes

$$g = G(1 - \gamma) \tag{VII.3.18}$$

a linear relation (see Fig. VII.2).

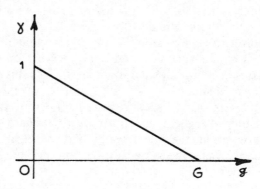

FIG. VII.2. Linear relation between rate of growth and per capita consumption when either $\mathbf{q} = \mathbf{q}^*$ or $\mathbf{p} = \mathbf{p}^*$

It is noteworthy that the case of prices $\mathbf{p}^*$ was not considered in our analysis of a linear function between π and w in Chapter V because in that context it would have had no meaning. (More precisely, it would have had no meaning to consider prices characterized by a given rate of profit – in that case $\pi = \Pi$ – in a context aimed at examining *changes* in the rate of profit). What we did consider there is the case in which prices, which we called $\bar{\mathbf{p}}$, remain constant at all levels of the rate of profit, i.e., the case associated with Ricardo's and Marx's assumption of a uniform capital intensity all over the economic system. In such a special case the prices are always equal to $\mathbf{p}^*$ (as they do not vary over the whole range $0 \leq \pi \leq \Pi$) and hence do satisfy requirement (ii) above. Therefore the special case of uniform capital intensity is another case in which the linear relation (VII.3.18) of Fig. VII.2 obtains.

3.5. *The same relation valid for the actual system, provided that the net product and capital are evaluated at prices p^*.* An interesting implication of what has just been said is that, as far as prices are concerned, the condition for obtaining a linear relation between g and γ (namely, $\mathbf{p} = \mathbf{p}^*$), is far less restrictive than the condition necessary to obtain a linear relation between π and w (namely, $\mathbf{p} = \mathbf{p}^* = \bar{\mathbf{p}}$; i.e., $\mathbf{p} = \mathbf{p}^*$ at *all* levels of the rate of profit). This would seem to confer on prices $\mathbf{p}^*$ – the particular prices that express a pure capital theory of value – a special relevance, which is worth investigating further.

We may recall, first of all, that prices $\mathbf{p}^*$ are the solution of a linear and homogeneous system of equations which is formally "dual" to the one defining the physical quantities $\mathbf{q}^*$, i.e., Sraffa's standard system. Therefore we should expect them to play a kind of dual role with respect to the one played by the standard system. It is also worth noting now that, as far as physical quantities are concerned, the condition necessary to obtain a linear relation between π and w (which we found in Chapter V, Sections 12.2, 12.3) is also far less restrictive than the one emerging here in connection with a linear relation between g and γ. For to obtain (VII.3.18) we need a system which is actually in standard proportions, while to obtain (V.12.9) the standard proportions are not needed at all. The only proviso required is that a certain (arbitrary) fraction of the standard system be used as the *numéraire* of the price system. As will be remembered, this is the remarkable property that allowed us to make use of the linear relation between π and w for any actual economic system (and not only for the standard system).

A similar, or rather a "dual," property emerges now with reference to prices $\mathbf{p}^*$. Any actual economic system (whatever its composition and prices may be) will in fact yield the linear relation (VII.3.18) between g and γ if, for the purpose of this relation, capital and net product are evaluated at the prices $\mathbf{p}^*$, thus satisfying requirement (ii) of the previous section.

It must be admitted that this linearity property of the g-γ relation associated with the prices $\mathbf{p}^*$, though formally "dual" to the linearity property of the π-w relation associated with the quantities $\mathbf{q}^*$, seems to have less force in it. For, while the choice of any commodity as the *numéraire* of the price system is really arbitrary, the choice of the prices at which to evaluate capital and income is not arbitrary, but needs justification. And this would not be easy to provide in the case of prices $\mathbf{p}^*$.

Yet the analytical result is a remarkable one. When considering the division of the net product between consumption and investment (i.e., for purposes of capital accumulation), the prices expressing a pure capital theory of value have the property of rendering the relation between the per capita consumption (as a proportion of per capita net product) and the rate of growth a linear one, whatever the composition of the net product and of capital may be.

4   Choice of Proportions and Rate of Growth

4.1. *The physical rate of net surplus.* We can now turn to an alternative way of representing the system of physical quantities, similarly to what was done in Chapter V, Section 8. That is, we can express the physical quantities which enter the net product of the economic system as proportions of the physical quantities which enter its means of production. Net investment has, in fact, already been expressed in this way, i.e., as a proportion of the means of production, in Section 2.5 above. But the same may also be done for consumption goods.

It will be recalled from Chapter V, Section 8, that the physical rate of surplus for each commodity i in the economic system as a whole is given by

$$R_i = \frac{Y_i}{Q_i - Y_i} \qquad\qquad i = 1, 2, \ldots, n - 1 \qquad (\text{VII.4.1})$$

Now, if the system is growing, the physical surplus cannot be devoted wholly to consumption, since a part of it corresponding to a percentage $\bar{g}$ of the means of production must be set aside for net investment. Consequently, only the difference $(R_i - \bar{g})$, which we shall call $R_i^{\ominus}$, or the physical rate of strictly net surplus, or for simplicity the physical rate of net surplus:

$$R_i^{\ominus} = R_i - \bar{g}, \qquad\qquad i = 1, 2, \ldots, n - 1 \qquad (\text{VII.4.2})$$

can be devoted to consumption. The $R_i^{\ominus}$ must, of course, satisfy the condition

$$R_i^{\ominus} \geq 0, \qquad\qquad i = 1, 2, \ldots, n - 1 \qquad (\text{VII.4.3})$$

These definitions enable us to rewrite the system of physical quantities as

$$\mathbf{Q}(t) - \mathbf{AQ}(t) - \bar{g}\mathbf{AQ}(t) - \hat{\mathbf{R}}_i^{\ominus}\mathbf{AQ}(t) = \mathbf{0} \qquad \text{(VII.4.4)}$$

or

$$[\mathbf{I} - \mathbf{A} \doteq (\mathbf{I}\bar{g} + \hat{\mathbf{R}}_i^{\ominus})\mathbf{A}]\mathbf{Q}(t) = \mathbf{0} \qquad \text{(VII.4.4a)}$$

where $\hat{\mathbf{R}}_i^{\ominus}$ is the diagonal matrix with the $(n - 1)$ $R_i^{\ominus}$, defined by (VII.4.2), on its principal diagonal. It will be noted that (VII.4.4) is a generalization of (V.8.5), which is obviously the special case in which $\bar{g} = 0$.

Similarly to what was said of (V.8.5), we can now say that, the technique $\mathbf{A}$ and the growth rate $\bar{g}$ being given, (VII.4.4) is a linear and homogeneous system of equations. A necessary condition for the existence of nonzero solutions is that

$$\det[\mathbf{I} - \mathbf{A} - (\mathbf{I}\bar{g} + \hat{\mathbf{R}}_i^{\ominus})\mathbf{A}] = 0 \qquad \text{(VII.4.5)}$$

This means that at most $(n - 2)$ physical rates of net surplus can be fixed at will. The remaining $(n - 1)$th rate must then be such as to satisfy (VII.4.5).

To conclude, when at most $(n - 2)$ physical rates of net surplus have been fixed, and when the remaining physical rate of net surplus has been found by solving the characteristic equation (VII.4.5), expression (VII.4.4) becomes a linear and homogeneous system of equations with a null determinant. Such a system contains at most $(n - 2)$ independent equations, i.e., it has at least one degree of freedom. And this degree of freedom allows us to add the equation

$$Q_n(t) = \mathbf{a}_n\mathbf{Q}(t) \qquad \text{(VII.4.6)}$$

concerning the full employment of the labor force. Equations (VII.4.4) and (VII.4.6) now form a system of equations which will, in general, be determinate, i.e., will contain $(n - 1)$ independent equations in the $(n - 1)$ unknowns: $Q_1(t), Q_2(t), \ldots, Q_{n-1}(t)$. For any given t, (VII.4.4) determines $(n - 2)$ relative quantities and (VII.4.6) determines the scale of operation at which full employment of the labor force is assured. And, as t increases, $Q_n(t)$ grows at the rate of growth $\bar{g}$. Therefore all the physical quantities $Q_1(t), Q_2(t), \ldots, Q_{n-1}(t)$ will also have to grow at exactly the same rate of growth.

4.2. *Restriction on choice imposed by the rate of growth.* The consumption possibilities open to the economic system, expressed in the previous sections by the per capita consumption coefficients $c_1, c_2, \ldots, c_{n-1}$, are now expressed by the physical rates of net surplus

$R_1^{\ominus}, R_2^{\ominus}, \ldots, R_{n-1}^{\ominus}$. Just as in the version of the previous sections all but one of the non-negative coefficients $c_1, c_2, \ldots, c_{n-1}$ could be chosen at will, so in the present formulation all but one of the physical rates of net surplus can be chosen at will. Like the coefficients of consumption, the physical rates of net surplus are, of course, restricted to be non-negative:

$$R_i^{\ominus} = R_i - \bar{g} \geq 0, \qquad\qquad i = 1, 2, \ldots, n - 1 \qquad \text{(VII.4.7)}$$

It may now be pointed out that condition (VII.4.7) becomes increasingly restrictive the higher is the rate of growth $\bar{g}$. For, the higher is $\bar{g}$, the smaller become the differences $R_i - \bar{g}$, $i = 1, 2, \ldots, n - 1$, subject to the constraint that none of them can become negative. Starting, for example, from a situation in which the proportions are defined by a particular set of physical rates of surplus $\bar{R}_1, \bar{R}_2, \ldots, \bar{R}_{n-1}$, it is quickly verified that, if $\bar{g}$ were to become greater than any one of these rates (and were thus to make the corresponding physical rate of net surplus negative), these particular proportions could no longer be chosen. It would be necessary to change the proportions in such a way as to restore non-negativity for all the physical rates of net surplus.

The range of possible choice of proportions thus becomes increasingly restricted as $\bar{g}$ increases and is eventually destined to disappear completely when the growth rate of the economic system reaches its maximum level G. At this growth rate every possibility of choice has vanished entirely. There is only one structure which permits growth at the maximum rate G; and it is the one that corresponds to the eigenvector associated with the maximum eigenvalue of $\mathbf{A}$. This is the structure which characterizes the "standard system." The proportions associated with this structure are open to no choice at all; they are rigidly determined by the technique of the economic system.

4.3. *Numerical example*. To elucidate these concepts, it may prove helpful to return to our numerical example introduced in Chapter II and used on several subsequent occasions.

In preceding chapters we have considered a situation with a stationary population and with physical rates of surplus for wheat (commodity No. 1), iron (No. 2) and pigs (No. 3) of: 66.6% (R_1), 0% (R_2) and 100% (R_3), respectively (see Table V.1, p. 95). If we now assume that the labor force, instead of remaining constant through time, increases at, for example, 2% per year ($\bar{g} = 2\%$), a necessary condition for the maintenance of dynamic equilibrium is that the means of production, consisting of all three produced commodities, must be increased at 2% per year. Now, if the economic system were to remain in the proportions which we assume to have been observed, the three physical rates of net surplus would become: $R_1^{\ominus} = 64.6\%$, $R_2^{\ominus} = -2\%$, and $R_3^{\ominus} = 98\%$, respectively. As can be seen, the second of these physical rates of net surplus would be negative, and that has no economic meaning. Thus the economic system under consideration, in the proportions which we have assumed to be observed, is not able to grow. Or, if one wishes, it can at most grow at zero percent per year, i.e., it can at best remain a stationary system.

But it is of course possible, given the technique, to increase the growth potential of the economic system by changing its proportions, provided that one is prepared to accept a restriction on the range of possible choices. In our example a growth of 2% per year necessitates a change of proportions which will increase the physical rate of surplus for iron to at least 2% (so that the physical rate of net surplus for iron is at least equal to zero). But this will imply a decrease in one or both of the other physical rates of surplus, i.e., a restriction of the possible choices open to the economic system (R_1 will have to fall below 66.6% and/or R_3 will have to fall below 100%; and, correspondingly, $R_1^{\ominus}$ will have to fall below 64.6% and/or $R_3^{\ominus}$ below 98%).

It is clear that the higher the rate of growth of population, the higher must be the minimum rate of surplus in order that the corresponding rate of net surplus may at least be equal to zero. And since, when changing the proportions, an increase in the minimum rate of surplus necessarily requires a decrease in at least one of the other rates of surplus, it follows that the range of possible choices open to the economic system is progressively narrowed down. The eventual outcome is clear. By continually increasing the minimum among the various rates of surplus, *all* the rates of surplus are bound to move closer to one another. In the limit, they all become equal to one another.[8] And this will happen at that rate of surplus which characterizes the standard system (in our particular example, 48%). At this rate the economic system can certainly grow at its maximum rate of growth, but no possibility of choice is open any more. The proportions become rigidly determined by the technology of the economic system.

4.4. *Concluding remarks.* We can reexpress the same ideas from a different point of view. We may say that there is a conflict between the range of choice of proportions which one wishes to leave open and the growth possibilities of the economic system.

Once the growth rate of the system, $\bar{g}$, has been fixed, it sets a minimum level for all the rates of surplus, none of which can fall below

---

[8] The arguments refer, of course, to basic commodities. If there were also non-basic commodities, their rates of surplus would in the limit become indeterminate because both numerators and denominators would tend to zero.

$\bar{g}$. The possible choice of proportions is thus restricted by the necessity of satisfying this constraint.

Similarly, if one wishes to start with the choice of certain particular proportions, expressed by a particular set of physical rates of surplus,

$$\bar{R}_1, \bar{R}_2, \ldots, \bar{R}_{n-1} \tag{VII.4.8}$$

the growth possibilities of the economic system are constrained by the smallest of these rates. Or, rather, the minimum rate of surplus represents the growth bottleneck of the system; it represents the maximum rate at which the economic system can grow, given the proportions which have been chosen.

In brief, the possibilities of choice open to the economic system are greatest when the growth rate of the system is reduced to zero (if zero is thought of as the minimum growth rate). And, similarly, the possibilities of growth are greatest when the choice of proportions is reduced to nil, by a technical determination of the proportions which correspond to the standard system.

5 The von Neumann Model

5.1. *A multiplicity of techniques.* After considering the relation between the rate of growth and per capita consumption for any given technique of production, we shall proceed to consider the same relation in the presence of a multiplicity of techniques.

We begin, however, by examining a special case suggested by the mathematician John von Neumann[9] even before publication of the works of Leontief and Sraffa.

5.2. *The technique which maximizes the rate of growth.* The model of economic growth suggested by von Neumann can be briefly summarized as follows. One considers an economic system in which the technology is represented by a finite number of production processes, each of which requires some physical inputs and produces some physical outputs. In each production process the various commodities that emerge as outputs may well be produced jointly. Labor is treated as if it were just another commodity. Like any other commodity, it requires certain inputs (subsistence consumption goods, which are thought of as being rigidly determined by physiological necessity) and produces certain outputs (labor services).

Such an economic system could obviously be interpreted as referring to a slave society, the workers being slaves and therefore being themselves means of production in the same way as are the beasts of burden and draft animals. (This is the old approach, which can be

[9] Von Neumann [16].

traced back to Classical analysis.)[10] But this same schema has also been interpreted as referring to a dual economy in which the production process analyzed is that belonging to the industrialized sector of the economy, which can absorb labor in virtually unlimited quantities (from the nonindustrialized sector, thought of as self-sufficient), at a wage rate which is rigidly determined in physical terms.

In any case, whichever interpretation one wishes to give to the schema, one consequence of this formulation is that it renders the destination of the net product completely determinate. The entire surplus, which remains in the economic system after having replaced the means of production (which in the present context also include the commodities advanced for the maintenance of the workers), is wholly distributed in the form of profits. Von Neumann specifically assumes, moreover, that all profits are devoted to accumulation. Hence the growth rate of the means of production of the economic system comes to coincide with the rate of profit.

The problem which von Neumann set himself can thus be presented as follows. Given the technology and assuming that the entire net product is accumulated, which configuration of methods of production and of relative outputs will yield the greatest uniform rate of growth of the system? Clearly, there might be some commodities which one could not avoid reproducing with a greater percentage surplus than holds for the other commodities. Von Neumann therefore introduces two restrictions: (i) production of all the commodities which have positive prices (i.e., the economic goods) must expand at a uniform rate of growth; (ii) commodities the outputs of which unavoidably grow at a rate greater than the (uniform) rate applying to economic goods have a price equal to zero (free goods).

A clearly defined choice-of-technique problem is thus formulated. The problem is that of choosing from among all the available alternative techniques the one which yields, for all the commodities with positive prices, the highest uniform rate of growth. And by applying a particular mathematical theorem (Brouwer's fixed point theorem) von Neumann has been able to prove that there always exists a configuration of methods of production and of relative outputs with which a maximum uniform rate of growth is associated.[11]

---

[10] We have had many opportunities of talking of this approach with reference to the works of Ricardo and Marx.

[11] To be precise, von Neumann set the problem in a more complex way. He chose to look for those relative quantities and rate of growth, and at the same time for those relative prices and rate of profit, which can remain constant through time. A typical mini-max problem has thereby emerged. The solution of this problem leads to the determination of the maximum among the possible rates of growth and of the minimum among the possible (maximum) rates of profit; and the two turn out to be the same.

5.3. *Relations with the standard system and with Sraffa's prices.* Within the more restrictive case of single-product industries, which is the case considered in this work, the von Neumann growth model appears as a particular case of the analysis developed in the previous pages.

In our analysis the technology of the economic system, i.e., the set of alternative techniques which are available, was represented by the set of matrices (VII.2.2). To each of these matrices, however, we must now add the matrix of interindustry coefficients of subsistence wage goods, which we called $\mathbf{da}_n$ in the Appendix to Chapter V. We thereby have

$$\mathbf{A}^{(x+)} = \mathbf{A}^{(x)} + \mathbf{da}_n^{(x)}, \qquad\qquad x = \alpha, \beta, \ldots, \omega$$

Moreover, since the surplus wage is zero *ex hypothesi*, all vectors of labor coefficients in (VII.2.1) become irrelevant, and the choice of technique reduces to a choice of one of the alternative matrices:

$$\mathbf{A}^{(\alpha+)}, \mathbf{A}^{(\beta+)}, \ldots, \mathbf{A}^{(\omega+)} \qquad\qquad\qquad \text{(VII.5.1)}$$

We know from our earlier analysis that each of these matrices is characterized by its own maximum eigenvalue:

$$\lambda_m^{(\alpha+)}, \lambda_m^{(\beta+)}, \ldots, \lambda_m^{(\omega+)} \qquad\qquad\qquad \text{(VII.5.2)}$$

respectively, and that there is associated with each of these eigenvalues a right-hand eigenvector (of physical quantities) and a left-hand eigenvector (of prices), both of which are non-negative. We know, furthermore, that to each of these eigenvalues there corresponds a maximum rate of growth, given by

$$G^{(x+)} = \frac{1}{\lambda_m^{(x+)}} - 1 \qquad\qquad x = \alpha, \beta, \ldots, \omega \qquad \text{(VII.5.3)}$$

Von Neumann's problem therefore reduces to choosing that technique, i.e., that matrix from (VII.5.1), to which corresponds the greatest of the growth rates (VII.5.3), or, which is the same thing, the smallest of the eigenvalues (VII.5.2). If such a technique is actually to yield the maximum growth rate, it is of course necessary that the various commodities be produced in the particular proportions associated with the "standard system," characterized by a uniform rate of surplus. Furthermore, since the (surplus) wage rate is zero, the system of prices will have to be that associated with the maximum rate of profit (which coincides with the uniform rate of surplus and thus with the maximum rate of growth).

The solution of von Neumann's problem thus entails: (i) the choice of the technique which is associated with the maximum rate of growth; (ii) given this technique, the choice of that system of physical quantities and that system of prices, dual to each other, which correspond to the uniform rate of surplus and to the maximum rate of profit, respectively (both these rates coinciding with the maximum rate of growth).[12]

5.4. *A restriction similar to that of the Sraffa system.* Our analysis, by being focused on the case of single-product industries, now allows us to make explicit a few properties of the von Neumann model which do not appear immediately from its original formulation.

We can say, first of all, that in the case of single-product industries there can be no production of free goods (goods which have zero prices because their production expands at a rate of growth greater than the uniform growth rate of the system). As we saw in Chapter V, the standard system contains commodities (basic commodities) which are produced at a uniform rate of surplus and which therefore, in the von Neumann schema, grow at a uniform rate of growth. All the other commodities (non-basic commodities) are not produced at all, and thus their processes of production will never enter the technique of production chosen on the basis of the von Neumann criterion.

More precisely, since the basic commodities which make up the standard system (i.e., the system able to grow at the maximum rate of growth) give rise to a matrix of interindustry coefficients which is irreducible, the associated vectors of physical quantities and of prices are both *strictly* positive.

However, the results above are subject to the important restriction, previously encountered in dealing with Sraffa's system,[13] that the maximum eigenvalue of the matrix of interindustry coefficients be also the maximum eigenvalue of the submatrix $A_{11}^{(+)}$ formed by the basic commodities. (The reference in this context must obviously be to the matrix $A^{(+)}$.) If this were not so, the von Neumann criterion would no doubt still lead to a solution in mathematical terms, but such a mathematical solution would have no economic meaning.

To grasp the meaning of this assertion we may consider for a moment the case in which the matrix associated with the maximum rate of growth were: (i) reducible, and (ii) such that the maximum eigenvalue of one of the submatrices on its principal diagonal, referring to non-basic commodities, were greater than the maximum eigenvalue

---

[12] It may be of interest to note that such an economic system satisfies those particular proportions at which, as shown above (Section 6 of the Appendix to Chapter V), all three inequalities (V.A.24), (V.A.25), (V.A.26) become equalities. In other words, von Neumann's system, like Sraffa's standard system, has the property of satisfying the three Marxian equalities between: total "values" and total prices, total surplus and total profits, rate of profit in terms of "values" and rate of profit in terms of prices.

[13] See p. 109.

of the submatrix referring to the basic commodities. Then the application of the von Neumann criterion would lead to a technique yielding a rate of growth equal to that permitted by the non-basic commodities. And since the own-rate of reproduction of the basic commodities would be greater, the prices of all the basic commodities would turn out to be zero.[14] This would have no economic meaning.

One may of course wonder what would happen in practice if such a system existed. And the answer is that, if an economic system required a rate of growth greater than that which is possible for the non-basic commodities (provided, of course, that it were not greater than the own-rate of reproduction of the basic commodities), such a rate of growth would indeed be achieved for the basic commodities (with positive prices), but a lower growth rate would have to be accepted for the non-basic commodities. In other words, the system could certainly exist; but it would not satisfy the basic requirement of the von Neumann model for a uniform rate of growth and a uniform rate of profit.[15]

6 A Relation Between the Rate of Growth and the Rate of Profit

6.1. *A capitalists' propensity to save smaller than unity.* The von Neumann model (by contrast with that of Sraffa) involves a perfectly determinate system of equations for relative prices. This determinateness of the price system is achieved, however, by means of rather drastic assumptions. It is assumed that the rate of growth is the highest technologically possible rate (and that the labor force increases at such a rate). It is assumed that the wage rate is kept down to the pure subsistence level. And finally it is assumed that the whole surplus that goes to profits is saved and invested.

Yet it is not necessary to make all these extreme assumptions in order to obtain a determinate system of relative prices. We may well

---

[14] This proposition can be proved with the aid of a theorem stated in footnote 9 on p. 275 of the *Mathematical Appendix*. If we take the matrix indicated there to represent the technique of the economic system, and if we suppose that its maximum eigenvalue coincides with the maximum eigenvalue of the submatrix A_{22} concerning the non-basic commodities, then it follows that the right-hand eigenvector (physical quantities) is strictly positive, whereas the left-hand eigenvector (prices) is semipositive in such a way as to contain zero prices for the basic commodities and positive prices for the non-basic commodities.

[15] To avoid complications of this kind, von Neumann found it convenient to assume straightaway that all possible interindustry matrices are irreducible, which is equivalent to assuming that there are no non-basic commodities.

adhere to our earlier analysis in which

$$\bar{g} \leq G \tag{VII.6.1}$$

$$\pi \leq \Pi \tag{VII.6.2}$$

and introduce a specific assumption about the division of incomes between consumption and savings.

In this respect some economists[16] have made the assumption that income recipients save a constant fraction of their incomes and moreover that they can, for simplicity, be divided into just two categories: workers, who save a fraction s_w (the propensity to save of workers), and "capitalists," who save a fraction s_c (the propensity to save of capitalists). These fractions are assumed to satisfy the inequalities

$$0 \leq s_w < s_c \leq 1 \tag{VII.6.3}$$

The adoption of this simple assumption suffices to provide an additional relation which is more general than that of von Neumann and at the same time is sufficient to close the system of relative prices.

6.2. *The "Cambridge equation."* For simplicity's sake consider first the special case in which $s_w = 0$ and $s_c < 1$. In this case, while all wages are devoted to the purchase of consumer goods, not all profits are devoted to the purchase of investment goods, the fraction $(1 - s_c)$ of profits being used for the purchase of consumer goods.

Since all new investment is carried out with that part of profits which is not consumed, it follows that in equilibrium total profits must exceed total new investment by an amount exactly equal to capitalist consumption.[17] Under our particular assumptions, this implies that

$$\text{Total profits} = \frac{\text{total investments}}{s_c} \tag{VII.6.4}$$

On dividing both sides of this equality by the total value of capital goods, we obtain the equilibrium relation

$$\pi = \frac{1}{s_c}\bar{g} \tag{VII.6.5}$$

which shows the equilibrium rate of profit corresponding to a given rate of growth and to a given propensity of capitalists to save.

This equation, which has become known as the "Cambridge equation," after the group of Cambridge economists[18] who first proposed it,

---

[16] Particularly Kalecki [6], Kaldor [4], J. Robinson [13], Kahn [3].

[17] This relation was originally proposed by Kalecki [6].

[18] Kaldor [5], J. Robinson [13], Kahn [3]. See also Pasinetti [9], [10].

is sufficient to close the system of relative prices considered above. In fact, expressions (VII.2.22) and (VII.6.5), taken together, constitute a system of n equations which, given the technology, the rate of growth of population, and the capitalists' propensity to save, determines n unknowns, namely: a wage rate (w), a rate of profit (π), and $(n - 2)$ relative prices (**p**), expressed in terms of any commodity or set of commodities arbitrarily chosen as *numéraire*.

6.3. *Extension to the case of a positive workers' propensity to save.* The "Cambridge equation" (VII.6.5) is in fact far more general than it might seem to be from the argument just given. It has been proved[19] that (VII.6.5) remains valid as a long-period, dynamic equilibrium relation, even when $s_w > 0$, provided that s_w is not so large as to make workers' savings exceed the amount which is sufficient, by itself (without any saving by capitalists), to finance the whole of new investment. (If this condition were not satisfied, the economic system would be fated to have a chronic tendency to excess savings and thus a chronic deficiency of effective demand, which would prevent its remaining on a dynamic equilibrium path).

Without giving a full exposition of the above-mentioned proof, it will simply be noted here that in the long run the capital owned by each group of savers tends to become proportional to the saving of that group. Consequently, under the simplifying assumption that the workers lend their savings to the capitalists at a rate of interest equal to the rate of profit, the total profits which workers collectively obtain each year on the capital lent to the capitalists tends to become equal in the long run to the amount of savings which the workers transfer to the capitalists in the form of loans. Thus total workers' savings tend to equal their total profits. The two flows exactly offset, and thus eliminate, each other from the equilibrium relations. As a consequence, only capitalists' savings turn out to be relevant to the determination of the rate of profit.[20] It is precisely this result which is expressed by the simple relationship (VII.6.5), independently of any savings by workers.

6.4. *Determinants of the composition of consumption.* At this point we may complete our previous discussion on the possible choices open to the economic system on consumption. It was stated in Section 2.8 above that consumers considered as a whole are free to choose the composition of per capita consumption but not its absolute level. However, at that point we did not wish to consider the question of the determinants of this choice. It is now possible to complete that discussion in the context of the savings assumptions made above.

[19] The proof is contained in Pasinetti [9].

[20] The interested reader may see Pasinetti [9], [10].

Because of our assumption that individual preferences remain unchanged over time, consumers' choices will depend on their per capita income and on the relative prices of the various goods and services. But per capita income depends, in turn, on technology and on the growth rate of the system, while relative prices depend on technology and on the rate of profit. The rate of profit finally depends, according to (VII.6.5), on the rate of growth and on the capitalists' propensity to save. Eventually, therefore, given consumers' preferences, the composition of consumption will, in dynamic equilibrium, depend on technology, on the rate of growth of population, and on the capitalists' propensity to save.

7 The Efficiency Criterion in the Process of Capital Accumulation

7.1. *The rate of growth of the labor force as an exogenously given datum.* We can at last resume our discussion of the multiplicity of production techniques. By contrast with von Neumann, we have adopted the approach, which is more typical of modern economists, of considering the rate of growth of the labor force as an exogenous datum (assumed, for simplicity, to be steady). This rate of growth of the labor force is usually much smaller than the maximum rate at which the system could grow; and this implies that a surplus of consumption over the subsistence minimum is normally available.

As a result, however, the problem of the choice of technique becomes more complex. In the von Neumann model the choice of technique is made according to the criterion of maximizing the rate of growth. But, if the growth rate of the system is constrained by the growth rate of the labor force, which is given exogenously, then the von Neumann criterion is no longer applicable. An alternative criterion must be found.

7.2. *The technological frontier of the consumption-and-growth possibilities.* Let us first try to figure out what possibilities are provided by the technology. It was seen in Section 3.2 above that each given technique of production $[\mathbf{A}, \mathbf{a}_n]'$ yields an inverse monotonic relation between the growth rate of the economic system and per capita consumption expressed in terms of any commodity. If there is more than one technique, there will clearly be as many relations between the rate of growth and per capita consumption as there are techniques. In the present case in which, from (VII.2.2), there are ω techniques, there will be ω such relations. Now, if per capita consumption is expressed in terms of the same commodity for all techniques, for example in terms of the ith commodity, we can represent and compare all the ω

alternative relations between g and c_i on the same diagram (see Fig. VII.3).

These relations (apart from the factor μ^{-1} which transforms per capita consumption into consumption per worker) are clearly the same relations already considered in Chapter VI and which were shown in Fig. VI.3. Indeed, since each relation between the rate of growth and consumption per worker, expressed in terms of the ith commodity, coincides (as pointed out in Section 3.2 above) with the relation between the rate of profit and the wage rate, expressed in terms of the same commodity, it follows that the set of relations between g and $\mu^{-1}c_i$ coincides with the set of relations between π and $w^{(i)}$.

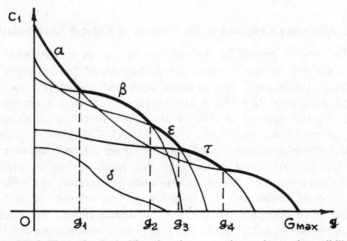

FIG. VII.3. The technological frontier of consumption-and-growth possibilities

However, although the mathematical functions are exactly the same, their meaning is quite different. Each relation in Fig. VII.3 represents the equilibrium per capita consumption which each technique makes possible at any given rate of growth. Hence the set of outermost segments in Fig. VII.3, or the envelope of the various curves (which is again shown boldface), represents the maximum equilibrium per capita consumption that the technology can offer at any predetermined rate of growth; or – which is the same thing – the maximum rate of growth which the technology can offer at any predetermined level of equilibrium per capita consumption.

This envelope thus represents what we may call the *technological frontier of consumption-and-growth possibilities* of the economic system.

The remarkable outcome is that this technological frontier (the boldface line in Fig. VII.3, multiplied by μ^{-1}) is exactly the same technological frontier as that representing the income distribution possibilities we encountered in Chapter VI (the boldface line in Fig. VI.3). In other words, given the technology of an economic system, the same envelope-function represents both the technological frontier of consumption-and-growth possibilities and the technological frontier of income distribution possibilities. Hence *there is only one technological frontier* which represents at the same time the relation between the rate of growth and consumption per worker, and the relation between the rate of profit and the wage rate.

7.3. *Properties of the technological frontier.* On the technological frontier of consumption and growth possibilities (as on the frontier of income distribution possibilities) the various techniques follow one another, as the rate of growth varies, without it being possible to relate their ordering *a priori* to any well definable objective property. In our example, for rates of growth between 0 and g_1, technique α is the technique which offers the highest equilibrium per capita consumption. For rates of growth between g_1 and g_2, the same role is played by technique β; for rates of growth between g_2 and g_3 by technique ε; for rates of growth between g_3 and g_4 by technique τ. And finally, for rates of growth greater than g_4, technique α, although discarded at intermediate rates of growth, comes back to become again the technique which offers the highest per capita consumption (the *reswitching of techniques* phenomenon). Corresponding to any given rate of growth, there is therefore normally only one technique which yields the highest equilibrium per capita consumption, except at the singular points g_1, g_2, g_3, g_4 (the *switch points*) at which there are two distinct techniques (or any linear combinations of them) which yield the same equilibrium per capita consumption.

There are then all the other techniques (of which only one, technique δ, is shown in Fig. VII.3) which never appear on the technological frontier. These techniques are inferior ones, in the sense that they would yield per capita consumption levels lower than those obtainable with some other technique, at *all* levels of the rate of growth (from zero to its maximum). These inferior techniques are thus economically irrelevant (though in practice they may be the majority).

We need not discuss the properties of this technological frontier at length here, since they coincide with the properties of the technological frontier of income distribution possibilities, which we have already examined in detail in Chapter VI. Yet it may be useful to recall that the shape of the technological frontier varies according to the commodity in terms of which per capita consumption is expressed. Nevertheless, the switches of technique always occur at the same rates of growth (just as they always occur at the same rates of profit). In other words, the switch points on the technological frontier are invariant with respect to the commodity in terms of which per capita consumption is expressed (just as they are invariant with respect to the commodity in terms of which the wage rate is expressed).

This means that the foregoing analysis, though conducted in terms of a specific commodity, is in fact valid with reference to any commodity.

7.4. *The criterion of efficiency.* We set out (Section 7.1) with the aim of seeking a criterion for choosing the technique of production, when the rate of growth of population is exogenously given. And at this point there emerges rather naturally a criterion of choice which we may call the *criterion of efficiency*. We can formulate it as follows: From among all the available techniques, choose that technique which, at the given rate of growth of population, $\bar{g}$, yields the dynamic equilibrium path characterized by the highest level of per capita consumption.

It is to be noted that the path referred to is one of dynamic equilibrium. The comparisons which can be made with the kind of analysis carried out above, and hence with diagrams such as that in Fig. VII.3, are all comparisons of the *comparative dynamics* type. All the points on the technological frontier of Fig. VII.3 refer to alternative economic systems for which the production techniques are indeed chosen from the same technology, but each of which is growing along its own dynamic equilibrium path, characterized by a particular rate of growth, a particular level of per capita consumption, and those particular proportions which are appropriate to it in equilibrium growth.

7.5. *The efficiency criterion and the profitability criterion.* It is clear from Figs. VI.3 and VII.3 that the efficiency criterion (considered in this chapter) and the profitability criterion (examined in Chapter VI) do not necessarily lead to the choice of the same technique. On the contrary, we can say that, in general, the two criteria lead to the choice of different techniques, unless the rate of profit happens to coincide with the rate of growth. In other words, the technique which secures the maximum per capita consumption, given the rate of growth, is not necessarily the technique which yields the maximum wage rate, given the rate of profit, except in the special case in which the rate of profit is equal to the rate of growth.

In the von Neumann model the rate of growth and the rate of profit are always equal to each other by assumption. But in the more general model considered in Sections 6.1–6.4 above, this is not so. Only in the special case in which $s_c = 1$ do we have

$$\pi = g \tag{VII.7.1}$$

This means that the equality of the rate of profit and the rate of growth, and hence the coincidence of the techniques chosen according to the two criteria of profitability and efficiency, will necessarily occur only in the special case in which all capitalists' profits are saved.

7.6. *The "golden rule" of capital accumulation.* From the standpoint of an economic system considered as a whole, it would seem that the efficiency criterion (the choice of that technique which secures the maximum equilibrium per capita consumption) is the only relevant one. Yet the fact is that the direct application of this criterion would be extremely laborious, as it would require centralized planning of the choice of all the methods of production in even the most remote sections of the economic system. The application of the profitability criterion, by contrast, permits a decentralized choice of production methods at the level of individual industries or even firms. Each single producer, when applying the profitability criterion, simply chooses that method of production which, given the wage rate, maximizes his profits (which is equivalent, in equilibrium, to choosing that method of production which, given the rate of profit, maximizes the wage rate). He does not need to consider what happens elsewhere in the economic system.[21] In organizational terms, the advantages of the profitability criterion are undoubtedly enormous.

Thus, even if one might in principle wish to adopt the efficiency criterion, it is the profitability criterion that has the higher chance to be applied in practice. This gives great significance and importance to the rule in (VII.7.1): a rate of profit equal to the rate of growth. This rule has become well known in the economic literature as the *golden rule of capital accumulation.*[22]

In the special case in which $\pi = g$, the application of the profitability criterion automatically becomes an application of the efficiency criterion.

References

[1] Desrousseaux, J., "Expansion stable et taux d'intérêt optimal," *Annales des Mines*, 1961, pp. 829–844.
[2] Jorgenson, Dale W., "On a Dual Stability Theorem," *Econometrica*, 1960, pp. 892–899.

[21] These propositions, of course, presuppose the assumption of constant returns to scale.

[22] See von Weizsäcker [17], Swan [15], Phelps [12], Desrousseaux [1], J. Robinson [14].

[3] Kahn, Richard F., "Exercises in the Analysis of Growth," *Oxford Economic Papers*, 1959, pp. 143–156; reprinted in *Selected Essays in Employment and Growth*, Cambridge: Cambridge University Press, 1972.

[4] Kaldor, Nicholas, "Alternative Theories of Distribution," *Review of Economic Studies*, 1955–1956, pp. 83–100; reprinted in *Essays on Value and Distribution*, London: G. Duckworth and Co., 1960.

[5] ———, "A Model of Economic Growth," *Economic Journal*, 1957, pp. 591–624; reprinted in *Essays on Economic Stability and Growth*, London: G. Duckworth and Co., 1960.

[6] Kalecki, Michal, *Essays in the Theory of Economic Fluctuations*, London, George Allen and Unwin: 1938.

[7] Leontief, Wassily W., "Static and Dynamic Theory," Part I of *Studies in the Structure of the American Economy*, ed. by W. W. Leontief, New York: Oxford University Press, 1953.

[8] ———, "The Dynamic Inverse," in *Contributions to Input-Output Analysis*, ed. by A. P. Carter and A. Bródy, Amsterdam: North-Holland Publishing Co., 1970, vol. I.

[9] Pasinetti, Luigi, "Rate of Profit and Income Distribution in Relation to the Rate of Economic Growth," *Review of Economic Studies*, 1962, pp. 267–279, reprinted in [10].

[10] ———, *Growth and Income Distribution – Essays in Economic Theory*, Cambridge: Cambridge University Press, 1974.

[11] ———, "A New Theoretical Approach to the Problems of Economic Growth," *Academiae Pontificiae Scientiarum Scripta Varia*, No. 28, Vatican City, 1965, pp. 571–696. (Republished in *The Econometric Approach to Development Planning*, Amsterdam, North-Holland Publ. Co., 1965.)

[12] Phelps, Edmund, "The Golden Rule of Accumulation: A Fable for Growthmen," *American Economy Review*, 1961, pp. 638–643.

[13] Robinson, Joan, *The Accumulation of Capital*, London: Macmillan, 1956.

[14] ———, "A Neo-classical Theorem," *Review of Economic Studies*, 1961–1962, pp. 219–226.

[15] Swan, Trevor W., "Growth Models: Of Golden Ages and Production Functions," *Economic Development. Proceedings of a Conference Held by the I.E.A.*, 1960, ed. by K. Berrill, London: Macmillan, 1964, pp. 3–18.

[16] Von Neumann, John, "Über ein ökonomisches Gleichungssystem und eine Verallgemeinerung des Brouwerschen Fixpunktsatzes," *Ergebnisse eines Matematischen Kolloquiums*," Vienna, 1937, vol.

VIII, pp. 73–83; English translation: "A Model of General Equilibrium," *Review of Economic Studies*, 1945–1946, pp. 1–9.
[17] Von Weizsäcker, Christian, *Wachstum, Zins und optimale Investitionsquote*, Basel: Kyklos Verlag, 1962.

MATHEMATICAL APPENDIX

An Elementary Introduction to Matrix Algebra

Warning. *This Appendix has been written for the benefit of those readers whose knowledge of mathematics is limited to elementary algebra. Its purpose is simply to introduce the concepts needed to understand the arguments developed in the preceding text. It is not, therefore, meant to be a substitute for a mathematics textbook. The reader interested in learning matrix algebra thoroughly is advised to refer to a good treatment of the subject.*[1]

1 Introductory Remarks

MATRIX algebra was developed primarily for the purpose of the analysis of systems of linear equations. Indeed, as long as one is concerned with systems of two or three equations, the problem can easily be solved by using elementary algebra and the solutions can be represented graphically as well. But, whenever these systems contain more than three equations, elementary algebra becomes cumbersome and a geometric treatment is no longer possible. It then becomes necessary to develop more powerful analytical tools, which is exactly what matrix algebra is designed to do.

2 Definitions

We begin with some definitions.

A *matrix* is defined as an ordered array of elements arranged on m rows and n columns written as

$$\begin{bmatrix} a_{11} & a_{12} & a_{13} & \cdots & a_{1n} \\ a_{21} & a_{22} & a_{23} & \cdots & a_{2n} \\ \cdot & \cdot & \cdot & \cdot & \cdot \\ \cdot & \cdot & \cdot & \cdot & \cdot \\ \cdot & \cdot & \cdot & \cdot & \cdot \\ a_{m1} & a_{m2} & a_{m3} & \cdots & a_{mn} \end{bmatrix} \qquad (A.2.1)$$

[1] See, for example, Hadley [8], Bellman [2], Shilov [11], Faddeev [5], Gantmacher [7].

Each element here is identified by two subscripts. The first subscript indicates the row and the second subscript indicates the column. Hence a_{ij} represents the element on the ith row and jth column. More compactly, a matrix can be represented by a capital letter (in boldface) **A**, or by a symbol $\|a_{ij}\|$, or $[a_{ij}]$, for $i = 1, 2, \ldots, m$; $j = 1, 2, \ldots, n$; or by $[a_{ij}]_{m \times n}$.

Notice that a matrix is simply an ordered array of elements. These elements may be several things: objects, polynomials, complex numbers, real numbers, etc. In our treatment we confine ourselves to matrices the elements of which are real numbers.

A matrix with m rows and n columns is said to be of order m by n or simply an $m \times n$ matrix. If $m \neq n$, the matrix is said to be rectangular. If $m = n$, the matrix is said to be a square matrix of the nth order, where n is the number of rows and columns. In a square matrix the *principal diagonal* consists of all elements having the same row and column subscript.

In this context the numbers of elementary algebra may be interpreted as square matrices with just one row and one column. This particular type of square matrix, with just one row and one column, is called a *scalar*.

Some square matrices have particular properties:

A square matrix is said to be *upper triangular* (or *lower triangular*) if all elements below (or above) its principal diagonal are zeros. For example, the matrix

$$
\begin{bmatrix}
a_{11} & a_{12} & a_{13} & \cdots & a_{1n} \\
0 & a_{22} & a_{23} & \cdots & a_{2n} \\
0 & 0 & a_{33} & \cdots & a_{3n} \\
\vdots & \vdots & \vdots & \ddots & \vdots \\
0 & 0 & 0 & \cdots & a_{nn}
\end{bmatrix}
\tag{A.2.2}
$$

is an upper triangular matrix.

A square matrix is said to be a *diagonal matrix* if all off-diagonal elements are zeros. It may be represented by

$$
\mathbf{D} = [\lambda_i \delta_{ij}], \qquad\qquad i, j = 1, 2, \ldots, n \tag{A.2.3}
$$

where λ_i is a scalar and δ_{ij} is the so-called "Kronecker delta." By definition the "Kronecker delta" is equal to 1 for $i = j$ and equal to zero for $i \neq j$ $(i, j = 1, 2, \ldots, n)$.

Observe that a diagonal matrix is simultaneously upper and lower triangular.

A diagonal matrix in which every element on the principal diagonal is the number 1 is called a *unit matrix, or identity matrix*, and is written

$$\mathbf{I} = [\delta_{ij}] = \begin{bmatrix} 1 & 0 & \cdots & 0 \\ 0 & 1 & \cdots & 0 \\ \vdots & \vdots & \ddots & \vdots \\ 0 & 0 & \cdots & 1 \end{bmatrix} \tag{A.2.4}$$

The identity matrix is written $\mathbf{I}_n$ whenever its order needs to be specified. In matrix algebra this matrix plays a role similar to that played by the number 1 (unity) in elementary algebra.

A diagonal matrix in which every element on the principal diagonal is the same number is called *scalar matrix* and is written

$$\lambda \mathbf{I} = [\lambda \delta_{ij}] \tag{A.2.5}$$

i.e., as the product of a scalar and a unit matrix (see also Section 4.4 below).

Among rectangular matrices there are some that have interesting properties:

A matrix (rectangular or square) the elements of which are all zeros is called a *null matrix*. We indicate it by $\mathbf{O}$. A $1 \times n$ matrix, i.e., a matrix with one row and n columns, is called a *row vector*. Similarly, an $m \times 1$ matrix (m rows and one column) is called a *column vector*.

As one may realize from these definitions, matrices – unlike numbers – are magnitudes with many dimensions. Rules and operations have been developed, however, to allow us to handle them in a similar way to numbers. It is this set of rules and operations that we refer to as matrix algebra.

3   Vectors

3.1. To introduce the subject it may be useful to illustrate briefly some concepts relating to vectors. The notion of a vector was initially devised by physicists concerned with the treatment and measurement of magnitudes which could not be represented by a single number. For example, the notion of *force*, which is encountered in elementary physics, is characterized by a given intensity and a given direction. To represent it, at least two numbers are required. And the physicists have traditionally represented it by an arrow, called a *vector*, the length of which indicates the intensity of the force and the slope of which indicates its direction (Fig. A.1.).

Suppose that the vector is drawn from the origin of two Cartesian axes (x_1, x_2); then the vector itself may be indicated by the coordinates of its extreme point (a_1, a_2), which enable us to identify its length – or modulus – and its direction. Indeed, its length or *modulus* will be $(a_1^2 + a_2^2)^{1/2}$, and its direction $\tan \alpha = a_2/a_1$.

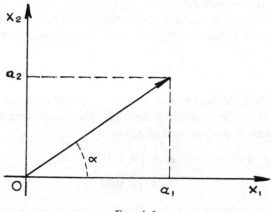

FIG. A.1.

It will be noted immediately from this graphical representation that there is a one-to-one correspondence between points in a space and vectors. Every point in a space is associated with a vector, expressed by the coordinates of that point. And every vector is associated with a point in the corresponding space.

3.2. The notion of a vector used in the following pages comes from a generalization of the notion presented in the section above.

An n-component *vector* is defined as an ordered n-tuple of components arranged in a row (row vector) or in a column (column vector). A vector is usually denoted by a small letter in boldface (for example, **a**) or, more explicitly, referring to its components, as

$$[a_1, a_2, a_3, \ldots, a_n]$$ (row vector)

or

$$\begin{bmatrix} a_1 \\ a_2 \\ \vdots \\ a_m \end{bmatrix}$$ (column vector)

If, by convention, a row vector is denoted by a small boldface letter **a**, a column vector will be denoted by the same letter with a prime (e.g., **a**′). Similarly, if by convention a column vector is denoted by a small boldface letter, a row vector will then be denoted by the same letter with a prime.

As already mentioned, vectors may also be interpreted as particular rectangular matrices with only one row (and n columns) or with only one column (and m rows).

Some vectors have particular properties which deserve our attention.

The *null vector*, defined as **0**, is a vector every component of which is a zero:

$$\mathbf{0} = [0, 0, \ldots, 0]. \tag{A.3.1}$$

The *unit vector*, defined as $\mathbf{e}_i$, $i = 1, 2, \ldots, n$, is a vector in which the ith component is the number 1 and all other components are zeros. There are hence n unit vectors of order n:

$$\mathbf{e}_1 = [1, 0, 0, \ldots, 0] \quad \mathbf{e}_2 = [0, 1, 0, \ldots, 0]$$
$$\ldots\ldots\ldots\ldots\ldots \quad \mathbf{e}_n = [0, 0, 0, \ldots, 1] \tag{A.3.2}$$

The *sum vector*, defined as **1** is a vector every component of which is equal to unity:

$$\mathbf{1} = [1, 1, \ldots, 1] \tag{A.3.3}$$

3.3. The following relations and operations are defined between vectors.

Equality. Two vectors **a** and **b** are equal if, and only if, each component of vector **a** is equal to the corresponding component of vector **b**. That is, if

$$a_i = b_i, \qquad\qquad i = 1, 2, \ldots, n \tag{A.3.4}$$

In order to grasp the meaning of this definition it may be helpful to consider vectors with two components, which can be represented

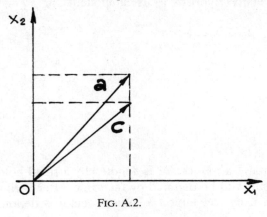

FIG. A.2.

graphically. For example, in Fig. A.2, vectors **a** and **c** are not equal even though they have a common coordinate.

It may be noted at once that the equality relation between vectors satisfies the reflexive, symmetric, and transitive properties. That is,

$$\mathbf{a} = \mathbf{a} \tag{A.3.5}$$

$$\text{if} \quad \mathbf{a} = \mathbf{b} \quad \text{then} \quad \mathbf{b} = \mathbf{a} \tag{A.3.6}$$

$$\text{if} \quad \mathbf{a} = \mathbf{b} \quad \text{and} \quad \mathbf{b} = \mathbf{c} \quad \text{then} \quad \mathbf{a} = \mathbf{c} \tag{A.3.7}$$

Scalar multiplication. Given a scalar λ and a vector **a**, their product is defined as another vector $\lambda\mathbf{a}$, the components of which are the components of vector **a** multiplied by the scalar λ:

$$\lambda\mathbf{a} = [\lambda a_1, \lambda a_2, \ldots, \lambda a_n] \tag{A.3.8}$$

For example, consider a scalar $\lambda = 2$ and a two-component vector $[a_1, a_2]$. Graphically, it can be seen at once that their product $[2a_1, 2a_2]$ is a vector which has the same direction as the former and twice its length (see Fig. A.3).

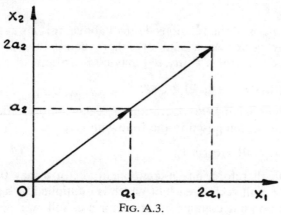

FIG. A.3.

Addition. Given two n-component vectors **a** and **b**, their sum is defined as the vector $(\mathbf{a} + \mathbf{b})$, the components of which are the sum of the corresponding components of the two vectors being added:

$$\mathbf{a} + \mathbf{b} = [a_1 + b_1, a_2 + b_2, \ldots, a_n + b_n] \tag{A.3.9}$$

Observe that the operation of addition (as well as the relation of equality) is defined only for vectors with the same number of components. It satisfies the commutative and associative properties. That is,

$$\mathbf{a} + \mathbf{b} = \mathbf{b} + \mathbf{a} \tag{A.3.10}$$

$$(\mathbf{a} + \mathbf{b}) + \mathbf{c} = \mathbf{a} + (\mathbf{b} + \mathbf{c}) \tag{A.3.11}$$

For two-component vectors one can show the operation of addition on a diagram (see Fig. A.4). The sum vector turns out to be the diagonal of the parallelogram obtained by adjoining each of the two vectors to the other. (This rule is known in physics as the parallelogram rule.)

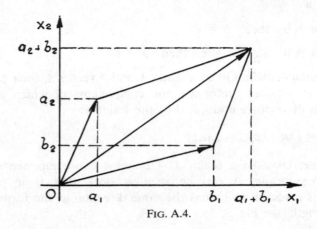

FIG. A.4.

3.4. On the basis of the relations defined above, it is always possible to consider any vector as a sum of other vectors. For example, the two-component vector $\mathbf{a} = [a_1, a_2]$ may be rewritten

$$\mathbf{a} = [a_1, a_2] = [a_1, 0] + [0, a_2] \tag{A.3.12}$$

Moreover, by applying the operation of scalar multiplication, vector $\mathbf{a}$ can be further decomposed in the following way:

$$\mathbf{a} = a_1[1, 0] + a_2[0, 1] \tag{A.3.13}$$

In general, therefore, any n-component vector $\mathbf{a}$ may be expressed as a sum of n unit vectors each of which is multiplied by a scalar equal to the corresponding component of vector $\mathbf{a}$ as follows:

$$\mathbf{a} = [a_1, a_2, a_3, \ldots, a_n] = a_1[1, 0, 0, \ldots, 0]$$
$$+ a_2[0, 1, 0, \ldots, 0] + a_3[0, 0, 1, \ldots, 0] + \cdots$$
$$+ a_n[0, 0, 0, \ldots, 1] \tag{A.3.14}$$

Vector $\mathbf{a}$ is then said to be expressed as a *linear combination* of vectors, i.e., a combination obtained by applying the operations of addition and scalar multiplication.

More generally, let there be m n-component vectors, $\mathbf{a}_1, \mathbf{a}_2, \ldots, \mathbf{a}_m$. Consider now the n-component vector $\mathbf{z}$, defined as

$$\mathbf{z} = \lambda_1\mathbf{a}_1 + \lambda_2\mathbf{a}_2 + \cdots, \lambda_m\mathbf{a}_m \tag{A.3.15}$$

where $\lambda_1, \lambda_2, \ldots, \lambda_m$ are real numbers. The vector $\mathbf{z}$ is said to be a *linear combination* of the vectors $\mathbf{a}_1, \mathbf{a}_2, \ldots, \mathbf{a}_m$.

The set of all vectors $\mathbf{z}$ obtained from the vectors $\mathbf{a}_1, \mathbf{a}_2, \ldots, \mathbf{a}_m$ by applying operation (A.3.15) is called a *vector space* (or also *linear space*).

Let us now consider the following special linear combination:

$$\mathbf{0} = \lambda_1 \mathbf{a}_1 + \lambda_2 \mathbf{a}_2 + \cdots + \lambda_m \mathbf{a}_m \qquad (A.3.16)$$

If $\mathbf{a}_1, \mathbf{a}_2, \ldots, \mathbf{a}_m$ are such that the only $\lambda_1, \lambda_2, \ldots, \lambda_m$ which satisfy (A.3.16) are $\lambda_1 = \lambda_2 = \cdots = \lambda_m = 0$, then the m vectors are said to be *linearly independent*. If, by contrast, at least one $\lambda_i \neq 0$ can be found, $i = 1, 2, \ldots, m$, then the m vectors are said to be *linearly dependent*. It should be noted that, if the m vectors are linearly dependent, at least one among them can be expressed as a linear combination of the others. Indeed, supposing that $\lambda_1 \neq 0$, we can write

$$\mathbf{a}_1 = \frac{\lambda_2}{-\lambda_1} \mathbf{a}_2 + \frac{\lambda_3}{-\lambda_1} \mathbf{a}_3 + \cdots + \frac{\lambda_m}{-\lambda_1} \mathbf{a}_m \qquad (A.3.17)$$

Let us go back for a moment to a two-dimensional vector space. In this space two vectors are linearly dependent if one is a scalar multiple of the other, i.e., if the two vectors lie on the same straight line drawn from the origin. Conversely, any given pair of vectors which do not lie on the same straight line drawn from the origin is a pair of linearly independent vectors. In such a space then, given any two linearly independent vectors, it can be immediately shown that any other vector can be obtained as a linear combination of them. In particular, it can be immediately shown that any vector can be obtained as a linear combination of the two unit vectors $[1, 0], [0, 1]$. It follows that a two-dimensional vector space cannot contain more than two linearly independent vectors.

3.5. We have just seen that in a two-dimensional vector space (V^2), given any set of two linearly independent vectors, all the other vectors can be obtained as linear combinations of them. Similarly, in any n-dimensional vector space, given a certain set of n vectors, it should always be possible to obtain from them the others as linear combinations.

We shall call the *set of vectors spanning a vector space V^n*, any subset of vectors of V^n from which the whole space can be obtained by linear combinations. It will obviously be of interest to select those sets which contain the minimum number of vectors. For this purpose it will be necessary to eliminate all linearly dependent vectors in order to be left with linearly independent vectors only. These sets which contain the minimum number of (linearly independent) vectors are called bases for V^n.

Thus we define the *basis for* V^n as a subset of linearly independent vectors spanning the whole vector space. For any given space V^n there exists an infinite number of bases. It can be shown, however, that each of these bases contains the same number of vectors. In particular, it can be immediately verified that the n unit vectors of V^n form a basis for V^n. This basis is called the *natural* or *canonical* basis for V^n. It follows that the number of vectors in any given basis for a space V^n is given by the number n, which also represents the maximum number of linearly independent vectors in V^n.

We may therefore also define as the *dimension of a vector space* the maximum number of linearly independent vectors which the space contains.

3.6. Let V^n be an n-dimensional vector space and let **a** and **b** be two n-component row vectors. We define the *scalar product* (or *inner product*) of **a** and **b**, written as **ab′**, as a scalar obtained by multiplying each component of the first vector by the corresponding component of the second vector and then summing the products thus obtained:

$$\mathbf{ab}' = [a_1, a_2, \ldots, a_n] \begin{bmatrix} b_1 \\ b_2 \\ \vdots \\ b_n \end{bmatrix} = \sum_{i=1}^{n} a_i b_i \tag{A.3.18}$$

Two vectors **a** and **b** are said to be *orthogonal* if their scalar product is zero, i.e., if

$$\mathbf{ab}' = 0 \tag{A.3.19}$$

The *modulus*, or *Euclidean length*, of a vector **a**, denoted by $|\mathbf{a}|$, is defined as the square root of the scalar product of vector **a** by itself:

$$|\mathbf{a}| = (\mathbf{aa}')^{1/2} = \left[\sum_{i=1}^{n} a_i^2 \right]^{1/2} \tag{A.3.20}$$

The *Euclidean length* satisfies the properties

$$|\mathbf{a}| > 0 \quad \text{except in the case} \quad \mathbf{a} = \mathbf{0} \tag{A.3.21}$$

$$|\mathbf{a} + \mathbf{b}| \leq |\mathbf{a}| + |\mathbf{b}| \tag{A.3.22}$$

$$|\lambda \mathbf{a}| = |\lambda| |\mathbf{a}| \tag{A.3.23}$$

The vector space V^n for which the notion of Euclidean length is defined is called *Euclidean space* and is denoted by E^n. We shall confine our analysis to Euclidean spaces. For any Euclidean space we also define the notion of:

Distance between a vector (point) **a** and a vector (point) **b**, which is denoted by $|\mathbf{a} - \mathbf{b}|$ and is defined as the square root of the scalar product of the vector $(\mathbf{a} - \mathbf{b})$ by itself:

$$|\mathbf{a} - \mathbf{b}| = [(\mathbf{a} - \mathbf{b}) \cdot (\mathbf{a} - \mathbf{b})']^{1/2} = \left[\sum_{i=1}^{n} (a_i - b_i)^2 \right]^{1/2} \quad \text{(A.3.24)}$$

It can immediately be verified that

$$|\mathbf{a} - \mathbf{b}| > 0 \quad \text{except in the case} \quad \mathbf{a} = \mathbf{b} \quad \text{(A.3.25)}$$

$$|\mathbf{a} - \mathbf{b}| = |\mathbf{b} - \mathbf{a}| \quad \text{(A.3.26)}$$

$$|\mathbf{a} - \mathbf{b}| + |\mathbf{b} - \mathbf{c}| \geq |\mathbf{a} - \mathbf{c}| \quad \text{(triangular inequality)} \quad \text{(A.3.27)}$$

Observe now that the length of a vector is a special case of distance (distance of the vector itself from vector **0**).

4 Matrices

4.1. We may now return to the more general concepts concerning matrices. It may be noted immediately that any $m \times n$ matrix may be looked at as being obtained by adjoining m row vectors or by adjoining n column vectors. We now define a set of relations and operations between matrices.

4.2. *Equality*. Two matrices **A** and **B**, which have the same number of rows and the same number of columns, are said to be equal $(\mathbf{A} = \mathbf{B})$ if every element of **A** is equal to the corresponding element of **B**, i.e., if $a_{ij} = b_{ij}$, for each i and j. The equality relation between matrices satisfies the reflexive, symmetric, and transitive properties:

$$\mathbf{A} = \mathbf{A} \quad \text{(A.4.1)}$$

$$\text{if} \quad \mathbf{A} = \mathbf{B} \quad \text{then} \quad \mathbf{B} = \mathbf{A} \quad \text{(A.4.2)}$$

$$\text{if} \quad \mathbf{A} = \mathbf{B} \quad \text{and} \quad \mathbf{B} = \mathbf{C} \quad \text{then} \quad \mathbf{A} = \mathbf{C} \quad \text{(A.4.3)}$$

4.3. *Addition*. The sum of two matrices **A** and **B**, both with the same number of rows and columns, is defined as a third matrix $\mathbf{C} = \mathbf{A} + \mathbf{B}$, the elements of which are the sum of the corresponding elements of **A** and **B**, i.e., $c_{ij} = a_{ij} + b_{ij}$ for all i and j. It follows from the definition that the operation of addition is defined solely for matrices with the same number of rows and the same number of columns.

The addition of matrices satisfies the commutative and associative properties:

$$\mathbf{A} + \mathbf{B} = \mathbf{B} + \mathbf{A} \tag{A.4.4}$$

$$(\mathbf{A} + \mathbf{B}) + \mathbf{C} = \mathbf{A} + (\mathbf{B} + \mathbf{C}) \tag{A.4.5}$$

4.4. *Multiplication by a scalar.* Given a matrix $\mathbf{A}$ and a scalar λ, their product is defined as another matrix each element of which is given by the corresponding element of $\mathbf{A}$ multiplied by λ:

$$\lambda \mathbf{A} = [\lambda a_{ij}]_{m \times n} \tag{A.4.6}$$

This operation has been defined to enable us to make sense of the operation $\mathbf{A} + \mathbf{A}$ and write it as $2\mathbf{A}$.

4.5. *Transposition.* Given a matrix $\mathbf{A}$, the transpose of $\mathbf{A}$, which is written $\mathbf{A}'$, is a matrix in which the rows and columns of $\mathbf{A}$ have been interchanged, i.e.,

$$\text{if} \quad \mathbf{A} = [a_{ik}]_{m \times n} \quad \text{then} \quad \mathbf{A}' = [a'_{ik}]_{n \times m} = [a_{ki}]_{n \times m} \tag{A.4.7}$$

It follows from the definition that

$$(\mathbf{A}')' = \mathbf{A} \quad \text{since} \quad (a'_{ik})' = a_{ik} \tag{A.4.8}$$

and also that

$$(\mathbf{A} + \mathbf{B})' = \mathbf{A}' + \mathbf{B}' \tag{A.4.9}$$

It can immediately be verified that

$$\mathbf{D} = \mathbf{D}' \quad \text{and therefore also that} \quad \mathbf{I} = \mathbf{I}' \tag{A.4.10}$$

Any matrix $\mathbf{A}$ which has the property of being equal to its transpose so that

$$\mathbf{A} = \mathbf{A}' \quad \text{and therefore} \quad \mathbf{A} - \mathbf{A}' = \mathbf{O} \tag{A.4.11}$$

is called a *symmetric matrix*. A symmetric matrix is necessarily a square matrix in which each row is equal to the corresponding column.

Any matrix $\mathbf{B}$ which has the property of being equal to its transpose with a changed sign, so that

$$\mathbf{B} = -\mathbf{B}' \quad \text{and therefore} \quad \mathbf{B} + \mathbf{B}' = \mathbf{O} \tag{A.4.12}$$

is called a *skew-symmetric matrix*. A skew-symmetric matrix is necessarily a square matrix in which each row is equal to the corresponding column with a changed sign. It follows that all the elements on the principal diagonal of a skew-symmetric matrix are always necessarily zeros.

4.6. *Matrix multiplication.* Given an $m \times n$ matrix $\mathbf{A}$ and an $n \times q$ matrix $\mathbf{B}$, their product is defined as a third matrix $\mathbf{C}$, of order $m \times q$, in which each element c_{ij} is the scalar product of the ith row of $\mathbf{A}$ and the jth column of $\mathbf{B}$, i.e.,

$$c_{ij} = \sum_{k=1}^{n} a_{ik}b_{kj} \qquad \begin{aligned} i &= 1, 2, \ldots, m \\ j &= 1, 2, \ldots, q \end{aligned} \qquad \text{(A.4.13)}$$

The operation of matrix multiplication is therefore defined only if the number of columns of the first matrix is equal to the number of rows of the second matrix. When this is so, the two matrices are said to be *conformable* for multiplication. The product matrix $\mathbf{C}$ necessarily has the same number of rows as the first matrix $\mathbf{A}$ and the same number of columns as the second matrix $\mathbf{B}$.

Note that, when $\mathbf{A}$ can be *post-multiplied* by $\mathbf{B}$, this does not necessarily mean that $\mathbf{A}$ can be *pre-multiplied* by $\mathbf{B}$. In fact, if $m \neq q$, pre-multiplication of $\mathbf{A}$ by $\mathbf{B}$ is not possible (i.e., is not defined, even though post-multiplication is defined). Moreover, even when $m = q$ (i.e., when both post- and pre-multiplication are defined), the product $\mathbf{AB}$ is not necessarily equal to the product $\mathbf{BA}$, i.e., in general

$$\mathbf{AB} \neq \mathbf{BA} \qquad \text{(A.4.14)}$$

This means that matrix multiplication *does not* satisfy the commutative property. It does, however, satisfy (if matrices are conformable for multiplication) both the associative property and the distributive property, i.e.,

$$(\mathbf{AB})\mathbf{C} = \mathbf{A}(\mathbf{BC}) \qquad \text{(A.4.15)}$$

$$\mathbf{A}(\mathbf{B} + \mathbf{C}) = \mathbf{AB} + \mathbf{AC} \qquad \text{(A.4.16)}$$

4.7. Let us briefly consider the multiplication of a few particular matrices, which we shall suppose to be conformable for multiplication.

The product of any matrix $\mathbf{A}$ and the identity matrix $\mathbf{I}$ is the matrix $\mathbf{A}$:

$$\mathbf{IA} = \mathbf{A} \qquad \text{(A.4.17)}$$

$$\mathbf{AI} = \mathbf{A} \qquad \text{(A.4.18)}$$

The product of any matrix $\mathbf{A}$ and the scalar matrix $\lambda \mathbf{I}$ is equivalent to the product of $\mathbf{A}$ and the scalar λ:

$$\lambda \mathbf{IA} = \lambda \mathbf{A} \qquad \text{(A.4.19)}$$

$$\mathbf{A}\lambda \mathbf{I} = \lambda \mathbf{A} \qquad \text{(A.4.20)}$$

The product of any matrix $\mathbf{A}$ by the null matrix is the null matrix

$$\mathbf{OA} = \mathbf{O} \tag{A.4.21}$$

$$\mathbf{AO} = \mathbf{O} \tag{A.4.22}$$

Note that, if $\mathbf{AB} = \mathbf{O}$, it does not necessarily follow that both $\mathbf{A}$ and $\mathbf{B}$ are null matrices. For example,

$$\mathbf{A} = \begin{bmatrix} 3 & 4 \\ 3 & 4 \end{bmatrix}, \quad \mathbf{B} = \begin{bmatrix} 4 & 4 \\ -3 & -3 \end{bmatrix}, \quad \mathbf{AB} = \begin{bmatrix} 0 & 0 \\ 0 & 0 \end{bmatrix}$$

If a matrix $\mathbf{A}$ is post-multiplied by a diagonal matrix $\mathbf{D}$, the product is a matrix whose columns are the columns of $\mathbf{A}$ multiplied by the corresponding scalars on the principal diagonal of $\mathbf{D}$. Similarly, if a matrix $\mathbf{A}$ is pre-multiplied by a diagonal matrix $\mathbf{D}$, the product is a matrix the rows of which are the rows of $\mathbf{A}$ multiplied by the corresponding scalars on the principal diagonal of $\mathbf{D}$. That is, if $\mathbf{A} = [a_{ij}]$ and $\mathbf{D} = [\delta_{ij}\lambda_i]$,

$$\mathbf{AD} = [\lambda_j a_{ij}] \tag{A.4.23}$$

$$\mathbf{DA} = [\lambda_i a_{ij}] \tag{A.4.24}$$

The transpose of the product of two matrices $\mathbf{A}$ and $\mathbf{B}$ is the product of the two transposes in reverse order, i.e.,

$$(\mathbf{AB})' = \mathbf{B}'\mathbf{A}' \tag{A.4.25}$$

For, each element of $\mathbf{AB}$ is $\sum a_{ik}b_{kj} = \sum a'_{ki}b'_{jk} = \sum b'_{jk}a'_{ki}$, from which it follows that $\mathbf{B}'\mathbf{A}' = (\mathbf{AB})'$.

4.8. *Inversion.* Given a matrix $\mathbf{A}$, if there exists a matrix, to be denoted by $\mathbf{A}^{-1}$, such that

$$\mathbf{AA}^{-1} = \mathbf{A}^{-1}\mathbf{A} = \mathbf{I} \tag{A.4.26}$$

matrix $\mathbf{A}^{-1}$ is called the *inverse matrix* of $\mathbf{A}$. If $\mathbf{A}^{-1}$ exists, the matrix $\mathbf{A}$ is said to be *nonsingular*. If $\mathbf{A}^{-1}$ does not exist, the matrix $\mathbf{A}$ is said to be *singular*. It follows from the definition that the operation of inversion is defined only for square matrices.

Observe the analogy with the algebra of numbers. Given a number a the *inverse* or reciprocal of a is a number a^{-1} such that $aa^{-1} = 1$. It immediately follows that $a^{-1} = 1/a$. Thus it is not difficult to see that in matrix algebra the operation of matrix inversion plays a role similar to that played in elementary algebra by the operation of division.

4.9. The inverse of a square matrix $\mathbf{A}$, when it exists, satisfies the following remarkable properties:

(i) $\mathbf{A}^{-1}$ is unique. For suppose that $\mathbf{B}$ is such that $\mathbf{BA} = \mathbf{AB} = \mathbf{I}$; and suppose also that $\mathbf{C}$ is such that $\mathbf{CA} = \mathbf{AC} = \mathbf{I}$. It follows that

$$\mathbf{CAB} = \mathbf{CI} = \mathbf{C}$$

$$\mathbf{CAB} = \mathbf{IB} = \mathbf{B} \qquad \text{Therefore} \quad \mathbf{C} = \mathbf{B}$$

(ii) $(\mathbf{A}^{-1})^{-1} = \mathbf{A}$. For, by the definition of inverse,

$$\mathbf{A}^{-1}(\mathbf{A}^{-1})^{-1} = (\mathbf{A}^{-1})^{-1}\mathbf{A}^{-1} = \mathbf{I}$$

It follows from the definition of inverse and from property (i) that

$$(\mathbf{A}^{-1})^{-1} = \mathbf{A}$$

(iii) $(\mathbf{A}')^{-1} = (\mathbf{A}^{-1})'$. For by definition

$$\mathbf{AA}^{-1} = \mathbf{I} = \mathbf{A}^{-1}\mathbf{A} \qquad\qquad\qquad\qquad (A.4.27)$$

By now taking the transpose of (A.4.27), according to (A.4.25), and noting that $\mathbf{I}' = \mathbf{I}$,

$$(\mathbf{A}^{-1})'\mathbf{A}' = \mathbf{I}' = \mathbf{I} = \mathbf{A}'(\mathbf{A}^{-1})'$$

Therefore $(\mathbf{A}^{-1})'$ is the inverse of $\mathbf{A}'$, i.e., $(\mathbf{A}')^{-1} = (\mathbf{A}^{-1})'$.

(iv) The inverse of the product of two nonsingular matrices $\mathbf{A}$ and $\mathbf{B}$ is the product of the two inverse matrices in reverse order, i.e., $(\mathbf{AB})^{-1} = \mathbf{B}^{-1}\mathbf{A}^{-1}$. For

$$(\mathbf{B}^{-1}\mathbf{A}^{-1})(\mathbf{AB}) = \mathbf{B}^{-1}\mathbf{A}^{-1}\mathbf{AB} = \mathbf{B}^{-1}\mathbf{IB} = \mathbf{B}^{-1}\mathbf{B} = \mathbf{I}$$

$$(\mathbf{AB})(\mathbf{B}^{-1}\mathbf{A}^{-1}) = \mathbf{ABB}^{-1}\mathbf{A}^{-1} = \mathbf{AIA}^{-1} = \mathbf{AA}^{-1} = \mathbf{I}$$

It follows that $\mathbf{B}^{-1}\mathbf{A}^{-1}$ satisfies the definition of inverse of $\mathbf{AB}$.

(v) If $\mathbf{AB} = \mathbf{O}$ and $\mathbf{A}$ is nonsingular, it necessarily follows that $\mathbf{B} = \mathbf{O}$.

For, if $\mathbf{AB} = \mathbf{O}$, then

$$\mathbf{A}^{-1}\mathbf{AB} = \mathbf{A}^{-1}\mathbf{O} = \mathbf{O}$$

$$\mathbf{IB} = \mathbf{O}$$

$$\mathbf{B} = \mathbf{O}$$

The same proof holds for the case of $\mathbf{BA} = \mathbf{O}$ (pre-multiplication).

4.10 The computation of an inverse matrix is almost immediate in some very special cases. For example,

$$\mathbf{I}^{-1} = \mathbf{I} \quad \text{since} \quad \mathbf{II} = \mathbf{I} \qquad\qquad\qquad\qquad (A.4.28)$$

It also can be easily verified that for the diagonal matrix $\mathbf{D} = [\delta_{ij}\lambda_i]$, the inverse is

$$\mathbf{D}^{-1} = \left[\delta_{ij}\frac{1}{\lambda_i}\right] \tag{A.4.29}$$

But, in general, the computation of an inverse is a rather laborious process, and we shall have to develop further concepts before being able to carry out such a computation.

4.11. *Powers of matrices.* Consider a square, nonsingular matrix $\mathbf{A}$. The product $\mathbf{AA}$ may be denoted by $\mathbf{A}^2$; the product $\mathbf{AAA}$ by $\mathbf{A}^3$; and in general the product $\mathbf{AA}^{k-1}$ (or, which is the same, $\mathbf{A}^{k-1}\mathbf{A}$) by $\mathbf{A}^k$.

Similarly, the product $\mathbf{A}^{-1}\mathbf{A}^{-1}$ may be denoted by $\mathbf{A}^{-2}$, and in general the product $\mathbf{A}^{-1}\mathbf{A}^{-k+1}$ (or $\mathbf{A}^{-k+1}\mathbf{A}^{-1}$) by $\mathbf{A}^{-k}$. If we now define, by analogy with numbers,

$$\mathbf{A}^0 = \mathbf{I} \tag{A.4.30}$$

we may notice that the product of powers of matrices satisfies the rule of the sum of the exponents, i.e.,

$$\mathbf{A}^n\mathbf{A}^m = \mathbf{A}^{n+m}$$

$$\mathbf{A}^n\mathbf{A}^{-n} = \mathbf{A}^0 = \mathbf{I}$$

We shall have, for example,

$$\mathbf{A}^3\mathbf{A}^{-3} = \mathbf{AAAA}^{-1}\mathbf{A}^{-1}\mathbf{A}^{-1} = \mathbf{AAA}^{-1}\mathbf{A}^{-1} = \mathbf{AA}^{-1} = \mathbf{I} = \mathbf{A}^0$$

It should be noted, moreover, that in the particular case in which $\mathbf{AB} = \mathbf{BA}$, the power of the matrix sum $(\mathbf{A} + \mathbf{B})^n$ satisfies the rule of the binomial expansion as power series:

$$(\mathbf{A} + \mathbf{B})^n = \mathbf{A}^n + \binom{n}{1}\mathbf{A}^{n-1}\mathbf{B} + \binom{n}{2}\mathbf{A}^{n-2}\mathbf{B}^2 + \ldots$$

$$+ \binom{n}{n-1}\mathbf{AB}^{n-1} + \mathbf{B}^n$$

5 Partitioning of Matrices

5.1. Given any $m \times n$ matrix $\mathbf{A}$, it may sometimes be useful to partition $\mathbf{A}$ into various subsets of its elements.

We shall call any matrix made up of h rows and k columns belonging to $\mathbf{A}$ and such that $h \leq m$ and $k \leq n$, where at least one of the two inequalities is a strict inequality, a *submatrix* of $\mathbf{A}$.

For example, an $m \times n$ matrix $\mathbf{A}$ may be partitioned into four submatrices in the following way:

$$\mathbf{A} = \begin{bmatrix} a_{11} & a_{12} & \vdots & \cdots & a_{1n} \\ a_{21} & a_{22} & \vdots & \cdots & a_{2n} \\ \hline \vdots & \vdots & \vdots & & \vdots \\ a_{m1} & a_{m2} & \vdots & \cdots & a_{mn} \end{bmatrix}$$

and written

$$\mathbf{A} = \begin{bmatrix} \mathbf{A}_{11} & \mathbf{A}_{12} \\ \mathbf{A}_{21} & \mathbf{A}_{22} \end{bmatrix} \tag{A.5.1}$$

where

$$\mathbf{A}_{11} = \begin{bmatrix} a_{11} & a_{12} \\ a_{21} & a_{22} \end{bmatrix}, \qquad \mathbf{A}_{12} = \begin{bmatrix} a_{13} & a_{14} & \cdots & a_{1n} \\ a_{23} & a_{24} & \cdots & a_{2n} \end{bmatrix}$$

$$\mathbf{A}_{21} = \begin{bmatrix} a_{31} & a_{32} \\ a_{41} & a_{42} \\ \vdots & \vdots \\ a_{m1} & a_{m2} \end{bmatrix}, \qquad \mathbf{A}_{22} = \begin{bmatrix} a_{33} & a_{34} & \cdots & a_{3n} \\ a_{43} & a_{44} & \cdots & a_{4n} \\ \vdots & \vdots & & \vdots \\ a_{m3} & a_{m4} & \cdots & a_{mn} \end{bmatrix}$$

5.2. As may be seen, (A.5.1) is a matrix whose elements are themselves matrices. It is of course possible, with partitioned matrices, to perform the matrix operations defined in Section 4 above, provided that certain rules are followed in their partitioning.

It is possible to add two partitioned matrices $\mathbf{A}$ and $\mathbf{B}$, of the same order, by adding up the corresponding submatrices, provided that the submatrices which are being added are of the same order. This means that, to be added, matrices $\mathbf{A}$ and $\mathbf{B}$ must be partitioned in the same way.

It is also possible to multiply two partitioned matrices $\mathbf{A}$ and $\mathbf{B}$, conformable for multiplication, by the usual rule

$$\mathbf{C}_{ij} = \sum_{k} \mathbf{A}_{ik} \mathbf{B}_{kj} \tag{A.5.2}$$

where the $\mathbf{C}_{ij}$ are submatrices of $\mathbf{C} = \mathbf{AB}$ and the $\mathbf{A}_{ik}$, $\mathbf{B}_{kj}$ are submatrices of $\mathbf{A}$ and $\mathbf{B}$, partitioned in such a way as to be conformable for multiplication. This means that, to perform the operation of multiplication in this way, the *columns* of the *first matrix* must be partitioned in the same way as the *rows* of the *second matrix*.

5.3. Let $\mathbf{A}$ be a square, nth-order matrix:

$$\mathbf{A} = [\mathbf{A}_{\alpha\beta}] \qquad\qquad \alpha, \beta = 1, 2, \ldots, s < n \qquad \text{(A.5.3)}$$

where the $\mathbf{A}_{\alpha\alpha}$ are square submatrices (not necessarily of the same order) and the $\mathbf{A}_{\alpha\beta}$, with $\alpha \neq \beta$, are rectangular (or square) submatrices. Such a matrix is called *upper block-triangular* if, for $\alpha > \beta$, $\mathbf{A}_{\alpha\beta} = \mathbf{O}$ (or *lower block-triangular* if, for $\alpha < \beta$, $\mathbf{A}_{\alpha\beta} = \mathbf{O}$).

A square matrix $\mathbf{A}$ which is, at the same time, upper block-triangular and lower block-triangular is called *block-diagonal*.

For example, the matrix

$$\begin{bmatrix} 3 & -2 & 7 & 2 \\ 2 & 1 & 3 & 3 \\ \hline 0 & 0 & 5 & 6 \\ 0 & 0 & 0 & 8 \end{bmatrix}$$

is upper block-triangular and the matrix

$$\begin{bmatrix} 3 & 1 & 0 \\ 2 & 1 & 0 \\ \hline 0 & 0 & 4 \end{bmatrix}$$

is block-diagonal.

5.4. When block-triangular matrices are nonsingular they can generally be inverted more easily by partitioning them. For example, consider a nonsingular nth-order block-triangular matrix $\mathbf{A}$ which has been partitioned in the following way:

$$\mathbf{A} = \begin{bmatrix} \mathbf{A}_{11} & \mathbf{A}_{12} \\ \mathbf{O} & \mathbf{A}_{22} \end{bmatrix}$$

where $\mathbf{A}_{11}$ and $\mathbf{A}_{22}$ are square submatrices of order k and $(n - k)$, respectively $(k < n)$; and $\mathbf{A}_{12}$ and $\mathbf{O}$ are submatrices of order $k \times (n - k)$ and $(n - k) \times k$, respectively.

Observe that, if $\mathbf{A}$ is nonsingular (i.e., if $\mathbf{A}^{-1}$ exists), then $\mathbf{A}_{11}$ and $\mathbf{A}_{22}$ must also both be nonsingular (i.e., both $\mathbf{A}_{11}^{-1}$ and $\mathbf{A}_{22}^{-1}$ exist). Now call $\mathbf{X} = \mathbf{A}^{-1}$ the inverse of $\mathbf{A}$ and partition it in the same way as $\mathbf{A}$, i.e.,

$$\mathbf{A}^{-1} = \mathbf{X} = \begin{bmatrix} \mathbf{X}_{11} & \mathbf{X}_{12} \\ \mathbf{X}_{21} & \mathbf{X}_{22} \end{bmatrix}$$

where $\mathbf{X}_{11}$ and $\mathbf{X}_{22}$ are square submatrices of order k and $(n - k)$, respectively; and $\mathbf{X}_{12}$ and $\mathbf{X}_{21}$ are submatrices of order $k \times (n - k)$ and $(n - k) \times k$, respectively.

From the definition of matrix inverse, we have

$$\begin{bmatrix} \mathbf{A}_{11} & \mathbf{A}_{12} \\ \mathbf{O} & \mathbf{A}_{22} \end{bmatrix} \begin{bmatrix} \mathbf{X}_{11} & \mathbf{X}_{12} \\ \mathbf{X}_{21} & \mathbf{X}_{22} \end{bmatrix} = \begin{bmatrix} \mathbf{I}_{11} & \mathbf{O} \\ \mathbf{O} & \mathbf{I}_{22} \end{bmatrix}$$

Now, by applying the multiplication rule (A.5.2) for partitioned matrices, we obtain

$$\mathbf{A}_{11}\mathbf{X}_{11} + \mathbf{A}_{12}\mathbf{X}_{21} = \mathbf{I}_{11} \tag{A.5.4}$$

$$\mathbf{A}_{11}\mathbf{X}_{12} + \mathbf{A}_{12}\mathbf{X}_{22} = \mathbf{O} \tag{A.5.5}$$

$$\mathbf{A}_{22}\mathbf{X}_{21} = \mathbf{O} \tag{A.5.6}$$

$$\mathbf{A}_{22}\mathbf{X}_{22} = \mathbf{I}_{22} \tag{A.5.7}$$

Since $\mathbf{A}_{22}^{-1}$ exists, we obtain from (A.5.6), (A.5.7)

$$\mathbf{X}_{21} = \mathbf{A}_{22}^{-1}\mathbf{O} = \mathbf{O}$$

$$\mathbf{X}_{22} = \mathbf{A}_{22}^{-1}$$

and, after substitution into (A.5.4), (A.5.5),

$$\mathbf{X}_{11} = \mathbf{A}_{11}^{-1}$$

$$\mathbf{X}_{12} = -\mathbf{A}_{11}^{-1}\mathbf{A}_{12}\mathbf{A}_{22}^{-1}$$

We can therefore write

$$\mathbf{X} = \begin{bmatrix} \mathbf{A}_{11}^{-1} & -\mathbf{A}_{11}^{-1}\mathbf{A}_{12}\mathbf{A}_{22}^{-1} \\ \mathbf{O} & \mathbf{A}_{22}^{-1} \end{bmatrix}$$

which expresses the inverse matrix $\mathbf{X}$ in terms of inverses of the submatrices of $\mathbf{A}$. It should be noted that both $\mathbf{A}$ and its inverse $\mathbf{X}$ are block-triangular matrices of the same type.

6   Determinants

6.1. Given any square matrix $\mathbf{A}$, there exists a scalar (a number) associated with it which is called the *determinant* of $\mathbf{A}$.

Definition. The determinant of an nth-order square matrix $\mathbf{A} = [a_{ij}]$ is a number, written $|\mathbf{A}|$, or det $\mathbf{A}$, obtained by the operation

$$|\mathbf{A}| = \sum (\pm) a_{1p}a_{2q}a_{3r} \ldots, a_{ns} \tag{A.6.1}$$

where the sum is over all possible permutations of the second (i.e., column) subscripts $p, q, r, \ldots, s$. Each addendum has the sign $(+)$ if it refers to an even permutation or the sign $(-)$ if it refers to an odd permutation.

6.2. *Permutations*. It may be useful to recall a few points concerning permutations. Given n integers, written in a certain order, they are said to be in *natural order* if each number is lower than all the following numbers. For example, the numbers

$$1, 2, 3, 4, \ldots, n$$

are written in natural order.

Any reordering of these numbers is called a *permutation*. Each permutation will contain a certain number of inversions. The number of inversions is defined as the number of pairs of elements (not necessarily adjacent) in which the second number is lower than the first number. For example: given the numbers $1, 2, 3, 4, 5$, the permutation $1, 5, 2, 3, 4$ contains three inversions, namely: $5, 2; 5, 3; 5, 4$.

A permutation is called an *even permutation* if the number of inversions it contains is even; it is called an *odd permutation* if the number of inversions it contains is odd.

By extension, the set of n numbers written in natural order $(1, 2, \ldots, n)$ is also called a permutation or, more specifically, the *natural permutation*. The natural permutation contains zero inversions and is therefore an even permutation.

Observe that, given the numbers $1, 2, \ldots, n$, we may obtain n permutations by simply changing the place of number 1. Then, given these n permutations, we may obtain additional $(n - 1)$ permutations by simply changing the place of number 2. Then we may obtain additional $(n - 2)$ permutations by changing the place of number 3. And so on. Altogether, we shall be able to obtain

$$n \cdot (n - 1) \cdot (n - 2) \cdot \ldots 2 \cdot 1 = n!$$

permutations.

6.3. Let us now return to the definition of a determinant. To obtain the sum (A.6.1), we may begin by writing, with a plus sign, the product of all the elements on the principal diagonal of $\mathbf{A}$, i.e.,

$$a_{11}a_{22}a_{33} \ldots a_{nn} \tag{A.6.2}$$

This is the first addendum. Then we may add the other addenda by performing, one by one, all the possible permutations of the second subscripts, and changing the sign at each inversion. The number of addenda will be $n!$

Observe that each addendum in the sum will contain one (and only one) element from each row and one (and only one) element from each column. This means that an alternative way to obtain det $\mathbf{A}$ would be to keep fixed the second (or column) subscripts and perform all the possible permutations of the first (or row) subscripts.

Example.

If

$$\mathbf{A} = \begin{bmatrix} a_{11} & a_{12} & a_{13} \\ a_{21} & a_{22} & a_{23} \\ a_{31} & a_{32} & a_{33} \end{bmatrix}$$

$$|\mathbf{A}| = a_{11}a_{22}a_{33} - a_{12}a_{21}a_{33}$$
$$+ a_{12}a_{23}a_{31} - a_{13}a_{22}a_{31}$$
$$+ a_{13}a_{21}a_{32} - a_{11}a_{23}a_{32} \tag{A.6.3}$$

if

$$\mathbf{B} = \begin{bmatrix} a_{11} & a_{12} \\ a_{21} & a_{22} \end{bmatrix}, \quad |\mathbf{B}| = a_{11}a_{22} - a_{21}a_{12}$$

where, as can be seen, $|\mathbf{A}|$ is the sum of $3! = 6$ addenda and $|\mathbf{B}|$ is the sum of $2! = 2$ addenda.

It may be noted that, if we consider a 1×1 matrix, i.e., a scalar, its determinant is the scalar itself. Or, given the scalar a,

$$\det a = a \tag{A.6.4}$$

It may also be noted that the determinant of a diagonal matrix is given by the product of the elements on its principal diagonal. For in this case the first addendum of (A.6.1) is the only nonzero addendum in the sum. For exactly the same reason, the determinant of a triangular matrix is also given by the product of the elements on its principal diagonal.

It can also be proved that the determinant of a block-triangular matrix (and by implication of a block-diagonal matrix) is given by the product of the determinants of the square submatrices on its principal diagonal.[2]

6.4. Given a square matrix $\mathbf{A} = [a_{ij}]$, a method of finding all the permutations of the second subscripts in the corresponding sum (A.6.1) is the so-called *expansion of the determinant* of $\mathbf{A}$ by the scalar

---

[2] See, for example, Hadley [8, pp. 99–100], Gantmacher [7, pp. 74 ff].

product of any row (or any column) of $\mathbf{A}$ and the vector of its cofactors.

As is well known, the cofactor, written A_{ij}, of any element a_{ij} of a square matrix $\mathbf{A}$ is a number obtained by multiplying $(-1)^{i+j}$ by the determinant of the submatrix obtained from $\mathbf{A}$ by deleting the ith row and the jth column. (The determinant of this submatrix is called the $(n-1)$th-order *minor* of $\mathbf{A}$). For example, if

$$\mathbf{A} = \begin{bmatrix} 0 & 1 & 2 \\ 3 & 1 & 0 \\ 2 & 1 & 2 \end{bmatrix}, \quad A_{11} = (-1)^2 \begin{vmatrix} 1 & 0 \\ 1 & 2 \end{vmatrix},$$

$$A_{12} = (-1)^3 \begin{vmatrix} 3 & 0 \\ 2 & 2 \end{vmatrix}, \quad A_{13} = (-1)^4 \begin{vmatrix} 3 & 1 \\ 2 & 1 \end{vmatrix}, \quad \text{etc.}$$

The expansion of the determinant by any one of the rows (or the columns) of $\mathbf{A}$ is therefore a method of computing the determinant itself. Hence, given any nth-order square matrix $\mathbf{A}$,

$$|\mathbf{A}| = \sum_{j=1}^{n} a_{ij} A_{ij} \tag{A.6.5}$$

where i is any one of the rows of $\mathbf{A}$, or

$$|\mathbf{A}| = \sum_{i=1}^{n} a_{ij} A_{ij} \tag{A.6.6}$$

where j is any one of the columns of $\mathbf{A}$.

6.5. *Some properties of determinants.*

(i) If $\mathbf{A}$ is a square matrix, the determinant of $\mathbf{A}$ and the determinant of the transpose of $\mathbf{A}$ are equal to each other, i.e.,

$$|\mathbf{A}| = |\mathbf{A}'| \tag{A.6.7}$$

The proof follows at once from the definition of the determinant. It also follows from this that all the properties of det $\mathbf{A}$ which refer to the rows of $\mathbf{A}$ also hold with reference to the columns of $\mathbf{A}$ and conversely.

(ii) Given a square matrix $\mathbf{A}$, the interchange of two rows (or of two columns) changes the sign of its determinant (while leaving its absolute value unchanged). In other words, if $\tilde{\mathbf{A}}$ is a matrix where two rows (or two columns) have been interchanged, with respect to $\mathbf{A}$,

$$|\tilde{\mathbf{A}}| = -|\mathbf{A}| \tag{A.6.8}$$

Proof: The interchange of two rows (or two columns) changes the signs of all permutations of the second subscripts in (A.6.1), i.e.,

changes the signs of all addenda, and therefore changes the sign of
their total sum.   Q.E.D.

(iii) The determinant of a square matrix in which two rows (or two
columns) are identical is zero.

Proof: In a matrix with two identical rows (or columns) the interchange of those two rows (or columns) leaves the matrix unchanged.
But, according to property (ii), the sign of its determinant must change.
Only one number is equal to itself with a changed sign: zero. Hence
the determinant of that matrix must be zero.   Q.E.D.

(iv) If a row (or a column) of a square matrix $\mathbf{A}$ is multiplied by a
scalar λ, the determinant of $\mathbf{A}$ is multiplied by λ. Hence, if all elements
of $\mathbf{A}$ are multiplied by λ, its determinant is multiplied by λ^n, i.e.,

$$|\lambda\mathbf{A}| = \lambda^n|\mathbf{A}| \tag{A.6.9}$$

It should be noticed, therefore, that $|\lambda\mathbf{A}| \neq \lambda|\mathbf{A}|$.

Proof. Each addendum of (A.6.1) contains one single element from
each row (and from each column). Therefore, if a row (or a column) of
$\mathbf{A}$ is multiplied by λ, all addenda – and therefore also their sum, i.e.,
the determinant – are multiplied by λ. If all elements of $\mathbf{A}$, i.e., all its
rows (and all its columns), are multiplied by λ, each addendum of
(A.6.1), by being the product of n elements, is multiplied by λ^n. Hence
their sum, too, i.e., the determinant, is multiplied by λ^n.   Q.E.D.

(v) The determinant of a square matrix in which a row (or a
column) is a linear combination of other rows (or columns) is zero.

Proof for the case of $n = 3$. Applying the definition of determinant
and properties (iii) and (iv), we have

$$\begin{vmatrix} a_{11} & a_{12} & (\lambda_1 a_{11} + \lambda_2 a_{12}) \\ a_{21} & a_{22} & (\lambda_1 a_{21} + \lambda_2 a_{22}) \\ a_{31} & a_{32} & (\lambda_1 a_{31} + \lambda_2 a_{32}) \end{vmatrix}$$

$$= \begin{vmatrix} a_{11} & a_{12} & \lambda_1 a_{11} \\ a_{21} & a_{22} & \lambda_1 a_{21} \\ a_{31} & a_{32} & \lambda_1 a_{31} \end{vmatrix} + \begin{vmatrix} a_{11} & a_{12} & \lambda_2 a_{12} \\ a_{21} & a_{22} & \lambda_2 a_{22} \\ a_{31} & a_{32} & \lambda_2 a_{32} \end{vmatrix}$$

$$= \lambda_1 \begin{vmatrix} a_{11} & a_{12} & a_{11} \\ a_{21} & a_{22} & a_{21} \\ a_{31} & a_{32} & a_{31} \end{vmatrix} + \lambda_2 \begin{vmatrix} a_{11} & a_{12} & a_{12} \\ a_{21} & a_{22} & a_{22} \\ a_{31} & a_{32} & a_{32} \end{vmatrix}$$

$$= \lambda_1 0 + \lambda_2 0 = 0 \qquad\qquad \text{Q.E.D.}$$

The proof can easily be extended to the case in which n is any positive
integer.

(vi) The determinant of a square matrix in which to a particular
row (or to a particular column) is added a linear combination of other
rows (or columns) remains unchanged.

The proof is similar to the one given for property (v).

It should be noted that, as a consequence, in general,

$$|\mathbf{A} + \mathbf{B}| \neq |\mathbf{A}| + |\mathbf{B}| \qquad\qquad (A.6.10)$$

(vii) It can be proved,[3] by contrast, that the determinant of the product of two square matrices is equal to the product of their determinants, i.e.,

$$|\mathbf{AB}| = |\mathbf{A}||\mathbf{B}| \qquad\qquad (A.6.11)$$

(viii) Given a square matrix $\mathbf{A}$, if one of its rows (or columns) is multiplied by the cofactors of another row (or column), the resulting expansion is equal to zero, i.e.,

$$\sum_{k=1}^{n} a_{ik}A_{jk} = 0 \qquad\qquad \text{for} \quad i \neq j \qquad (A.6.12)$$

Proof. Expression (A.6.12) is nothing but the determinant of a matrix in which two rows are identical. Therefore, from property (iii), it must be zero.   Q.E.D.

6.6. *Definition of the adjoint matrix.* Given a square matrix $\mathbf{A}$, the adjoint matrix of $\mathbf{A}$, written $\mathbf{A}^+$, is defined as the transpose of a matrix the elements of which are the cofactors of the correspondent elements of matrix $\mathbf{A}$. For example,

$$\text{if} \quad \mathbf{A} = \begin{bmatrix} 2 & 1 & 3 \\ 0 & 1 & 2 \\ 3 & 4 & 5 \end{bmatrix}, \quad \mathbf{A}^+ = \begin{bmatrix} \begin{vmatrix} 1 & 2 \\ 4 & 5 \end{vmatrix} & -\begin{vmatrix} 1 & 3 \\ 4 & 5 \end{vmatrix} & \begin{vmatrix} 1 & 3 \\ 1 & 2 \end{vmatrix} \\[2ex] -\begin{vmatrix} 0 & 2 \\ 3 & 5 \end{vmatrix} & \begin{vmatrix} 2 & 3 \\ 3 & 5 \end{vmatrix} & -\begin{vmatrix} 2 & 3 \\ 0 & 2 \end{vmatrix} \\[2ex] \begin{vmatrix} 0 & 1 \\ 3 & 4 \end{vmatrix} & -\begin{vmatrix} 2 & 1 \\ 3 & 4 \end{vmatrix} & \begin{vmatrix} 2 & 1 \\ 0 & 1 \end{vmatrix} \end{bmatrix}$$

6.7. *Computation of the inverse matrix.* The definition above and the properties of determinants may now be used to obtain a method for computing the matrix inverse. Given a square matrix $\mathbf{A}$, and thus its adjoint matrix $\mathbf{A}^+$, it follows from (A.6.5) and (A.6.12) that

$$\mathbf{AA}^+ = \mathbf{A}^+\mathbf{A} = |\mathbf{A}|\ \mathbf{I} \qquad\qquad (A.6.13)$$

Therefore, if $|\mathbf{A}| \neq 0$,

$$\mathbf{A}\frac{1}{|\mathbf{A}|}\mathbf{A}^+ = \frac{1}{|\mathbf{A}|}\mathbf{A}^+\mathbf{A} = \mathbf{I} \qquad\qquad (A.6.14)$$

[3] See, for example, Hadley [8, p. 99].

We have thus obtained an expression which, when multiplied by $\mathbf{A}$, gives the identity matrix. Such an expression, according to the definition (A.4.26), is the inverse of matrix $\mathbf{A}$. Hence

$$\frac{1}{|\mathbf{A}|}\mathbf{A}^+ = \mathbf{A}^{-1} \tag{A.6.15}$$

This expression in fact gives us a general method for computing the matrix inverse.

Numerical example. Consider the square matrix

$$\mathbf{A} = \begin{bmatrix} 1 & -0.6 \\ -0.3 & 1 \end{bmatrix}$$

To compute the inverse of this matrix, according to (A.6.15), we must first find the adjoint matrix and then divide each of its elements by the determinant of $\mathbf{A}$:

$$\mathbf{A}^+ = \begin{bmatrix} 1 & 0.6 \\ 0.3 & 1 \end{bmatrix}, \quad |\mathbf{A}| = 1 - 0.18 = 0.82$$

$$\mathbf{A}^{-1} = \frac{1}{|\mathbf{A}|}\mathbf{A}^+ = \begin{bmatrix} \dfrac{1}{0.82} & \dfrac{0.6}{0.82} \\ \dfrac{0.3}{0.82} & \dfrac{1}{0.82} \end{bmatrix} = \begin{bmatrix} 1.2195 & 0.7317 \\ 0.3658 & 1.2195 \end{bmatrix}$$

6.8. Expressions (A.6.14) and (A.6.15) are defined only if $|\mathbf{A}| \neq 0$. If $|\mathbf{A}| = 0$, neither of them is defined and $\mathbf{A}^{-1}$ does not exist. We are thus able at this stage to specify the conditions under which, given a square matrix $\mathbf{A}$, there exists an inverse $\mathbf{A}^{-1}$. We may say that a square matrix $\mathbf{A}$ is a *nonsingular matrix* if its determinant is not zero, and therefore its inverse exists. Conversely, we may say that a square matrix $\mathbf{A}$ is *singular,* if its determinant is zero and therefore its inverse does not exist.

7 The Rank of a Matrix

7.1. It may be interesting to explore a little further the meaning of a matrix with a zero determinant. Owing to properties (iii) and (v) of Section 6.5, we may say that the determinant of a square matrix is zero when: (i) one row is a linear combination of other rows, i.e., when the rows of the matrix are linearly dependent vectors; or (ii) one column is a linear combination of other columns, i.e., when the columns of the matrix are linearly dependent vectors.

In fact, it is not necessary to refer to both the rows and the columns; it suffices to refer to either of them, owing to the following

Theorem. If the rows of a square matrix are linearly dependent (or independent), the columns, too, are linearly dependent (or independent); and conversely.

A *proof* may easily be given by starting from a 2nd-order matrix

$$\begin{bmatrix} a_{11} & a_{12} \\ \lambda a_{11} & \lambda a_{12} \end{bmatrix}$$

where the second row is simply equal to the first row multiplied by $\lambda \neq 0$. It suffices to solve the equation $a_{11}x = a_{12}$ to obtain the scalar $x = a_{12}/a_{11}$ which, when multiplied by the first column, yields the second column; i.e., enables us to express the second column as a scalar multiple of the first. The proof can be extended to square matrices of any order.

We may therefore say that a square matrix **A** is nonsingular when its rows (or columns) are a set of linearly independent vectors. We know that in this case $\mathbf{A}^{-1}$ exists and $|\mathbf{A}| \neq 0$. Similarly we may say that a square matrix **A** is singular when its rows (or columns) are a set of linearly dependent vectors. In this case the matrix inverse does not exist and $|\mathbf{A}| = 0$. There is therefore a one-to-one correspondence between the notion of linear independence of the vectors constituting the rows or the columns of a square matrix and the notion of a matrix with a zero determinant.

7.2. So far we have referred only to square matrices. But the notion of vector linear independence allows us to explore the properties of rectangular matrices as well.

The *rank* of an $m \times n$ matrix **A**, written $r(\mathbf{A})$, is defined as the maximum number of linearly independent vectors it contains. It can be verified at once that

$$r(A_{m \times n}) \leq \min(m, n) \tag{A.7.1}$$

That is, the rank of a matrix cannot exceed the minimum of the two numbers m and n, denoting the number of rows and the number of columns, respectively. For suppose that $m > n$. This means that **A** contains m n-component row vectors, i.e., vectors belonging to an n-dimensional space. But an n-dimensional space cannot contain more than n linearly independent vectors. The converse argument holds when $n > m$.

As a corollary of the one-to-one correspondence between the notions of linear independence and of zero determinant, the rank of a matrix may also be defined as the maximum order of the nonvanishing determinants which may be found among its minors.

7.3. There are two important theorems concerning the rank of a matrix.

Theorem (i). If **A** and **B** are two matrices, conformable for multiplication, then

$$r(\mathbf{AB}) \le \min\left[r(\mathbf{A}), r(\mathbf{B})\right] \qquad (A.7.2)$$

In other words, a linear transformation cannot increase the rank of a matrix.

Proof. Suppose that **A** is an $m \times n$ matrix and **B** an $n \times q$ matrix. Then **AB** is an $m \times q$ matrix where each column is a linear combination of n vectors. Hence the rank of **AB** cannot be higher than the minimum of the three numbers m, q, n. Q.E.D.

Theorem (ii). Given a matrix **A** and two nonsingular matrices **B** and **C**, conformable to **A** for post- and pre-multiplication, respectively, then

$$r(\mathbf{AB}) = r(\mathbf{CA}) = r(\mathbf{A}) \qquad (A.7.3)$$

In other words, post- or pre-multiplication of any matrix by a nonsingular matrix does not change the rank of that matrix.

Proof. Let $r(\mathbf{A}) = k$ and $r(\mathbf{AB}) = h$. Owing to Theorem (i), $h \le k$. But $\mathbf{A} = \mathbf{ABB}^{-1}$ and therefore $r(\mathbf{A}) = r(\mathbf{ABB}^{-1}) = k$. Again, owing to Theorem (i), $r(\mathbf{AB}) = h \ge r[(\mathbf{AB})\mathbf{B}^{-1}] = k$. But, if $h \le k$ and $k \le h$, it follows that $k = h$. Q.E.D.

8 Systems of Linear Equations

8.1. We are at last in a position to inquire into the properties of systems of linear equations. It may be helpful to begin by considering the special case of a system of n equations in n unknowns, which we may write as

$$\left.\begin{aligned}
a_{11}x_1 + a_{12}x_2 + \cdots + a_{1n}x_n &= b_1 \\
a_{21}x_1 + a_{22}x_2 + \cdots + a_{2n}x_n &= b_2 \\
\vdots \\
a_{n1}x_1 + a_{n2}x_2 + \cdots + a_{nn}x_n &= b_n
\end{aligned}\right\} \qquad (A.8.1)$$

or, more compactly,

$$\mathbf{Ax} = \mathbf{b} \qquad (A.8.1a)$$

where **A** is an nth-order square coefficient matrix, **x** is an n-component column vector representing the unknowns, and **b** is an n-component column vector of known terms. If **A** is nonsingular, i.e., of rank n, this means that the system contains n linearly independent equations. In matrix notation the solution is immediate. Pre-multiplying both sides of (A.8.1a) by the inverse of $\mathbf{A}$, we obtain

$$\mathbf{A}^{-1}\mathbf{A}\mathbf{x} = \mathbf{A}^{-1}\mathbf{b}$$

$$\mathbf{x} = \mathbf{A}^{-1}\mathbf{b} \tag{A.8.2}$$

Since the inverse matrix is unique, it follows that the solution is unique. In other words, when $\mathbf{A}$ is a nonsingular matrix, there is a unique solution vector, given by (A.8.2), which satisfies (A.8.1).

Expression (A.8.2) enables us to look at the inverse matrix from a new point of view. In a system of n linearly independent equations, in n unknowns, the inverse of the coefficient matrix enables us to compute immediately all possible solutions of the system corresponding to *any* arbitrarily given set of values assigned to the components of the known vector $\mathbf{b}$.

Numerical example. Consider the simple system of two linear equations:

$$\begin{cases} x_1 - 0.6x_2 = b_1 \\ -0.3x_1 + x_2 = b_2 \end{cases}$$

which may be rewritten

$$\begin{bmatrix} 1 & -0.6 \\ -0.3 & 1 \end{bmatrix} \begin{bmatrix} x_1 \\ x_2 \end{bmatrix} = \begin{bmatrix} b_1 \\ b_2 \end{bmatrix}$$

By solving this system (for example, by applying any one of the methods known from elementary algebra), we obtain

$$\begin{cases} x_1 = 1.2195b_1 + 0.7317b_2 \\ x_2 = 0.3658b_1 + 1.2195b_2 \end{cases}$$

which may be rewritten

$$\begin{bmatrix} x_1 \\ x_2 \end{bmatrix} = \begin{bmatrix} 1.2195 & 0.7317 \\ 0.3658 & 1.2195 \end{bmatrix} \begin{bmatrix} b_1 \\ b_2 \end{bmatrix}$$

Observe now that the two matrices of this example are the same as those of the numerical example of Section 6.7 above. The matrix appearing in the solution is precisely the inverse of the coefficient matrix of the original system.

8.2. Consider now a more general system of m equations and n unknowns:

$$\left.\begin{array}{r}a_{11}x_1 + a_{12}x_2 + \quad \cdots \quad + a_{1n}x_n = b_1 \\ a_{21}x_1 + a_{22}x_2 + \quad \cdots \quad + a_{2n}x_n = b_2 \\ \vdots \\ a_{m1}x_1 + a_{m2}x_2 + \quad \cdots \quad + a_{mn}x_n = b_m\end{array}\right\} \qquad \text{(A.8.3)}$$

which may also be written

$$\mathbf{a}_1 x_1 + \mathbf{a}_2 x_2 + \quad \cdots \quad + \mathbf{a}_n x_n = \mathbf{b} \qquad \text{(A.8.3a)}$$

where $\mathbf{a}_1, \mathbf{a}_2, \ldots, \mathbf{a}_n, \mathbf{b}$, are m-component column vectors and $x_1, x_2, \ldots, x_n$ are scalars.

The solution of this system of equations may be interpreted as that particular n-tuple of scalars $x_1, x_2, \ldots, x_n$ which allows us to express vector $\mathbf{b}$ as a linear combination of vectors $\mathbf{a}_1, \mathbf{a}_2, \ldots, \mathbf{a}_n$. Clearly, if vector $\mathbf{b}$ were linearly independent of vectors $\mathbf{a}_1, \mathbf{a}_2, \ldots, \mathbf{a}_n$, it would be impossible to find that n-tuple of scalars $x_1, x_2, \ldots, x_n$. In this case the system (A.8.3) would have no solution. Hence, for a solution to exist, it is necessary that vector $\mathbf{b}$ be linearly dependent on vectors $\mathbf{a}_1, \mathbf{a}_2, \ldots, \mathbf{a}_n$.

More compactly, call $\mathbf{A}$ the coefficient matrix of system (A.8.3) and $(\mathbf{A}, \mathbf{b})$ the *augmented matrix* of the system, defined as

$$(\mathbf{A}, \mathbf{b}) = \begin{bmatrix} a_{11} & a_{12} & \cdots & a_{1n} & b_1 \\ a_{21} & a_{22} & \cdots & a_{2n} & b_2 \\ \vdots & \vdots & \cdot & \vdots & \vdots \\ a_{m1} & a_{m2} & \cdots & a_{mn} & b_m \end{bmatrix} \qquad \text{(A.8.4)}$$

If

$$r(\mathbf{A}, \mathbf{b}) > r(\mathbf{A}) \qquad \text{(A.8.5)}$$

then the system has no solution. (It obviously contains *inconsistent* equations.) If, on the other hand,

$$r(\mathbf{A}, \mathbf{b}) = r(\mathbf{A}) \qquad \text{(A.8.6)}$$

then vector $\mathbf{b}$ is linearly dependent on $\mathbf{a}_1, \mathbf{a}_2, \ldots, \mathbf{a}_n$. The system has at least one solution.

8.3. When (A.8.6) holds, and thus the system of equations has at least one solution, it is of interest to investigate whether the solution is unique.

Theorem. If a system of linear equations $\mathbf{Ax} = \mathbf{b}$ has more than one solution, then it has an infinite number of solutions.

Proof. Suppose that $\mathbf{x}^*$ is a solution of the system and suppose that $\mathbf{x}^{**}$ is another solution of the same system, i.e.,

$$\mathbf{Ax}^* = \mathbf{b} \quad \text{and also} \quad \mathbf{Ax}^{**} = \mathbf{b}$$

Now multiply the first system by any scalar $\lambda \neq 0$, and the second system by $(1 - \lambda)$, and then sum:

$$\lambda \mathbf{Ax}^* = \lambda \mathbf{b}$$

$$(1 - \lambda)\mathbf{Ax}^{**} = (1 - \lambda)\mathbf{b}$$

$$\mathbf{A}[\lambda\mathbf{x}^* + (1 - \lambda)\mathbf{x}^{**}] = \mathbf{b}$$

It follows that $[\lambda\mathbf{x}^* + (1 - \lambda)\mathbf{x}^{**}]$ is also a solution. And, since the only restriction on λ is $\lambda \neq 0$, this scalar may be arbitrarily assigned an infinite number of values. Hence the system has an infinite number of solutions.   Q.E.D.

We may conclude that, when solutions exist, either there exists a unique solution or there exists an infinite number of solutions.

8.4. Consider now a system of m linear equations in n unknowns for which solutions do exist, and call k the rank of its coefficient matrix. Clearly $k \leq m$. If $k < m$, the system contains $(m - k)$ equations that are redundant in the sense that they can be expressed as linear combinations of the others, and can therefore be dropped without any consequence on the solutions of the system itself. Suppose that the redundant equations have been dropped, so that we are left with the system

$$\mathbf{Ax} = \mathbf{b} \tag{A.8.7}$$

of k linearly independent equations in n unknowns.

Two cases are now possible: either $k = n$ or $k < n$. If

$$k = n \tag{A.8.8}$$

then the system contains a number of unknowns equal to the number of linearly independent equations. The matrix $\mathbf{A}$ is a square matrix of rank $k = n$, i.e., is a nonsingular matrix. This is the case examined in Section 8.1 above. The system has a unique solution.

But if

$$k < n \tag{A.8.9}$$

then the system contains a number of linearly independent equations which is smaller than the number of unknowns. In this case we may decompose the system into two parts:

$$A_1x_1 + A_2x_2 = b \tag{A.8.10}$$

where vector x_1 contains k unknowns and vector x_2 contains the remaining $(n - k)$ unknowns, the former being chosen in whatever way one likes, with the sole proviso that the matrix A_1 satisfy the condition of being of rank k (a square nonsingular matrix). After a few algebraic manipulations we have

$$A_1x_1 = b - A_2x_2$$

$$x_1 = A_1^{-1}(b - A_2x_2) \tag{A.8.11}$$

$$x_1 = A_1^{-1}b - A_1^{-1}A_2x_2 \tag{A.8.12}$$

from which we can see that the system has an infinite number of solutions, to be obtained by assigning arbitrary values to the $(n - k)$ unknowns of vector x_2 and then solving the system with respect to the k unknowns contained in vector x_1.

It may be noted that (A.8.12) provides the most general formula for the solution of a system of linear equations. Equation (A.8.2) appears as a special case in which $A_2 = O$ (and thus the second addendum on the right side vanishes).

Observe, moreover, that, since $x = [x_1', x_2']'$ is an n-component vector belonging to an n-dimensional Euclidean space E^n, all possible solutions x_1 given by (A.8.12) will generate an $(n - k)$-dimensional Euclidean subspace of E^n.

8.5. To summarize and conclude, a system of m linear equations in n unknowns may have:
  (i) no solution, if $r(A, b) > r(A)$;
  (ii) a unique solution if $r(A, b) = r(A) = k = n$;
  (iii) an infinite number of solutions, generating an $(n - k)$-dimensional Euclidean subspace of E^n, if $r(A, b) = r(A) = k < n$.

8.6. *Homogeneous linear systems.* The special case in which $b = 0$ is of particular interest. Linear systems of the type

$$Ax = 0 \tag{A.8.13}$$

are called *homogeneous*. It may be noted at once that:
  (i) The rank of the augmented matrix of a homogeneous system is always equal to the rank of the coefficient matrix, i.e.,

$$r(A, 0) = r(A) \tag{A.8.14}$$

since the null vector can never be linearly independent. Hence a homogeneous linear system always has at least one solution;

(ii) this solution, which always exists, is given by the null vector.

The solution $\mathbf{x} = \mathbf{0}$ is called the *trivial solution*. But the system might have other nonzero solutions, called *nontrivial solutions*. More specifically, we may say, following the rules of the previous sections, that if

$$r(\mathbf{A}) = k = n \qquad (A.8.15)$$

the system has a unique solution: the trivial solution $\mathbf{x} = \mathbf{0}$. If, by contrast,

$$r(\mathbf{A}) = k < n \qquad (A.8.16)$$

then, besides the solution $\mathbf{x} = \mathbf{0}$, the system also has an infinite number of nontrivial solutions. Hence the nontrivial solutions, when they exist, are infinitely many.

In the special case in which $n = m$ (case of a square $\mathbf{A}$ matrix), we may also say that, if $\mathbf{A}$ is nonsingular, the system has only the trivial (zero) solution. If, by contrast, $\mathbf{A}$ is singular, i.e., if its determinant is equal to zero, then the system also has an infinite number of nonzero solutions.

The nonzero solutions, when they exist, may be obtained by the procedure illustrated in Section 8.4 above, namely, by decomposing the system as in (A.8.10) and then solving it, as in (A.8.12), which takes the special form:

$$\mathbf{x}_1 = -\mathbf{A}_1^{-1}\mathbf{A}_2\mathbf{x}_2 \qquad (A.8.17)$$

where the $(n - k)$ unknowns of vector $\mathbf{x}_2$ may be assigned any arbitrary values. All the possible solutions will therefore generate an $(n - k)$-dimensional Euclidean subspace of E^n. The number $(n - k)$ is also called the *nullity* of $\mathbf{A}$. It defines the dimension of the subspace generated by the solutions of the system.

8.7. It will be noted that the solution of a homogeneous linear system derived above may be regarded as the special case of the general expression (A.8.12) in which the first term on the right side vanishes. We have already noted that the solution of the system of n independent equations in n unknowns considered in Section 8.1 is, on the other hand, the special case of (A.8.12) in which the *second* term on the right side vanishes. We may therefore also state that the general solution of a system of m linear equations in n unknowns $\mathbf{Ax} = \mathbf{b}$ is obtained, as may be seen from (A.8.12), by writing the particular solution $\mathbf{A}_1^{-1}\mathbf{b}$ plus all the solutions of the homogeneous linear system which one would get by replacing vector $\mathbf{b}$ with the null vector $\mathbf{0}$.

9 Eigenvalues and Eigenvectors

9.1. In numerous applications of linear algebra the following problem often arises. Given a square matrix $\mathbf{A}$, find those vectors $\mathbf{x} \neq \mathbf{0}$ such that

$$\mathbf{A}\mathbf{x} = \lambda \mathbf{x} \qquad (A.9.1)$$

where λ is a scalar. In other words, find those vectors $\mathbf{x} \neq \mathbf{0}$ such that the linear transformation $\mathbf{A}\mathbf{x}$ yields a vector which is a scalar multiple of $\mathbf{x}$.

This problem can be solved by writing (A.9.1) in the form

$$(\mathbf{A} - \lambda \mathbf{I})\mathbf{x} = \mathbf{0} \qquad (A.9.2)$$

which is a homogeneous linear system. Of course, such a system always has the solution $\mathbf{x} = \mathbf{0}$, which, however, does not satisfy the condition $\mathbf{x} \neq \mathbf{0}$ of our problem. For other (nonzero) solutions to exist, it is necessary and sufficient that

$$r(\mathbf{A} - \lambda \mathbf{I}) < n \qquad (A.9.3)$$

that is,

$$|\mathbf{A} - \lambda \mathbf{I}| = 0 \qquad (A.9.4)$$

or, in more detail,

$$\begin{vmatrix} (a_{11} - \lambda) & a_{12} & \cdots & a_{1n} \\ a_{21} & (a_{22} - \lambda) & \cdots & a_{2n} \\ \vdots & \vdots & \ddots & \vdots \\ a_{n1} & a_{n2} & \cdots & (a_{nn} - \lambda) \end{vmatrix} = 0 \qquad (A.9.4a)$$

This algebraic equation is called the *characteristic equation* of matrix $\mathbf{A}$. Observe that the expansion of the determinant is an nth-order polynomial in λ, i.e.,

$$|\mathbf{A} - \lambda \mathbf{I}| = (-\lambda)^n + b_{n-1}(-\lambda)^{n-1} + \cdots + b_1(-\lambda) + b_0$$

where $b_{n-1}, b_{n-2}, \ldots, b_1, b_0$ are sums of determinants of submatrices of $\mathbf{A}$. This polynomial is called the characteristic polynomial of matrix $\mathbf{A}$.

It follows that the equation (A.9.4) has n solutions, or roots, which will be denoted by

$$\lambda_1, \lambda_2, \lambda_3, \ldots, \lambda_n \qquad (A.9.5)$$

and which are called the *eigenvalues* or *characteristic roots* of matrix $\mathbf{A}$. The eigenvalues of $\mathbf{A}$ may be real numbers or complex numbers; they may all be distinct from one another, or some of them may be repeated. In any case they cannot be more than n, if n is the order of the matrix $\mathbf{A}$. If an eigenvalue is repeated h times, it is said to have *multiplicity h*.

It follows from these definitions that the eigenvalues of $\mathbf{A}$ and the eigenvalues of its transpose $\mathbf{A}'$ are the same. Moreover, it follows that a singular matrix must have at least one eigenvalue equal to zero. More generally, if $\mathbf{A}$ is a square matrix of order n and rank k, where $k < n$, then $\mathbf{A}$ must have $(n - k)$ eigenvalues equal to zero. (For, by deleting one row and one column at a time, one can obtain $(n - k)$ singular submatrices.)

It should be noted moreover, as a corollary to what was said at the end of Section 6.3, that the eigenvalues of a triangular matrix (and *a fortiori* the eigenvalues of a diagonal matrix) coincide with the elements on its principal diagonal. Similarly, the eigenvalues of a block-triangular matrix (and *a fortiori* the eigenvalues of a block-diagonal matrix) coincide with the eigenvalues of the (square) submatrices on its principal diagonal.

9.2. To each eigenvalue of $\mathbf{A}$, there corresponds a homogeneous linear system of type (A.9.2). For any nth-order matrix $\mathbf{A}$ there will therefore be n homogeneous linear systems of type (A.9.2). The vectors $\mathbf{x} \neq \mathbf{0}$ which satisfy these n systems are called the *eigenvectors* or *characteristic vectors* of matrix $\mathbf{A}$.

Let us begin by considering the homogeneous linear system associated with the first eigenvalue (λ_1) of matrix $\mathbf{A}$, i.e.,

$$(\mathbf{A} - \lambda_1\mathbf{I})\mathbf{x} = \mathbf{0} \tag{A.9.6}$$

Since $(\mathbf{A} - \lambda_1\mathbf{I})$ is a singular matrix, the number of vectors $\mathbf{x} \neq \mathbf{0}$ satisfying the system is infinite. If n is the order and k the rank $(k < n)$ of matrix $\mathbf{A}$, we may arbitrarily fix $(n - k)$ unknowns and then solve the system for the remaining k unknowns. This means, in particular, that, if $\mathbf{x}^*$ is an eigenvector-solution of (A.9.6),

$$\alpha\mathbf{x}^* \tag{A.9.7}$$

(where α is an arbitrarily chosen scalar) is also an eigenvector-solution of (A.9.6). It follows that, α being an arbitrary number, (A.9.7) represents an infinite number of solutions. The eigenvectors $\alpha\mathbf{x}^*$, however, though being infinite in number, are all linearly dependent.

Exactly the same argument may be repeated for $\lambda_2, \lambda_3, \ldots, \lambda_n$. To each of the n homogeneous linear systems $(\mathbf{A} - \lambda_i\mathbf{I})\mathbf{x} = \mathbf{0}$, $i = 1, 2, \ldots, n$, there corresponds an infinite number of linearly dependent eigenvectors. However, each of the eigenvectors associated with λ_1 might be linearly independent of the eigenvectors associated with the other eigenvalues. The same can be said of each of the eigenvectors associated with $\lambda_2, \lambda_3, \ldots, \lambda_n$. In any case, therefore, no square matrix **A** can have more than n linearly independent eigenvectors.

The same arguments could now be repeated for **A'**, the transpose of matrix **A**. It was pointed out above that the eigenvalues of **A** and the eigenvalues of **A'** are the same. But this is *not* the case for the eigenvectors. For any eigenvalue λ_i, $i = 1, 2, \ldots, n$, the eigenvectors of **A'** will in general be *different* from the eigenvectors of **A**. Of course, the matrix **A'** cannot have more than n linearly independent eigenvectors.

To conclude, each eigenvalue λ_i, $i = 1, 2, \ldots, n$, of any nth-order square matrix **A** is associated with two distinct eigenvectors: an eigenvector $\mathbf{x} \neq \mathbf{0}$, which is obtained as the solution of the homogeneous linear system

$$(\mathbf{A} - \lambda_i \mathbf{I})\mathbf{x} = \mathbf{0} \qquad (A.9.8)$$

and another eigenvector $\mathbf{y} \neq \mathbf{0}$, which is obtained as the solution of the homogeneous linear system

$$(\mathbf{A'} - \lambda_i \mathbf{I})\mathbf{y'} = \mathbf{0} \qquad (A.9.9)$$

To distinguish these two eigenvectors from each other, $\mathbf{y}$ is generally defined as a row vector and (A.9.9) is rewritten

$$\mathbf{y}(\mathbf{A} - \lambda_i \mathbf{I}) = \mathbf{0} \qquad (A.9.10)$$

Eigenvector $\mathbf{x}$ is also called an eigenvector according to the rows (as it multiplies the rows of **A**) or simply a *right-hand eigenvector* of **A**; and eigenvector $\mathbf{y}$ is called an eigenvector according to the columns (as it multiplies the columns of **A**) or simply a *left-hand eigenvector* of **A**.

In following sections the convention will be followed of carrying out all the arguments and proofs in terms of the right-hand eigenvectors of the matrices considered. It goes without saying that the same arguments and proofs could be repeated (and therefore would hold) with reference to the left-hand eigenvectors of the same matrices.

9.3. *Theorem.* Given a square matrix **A**, if its n eigenvalues $\lambda_1, \lambda_2, \ldots, \lambda_n$ are all distinct, matrix **A** has n linearly independent eigenvectors.

Proof (ab absurdo.) Let **A** be a square matrix with n eigenvalues $\lambda_1, \lambda_2, \ldots, \lambda_n$ all distinct from each other. Call $\mathbf{x}_1$ one of the eigenvectors associated with λ_1, $\mathbf{x}_2$ one of the eigenvectors associated with $\lambda_2, \ldots, \mathbf{x}_n$ one of the eigenvectors associated with λ_n. Suppose now that $(n - k)$ of these eigenvectors are linearly independent, while the remaining k vectors, for example, $x_1, x_2, \ldots, x_k$ are linear combinations of the former. Hence it must be possible to express each of the vectors $x_1, x_2, \ldots, x_k$ as a linear combination of the vectors $x_{k+1}, x_{k+2}, \ldots, x_n$. For example, it must be possible to write

$$x_1 = \sum_{i=k+1}^{n} \alpha_i x_i \tag{A.9.11}$$

where at least one $\alpha_i \neq 0$, $i = k + 1, \ldots, n$. Now multiply both sides of (A.9.11) by A:

$$Ax_1 = \sum_{i=k+1}^{n} \alpha_i A x_i$$

and thus, by definition,

$$\lambda_1 x_1 = \sum_{i=k+1}^{n} \alpha_i \lambda_i x_i \tag{A.9.12}$$

Multiply (A.9.11) by λ_1 and subtract it from (A.9.12) then obtain

$$(\lambda_1 - \lambda_1)x_1 = \sum_{i=k+1}^{n} \alpha_i(\lambda_i - \lambda_1)x_i$$

$$0 = \sum_{i=k+1}^{n} \alpha_i(\lambda_i - \lambda_1)x_i \tag{A.9.13}$$

It follows that, since the $x_{k+1}, x_{k+2}, \ldots, x_n$ are linearly independent, the following equalities must hold:

$$\alpha_{k+1}(\lambda_{k+1} - \lambda_1) = \alpha_{k+2}(\lambda_{k+2} - \lambda_1) = \ldots = \alpha_n(\lambda_n - \lambda_1) = 0$$

But we know, *ex hypothesi*, that all the eigenvalues are distinct, and hence that

$$\lambda_{k+1} - \lambda_1 \neq 0$$
$$\lambda_{k+2} - \lambda_1 \neq 0$$
$$\vdots$$
$$\lambda_n - \lambda_1 \neq 0$$

But, if this is so, then (A.9.13) is impossible, since the coefficients $\alpha_{k+1}, \alpha_{k+2}, \ldots, \alpha_n$ cannot all be zero. We must conclude that none of the eigenvectors $x_1, x_2, \ldots, x_n$ can be linearly dependent. And, if none of these eigenvectors can be linearly dependent, then they must all be linearly independent.   Q.E.D.

9.4. When the characteristic roots of any nth-order square matrix A are not all distinct (i.e., some of them are *simple* roots and others are repeated), it is not possible, in general, to state the number of linearly independent eigenvectors of $\mathbf{A}$. It is only possible to say that the number of linearly independent eigenvectors cannot be smaller than the number of distinct eigenvalues (i.e., of the simple roots) and cannot be larger than the number n (expressing the order of matrix $\mathbf{A}$).

9.5. More specific statements can be made for special types of matrices. For example, it can be proved[4] that, if $\mathbf{A}$ is a symmetric nth-order matrix, then the following propositions hold:

(i) The eigenvalues of $\mathbf{A}$ are all real numbers.

(ii) In all cases (whether the characteristic roots are all distinct or are repeated) $\mathbf{A}$ has n linearly independent eigenvectors.

(iii) The n (linearly independent) eigenvectors of $\mathbf{A}$ are othogonal to one another.

(iv) Right-hand eigenvectors and left-hand eigenvectors coincide.

9.6. *Similarity transformations.* It can easily be proved that, if λ is an eigenvalue of the square matrix $\mathbf{A}$ and $\mathbf{P}$ is a nonsingular square matrix, then λ is also an eigenvalue of the matrix $(\mathbf{PAP}^{-1})$. Let $\mathbf{x}$ be an eigenvector of $\mathbf{A}$ corresponding to the eigenvalue λ, i.e.,

$$\mathbf{Ax} = \lambda \mathbf{x} \tag{A.9.14}$$

Multiply both sides by $\mathbf{P}$:

$$\mathbf{PAx} = \lambda \mathbf{Px}$$

$$\mathbf{PAP}^{-1}\mathbf{Px} = \lambda \mathbf{Px}$$

Now let $\mathbf{y} = \mathbf{Px}$. It follows that

$$(\mathbf{PAP}^{-1})\mathbf{y} = \lambda \mathbf{y} \tag{A.9.15}$$

where $\mathbf{y}$ is an eigenvector of $(\mathbf{PAP}^{-1})$ and λ an eigenvalue of both $\mathbf{A}$ and $(\mathbf{PAP}^{-1})$.

The operation $\mathbf{PAP}^{-1}$ is said to be a *similarity transformation*. The two matrices $\mathbf{A}$ and $(\mathbf{PAP}^{-1})$, which have the same eigenvalues, are called *similar*.

9.7. *Diagonalization of a square matrix.* Let $\mathbf{A}$ be an nth-order square matrix with n linearly independent eigenvectors, $\mathbf{x}_1, \mathbf{x}_2, \ldots, \mathbf{x}_n$, corresponding to the eigenvalues $\lambda_1, \lambda_2, \ldots, \lambda_n$. Consider now the square matrix $\mathbf{X}$ defined as

$$\mathbf{X} = [\mathbf{x}_1, \mathbf{x}_2, \ldots, \mathbf{x}_n] \tag{A.9.16}$$

[4] See, for example, Almon [1, p. 117 ff].

By using the definitions of eigenvalue and eigenvector, we have

$$\mathbf{AX} = [\lambda_1\mathbf{x}_1, \lambda_2\mathbf{x}_2, \ldots, \lambda_n\mathbf{x}_n] \qquad \text{(A.9.17)}$$

Observe now that the right-hand side of (A.9.17) is a matrix whose columns are the columns of (A.9.16) multiplied by the corresponding eigenvalues. Therefore, by defining the diagonal matrix

$$\mathbf{D} = [\lambda_j\delta_{ij}] \qquad \text{(A.9.18)}$$

where the eigenvalues of $\mathbf{A}$ are on the principal diagonal, we may write

$$[\lambda_1\mathbf{x}_1, \lambda_2\mathbf{x}_2, \ldots, \lambda_n\mathbf{x}_n] = \mathbf{XD} \qquad \text{(A.9.19)}$$

Hence

$$\mathbf{AX} = \mathbf{XD} \qquad \text{(A.9.20)}$$

Since $\mathbf{X}$ is a nonsingular matrix (its columns are linearly independent vectors *ex hypothesi*), we may pre-multiply both sides of (A.9.20) by $\mathbf{X}^{-1}$:

$$\mathbf{X}^{-1}\mathbf{AX} = \mathbf{X}^{-1}\mathbf{XD}$$
$$\mathbf{X}^{-1}\mathbf{AX} = \mathbf{D} \qquad \text{(A.9.21)}$$

We have thereby obtained a similarity transformation of $\mathbf{A}$, which yields the diagonal matrix $\mathbf{D}$, i.e., a matrix which has the property not only of having the same eigenvalues of $\mathbf{A}$, but also of actually exhibiting them all on its principal diagonal. This particular similarity transformation of $\mathbf{A}$ is called the *diagonalization of matrix* $\mathbf{A}$.

Observe that the crucial property that has enabled us to diagonalize $\mathbf{A}$ is the existence of the inverse of matrix $\mathbf{X}$, i.e., the existence of n linearly independent eigenvectors of $\mathbf{A}$.

When the number of linearly independent eigenvectors of $\mathbf{A}$ is smaller than n, its diagonalization is not possible.

Numerical example. Consider the square matrix

$$\mathbf{A} = \begin{bmatrix} -4 & 9 \\ 4 & 5 \end{bmatrix}$$

The two eigenvalues are easily computed:

$$|\mathbf{A} - \lambda\mathbf{I}| = \begin{vmatrix} -4 - \lambda & 9 \\ 4 & 5 - \lambda \end{vmatrix} = (-4 - \lambda)(5 - \lambda) - 36 = 0$$

$$-20 + \lambda^2 + 4\lambda - 5\lambda - 36 = 0$$

$$\lambda^2 - \lambda - 56 = 0$$

$$\lambda_{1,2} = \tfrac{1}{2}(1 \pm \sqrt{1 + 224})$$

Hence $\lambda_1 = 8$, $\lambda_2 = -7$.

To find the corresponding (right-hand) eigenvectors, we may form the two homogeneous linear systems

$$\begin{cases} -12x_1 + 9x_2 = 0 \\ 4x_1 - 3x_2 = 0 \end{cases} \quad \text{and} \quad \begin{cases} 3x_1 + 9x_2 = 0 \\ 4x_1 + 12x_2 = 0 \end{cases}$$

the solutions of which are $x_1 = (3/4)x_2$ and $x_1 = -3x_2$, respectively. Now take one eigenvector from the first solution and one eigenvector from the second solution to form the matrix

$$\mathbf{X} = \begin{bmatrix} \dfrac{3}{4} & -3 \\ 1 & 1 \end{bmatrix}, \quad \mathbf{X}^{-1} = \begin{bmatrix} \dfrac{4}{15} & \dfrac{12}{15} \\ -\dfrac{4}{15} & \dfrac{3}{15} \end{bmatrix}$$

It can immediately be verified that

$$\mathbf{D} = \mathbf{X}^{-1}\mathbf{A}\mathbf{X} = \begin{bmatrix} 8 & 0 \\ 0 & -7 \end{bmatrix}$$

where, as can be seen, the eigenvalues $\lambda_1 = 8$ and $\lambda_2 = -7$ appear on the principal diagonal.

9.8. *Canonical Jordan form.* It was stated above that, when the number of linearly independent eigenvectors of $\mathbf{A}$ is less than n, diagonalization is impossible. It is always possible, however, to subject $\mathbf{A}$ to a similarity transformation, $\mathbf{J} = \mathbf{V}\mathbf{A}\mathbf{V}^{-1}$, where $\mathbf{V}$ is a nonsingular matrix which will reduce matrix $\mathbf{A}$ to its canonical Jordan form.[5]

The canonical Jordan form of any square matrix $\mathbf{A}$ is a square matrix $\mathbf{J}$ of the same order as $\mathbf{A}$ with the following properties:

(i) The elements on its principal diagonal are the eigenvalues of $\mathbf{A}$, and the multiple eigenvalues appear in adjacent positions.

(ii) The elements on the diagonal above the principal diagonal are either zero or unity. Only elements on the right-hand side of an eigenvalue which is going to be repeated can be equal to unity.

(iii) All other elements in the matrix are zero.

An example of a canonical Jordan form is the matrix

$$\mathbf{J} = \begin{bmatrix} \lambda_1 & 1 & 0 & 0 \\ 0 & \lambda_2 & 0 & 0 \\ 0 & 0 & \lambda_3 & 1 \\ 0 & 0 & 0 & \lambda_4 \end{bmatrix}$$

[5] See, for a proof, Zurmühl [14, pp. 245 ff]; also Birkhoff and MacLane [3, p. 333].

where $\lambda_1, \lambda_2, \lambda_3, \lambda_4$ ($\lambda_1 = \lambda_2, \lambda_3 = \lambda_4$) are the eigenvalues of a square matrix $\mathbf{A}$ from which matrix $\mathbf{J}$ has been obtained by a transformation of the type $\mathbf{J} = \mathbf{V}\mathbf{A}\mathbf{V}^{-1}$.

9.9. The Jordan canonical form $\mathbf{J}$ of $\mathbf{A}$ can always be written as a sum:

$$\mathbf{J} = \mathbf{D} + \mathbf{I}^{\ominus}$$

where $\mathbf{D}$ is the diagonal matrix with the eigenvalues of $\mathbf{A}$ on its principal diagonal and $\mathbf{I}^{\ominus}$ is a special matrix the elements of which are all zeros except some ones on the diagonal above the principal one.

Observe that the powers of matrix $\mathbf{I}^{\ominus}$ have the property that the diagonal containing the ones is shifted to the next diagonal at each multiplication by $\mathbf{I}^{\ominus}$. For example, in the case of a 4th-order matrix,

$$\mathbf{I}^{\ominus 2} = \begin{bmatrix} 0 & 1 & 0 & 0 \\ 0 & 0 & 1 & 0 \\ 0 & 0 & 0 & 1 \\ 0 & 0 & 0 & 0 \end{bmatrix} \begin{bmatrix} 0 & 1 & 0 & 0 \\ 0 & 0 & 1 & 0 \\ 0 & 0 & 0 & 1 \\ 0 & 0 & 0 & 0 \end{bmatrix} = \begin{bmatrix} 0 & 0 & 1 & 0 \\ 0 & 0 & 0 & 1 \\ 0 & 0 & 0 & 0 \\ 0 & 0 & 0 & 0 \end{bmatrix}$$

$$\mathbf{I}^{\ominus 3} = \begin{bmatrix} 0 & 0 & 0 & 1 \\ 0 & 0 & 0 & 0 \\ 0 & 0 & 0 & 0 \\ 0 & 0 & 0 & 0 \end{bmatrix} \qquad \mathbf{I}^{\ominus 4} = \mathbf{O}$$

Hence, if n is the order of $\mathbf{I}^{\ominus}$, then $\mathbf{I}^{\ominus n}$ is necessarily a null matrix.

9.10. *Convergence conditions for a square matrix.* Consider the powers of a square matrix $\mathbf{A}$, namely, $\mathbf{I}, \mathbf{A}, \mathbf{A}^2, \mathbf{A}^3, \ldots$ Matrix $\mathbf{A}$ is said to be a *convergent matrix* if

$$\lim_{N \to \infty} \mathbf{A}^N = \mathbf{O} \tag{A.9.22}$$

Otherwise it is said to be a nonconvergent matrix. Observe that, for matrix $\mathbf{A}^N$ to tend to the null matrix as N increases, it is necessary that *all* elements of $\mathbf{A}^N$ tend to zero as $N \to \infty$.

Theorem. Given a positive real number ν and a square matrix $\mathbf{A}$, the matrix $\nu\mathbf{A}$ is convergent if $\nu < (1/|\lambda_M|)$, where λ_M is the eigenvalue of $\mathbf{A}$ which is maximum in modulus.

Proof. Let $\mathbf{J}$ be the Jordan canonical form of matrix $\mathbf{A}$ obtained by a similarity transformation $\mathbf{V}\mathbf{A}\mathbf{V}^{-1}$, where $\mathbf{V}$ is a nonsingular matrix. It follows that $(\nu\mathbf{J})^N = \mathbf{V}(\nu\mathbf{A})^N\mathbf{V}^{-1}$ and hence that $\mathbf{V}^{-1}(\nu\mathbf{J})^N\mathbf{V} = (\nu\mathbf{A})^N$ from which it appears at once that the convergence conditions for $(\nu\mathbf{A})^N$ coincide with the convergence conditions for $(\nu\mathbf{J})^N$.

Consider first the special case $\mathbf{J} = \mathbf{D}$, i.e., the case in which matrix $\mathbf{A}$ can be diagonalized. In this case, if $\nu < (1/|\lambda_M|)$, then the elements on the principal diagonal of $\nu\mathbf{D}$ are smaller than 1 in modulus. Hence their powers converge to zero for $N \to \infty$. It follows that $\lim_{N\to\infty} (\nu\mathbf{D})^N = \mathbf{O}$ and therefore also that $\lim_{N\to\infty} (\nu\mathbf{A})^N = \mathbf{O}$.

If $\nu\mathbf{A}$ cannot be diagonalized, we can always write the powers of the corresponding Jordan canonical form (since $\mathbf{D}\mathbf{I}^\ominus = \mathbf{I}^\ominus\mathbf{D}$) by using the binomial power series (see Section 4.11 above); that is,

$$(\nu\mathbf{J})^N = (\nu\mathbf{D} + \nu\mathbf{I}^\ominus)^N = (\nu\mathbf{D})^N + N(\nu\mathbf{D})^{N-1}\nu\mathbf{I}^\ominus$$

$$+ \binom{N}{2}(\nu\mathbf{D})^{N-2}(\nu\mathbf{I}^\ominus)^2 + \ldots + \binom{N}{N-1}\nu\mathbf{D}(\nu\mathbf{I}^\ominus)^{N-1}$$

$$+ (\nu\mathbf{I}^\ominus)^N$$

Now matrix $\mathbf{I}^{\ominus N}$ is certainly null for all $N > n$, where n is the order of the matrix itself. Therefore only the first n addenda of the binomial expansion can be different from zero; all the remaining addenda vanish. Hence we may write

$$(\nu\mathbf{J})^N = \sum_{i=0}^{n} \frac{N!}{(N-i)!i!} \nu^N \mathbf{D}^{N-i}\mathbf{I}^{\ominus i}$$

And, since n is a given and *finite* number, the conditions of convergence of this *finite sum*, for $N \to \infty$, and hence also the conditions of convergence of matrix $\nu\mathbf{J}$, coincide with the conditions of convergence of matrix $\nu\mathbf{D}$. But it was shown above that, if $\nu < (1/|\lambda_M|)$, then $\lim_{N\to\infty} (\nu\mathbf{D})^N = \mathbf{O}$. It follows that in such a case $\lim_{N\to\infty} (\nu\mathbf{J})^N = \mathbf{O}$ and therefore also that $\lim_{N\to\infty} (\nu\mathbf{A})^N = \mathbf{O}$.

The proof is thereby complete.   Q.E.D

9.11. *An iterative method to compute the inverse matrix* $(\mathbf{I} - \nu\mathbf{A})^{-1}$. Given a positive real number ν and a square matrix $\mathbf{A}$, consider the sum of powers of $\nu\mathbf{A}$:

$$\sum_{i=0}^{N} (\nu\mathbf{A})^i = (\nu\mathbf{A})^0 + \nu\mathbf{A} + (\nu\mathbf{A})^2 + \ldots + (\nu\mathbf{A})^N \qquad (A.9.23)$$

Now multiply both sides by $(\mathbf{I} - \nu\mathbf{A})$:

$$(\mathbf{I} - \nu\mathbf{A}) \sum_{i=0}^{N} (\nu\mathbf{A})^i = (\mathbf{I} - \nu\mathbf{A})[\mathbf{I} + \nu\mathbf{A} + (\nu\mathbf{A})^2 + \ldots + (\nu\mathbf{A})^N]$$

$$= \mathbf{I} + \nu\mathbf{A} + (\nu\mathbf{A})^2 + \ldots + (\nu\mathbf{A})^N$$

$$-\nu\mathbf{A} - (\nu\mathbf{A})^2 - \ldots - (\nu\mathbf{A})^N - (\nu\mathbf{A})^{N+1}$$

$$= \mathbf{I} - (\nu\mathbf{A})^{N+1}$$

If $\nu < (1/|\lambda_M|)$, we know from the theorem of the previous section that $\lim_{N\to\infty} (\nu\mathbf{A})^{N+1} = \mathbf{O}$. Hence

$$(\mathbf{I} - \nu\mathbf{A})[\mathbf{I} + \nu\mathbf{A} + (\nu\mathbf{A})^2 + (\nu\mathbf{A})^3 + \ldots] = \mathbf{I}.$$

Observe now that the sum-matrix $[\mathbf{I} + \nu\mathbf{A} + (\nu\mathbf{A})^2 + (\nu\mathbf{A})^3 + \ldots]$ is a matrix which, when multiplied by $(\mathbf{I} - \nu\mathbf{A})$, yields the identity matrix. But this is precisely the definition of the inverse of matrix $(\mathbf{I} - \nu\mathbf{A})$. The remarkable conclusion follows that, when $\nu < (1/|\lambda_M|)$, we can write

$$(\mathbf{I} - \nu\mathbf{A})^{-1} = \mathbf{I} + \nu\mathbf{A} + (\nu\mathbf{A})^2 + (\nu\mathbf{A})^3 + \ldots \tag{A.9.24}$$

The sum on the right side may be regarded as the power series expansion of matrix $(\mathbf{I} - \nu\mathbf{A})^{-1}$.

The interest of this power series expansion is that in all cases in which $\nu < (1/|\lambda_M|)$ it provides us with an iterative method for the computation of the inverse matrix $(\mathbf{I} - \nu\mathbf{A})^{-1}$.

9.12. Now define $\mu = 1/\nu$. Then

$$(\mathbf{I} - \nu\mathbf{A}) = \frac{1}{\mu}(\mu\mathbf{I} - \mathbf{A})$$

and hence

$$(\mathbf{I} - \nu\mathbf{A})^{-1} = \left[\frac{1}{\mu}(\mu\mathbf{I} - \mathbf{A})\right]^{-1} = \mu(\mu\mathbf{I} - \mathbf{A})^{-1} \tag{A.9.25}$$

Thus, provided that $\mu > |\lambda_M|$, where λ_M is the eigenvalue of $\mathbf{A}$ which is maximum in modulus, the power series expansion (A.9.24) may also be written

$$(\mu\mathbf{I} - \mathbf{A})^{-1} = \frac{1}{\mu}\left[\mathbf{I} + \frac{1}{\mu}\mathbf{A} + \left(\frac{1}{\mu}\mathbf{A}\right)^2 + \left(\frac{1}{\mu}\mathbf{A}\right)^3 + \ldots\right] \tag{A.9.26}$$

This is an expansion, alternative to (A.9.24), which allows us to compute by successive iterations the inverse matrix $(\mu\mathbf{I} - \mathbf{A})^{-1}$, whenever $\mu > |\lambda_M|$.

10   Non-negative Matrices

10.1. Non-negative matrices have found widespread application in economic analysis and in probability theory. Since they have peculiar properties of their own, it is important to investigate them.

10.2. *Definitions.* A matrix $\mathbf{A}$ is called a positive matrix, and is written $\mathbf{A} > \mathbf{O}$, if all its elements are positive numbers.

A matrix **A** is called a *non-negative matrix*, and is written **A** ≥ **O** or **A** ≧ **O**, if none of its elements is a negative number. The inequality **A** ≥ **O** denotes a non-negative matrix in which at least one element is strictly positive (and is also called a *semipositive matrix*). The inequality **A** ≧ **Ò**, on the other hand, denotes a non-negative matrix in which there is no restriction on the number of zero elements; all elements might be zeros.

A square matrix **A** is called a *reducible matrix* (or also a *decomposable* matrix) if it is possible, by the operation of interchanging some rows *and the corresponding columns*, to reduce it to the form:

$$\mathbf{A} = \begin{bmatrix} \mathbf{A}_{11} & \mathbf{A}_{12} \\ \mathbf{O} & \mathbf{A}_{22} \end{bmatrix} \tag{A.10.1}$$

where **A**$_{11}$ and **A**$_{22}$ are square submatrices and **O** is a null submatrix.

Conversely, a square matrix **A** is called an *irreducible matrix* (or also an *indecomposable* matrix) if it is not possible, by the operation of interchanging rows and corresponding columns, to reduce it to the form (A.10.1).

The submatrices **A**$_{11}$ and **A**$_{22}$ in (A.10.1) may themselves be reducible matrices; so that, in general, a reducible matrix may always be reduced to the block-diagonal form:

$$\begin{bmatrix} \mathbf{A}_{11} & \mathbf{A}_{12} & \cdots & \mathbf{A}_{1s} \\ \mathbf{O} & \mathbf{A}_{22} & \cdots & \mathbf{A}_{2s} \\ \cdot & \cdot & \cdot & \cdot \\ \cdot & \cdot & \cdot & \cdot \\ \cdot & \cdot & \cdot & \cdot \\ \mathbf{O} & \mathbf{O} & \cdots & \mathbf{A}_{ss} \end{bmatrix} \tag{A.10.2}$$

where **A**$_{11}$, **A**$_{22}$, ..., **A**$_{ss}$, are irreducible square matrices not necessarily of the same order.

11 The Perron-Frobenius Theorems

11.1. A number of mathematicians, and particularly Perron and Frobenius,[6] have developed a whole set of remarkable theorems concerning the eigenvalues and the eigenvectors of non-negative matrices. In the following pages we consider the theorems of Perron and Frobenius which are used in the text. These theorems normally have two versions – a strong version concerning irreducible matrices and a weak version concerning reducible matrices. Proofs will be given for

---

[6] The original references are Perron [10] and Frobenius [6]. But the proofs developed in the following pages will follow more closely the versions given by Wielandt [13] and Manara and Nicola [9]. See also Debreu and Herstein [4].

the strong version. The corresponding weak version will then simply be stated.

11.2. Perron-Frobenius theorems concerning irreducible non-negative matrices. Let $\mathbf{A} \geq \mathbf{O}$ be an irreducible non-negative nth-order square matrix, and $\mathbf{x} \geq 0$ an n-component non-negative vector.

Lemma 1. The matrix $(\mathbf{I} + \mathbf{A})^n$ is positive.

Proof. We may always write vector $\mathbf{x} \geq 0$, after suitable rearrangement of its components, as

$$\mathbf{x} = \begin{bmatrix} \mathbf{y} \\ \mathbf{0} \end{bmatrix} \tag{A.11.1}$$

where $\mathbf{y}$ is an h-component positive vector ($h < n$). After rearranging the rows and columns of $\mathbf{A}$ in the same way as for vector (A.11.1), we may write it

$$\mathbf{A} = \begin{bmatrix} \mathbf{A}_{11} & \mathbf{A}_{12} \\ \mathbf{A}_{21} & \mathbf{A}_{22} \end{bmatrix}$$

where $\mathbf{A}_{11}$ and $\mathbf{A}_{22}$ are square matrices of order h and $(n - h)$, respectively. The expression $(\mathbf{I} + \mathbf{A})\mathbf{x} = \mathbf{x} + \mathbf{A}\mathbf{x}$ may then be rewritten

$$(\mathbf{I} + \mathbf{A})\mathbf{x} = \begin{bmatrix} \mathbf{y} \\ \mathbf{0} \end{bmatrix} + \begin{bmatrix} \mathbf{A}_{11} & \mathbf{A}_{12} \\ \mathbf{A}_{21} & \mathbf{A}_{22} \end{bmatrix} \begin{bmatrix} \mathbf{y} \\ \mathbf{0} \end{bmatrix} = \begin{bmatrix} \mathbf{y} + \mathbf{A}_{11}\mathbf{y} \\ \mathbf{A}_{21}\mathbf{y} \end{bmatrix}$$

Now the first h components of the vector on the extreme right side are certainly positive. As to the other $(n - h)$ components, we cannot have

$$\mathbf{A}_{21}\mathbf{y} = \mathbf{0}$$

for this would imply $\mathbf{A}_{21} = \mathbf{0}$, contrary to the hypothesis that $\mathbf{A}$ is irreducible. Hence vector $(\mathbf{I} + \mathbf{A})\mathbf{x}$ must have at least one more positive component than vector $\mathbf{x}$.

Repeating the same operation n times, we obtain

$$(\mathbf{I} + \mathbf{A})^n\mathbf{x} > \mathbf{O}$$

And, since the non-negative vector $\mathbf{x}$ can be chosen arbitrarily, it follows that

$$(\mathbf{I} + \mathbf{A})^n > \mathbf{O}$$

That is, that matrix $(\mathbf{I} + \mathbf{A})^n$ must contain all positive elements.

Q.E.D.

Now let S be the set of non-negative n-component vectors $\mathbf{x}$ such that

$$\sum_{i=1}^{n} x_i = 1 \tag{A.11.2}$$

Call $\lambda(\mathbf{x})$ the maximum real number for which the relation

$$(\mathbf{I} + \mathbf{A})^n \mathbf{A}\mathbf{x} \geq \lambda(\mathbf{x})(\mathbf{I} + \mathbf{A})^n \mathbf{x} \qquad (A.11.3)$$

holds. Clearly, for any other real number λ, such that $\lambda < \lambda(\mathbf{x})$, the strict inequality $(\mathbf{I} + \mathbf{A})^n \mathbf{A}\mathbf{x} > \lambda(\mathbf{I} + \mathbf{A})^n \mathbf{x}$ holds. Observe that $(\mathbf{I} + \mathbf{A})^n \mathbf{A} = \mathbf{A}(\mathbf{I} + \mathbf{A})^n$, and that $(\mathbf{I} + \mathbf{A})^n \mathbf{A}\mathbf{x} > \mathbf{0}$ and $(\mathbf{I} + \mathbf{A})^n \mathbf{x} > \mathbf{0}$. We may now state the following.

Lemma 2. The function $\lambda(\mathbf{x})$ has a positive maximum λ_m in S.

Proof. The existence of a maximum follows from Weierstrass' theorem, since $\lambda(\mathbf{x})$ is continuous in S, and S is a closed and bounded set. The positivity of $\lambda(\mathbf{x})$ follows from the observation above that its upper bound is positive. Q.E.D.

Theorem 1. The maximum λ_m of the function $\lambda(\mathbf{x})$ in S is an eigenvalue of matrix $\mathbf{A}$. Such an eigenvalue is associated with an eigenvector $\bar{\mathbf{x}}$ which is positive. That is,

$$\mathbf{A}\bar{\mathbf{x}} = \lambda_m \bar{\mathbf{x}} \qquad (A.11.4)$$

and

$$\bar{\mathbf{x}} > \mathbf{0} \qquad (A.11.5)$$

Proof. Let $\tilde{\mathbf{x}}$ be the vector in S for which $\lambda(\tilde{\mathbf{x}})$ takes the maximum value λ_m. We know by construction that at least

$$(\mathbf{I} + \mathbf{A})^n \mathbf{A}\tilde{\mathbf{x}} \geq \lambda_m (\mathbf{I} + \mathbf{A})^n \tilde{\mathbf{x}} \qquad (A.11.6)$$

must hold; while we must exclude the existence of any vector $\mathbf{y}$ such that

$$(\mathbf{I} + \mathbf{A})^n \mathbf{A}\mathbf{y} > \lambda_m (\mathbf{I} + \mathbf{A})^n \mathbf{y} \qquad (A.11.7)$$

since λ_m is the maximum of $\lambda(\mathbf{x})$ in S (Lemma 2), defined in such a way as to satisfy (A.11.3). Now call $\bar{\mathbf{x}} = (\mathbf{I} + \mathbf{A})^n \tilde{\mathbf{x}}$ and note that, if (A.11.6) should hold, but not (A.11.4), then, if we called

$$\bar{\mathbf{z}} = \mathbf{A}\bar{\mathbf{x}} - \lambda_m \bar{\mathbf{x}} \qquad (A.11.8)$$

we would have

$$\bar{\mathbf{z}} \geq \mathbf{0}$$

where at least one component is zero. But from Lemma 1 we know that

$$(\mathbf{I} + \mathbf{A})^n \bar{\mathbf{z}} > \mathbf{0}$$

Thus, after multiplying both sides of (A.11.8) by $(\mathbf{I} + \mathbf{A})^n$, we have

$$(\mathbf{I} + \mathbf{A})^n \bar{\mathbf{z}} = (\mathbf{I} + \mathbf{A})^n \mathbf{A}\bar{\mathbf{x}} - \lambda_m (\mathbf{I} + \mathbf{A})^n \bar{\mathbf{x}} > \mathbf{0}$$

Vector $(\mathbf{I} + \mathbf{A})^n \tilde{\mathbf{x}}$ would thus satisfy (A.11.7) But that is impossible. Therefore we must have

$$\tilde{\mathbf{z}} = \mathbf{A}\tilde{\mathbf{x}} - \lambda_m \tilde{\mathbf{x}} = \mathbf{0}$$

That is, λ_m *must* be an eigenvalue of $\mathbf{A}$.

To prove (A.11.5) note that, if it were possible to rearrange the components of $\tilde{\mathbf{x}}$, as for (A.11.1), and the corresponding rows and columns of $\mathbf{A}$ in such a way as to write

$$\begin{bmatrix} \mathbf{A}_{11} & \mathbf{A}_{12} \\ \mathbf{A}_{21} & \mathbf{A}_{22} \end{bmatrix} \begin{bmatrix} \bar{\mathbf{y}} \\ \mathbf{0} \end{bmatrix} = \lambda_m \begin{bmatrix} \bar{\mathbf{y}} \\ \mathbf{0} \end{bmatrix} \qquad \text{where} \quad \bar{\mathbf{y}} > \mathbf{0}$$

or

$$\mathbf{A}_{11}\bar{\mathbf{y}} = \lambda_m \bar{\mathbf{y}}$$

$$\mathbf{A}_{21}\bar{\mathbf{y}} = \mathbf{0}$$

then it would follow that $\mathbf{A}_{21} = \mathbf{O}$. But that is contrary to the hypothesis that $\mathbf{A}$ is irreducible. The strict inequality $\tilde{\mathbf{x}} > \mathbf{0}$ must therefore hold. *A fortiori* $\bar{\mathbf{x}} > \mathbf{0}$. Q.E.D.

Remark. The proof has been carried out with reference to the right-hand eigenvector of $\mathbf{A}$. The same proof could be repeated for the left-hand eigenvector.

Now let $\mathbf{B}$ be a non-negative nth-order square matrix; let α be any eigenvalue of $\mathbf{B}$ and $\mathbf{p}$ the corresponding left-hand eigenvector. (Both α and the components of $\mathbf{p}$ might be complex numbers). By definition,

$$\mathbf{pB} = \alpha\mathbf{p} \tag{A.11.9}$$

or

$$\sum_{i=1}^{n} p_i b_{ij} = \alpha p_j \qquad j = 1, 2, \ldots, n$$

The triangular inequality allows us to write

$$\sum_{i=1}^{n} |p_i| b_{ij} \geq |\alpha| \, |p_j| \qquad j = 1, 2, \ldots, n \tag{A.11.10}$$

where we have taken the moduli of all numbers. (It was not necessary to do this for the b_{ij}, since they are all non-negative real numbers *ex hypothesi*). Now let $\mathbf{p}^*$ be a vector the components of which are the moduli of the corresponding components of vector $\mathbf{p}$. Then (A.11.10) may be rewritten

$$\mathbf{p}^*\mathbf{B} \geq |\alpha|\mathbf{p}^* \tag{A.11.10a}$$

Theorem 2. If α is any eigenvalue of matrix **A**, then $|\alpha| \leq \lambda_m$. (In other words, no eigenvalue of **A** can be greater, in modulus, than λ_m).[7]

Proof. Consider a matrix **B** such that

$$\mathbf{O} \leq \mathbf{B} \leq \mathbf{A} \tag{A.11.11}$$

Now let α be an eigenvalue of **B** and **p** be the left-hand eigenvector associated with it. Moreover, let λ_m and **x** be the eigenvalue and the eigenvector of **A**, respectively, as defined in Theorem 1 above. From (A.11.10a) and (A.11.11), we can write

$$|\alpha|\mathbf{p}^* \leq \mathbf{p}^*\mathbf{B} \leq \mathbf{p}^*\mathbf{A} \tag{A.11.12}$$

On post-multiplying by $\bar{\mathbf{x}}$ we obtain

$$|\alpha|\mathbf{p}^*\bar{\mathbf{x}} \leq \mathbf{p}^*\mathbf{A}\bar{\mathbf{x}}$$

and hence

$$|\alpha|\mathbf{p}^*\bar{\mathbf{x}} \leq \lambda_m\mathbf{p}^*\bar{\mathbf{x}}$$

But $\bar{\mathbf{x}} > \mathbf{0}$. It follows that

$$|\alpha| \leq \lambda_m \tag{A.11.13}$$

In particular, by letting $\mathbf{B} = \mathbf{A}$ we obtain the theorem.   Q.E.D.

Lemma 3. Let $\mathbf{O} \leq \mathbf{B} \leq \mathbf{A}$, and let α be an eigenvalue of **B**. If $|\alpha| = \lambda_m$, then it follows that $\mathbf{B} = \mathbf{A}$.

Proof. Since $|\alpha| = \lambda_m$, (A.11.12) becomes

$$\lambda_m\mathbf{p}^* \leq \mathbf{p}^*\mathbf{B} \leq \mathbf{p}^*\mathbf{A} \tag{A.11.14}$$

Observe now that, if we had

$$\lambda_m\mathbf{p}^* \leq \mathbf{p}^*\mathbf{A}$$

then, by the argument used in the proof of Theorem 1, we could construct a vector $\mathbf{z} > \mathbf{0}$ such that

$$\lambda_m\mathbf{z} < \mathbf{z}\mathbf{A}$$

But this is impossible, as we have seen. The first term of (A.11.14) must therefore be equal to the last term and, by implication, to the intermediate term as well, i.e.,

$$\lambda_m\mathbf{p}^* = \mathbf{p}^*\mathbf{A} \tag{A.11.15}$$

$$\mathbf{p}^*\mathbf{B} = \mathbf{p}^*\mathbf{A} \tag{A.11.16}$$

[7] A matrix whose other eigenvalues are all strictly smaller than λ_m is called a *primitive matrix*. It can be shown that a sufficient condition for a non-negative matrix to be primitive is that at least one element on its principal diagonal be positive. See Solow [12].

It now follows that, in (A.11.15), $\mathbf{p}^*$ is the eigenvector of $\mathbf{A}$ associated with eigenvalue λ_m. Since $\mathbf{p}^* > \mathbf{0}$ and $\mathbf{p}^*(\mathbf{A} - \mathbf{B}) = \mathbf{0}$, it follows from (A.11.16) that $\mathbf{A} = \mathbf{B}$.   Q.E.D.

Theorem 3. The eigenvalue λ_m of $\mathbf{A}$ is a continuous, increasing function of the elements of $\mathbf{A}$.

Proof. By letting $\mathbf{O} \le \mathbf{B} \le \mathbf{A}$, as in Lemma 3, and using the proof of Theorem 2, we may write

$$\lambda_m(\mathbf{B}) \le \lambda_m(\mathbf{A}) \tag{A.11.17}$$

If, more specifically, we now set $\mathbf{B} \ne \mathbf{A}$, then necessarily

$$\lambda_m(\mathbf{B}) < \lambda_m(\mathbf{A})$$

For, if the equality sign were to hold in (A.11.17), we should then have $\mathbf{B} = \mathbf{A}$, from Lemma 3, contrary to the hypothesis $\mathbf{B} \ne \mathbf{A}$. (The continuity of λ_m follows from well-known theorems on the continuity of the roots of any algebraic equation, when considered as functions of the coefficients.)   Q.E.D.

Two remarkable corollaries follow from this theorem.

Corollary 1. The maximum eigenvalue of any square submatrix of $\mathbf{A}$ is smaller than the maximum eigenvalue λ_m of $\mathbf{A}$. For, by taking any submatrix of $\mathbf{A}$ and augmenting it with zeros, we obtain a matrix such as matrix $\mathbf{B}$ considered in the proof of Theorem 3.

Corollary 2. The eigenvalue λ_m is a simple root of the characteristic equation of $\mathbf{A}$:

$$\varphi(\lambda) = \det(\lambda\mathbf{I} - \mathbf{A}) = 0.$$

For, the first derivative of $\varphi(\lambda)$ is a sum of determinants of submatrices of $(\lambda\mathbf{I} - \mathbf{A})$. Owing to Corollary 1, λ_m cannot make any one of these determinants (nor their sum) vanish. This means that λ_m cannot be a root of the first derivative of $\varphi(\lambda)$, which is a necessary and sufficient condition for it to be a simple root of $\varphi(\lambda)$.

Theorem 4. To each real eigenvalue α of $\mathbf{A}$ different from λ_m there corresponds an eigenvector $\mathbf{x} \ne \mathbf{0}$ which has at least one negative component.

Proof. By definition we have

$$\mathbf{A}\mathbf{x} = \alpha\mathbf{x} \tag{A.11.18}$$

We know, moreover, from Theorem 2, that $|\alpha| \le \lambda_m$, and therefore in our case that

$$\alpha < \lambda_m \tag{A.11.19}$$

Now, if $\alpha < 0$, we can see immediately that $\mathbf{x}$ must contain at least one negative component for (A.11.18) to be satisfied. If $\alpha > 0$, recall first that

$$\bar{\mathbf{p}}\mathbf{A} = \lambda_m\bar{\mathbf{p}}, \qquad\qquad \bar{\mathbf{p}} > 0 \qquad\qquad\qquad \text{(A.11.20)}$$

By post-multiplying both sides of (A.11.20) by $\mathbf{x}$, pre-multiplying both sides of (A.11.18) by $\bar{\mathbf{p}}$, and subtracting the one from the other we obtain

$$(\lambda_m - \alpha)\bar{\mathbf{p}}\mathbf{x} = 0$$

Given (A.11.19), we must have

$$\bar{\mathbf{p}}\mathbf{x} = 0$$

But $\bar{\mathbf{p}} > 0$. Vector $\mathbf{x}$ must therefore contain at least one negative component. Q.E.D.

Remark. Again the proof has been carried out with reference to the right-hand eigenvector of $\mathbf{A}$. The same proof could be repeated for the left-hand eigenvector.

Theorem 5. Given a real number $\mu = (1/\nu) > 0$, if $\mu > \lambda_m$ (and therefore $\nu < 1/\lambda_m$), then

$$(\mu\mathbf{I} - \mathbf{A})^{-1} > \mathbf{O} \qquad\qquad\qquad \text{(A.11.21)}$$

$$(\mathbf{I} - \nu\mathbf{A})^{-1} > \mathbf{O} \qquad\qquad\qquad \text{(A.11.22)}$$

That is, all the element of matrices (A.11.21) and (A.11.22) are positive real numbers. Moreover, all the elements of matrices (A.11.21) and (A.11.22) are continuous, increasing functions of ν and continuous, decreasing functions of μ.

Proof. We know from (A.9.24) and (A.9.26) that

$$(\mathbf{I} - \nu\mathbf{A})^{-1} = \mathbf{I} + \nu\mathbf{A} + (\nu\mathbf{A})^2 + (\nu\mathbf{A})^3 + \ldots \qquad \text{(A.9.24)}$$

$$(\mu\mathbf{I} - \mathbf{A})^{-1} = \frac{1}{\mu}\left[\mathbf{I} + \frac{1}{\mu}\mathbf{A} + \left(\frac{1}{\mu}\mathbf{A}\right)^2 + \cdots\right] \qquad \text{(A.9.26)}$$

Observe now that the first n addenda on the right-hand sides of both (A.9.24) and (A.9.26) are, except for the coefficients, the same addenda that appear in the following binomial power series expansion:

$$(\mathbf{I} + \mathbf{A})^n = \mathbf{I} + n\mathbf{A} + \binom{n}{2}\mathbf{A}^2 + \ldots + \binom{n}{n-1}\mathbf{A} + \mathbf{A}^n$$

$$\text{(A.11.23)}$$

We know that all the coefficients in (A.11.23) are real positive numbers, and that $\nu = 1/\mu$ in (A.9.24) and (A.9.26) is a real positive number. Moreover, we know from Lemma 1 above that $(\mathbf{I} + \mathbf{A})^n > \mathbf{O}$.

It follows that, even if we confine ourselves to considering the sum of the first n addenda in each of (A.9.24) and (A.9.26), such a sum is certainly strictly positive. A *fortiori* the sum of the infinite series is strictly positive, or

$$(\mathbf{I} - \nu\mathbf{A})^{-1} > \mathbf{O} \quad \text{and} \quad (\mu\mathbf{I} - \mathbf{A})^{-1} > \mathbf{O}$$

Moreover, it can be seen at once that, in each matrix appearing in the sums on the right-hand sides of (A.9.24) and (A.9.26), each positive element is a continuous increasing function of $\nu = 1/\mu$. Since the sum is strictly positive, it follows that each single element of the sum matrix is a continuous increasing function of $\nu = 1/\mu$.   Q.E.D.

Theorem 6. Denote by $\mathbf{a}^{(i)}$, $i = 1, 2, \ldots, n$, the rows of $\mathbf{A}$, and by $\mathbf{1}$ the (column) sum vector. Then

$$\max_i \mathbf{a}^{(i)}\mathbf{1} \geq \lambda_m \geq \min_i \mathbf{a}^{(i)}\mathbf{1} \tag{A.11.24}$$

That is, the maximum eigenvalue λ_m lies between the maximum and the minimum of the row sums of matrix $\mathbf{A}$.

Proof. We may go back to Lemma 2 above, where λ_m was defined as the maximum of the function $\lambda(\mathbf{x})$ which satisfies relation (A.11.3). We can therefore also write

$$\mathbf{A}\mathbf{x} \geq \lambda(\mathbf{x})\,\mathbf{x}$$

for any $\mathbf{x}$ belonging to the set S in which $\sum_{i=1}^{n} x_i = 1$. Let us now choose the following $\mathbf{x}$:

$$\mathbf{x} = \frac{1}{n}\mathbf{1}$$

We obtain:

$$\mathbf{A}\mathbf{1} \geq \lambda\mathbf{1}$$

or

$$\mathbf{a}^{(i)}\mathbf{1} \geq \lambda \qquad\qquad i = 1, 2, \ldots, n$$

where $\lambda = \min_i \mathbf{a}^{(i)}\mathbf{1}$. But $\lambda_m \geq \lambda$: hence $\lambda_m \geq \min_i \mathbf{a}^{(i)}\mathbf{1}$.

Now consider the matrix

$$(\alpha\mathbf{I} - \mathbf{A}) \tag{A.11.25}$$

If we choose $\alpha \geq \max_i \mathbf{a}^{(i)}\mathbf{1}$, then the determinant of the matrix (A.11.25) cannot be zero; this means that (A.11.25) is nonsingular, which in turn implies that an α so chosen cannot be an eigenvalue of $\mathbf{A}$. We can therefore write $\lambda_m \leq \max_i \mathbf{a}^{(i)}\mathbf{1}$, unless all the $\mathbf{a}^{(i)}\mathbf{1}$ are equal to one another, $i = 1, 2, \ldots, n$, in which case $\min_i \mathbf{a}^{(i)}\mathbf{1} = \max_i \mathbf{a}^{(i)}\mathbf{1} = \lambda_m$. The proof is thus complete.   Q.E.D.

A similar proof can be repeated with reference to the columns of $\mathbf{A}$.

11.3. *Perron-Frobenius theorems concerning reducible non-negative matrices.* With reference to *reducible* non-negative matrices, the theorems considered above must be stated in a weaker version. By following the same order as above, the corresponding statements (weak versions) may be given as follows.[8]

Let **A** be a reducible non-negative nth-order square matrix, and let **x** and **p** be an n-component non-negative column vector and an n-component non-negative row vector, respectively. Then the following theorems hold.

Theorem 1a. The maximum λ_m of the function $\lambda(\mathbf{x})$, defined by (A.11.3), is an eigenvalue of matrix **A**. Such an eigenvalue is associated with an eigenvector **x** which is non-negative. (The same statement holds for the left-hand eigenvector **p**).[9]

Theorem 2a. The same as Theorem 2.

Theorem 3a. The eigenvalue λ_m of **A** is a continuous nondecreasing function of the elements of **A**.

Corollary 1a. The maximum eigenvalue of any square submatrix of **A** cannot be greater than the maximum eigenvalue of **A**.

Corollary 2a. The eigenvalue λ_m is not necessarily a simple root of the characteristic equation of **A**.

There is no theorem, for reducible matrices, corresponding to Theorem 4 of the preceding section.

---

[8] The proofs may be found, for example, in Gantmacher [7, Vol. II, pp. 6–74].

[9] There is one case (which is relevant for certain economic problems) in which it can be shown that even with a reducible non-negative matrix, at least one of the two eigenvectors associated with the maximum eigenvalue has all positive components. This occurs when in a reducible matrix (reduced to a block-triangular form), that irreducible submatrix on the principal diagonal, which is followed on the same column by zero submatrices, has a maximum eigenvalue which is greater than the maximum eigenvalues of all the other submatrices on the principal diagonal.

For example, it can be shown for the matrix

$$\mathbf{A} = \begin{bmatrix} \mathbf{A}_{11} & \mathbf{A}_{12} \\ \mathbf{O} & \mathbf{A}_{22} \end{bmatrix}$$

that, if the maximum eigenvalue of $\mathbf{A}_{11}$ is greater than the maximum eigenvalue of $\mathbf{A}_{22}$, then the left-hand eigenvector of **A** has all positive components. The right-hand eigenvector, on the other hand, will be semipositive; and, more precisely, its first k components will be positive (k being the order of matrix $\mathbf{A}_{11}$) and the other $(n-k)$ components will be zero. By way of symmetry, if the maximum eigenvalue of $\mathbf{A}_{22}$ is larger than the maximum eigenvalue of $\mathbf{A}_{11}$, then the right-hand eigenvector of **A** has all positive components. On the other hand, the left-hand eigenvector will be semipositive, in such a way that its last h components will be positive (h being the order of matrix $\mathbf{A}_{22}$) and its first $(n-h)$ components will be zero. See Gantmacher [7, Vol. II, pp. 77 ff].

Theorem 5a. Given a real number $\mu = (1/\nu) > 0$, if $\mu > \lambda_m$ (and thus $\nu < 1/\lambda_m$), then

$$(\mu \mathbf{I} - \mathbf{A})^{-1} \geq \mathbf{O} \tag{A.11.26}$$

$$(\mathbf{I} - \nu \mathbf{A})^{-1} \geq \mathbf{O} \tag{A.11.27}$$

That is, all the elements of matrices (A.11.26) and (A.11.27) are non-negative real numbers. Moreover, all the elements of matrices (A.11.26) and (A.11.27) are continuous nondecreasing functions of ν and continuous, nonincreasing functions of μ. (The proof of this theorem is actually similar to the one given for Theorem 5 in the previous section).

Theorem 6a. The same as theorem 6.

References

[1] Almon, Clopper, Jr., *Matrix Methods in Economics*, New York: Addison-Wesley, 1967.

[2] Bellman, Richard, *Introduction to Matrix Analysis*, 2nd ed., New York; McGraw-Hill Book Co., 1970.

[3] Birkhoff, Garret, and MacLane, Saunders, *A Survey of Modern Algebra*, rev. ed., New York: Macmillan, 1953.

[4] Debreu, Gerard, and Herstein, I. N. "Non-negative Square Matrices," *Econometrica*, 1953, pp. 597–607.

[5] Faddeev, D. K., "Linear Algebra," Chap. XVI of Aleksandrov, A. D., Kolmogorov, Andrej N., and Lavrent'ev, M. A., (eds.), *Mathematics. Its Content, Methods, and Meaning*, 3 vols., Cambridge, Mass.: MIT Press, 1969.

[6] Frobenius, Georg, "Über Matrizen aus positiven Elemente," and "Über Matrizen aus nicht negativen Elemente," *Sitzungsberichte der königlichen preussischen Akademie der Wissenschaften*, 1908, pp. 471–476; 1909, pp. 514–518; 1912, pp. 456–477.

[7] Gantmacher, Feliks R., *The Theory of Matrices*, 2 vols., New York: Chelsea Publishing Co., 1959.

[8] Hadley, George, *Linear Algebra*, London: Addison-Wesley Publishing Co., 1961.

[9] Manara, Carlo Felice, and Nicola, Pier Carlo, *Elementi di economia matematica*, 2nd ed., Milano: Viscontea, 1970.

[10] Perron, Oskar, "Über Matrizen," *Mathematische Annalen*, Vol. LXIV, 1907, pp. 248–263.

[11] Shilov, Georgi E., *An Introduction to the Theory of Linear Spaces*, Englewood Cliffs, N.J.: Prentice-Hall Inc., 1961.

[12] Solow, Robert M., "On the Structure of Linear Models," *Econometrica*, 1952, pp. 29–46.
[13] Wielandt, H., "Unzerlegbare nicht negative Matrizen," *Mathematische Zeitschrift*, 1950, pp. 642–648.
[14] Żurmühl, Rudolf, *Matrizen*, Berlin, Springer Verlag, 1964.

AUTHOR INDEX

The numbers refer to pages; when followed by n they refer to footnotes

SUBJECT INDEX

Accumulation of capital: in Ricardo, 12, 16; in dynamic models, 194–5; difficulties for marginal theory, 26–7

Agricultural Revolution, 1

Basic and non-basic commodities, 104–11; relevance of this distinction, 108, 155, 156, 161–2, 215–16; vs. subsistence and luxury goods, 108–9

"Cambridge equation", 217

Capital intensity effect and price effect, 83

Circular process: *see* Production of goods

Circulating capital and fixed capital, 43–4, 71n

Coefficients of consumption, 56, 194, 197, 209, 219

Coefficients of production: in Walras, 26; in linear production models, 50, 51–2; in Leontief, 54; in Sraffa, 72; vs. consumption coefficients, 56, 59–60; in terms of embodied labor, 135; "augmented" of subsistence consumption coefficients, 127, 214

"Constant capital" and "variable capital" (Marx), 19, 125, 138, 148

Constant vs. non-constant coefficients, 52, 69, 72, 116, 187–8

Consumption, per capita:
in Leontief, 55, 56; 59
subsistence, 124, 127; numerical example, 146
vertically integrated subsistence, 125n
in dynamic models, 194, 218; its maximum level, 203; structure open to choice but not absolute level, 197; expressed in terms of rates of net surplus, 209–10, 211–12
its relation with rate of growth, 201–2, 219–20; same relation as that of wage rate and rate of profit, 202, 220; case of linearity, 206–8

Cost of production: and "natural price", in Ricardo, 14; and competitive prices, in Marx, 19; and prices, in Sraffa, 72–3, 153, 155; not the same thing as "imputed" cost, 182

Demand:
in the Ricardian system, 14; in the traditional model, 24–5, 184
final: in the open Leontief system, 60–1; in proportional dynamic models, 194–5
does not affect the choice of technique, 167

Duality:
price system and physical quantity system, 50, 61, 92, 111, 199–200
wage rate/rate of profit relation and per capita consumption/growth rate relation, 201–2, 220; linearity conditions, 204–8
standard system and uniform capital intensity hypothesis, 100n, 119n, 204n, 207

Dynamics: proportional, 191–2, 195; comparative, 201, 222; as against quasi-dynamics, 191

Economic goods vs. free goods, 213, 215

Efficiency criterion, 222; and profitability criterion, 222–3

Equilibrium: "natural", in Ricardo's system, 10–11, 15; general, in marginal theory, 25; dynamic, 192, 195–6

Exports and imports, 42, 42n

Final sector, 7, 37; its components, 42–3; considered as any other industry in Leontief's closed system, 55; considered as exogenous in Leontief's open system, 61; in dynamic models, 193–4; vs. technical interindustry relations, 39